New Voices in the Nation

NEW VOICES IN THE NATION

Women and the Greek Resistance, 1941–1964

JANET HART

Cornell University Press

Ithaca and London

This book has been published with the aid of a grant from the University
of Michigan, Ann Arbor.

First published 1996 by Cornell University Press.

Printed in the United States of America

☺ The paper in this book meets the minimum requirements of the
American National Standard for Information Sciences—Permanence of
Paper for Printed Library Materials, ANSI Z39.48-1984.

Library of Congress Cataloging-in-Publication Data

Hart, Janet, 1953–
    New voices in the nation : women and the Greek Resistance,
  1941–1964 / Janet Hart.
      p. cm. — (The Wilder house series in politics, history, and
  culture)
    Includes bibliographical references (p.   ) and index.
    ISBN 0-8014-3044-5. — ISBN 0-8014-8219-4 (pbk.)
      1. World War, 1939–1945—Underground movements—Greece. 2. World
  War, 1939–1945—Women—Greece. 3. Women—Greece—History—20th
  century. 4. Greece—History—Occupation, 1941–1944. I. Title.
  II. Series.
  D802.G8H37 1995
  940.53′495′082—dc20   95-38746

To Jared

You don't give up: I do not give up hope: I am not a pessimist. I am a utopian romantic who always sees a spark somewhere flying, but with some melancholy and mourning and fears.

—Leo Lowenthal

Contents

Illustrations

Acknowledgments

In the ten-year span of this research project, many people have contributed their sympathy, knowledge, material and intellectual support, and time. They are, however, far too numerous to mention, and so I can only hope they know who they are and that they will accept my thanks and apologies for not identifying them by name. I will instead shine the light of gratitude on those people without whom this book absolutely, categorically, could not have been written. If, in fact, any one of them had been missing from the process, the book would not have become a tangible thing, and its insights certainly would have been far poorer. But of course they should not be held accountable for any mistakes or misinterpretations.

This vital list includes Chip Ammerman, director of the Fulbright-Greece Program; Nick Diamandouros, an early supporter; Eleni Fourtouni, for long, intriguing talks and initial contacts; James House, former chair of the University of Michigan Sociology Department; John Iatrides, a guiding light of the Modern Greek Studies Association; David Laitin, Wilder House series editor, who believed in me even when to others this book seemed a risky bet; various folks at the University of Michigan and elsewhere who helped me navigate shark-infested waters without somehow turning into sharks themselves; John Weiss, who reviewed my original Fulbright application; and three anonymous reviewers for Cornell University Press. On a slightly more personal note, thanks to Penny and Lena Katsika, my "Greek sisters," for their generosity and all manner of help; their mother, Mairi Katsika, for teaching me much of what I know about *filotimo;* Deone Terrio and Lynne Wozniak, without whose caring, humor, and devoted friendship I undoubtedly would have foundered somewhere between graduate school, fieldwork, and the completion of this manuscript—and whose moral courage I will always cherish; my three "grandmothers," Jersey Bell Johnson Reed, Cynthia Holloway and Lida Richardson, for teaching me to love survivors' words; Ron Aminzade, Maria Fanis, Linda Gregerson, Frances Hasso, Lela Jacobson, Judy Mackey and the Van Dyck family for their bedrock support and indulgence at crucial stages; Amy Chasteen, my clever, humorous, and dependable research assistant; Marion Sarafis, for her infinite assistance, kindness, enthusiasm, and wisdom. As is now our custom, I also thank the other members of the Fab Four: Jane Cowan, Karen Van Dyck, Charles Stewart, and honorary member Nelson Moe. Little did we know what ties would bind when we climbed aboard that bus parked on Vas. Sofias Street on the way to the Fulbright orientation on Hydra.

The book is dedicated, as promised, to my nephew Jared, who has been a rare and wonderful combination of son, friend, brother, and emotional next-door neighbor. His ability to remain playful while keeping the people around him honest, I greatly admire. Finally, my profound and heartfelt thanks to the women and men of the Greek resistance movement, some of whom I was lucky enough to speak with in person and all of whom—including those who are now "in spirit"—I credit with teaching me about life-blood causes that can in their way help us all to prosper.

J. H.

Thanks to

N. Apostolopoulou

M. Bikia-Aroni

M. Beikou

E. Christoforaki-Alexaki

V. Damianakou

D. DeKavalla

K. Desilla-Halikia

E. Drosaki

T. Drosou

K. Floutzi

D. Fouka-Reze

V. Franzeskaki

K. Hariati-Sismani

E. Kamoulakou

S. Karanika

M. Karra

V. Katraki

A. Kokovli

T. Lagoudaki

A. Laloupoulou

F. Lazarou

P. Liakata

L. Litina

K. Marangoudaki

A. Mavroeidi-Pandeleskou

K. Mendrakou

E. Moriki-Gravari

O. Papadouka

M. Piniatidou-Benaki

A. Potamianou

V. Psitakidou

D. Pym

G. Sakka

M. Sideri

Y. Terentsio

V. Theordorou

K. Tsatsaronaki-Papapanayiotaki

L. Tzima

E. Tsirou

Z. Sari

M. Vardaki

X. Vardaki

T. Vasilaki

L. Vouloudaki

M. Xanthopoulou

New Voices in the Nation

Political Fables

When we speak to those who want to hear us, we do not essentially address their political finesse. The reactions we hope for from them are not calculations of positions, nor are they new political alliances. What we hope for is of a different nature. . . . [We know] above all that the forces destined to prevail are those that not only overcome their crises but are capable of profiting by them.
—Bataille 1935, "Popular Front in the Street"

Six years ago, after half-heartedly watching my mother's soap operas and wondering whether there wasn't something more to be asked of life, the Civil Rights Movement came into my life. Like a good omen for the future, the face of Dr. Martin Luther King, Jr., was the first black face I saw on our new television screen. And, as in a fairy tale, my soul was stirred by the meaning for me of his mission . . . and I fell in love with the sober and determined face of the Movement.
—Alice Walker 1983, "The Civil Rights Movement: What Good Was It?" (1966–67)

"I think I'm really not interested in the quest for the self any more. Oh, I suppose everyone continues to be interested in the quest for the self, but what you feel when you're older, I think, is that—how to express this—that you really must *make* the self. It's absolutely useless to look for it, you won't find it, but it's possible in some sense to make it." . . . The lesson of [Mary] McCarthy's experience of the autobiographical act is that the process of self-discovery is finally inseparable from the art of self-invention.
—Eakin 1985, "Mary McCarthy"

In this book I explore events in Greek political history that occurred during the 1940s. The above three quotations contain an essentially anti-nihilistic view of how adverse conditions can be manipulated to advantage, and each represents one of the stories that I seek to tell. Although crucial to my tale as a whole, later on the seams of these predominant fables will not always be visible. For this reason, I begin by delimiting the fables and by examining some of the reasons for their existence and symbiosis.

I

The first is a tale about how centrally placed leaders of Greece's largest resistance organization, the Ethniko Apeleftherotiko Metopo (EAM) or National Liberation Front conceived of the Nazi occupation as a broader mandate for social transformation. The organization was formed in September 1941 for military and defensive purposes. It is, however, the social and political transformations that the EAM eventually also tried to bring about which this book seeks to illuminate. By 1944, the organization was around 1.5 million strong, even by conservative estimates, and had managed to gain a mass following by engaging in several kinds of "resistance," becoming in effect a quasi governmental regime. Attempts by the EAM to institute a new social order that included, among other things, unprecedented numbers of female citizens, are best understood as part of a bid for national modernity or a "modernist moment." Here, sentiments in Georges Bataille's 1935 speech on the French Popular Front parallel those of the Greek leaders who are among this book's protagonists. This is especially true of Bataille's assertions about the French movement's future role in creating and harnessing popular energy to defy business-as-usual in the traditional political world, while in the process also devising a brazen mass response to fascism. "What we demand," declares Bataille, "is a coherent, disciplined organization, its entire will straining with enthusiasm toward popular power."[1]

Across the left political spectrum, various forms of *radical syndicalism* had captured leaders' imaginations in a particularly vivid way throughout the 1920s and 1930s. These were based on the notion that solidly constructed organizations could create and channel mass participatory zeal to effect political change. In Greece the discourse of organization became part of a secular religion central to the popular revolution taking place during the war. "Strong and disciplined organizations [*sindhikata*] are the main battlefronts, not only for the working class but also for every popular struggle," enthuses a typical resistance monograph. "All such initiatives will be effective only if they are organized and coordinated as part of a broader program whose purpose is to help the people to survive and to deliver them not only from German and Italian slavery, but also from the violence perpetuated by our internal fascist enemies."[2]

At a broader level, the "modern" innovations that I address in this book were inspired by some of the same oppositional, pangenerational impulses that had assumed indigenous form elsewhere after the turn of the century. As Eric

[1] Some maintain that Bataille and his contingent failed to recognize that mass mobilization in the absence of strong theoretical direction actually left insurgents vulnerable to fascist appeals. Bataille challenged and ridiculed the closed, ordered, rational systems of society and economy advocated by many of his contemporaries, which is why he is often seen as a predecessor of postmodern thinkers. Nevertheless, he mirrors the spirit of modernist times when he insists that syndicalists use popular emotion as part of their organizing strategy.

[2] "Pos prepei na dhoulevi i yineka sto Ethniko Apeleftherotiko Metopo" (The role of the woman in the National Liberation Front), Documents of the National Progressive Movement, EAM Central Committee, February 1943, 7, 38.

Hobsbawm notes, between 1870 and 1914, when influential wartime leaders came of political age, "the western world, including after 1905 even tsarist Russia, was plainly moving towards systems of politics based on an increasingly wide electorate dominated by the common people. . . . Religion, nationalism, democracy, socialism, the precursor ideologies of inter-war fascism: these held together the newly mobilized masses, whatever material interests their movements also represented."[3]

The modern orientation was rooted in Enlightenment and French revolutionary opposition to previous structures of domination. Features of modernist political culture were evident in many polities during the nineteenth and twentieth centuries. These included a utopian quest for communal "reason" and "rationality"; the desire to break with the old regimes of governance and to "catch up" in terms of economy and education with other countries perceived to be more advanced; "freedom" and universal rights discourse; and foundational questions about how the interests of certain social classes and economic groupings might be justly represented, but in a way that ensured public stability. A crucial part of the modern identity crisis involved gender as both a personal and an associational problem. At critical junctures as well as in everyday life, what it meant to be a male or female member of the polity, community, or workforce, was subject to debate (though sometimes couched in conversations about other topics) and attempts to emulate a "modern" standard of female participation created the situation that will be this book's primary focus.

Like their counterparts in other lands, in Greece influential figures based their prescriptions for change on a strong faith in the power of social engineering and more rational management of politics and economy. Moreover, as the 1930s progressed, members of the so-called generation of 1914 in continental Europe, the Balkans, and the Mediterranean struggled to respond to the up-and-coming ideology of fascism by bringing a range of human and material resources to bear on the problem. Here, one is reminded of contemporary (by no means unproblematic) efforts in the Arab world to shore up secular institutions against the claims of fundamentalist extremism.[4] But the clarity of hindsight has also revealed that modernism's endemic sense of urgency, combined with the stubborn nature of many of the era's social predicaments, left many problems and conflicts undetected, unacknowledged or simply pending.

Revolutionary syndicalism, with organizations begun by knowledgeable ac-

---

[3] Hobsbawm 1989, 87, 93, and see his extensive discussion of these processes.

[4] Fascism was not the binary opposite of "modernism," but rather combined elements of modern mass politics with its own perverse ideologies. Here the analogy to events in the Middle East holds, since secularism and terroristic religious fundamentalism share some common lineages and rhetorics; and as they look to the past in formulating strategies, both attempt to transcend complications associated with the current political era. See Al-Azmeh 1993.

tivists and used as strategic weapons against old regime and big industrial interests, originated in the period before 1914. As time went on, mass movements of the era were increasingly careful to distance themselves from violent anarchism when extolling the virtues of political organization. Thus although some branches of syndicalism stressed "direct action," popular organizations usually succeeded in mobilizing greater numbers of people when not too closely associated in the public mind with tactics perceived as too militant. On this score, for example, Lenin warned against terrorism in his 1902 tract *What Is To Be Done?*, a piece that activists and would-be revolutionaries read and reread into the 1930s.

In keeping with earlier trends, the inclusive wartime policies that are my focus were conditioned by a Greek modernism combining "indigenized" Cominternist, populist, and liberal national ideals held by key resistance figures, under a sturdy organizational umbrella. Anxious to attract a wide spectrum of adherents without jarring their sensibilities, the EAM comprised heterogenous material that during a state of emergency was not closely examined for inconsistencies. Wartime expediency led to an at times awkward combination of popular and national front tendencies within the same movement. The coalition's hasty formation was to have some bearing on the turn of events when combined with authoritaive postwar repression.

More generally, the question of coalition building was related to the quintessentially modern problem of the survival and resilience of the new mass "catch-all" party, whereby it was often necessary to gloss over incongruities in order to accommodate a more expansive political ethic. The demarcation lines should not be drawn too inflexibly, but I suggest that there is an important historical distinction to be made between modern and subsequent postmodern attempts to unite popular participants in struggle. In this regard I contrast political modernism with contemporary postmodern political rhetorics and strategies that also center around the issue of how to manage coalitional politics. Postmodern political discourse, however, involves the rights of a multiplicity of groups, identities, and voices to be taken into account and somehow incorporated in a way that celebrates and maintains their distinctions. Significantly, in the contemporary world optimism appears to be waning about the possibility of clear boundaries for group membership and the regulation of universal standards. Fewer attempts are made—because it no longer seems quite so possible—to minister regimes of "modernity" and "modernization" to mass publics.

Before continuing, we must note the somewhat anomalous character of the Greek resistance movement in relation to the Holocaust, particularly regarding the fate of the country's Jewish population.[5] The central activities of most

---

[5] See Mazower 1993, 235–61. This subject is addressed in Hondros 1983, 90–94; Dalven 1990; Kitroeff 1985; Matsas 1991; Stavrianos 1948. Brief mention is made in Stavrianos and Panagopoulos 1948, along with the few references available then.

other European resistance movements involved hiding and rescuing Jewish victims of Hitler's "Final Solution." Although the EAM also served as a refuge and performed these functions, the issue of racial hatred *cum* religious persecution did not constitute the major thrust of the Greek movement. An estimated 98 percent of Greece's Jewish population perished in northern concentration camps. The reasons behind this tragedy are varied: the demographic concentration and therefore easy targetability of Greek Jews in Macedonia, particularly in the Salonika area; the overwhelming power of the Nazi "New Order" once the decision was made to systematically annihilate Jewish citizenry; the community's social isolation from other Greeks before the war, a situation that, to the extent that it existed, was both voluntary and the result of anti-Semitic sentiment within the dominant culture;[6] mass starvation during the winter of 1941–1942; and the failure of Salonika's Rabbi Koretz to dissuade Nazi authorities from registering a majority of his congregation, who were then deported to concentration camps in the spring of 1943. A full examination of this very moving and important topic is beyond the scope of this book.

2

My second story is a collective account of the experience[7] of the often adolescent women targeted by innovative social policies and given an unprecedented opportunity to become the agents of their own political fates. Alice Walker, removed from these Greek events by geography, ethnicity, and approximately twenty years, captures what an attraction to the resistance movement might have felt like to a young Greek woman recognizing for the first time that an identity she had previously understood as relatively permanent might be open to restructuring. The theme of incipient transformation is evident in the testimonies of nascent activists in other times and places. For example, a participant in the 1984–1985 British coalminers' strike declares: "I'd been involved almost from day one, my days of 'just a housewife' were over, and I'd actually enjoyed the awfulness of it all, because, through my

[6] Apparently, Greek popular reaction to Wehrmacht plans for Jewish annihilation was mixed. For example, Mazower (1993) describes an episode in which Jewish men were publicly humiliated during the forced registration in Salonika, while civilians watched the show from their balconies. At the same time, Axis attempts to stir up anti-Semitism to divert attention from the excesses of the occupation reportedly met widespread passive resistance. Newspapers refused to include anti-Semitic copy, and Jewish families were hidden by associates. "The Position of Greek Jewry," Post Zion, Buenos Aires, Lagoudakis Collection, Modern Greek Studies Association and Boston University Library.

[7] Throughout this book the term *experience* denotes scenes from the past as described by informants and seen by the historical protagonists themselves as causally linked to subsequent situations; what I would call, combining the notions of life history and experience, *life experience*. This concept is similar to E. P. Thompson's "lived experience," which stresses the experiences themselves in light of their particular histories and emphasizes subjects' memories and narrative accounts of those experiences.

involvement, I became a totally different woman. I became my own self, an entirely different person. A person in my own right, belonging not only to my husband and family, but to myself, discovering I'd a brain of my own, an independent soul, and a right to drop everything and go anywhere, because, for once, I was needed and depended on by others" (Ali 1987, 100).

Diamando Grizona, member of the EAM youth organization EPON (Enaia Panelladhiki Organosi Neon—United Panhellenic Organization of Youth) describes similar emotions:

> But before we could really do anything, we had to convince our parents—a difficult task for all of us, especially the girls. For the first time we were stepping outside the home, taking on roles other than those assigned to us by our fathers and strictly enforced by our mothers. "You are girls," they cried. Our reputations would be ruined, no one would want to marry us, we would shame our fathers' names. There was no end to the calamities we would bring upon our families. But we had decided to do this, nothing could dissuade us. We persisted and slowly managed to bring about the miracle of our parents' believing in us, seeing us as people, respecting us for our determination, seeing that our struggle would spare us all the shame of submitting to the enemy. . . . We organized EPON groups in every village we visited. (Fortouni 1984, 35)

My primary focus is the leaders and active participants to whom the movement appeared to dually signify resisting Nazi domination and complex personal and collective emancipation. Using participant oral histories, among other sources, this book examines aspects of such developmental processes as they unfolded in Greece which, not coincidentally, are frequently cited by girls and women in other revolutionary contexts. In fact, the testimonies I gathered and resistance literature generally all demonstrate enormous popular enthusiasm for reforms and revolutionary measures instituted. As noted above, this exhilaration—what Henri Bergson called *élan vital*—was by no means unusual for social movements of the modern period and was a key feature of female testimony about Greek resistance experiences. The women interviewed talked of learning more than they ever thought possible as young girls about the ways of politics; and of the joy of a new literacy and freedom of movement. Among the privileges and duties cited were the right to vote and other legal guarantees; participating in popular courts; learning to read and write; developing the ability learning to stand up and speak their own informed political opinions at meetings; fighting, going on missions, and even dying honorably beside male comrades; being able to compete with and be taken seriously by those male comrades; and discovering new life choices. As I see them, the implications for collective historical memory are twofold, suggesting that the organizing discourses propagated by movement architects to a large extent struck the intended chord and were internalized by initiates in a lasting way; and that these recollections were grounded in what we can assume to have been actual occurrences, incidents that went beyond fanciful speculation.

In other words, in spite of the many tragic consequences, reports of the resistance experience from the women I interviewed were overall extremely positive, and later on I will consider why this might have been so. In fact, this texture of experience, voiced by women in numerous settings, is reason to reconsider what have traditionally been assumed to be the two major sites of political socialization and empowerment in the modern moment—the family and the school. Another important site where citizenship norms develop is *social movements* and especially what I call "socializing" movements, where new participatory values are taught and national identities forged. For women and girls, the voltage from these positive feelings about participation and incorporation frequently persists years later. What is also striking (and surely not just a matter of "false consciousness") is that these sentiments are often not critiques of the masculinist public spheres that excluded women in the first place. Rather, visions of uniting with men in struggle are cherished memories in their own right in the minds of female former activists, as was the case for a significant portion of the women and girls who took part in the American civil rights movement. Thus, this book is about gender and politics in the widest possible sense. My aim is not to record women's experiences in the resistance separately but rather to determine how this unprecedented scenario became possible at all. This I do by linking the behavior of male founders to broader cultural and historical antecedents and by defining gender analysis as examining the ways in which critical male and female behaviors are interrelated and contingent in social movements.

There are several areas that I do not delve into in great detail. I do not attempt to trace the intricacies of mid-twentieth-century Balkan diplomatic history or of developments within the Greek Communist Party, the Kommounistiko Komma tis Ellados.[8] The book does not deal directly with those women and men who chose not to join the EAM, who joined other organizations, or "rank-and-file" men in the EAM. Nor is it my intention to theorize about "all Greek women" during this or any other historical period. Undoubtedly, my most immediate (though still secondhand) knowledge is about the lives of those avowed activists who agreed to tell me their version of the EAM story. Later on, I make liberal use of the women's own words to illustrate my broader theoretical points. To the extent that I do so, I want to convey their experience as they saw it when I interviewed them in 1985. Although I have

---

[8] The Communist party is the subject of books by Haris Vlavianos (1992), Peter Stavrakis (1989), and John Loulis (1982).

tried to be true to their words, hoping that I have done justice to my informants and that they might recognize themselves upon reading this, ultimately
I claim this account as my own, conditioned view of what happened in Greece
between 1941 and 1964. Many native and diaspora Greeks will sympathize with
my view of the resistance from a political-developmental as well as from a
gendered standpoint, but as we shall later see, many others would interpret the
events of this rather controversial case differently.

3

The third relevant narrative involves my own intellectual history, shedding
possible light on the questions, What would possess an African American
woman to write a book about Greece? and, What compelled me, in no less
than a flood of compulsion and contrariness, to write about these events in
particular? These are questions that I have often asked myself, and have occasionally also been asked (somewhat more tactfully) by others. For instance,
there is little doubt in my mind that the project would have been significantly
harder had I, as a black person, not been readily identified in the minds of my
interviewees with a historically oppressed group. Greek leftists whose political
awareness was formed during the resistance era self-consciously carry an image
of themselves as a persecuted group, that is to say, as members of an officially
condemned movement within a semiperipheral, recurrently colonized country. In their words I recognized aspects of emancipatory social movements and
personal struggles in which Africans and African Americans, some of them my
own relatives, sought to define political space within a larger framework of
power and domination.

Conversations in the academy have recently centered around questions of
responsible and responsive ethnography. Increasingly, authors have been challenged to recognize possible ethical and political uses and abuses of the knowledge they generate. From a more personal point of view, questions have been
raised about how one's own identity is implicated in the act of speaking for
another group. Most authors, whether of avowed fiction or of history, sociology, anthropology, or political "science" are at least latently attracted to and
perhaps, as the old advice goes, write best about cases they know or in some
larger allegorical sense wish to understand. If, then, as a black scholar I had
chosen to focus on an event involving a group identified as black, my story
might not have differed in certain key respects; and had I come to this analysis
as a native Greek, my story might have been different though not more or less
"valid." Conviction and some degree of personal involvement have for me
become an inseparable part of the act of research, and the parameters of what

constitutes an "authentic" community will always remain open to negotiation.[9] This expansive view results, I think, partly from positioning myself, almost as a matter of instinct, somewhere along the edge that surrounds the official center of many different communities. By this I do not mean instinct in any naturalized sense, but rather a specific interpretive strategy that defies the conventions and impermeability of social borders.

Without this third, subjective fable there would be no book. At the same time, of the three it is the least complete. I do not intend to give a formal account of my life, nor will I try to balance my subjects' narratives with my own. I would however, link certain moral and psychological imperatives as well as an underlying autodidacticism with the final product. To that end, this book is about a passage in a longer journey, propelling me toward a consciousness regarding my connection with the world. That world is a place where we at least try, often with mixed results, to comprehend the meaning of personal and collective responsibility. I take the commitment to self-exploration to be fundamental to research, teaching, orthodox and nontraditional education, and writing.

In an interview entitled "The Minimalist Self," Michel Foucault makes the point that the authorial self should be kept to modest proportions even though sociological study has the potential to reveal as much about the author's developing identity as it does about the genesis of the objects of knowledge. "Refer[ring] to my own personal experience I have the feeling knowledge can't do anything for us and that political power may destroy us," says Foucault, and I identify with his pessimism. "Anyway, my personal life is not at all interesting. If somebody thinks that my work cannot be understood without reference to such and such a part of my life, I accept to consider the question" (1988, 16) he says, laughing, and I recognize my own discomfort at the potential for spectacle; "making a spectacle of yourself" being something that generations of American children have been warned against repeatedly. It is tempting to join Foucault in his cynicism about knowledge as the driving force behind political practice, and in his disdain for intellectual autobiography. Similarly, questions of how much importance should be given to the autobiographical process in shaping the actual products of academic imagination and in bearing witness to overt political agendas are admittedly also matters of ongoing ambivalence for me.

But if Foucault's radical subject hesitates, skeptical of both closure and disclosure, his view of the existential worth of the writing experience is more emphatic. On the therapeutic value of adult learning, Foucault remarks,

[9] The idea of theoretical imaginings and political practice conceived from a marginal standpoint is examined in hooks 1990; Haraway 1988; and Harding 1986, to name a few, and is also central to Gramscian formulations.

You see, that's why I really work like a dog and I worked like a dog all my life. I am not interested in the academic status of what I am doing because my problem is my own transformation. That's the reason also why, when people say, "Well, you thought this a few years ago and now you say something else," my answer is, (Laughter) "Well, do you think I have worked like that all those years to say the same thing and not be changed?" This transformation of one's self by one's own knowledge is, I think, something rather close to the aesthetic experience. Why should a painter work if he is not transformed by his own painting? (1988, 14)

A further point needs to be made: my aim has not been to erase all traces of conflict in presenting the material I have gathered, as the reader might be tempted to assume given that my evaluation of events is often so blatantly positive. On the one hand, the idealism endemic to revolutionary movements needs to be scrutinized with a critical eye. But on the other, I do want to stress the point that in recounting events so contingent on a hard-won capacity for survival, narrators frequently express their stories in a triumphal register. I see the impulse to deprecate the quality of *quest-romance* so vital to these stories as the product of an often unexamined allegiance to the same objectivist discourse initiated in earnest in the mid-nineteenth century.[10] For some, this loyalty manifests itself in a distrust of emotion in social narrative.[11] Others, insisting on literal proof, cringe at the blending of "fact" and "fiction" that is nevertheless, I believe, intrinsic to historical narrative. We have recently witnessed a critical rejection of uncomplicated metanarratives, a trend I think is generally salutary. Moreover, those of us who consider ourselves progressives (in an era when clear alternatives seem scarce) are reluctant to allow potential bases for political advocacy to be completely eroded by sanguine expectations. Clearly, antipathy toward the idealism and romance that are key to political action is shared by a mixed group of skeptics.

And yet analyzing cultural transformations calls for some commitment to the practice of "creative hearing" so that audience preconceptions are at least temporarily suspended and multiple testimonial "truths" given room to emerge.[12] I join others in proposing that the mythological form is crucial to

[10] This literature has become vast. As an intrinsic part of Western philosophy, the so-called "objectivist fallacy" runs across the spectrum from conservative-cum-liberal individualism to literary realism to orthodox Marxism. For example, see Williams 1983, especially s.v. "Positivist" (238–39), "Rational" (252–56), "Realism" (257–62), and "Science" (276–80); and Lakoff and Johnson 1980.

[11] Peter Middleton (1990) notes a more recent cerebralizing trend in the human sciences. Also see Jaggar 1989 on emotional affect and feminist scholarship and Lutz and Abu-Lughod 1990.

[12] "Creative hearing" is William L. Andrews's suggested approach to the slave narratives, quoted in Eakin 1991, 9. Also see Anderson and Jack 1991; Anderson et al. 1990, 94–112.

collective action. Here, "mythology" should be taken to mean not a network of falsehoods but rather scenarios woven together in human consciousness which guide and influence human behavior.[13] Acknowledging the mythological element is logically prior to isolating whatever motives, intentions, or understandings might have given rise to radical energies. It is certainly a good idea to reserve suspicions about elegiac or vainglorious narrative content, for "tall tales" may entirely defeat the meaning of research about the past.[14] As important as these qualms are, however, our apprehension should not, it seems to me, approach a level that interferes with our capacity to hear what protagonists have to say when voiced in a utopian syntax and similarly, to accept our own enchantment with particular topics. In this spirit Ernst Bloch, attempting to construe popular political attractions, asserted: "We need not be afraid of taking note of and distinguishing the hunger for happiness and freedom, the images of freedom for human beings deprived of their rights, images which are contained in these dreams."[15]

In view of the expansive, but often inchoate nature of national aspirations (as opposed to the conditions that produce them), to round out the picture it will be necessary to identify disharmonious or absent elements in this narrative, as well as problems that may never be resolved given the available data. In the end, however, this book is not about people who were fundamentally dissatisfied with the movement that is my focus. Nonetheless, I do see value in trying to figure out how participants who seemed to view this as their finest hour, undoubtedly repressing certain misgivings, could make statements like "I believed in the cause of EAM very much," or, "Without the resistance, I would have been a nobody."

In short, social movements trade heavily in paragons. The success of any social movement depends almost entirely on the extent to which it can convert bitter ore into idealistic gold. Powerless to communicate optimistic readings of possible futures and to generate resilient faith in members, it is difficult for any social movement to exist long enough to be taken account of by history.

Dominick LaCapra (1983, esp. 64) makes a similar point in opposing traditional intellectual to popular cultural history.

[13] An important source on this subject is Samuel and Thompson 1990.

[14] Tall tales or dramaturgical exaggerations are themselves noteworthy objects of study especially when so designated by the tellers themselves. That most historical narratives contain fictional elements is a separate point. For a discussion of the application of narrative analysis to deliberately fabricated stories labeled as "lies" by speakers and not meant to describe actual incidents from the past, see R. Bauman 1986.

[15] Ernst Bloch, quoted in Rabinbach 1977, 12. Bloch is asserting a view of fascism as "a cultural (and temporal) synthesis" rather than as an altogether irrational historical moment. The passage hints at his more general critique of what he saw as the tragic inability of German Marxism in the 1920s and 1930s to perceive the "everyday" facet of National Socialism and so to offer equally compelling solutions to vulnerable segments of the population.

Considering the vital role it plays in the mobilization of popular movements generally and as a quintessentially modern way of thinking, which is foundational to its core, idealism should not be equated a priori with simplism, delusional thinking, or cynical self-promotion on the part of historical protagonists, and be allowed to float away unexamined.

The book is organized into chapters each of which is connected in some way to the central themes that began this Prologue. In Chapter 1, I start with a historical overview of the period between 1941 and 1964. Next, I trace leadership mentalities to *modernism* as a major source of inspiration and vital "structure of feeling" for nineteenth- and twentieth-century political leaders. It is the era's specifically modern political orientations that reveal why this and other twentieth-century movements concentrated such passionate efforts on certain policies and goals, and it is modernism that imprinted them with the authoritative (though also on some matters fundamentally ambivalent) style of their times. In Chapter 1, I also discuss the epistemology and methodology of "narrative analysis," which has been an especially useful approach to understanding political activities during the modern age.

In Chapter 2, I present some of the ideas of Italian leader and political theorist Antonio Gramsci, whose writings provide the main analytic frame for this book. I highlight several conjunctures in Gramsci's early years which I find useful to my analysis, but my primary source of theoretical insight is the notebooks produced during his stint as a political prisoner under Mussolini. Usually among the first targets of repression, Communists were understandably also among the first to recognize the menace looming on the horizon and played a leading role in theorizing and organizing resistance against it. Like certain prominent Greek leaders imprisoned during the 1930s, Gramsci was a Communist thinker during a critical period and was also, in the end, a mortal casualty of fascism.

From a wider perspective, by weaving Gramscian thought and Greek radical history together, I aim to demonstrate that communists of the 1920s, 1930s and 1940s often sought ways to solve problems of national unity and state formation through the creative use of internationalist guidelines and their own readings of history. Whereas there was no shortage of doctrinaire thinking in regional parties, engendering many a debate about strategy behind closed doors, nonetheless responses to Comintern policies displayed some flexibility. In practice, such strategies were not always as uniformly acquiescent as is sometimes assumed, and might in fact be left open to debate or local implementation. Some, perhaps more independent-minded than most and adhering more to Leninist tradition than to emergent Stalinism, hoped to create working models of socialism, adjusted to fit indigenous requirements, rather than to replicate any essentialized notion of communism, especially where that might interfere with attracting and conditioning a mass following. Such agendas are strongly evident in Lenin's recurrently influential call to resist "subservience to spontaneity" and "artificial stimulants" (Lenin 1987, 108, 111). They are prominent in Gramsci's writings, too, and also characterized Greek thought in some quarters before and during the resistance period.

In Chapter 3, I reconstruct salient themes advanced by the EAM and place the actions of the Greek "organic intellectuals," whose authoritative policy decisions shaped the movement in specific directions, in a broader context of collective action. Here I summarize two types of nationalist narrative as they were framed, in a very public way, by movement organizers. These narratives, I contend, were what persuaded so many people, including a significant number of young women, to join the EAM and to believe in its basic goals. In Chapters 3 and 4, my "evidence" comes from interview testimony as well as from movement organizing lore and literature—pamphlets, newspaper articles, songs, photographs, and handbills.

In Chapter 4, I turn my attention to key gender issues and explore some of the possible motivations and underlying justifications for incorporating ideals of social justice and greater involvement for women into the movement. My premise is that despite the importance of women's own agency throughout the period, had at least some of the primarily male leaders not hoped to drive a wedge between traditional and "modern" values, a macrostructural picture of the movement might have looked very different. This position will tend to be unpopular in those parts of the feminist landscape lit by the fantasies that patriarchal structures cannot really thwart independent initiatives, that discussions about the "woman question" were not part of a more comprehensive discourse, and that ideas about women's place in the modern world were immaculately conceived by women alone. Nevertheless, the limits imposed on my informants by prevailing hegemonies cannot really be dismissed by such hopeful sleights of hand.

Also in Chapter 4, I relate Gramsci's prison writings to analogous themes in the writings of the EAM strategist Dimitris Glinos. On the question of subaltern political mobilization, Gramsci and Glinos exhibit similarities because both had been exposed to homologous intellectual networks and worldviews-in-process. The modern generation mined a common quarry for answers to problems of mass politics, and in the communist world this was not the monolithic terrain that has generally been assumed. It no doubt included such diverse ideological deposits as Leninist vanguardism; August Bebel, Friedrich Engels, and probably also narratives gleaned from John Stuart Mill; Clara Zetkin and local feminist thinkers on "the woman question"; classical and neoclassical theories about public speech, effective governance, literacy and education; syndicalism's passionate organizational and representational claims; and ideas about democratic practice and its relationship to culture and language. The point is that Gramsci, Glinos, and notable others struggled to find solutions to some of the same thorny material and intellectual dilemmas. Like present-day leaders, what they took away from conversations that tended to be international in scope, they blended with innovations inspired by domestic developments, to serve national ends. These conversations foregrounded the need for their societies to "catch up" with a West less scarred by, in Gramsci's parlance, "narrow egoism" on the part of elites, and by a woefully underdeveloped consciousness (Gramsci's "common sense") that blocked and distorted mass potential. Glinos wrote more extensively on "the woman question" per se than did Gramsci, both in composing resistance organizing material and earlier, as founder of a women's university in 1921. Gramsci, however, was not completely indifferent to feminist goals and from a broader perspective his writings engage such relevant themes as the role of the revolutionary party in inducing collective action, the importance of popular education and political learning for dynamic citizenship, and the need for counterhegemonic strategy. From an experiential point of view, in *The Prison Notebooks* Gramsci drew heavily on his work with the Turinese "factory councils" during the so-called two red years of 1919 and 1920. Thus, with similar emotional intensity and commitment, both men tackled questions of nation building and popular organization at great length in their writings and in related efforts at "ground level."

In Chapters 5 and 6, I investigate how latent rank-and-file identities become open to change during crises, and then go on to consider the mobilization of Greek women into the mixed-sex organizations that dominated the resistance landscape. In this portion of the book, I examine the mobilization based on gender (but not unconcerned with class and region) that occurred in wartime Greece. My aim is to isolate facets of the popular social imaginary that civil insurgencies tap into in creating what C. Wright Mills (1984) called "situated actions and vocabularies of motive." The discussion is based on the oral histories elicited from the women who participated in the activities of the EAM from 1941 to 1944, along with other types of archival material.

Chapter 7 also relies heavily on the eyewitness testimonies of participants. By the early 1950s, many had become political prisoners and casualties of the early years of the Cold War. Here I relate the initial blossoming of popular enthusiasm for social and political change—most closely akin perhaps to the powerful early stages of a romance—to those long-term effects of the mobilization process which by all appearances managed to survive the sombre postwar years. In this sense, Chapter 7 is my reading of the "rest of the story" focusing on the demobilization phase (1945–1964), and partisan women's experiences during that period. Here, I direct my attention to the conjuncture that was marked by political repression and by the rescinding of participants' civil rights by the Greek state.

In the Epilogue, I return to my major theoretical, empirical, and subjective themes, but with added "hindsight"—or is it newer fictions, as vivid and personal for me as Cavafy's Ithakas? I end the book with afterthoughts about the Greek resistance as historical example and contemporary lesson, mindful of the postmodern trope that the past is meaningful only through the drama of the present.

This brings me to several final points about my case selection and approach. Greece is not a country that non-Greeks tend to know very much about, beyond images of an ancient past, some vague familiarity with the dictatorship and events in Cyprus, occasional tourism, and contacts with cabdrivers, diner owners, and maybe a neighbor or two. It is geographically small and not a major power within the world hierarchy of states, for what that's worth. For many blacks and other people of color, Greece has come to signify whiteness at its whitest, and my dissenting view here will be addressed in the second part of this Prologue. The relegation to a status of obscurity and supposed "minorness"—even though for Greeks living in Greece the country is anything but minor—is a reaction that many Greeks and Greek-Americans have become accustomed to, and indeed often accept. In the course of this research, I have often faced wrinkled noses and the question, Why Greece?

What I have been concerned with in this work, and what I have found most intriguing, is the question of how events in Greece, a land however small and located at the semiperiphery of core states on the world map, might fit into a panoramic picture of social and political processes. This is why I have often resisted talk of "anomaly" and the idea that the patterns I have identified are relevant only to a tiny part of the world. Metaphorically, the point is that what I have been looking at is not merely a snapshot of Greece itself but rather, in my scope of vision, a series of large murals telling stories about particular kinds of social transformations. In each case, the Greek version suggests what conceivably might have taken place in other parts of the world. What kinds of stories do the larger murals tell? What is the broader picture of social change? This is what I ask readers to join me in exploring.

I devote the remainder of this Prologue to the business of "interrogating my own subjectivity," as bell hooks puts it. Entering the gray area where one attempts to think about how epistemology and research inform and transform each other has been for me the most daunting yet instructive part of this project. By what authority do I speak? What are some of the sources of my critical judgments about these data? My purpose is to reflect upon decisions made and insights uncovered in the course of the research process and to think about research as an autobiographical event, a theme I revisit in the Epilogue.

Bearing Witness

As a graduate student in comparative politics, I arrived in Athens in June 1983; planning to use my Fulbright grant to study the internal and external policies of the recently elected Socialist party (PASOK) with regard to gender-related issues. As a black American woman, I knew that my choice of topic was *different,* to say the least. I wasn't and could never be "Greek," nor was I trying somehow to release myself from a meaningful black identity. My motives in electing to cross intellectual and physical borders had little to do with a desire to negate a consciousness of the African diaspora past as it has shaped me. Rather than adopt, I wanted to *adapt* a belief system both similar to and different from my own, and I hoped to do so without a lot of fanfare. Just as any white scholar might elect to study another culture without feeling constrained to choose "caucasian" subject matter, so I would make my choice based on something that happened to catch my interest. In any case, halfway through the first year my original plans were curtailed by circumstances I still do not fully understand, having to do with the political climate in Greece at the time. After some soul-searching and reformulation, I switched my thesis topic to the "safer," historical subject of Greek women's experience in the resistance and began to conduct the oral histories and dig up the necessary archival data on which this project is based.

An important piece of my decision to pursue this research is embedded in my response to African American sisters and brothers who suggest that there is too much at home to study which is directly related to black people. My answer to "my own" (*stous dhikous mou, oi dhikoi* being an important concept in Greek culture also) is that what I have explored, and learned and cried about in studying the Greek resistance *is* about black people, certainly metaphorically if not, as some scholars of the ancient world suggest, literally. Far from disloyalty and distraction, my topic selection represents a black person conducting herself with a fuller agency within the academy. The case itself, about individual and collective resistance, in various aspects parallels how black people have survived an "occupation" of our own; and suggests ways that any community in crisis might begin to think about redressing grievances through organization, strategic alliances, education, and political nationalism.

In the 1980s, Greek leftists in particular tended to be aware of and to identify with the slavery and civil rights struggles in America. Images of slaves in chains and police dogs turned on children in Birmingham, Alabama, were familiar to many of the women I spoke with, whose country was under Ottoman domination during the eighteenth and part of the nineteenth centuries, some of whom remained political prisoners as a result of their resistance activities into the 1950s and early 1960s. In their minds such facsimiles of the hardships of black life in America were often juxtaposed with, for example, more recent television scenes of police brutality in Soweto. The women would often say, with no prompting from me, "You can understand. Your people have been oppressed too." Or, "We respect the brave struggles of your people for freedom and justice." Many added, "I don't know if I would have shared my life with you if you had been a white American." Vasso Katraki, the well-known woodcut artist and former EAM member originally from Crete, gave me a smooth, round rock on which she had painted the image of Martin Luther King Jr. when she was imprisoned during the Colonels' dictatorship, saying, "Here, you should have this. He's your martyr."

Oral histories are in effect managed conversations, in which it is best to control one's self-presentation as carefully as one would a performance in a play. There is also the initial awkwardness of meeting someone new. But with each interview, I felt more drawn into the "community," especially as I learned more about critical battles, heroic icons, and song lyrics. I even went to a former partisan social gathering in a big windy hall in downtown Athens and sang along with the anthems to the tune of a tinny old piano. Afterward, some of the old people came up to me and expressed how delighted they were that a black person, of all unexpected things, had joined their chorus. They congratulated me on the civil rights movement's struggles for freedom, which they likened to their own in the face of postwar political repression, citing the courage of "Luther King."

So I was treated with some respect and given access to sources because I was declared "one of us" (*i dhiki mas*), someone to be trusted. I began to feel very much at home in my day-to-day negotiations, developing a love-hate relationship with the country, and now feel a painful longing (*enas kaiimos*) to go back if I'm ever away from Greece for too many years. Yet I was also the target of an odd, nuanced kind of racism, which, although it took longer to identify than the more direct variety, and was somewhat easier to swallow, nonetheless served to remind me of the power of typecasting.

As a resident expatriate, I had no doubt that in its daily life Greece resembled a Third World country more than it did England, France, or Denmark. Like other scholars and expatriates, I too was struck by the phrase *Tha pame Evropi* ("We're going to Europe"), which suggested that we weren't there already. Often I would wend my way through the streets, buying olives and cheese wrapped in paper, chatting and commiserating and arguing with merchants and acquaintances and "strangers" about politics, life, and law, about death and taxes. This constant communication, in a country where no word for privacy exists, save "loneliness" (*monaksia*),[16] helped me to develop the

---

[16] It is also possible to translate "privacy" as "peace," or *isihia*, as in "They don't respect my privacy" (*Dhen m'afinoun isiho*). See Pring 1982, 247. Generally, however, the idea that a person would regularly seek something called "privacy," is considered a sign of dysfunctionality and rejection of communal values in Greek society.

fluency in modern Greek language and culture I needed for my work, but it also, after a while, just became a way of life, *my* way of life. I was told, "We admire the struggles of your people toward freedom; we Greeks are like black people." But I also heard friendly and yet disconcerting warning shouts of *mavri* ("Here comes a black one!") as I walked down many village or neighborhood streets. An African American friend and I would joke about how often we heard references to sexy dark women in the songs, saying, "They're talking about us again," even though the references were barbed— degrading in one sense, exalting in another. The black woman's presence in the art and popular culture of what might broadly be called the Middle East can be double edged, marked by a tendency to slip from appreciation to inappropriate sexualization and objectification. At times, being stared at in the street was flattering, stemming as it seemed to from curiosity and admiration rather than malicious hatred—at times it seemed obtrusive and to signal disrespect. It should also be noted that in Greece staring, discrimination, and blatant teasing are fairly standard initial reactions to difference of any kind. Thus, the possibility always exists that conspicuous traits other than race could engender similar responses.

I formed quasi-family relationships with neighbors, interviewees, people I met on buses. Sitting around the table, I often felt a sense of déjà vu in the way in which families related to one another. These interactions brought to mind visiting my relatives in Greensburg, Louisiana, or travels with Aunt Cynthia of Cleveland. Kyria So-and-So reminded me of Aunt Lida, who had spent her youth in Little Rock, Arkansas; Kyria Such-and-Such was as protective of me as my grandmother Jersey Bell Johnson Reed, raised in New Orleans. Here, I saw traces of Uncle A.P. in the kindly innkeeper and former resistance fighter in Monemvassia, and there, of Uncle Ed in the father of friends from Thessaloniki. But naturally I was annoyed when a Greek housemate's *haut bourgeois* parents accused her of deliberately trying to torture them when she announced our plans to rent an apartment together. African students in Athens and Saloniki have faced serious race-related resistance from some quarters of Greek society. And when the possibility arose of my marrying into a Greek island family now residing, compound-style, in Athens, the reaction to the possible integration of an "Other" and fears of public ridicule and gossip from some members demonstrated that I was definitely not *i dhiki mas* in all situations. The first time (and not the last) I overheard parents disciplining their children in public, on the ferry to the Cycladic Islands, by warning, "If you don't behave, the Moor will come and eat you! [*O Arapis tha se faei*]," I was not really surprised. Historical contingencies and lack of prolonged contact do, however, tend to exempt blacks from the prejudice and disrespect frequently encountered by other groups such as Jews, Albanians, gypsies, and the politically dissident. Blacks have by no means been the main targets of negative stereotyping, although that could always change should a significant in-migration occur. Social constructions of race in Greece are also profoundly joined to issues of class, education, language facility, and cultural adaptation; these components, however, deserve a fuller treatment than is possible here.

So while in general my reception was remarkably good, it was admittedly multilayered and at times disturbing, indicating a popular ambivalence on questions of race, Greek history and collective identity. Yet it was because of these competing narratives, not all of them audible to the naked ear and a significant number of them quite sympathetic, that as a person shaped by the inevitable mix of influences of the late twentieth-century, I found Greece to be such a fascinating analogue. Apart from whatever visceral attachment I developed toward the country, Greece gave me the means to understand some of the intricacies of modern and postmodern identity formation.[17]

Patricia Hill Collins's book *Black Feminist Thought* pulls together diverse strands of theorizing through black female existence. The themes of Collins's book have been crucial to my project, stimulating my thinking about the case and bringing half-remembered lessons to mind. These memories are based on my own experiences and on those of my "subjects." I join others in arguing that researcher subjectivity, however multigrained, structures and elicits certain kinds of metanarratives that then take shape in the form of one's published work. What has been called the "context of discovery" is a critical factor, since exposure to incidents, accidents, events, or ideas is what creates the researcher-as-subject, the author who feels the need to articulate points that ought to be of collective concern.[18] In part, my particular take on these events is oriented by one of the core themes Collins identifies: that "all African-American women share the common experience of being Black women in a society that denigrates women of African descent" (1991, 22). For me, this constitutes a major "context of discovery" and the source of a good deal of my curiosity about wartime Greece, since "like African-American women, many others who occupy societally denigrated categories have been similarly silenced. So the voice that I now seek is both individual and collective, personal and political, one reflecting the intersection of my unique biography and the larger meaning of my historical times" (xii).

The voice I seek is rooted in my developing subjectivity, which combines an allegiance to historicity with a continuing desire to innovate, while maintaining control over my fundamental scholarly decisions. In spite of the hybrid

---

[17] See Stewart 1994 on Greek national qua religious syncretism.

[18] This phrase, first used by Hans Reichenbach, is discussed more fully by Margaret Somers (forthcoming), who defines this as "the context in which we 'discover' the questions we ask in our research, in which we define that which is considered problematic in the first place (or what is necessary to be explained), and in which we select our conceptual vocabulary to formulate those questions. Discovery thus comprises the pre-history of theory construction."

nature of late twentieth-century black identity, my claim to a special sensitivity regarding the experiences and lessons taught to me by my informants and coauthors and, in turn, my presentation of that material to a wider public are ultimately an assertion of a personal *authenticity*, itself a concept rooted in many perplexing and insolvable dilemmas.[19]

Like any book, this one will raise, but can never confidently answer the riddles, Why me? Why this book? Who has the right to engage what material? and finally, with a whole chorus of seekers, *Truth, whose* truth?

The Narrative Context

> Jesus told the crowds all these things in parables; without a parable he told them nothing.
>
> —Matthew 13:34

One of the tools with which I dig through the layers of experience and meaning comprised in the resistance event is narrative analysis. By this I mean that I try to discern the stories or narratives embedded in personal testimonies and other types of "evidence," on the logic that what often stands between activism and passiveness during periods of crisis and social movement activity is a plausible story about why people should act boldly, transmitted in a compelling way by highly credible figures. Social mobilization is an art form heavily dependent on storytelling—to the self to justify one's choices and by others as a catalyst for collection action.

Initially, certain questions intrigued me. Why did a range of women with virtually no previous political experience suddenly venture into male territory to become politically involved? Why, as I unearthed more narratives, did participants—even leaders—seem more interested in the ideals of a Greek participatory democracy than in becoming mock Soviet citizens? Was the Greek civil war the aggressive, Moscow-led insurgency that many (most, really) history books claim, a graphic vindication of the Domino Theory, or could it have been grounded in the kind of sovereign popular will that lay behind many so mislabeled movements of the period? Most striking of all, why did a putatively democratic government find it necessary to execute sixteen-year-old girls in a paroxysm of alarm about the meaning of their involvement in a popular movement?

Events in Greece during the 1940s remain controversial and emotionally charged. Represented among the characters in this ongoing and in many ways still unresolved controversy are the forces of resistance, collaboration, and survival, as well as parties to older, unconnected feuds that erupted during this

---

[19] On the question of authenticity, see Gates 1991b.

period of tremendous dislocation. Over subsequent decades a legacy of clashes typical of wartime combined with a bitter civil war, which followed almost immediately on the heels of the German evacuation, the demobilization of the EAM as a "seditionary" organization, and the large-scale persecution of the Greek Left during the 1950s. From a symbolic and affective point of view, the country continued to fight related battles well into the 1970s and strongly held beliefs about the resistance period remain a feature of the contemporary political landscape.[20] In broader epistemological terms, the fact that authors on different sides of the conflict dispute one another's stories, especially about highly polarized issues and events, presents narrative analysis with a problem that it has yet to solve at this point in its evolution. Whom one chooses to believe depends on the volume of available evidence, the character of the "witnesses," and arguably also on one's own moral code and reading of history. Like all books based on "original" research, this one was written without a comprehensive model and certainly in the beginning, with no visible street signs. Indeed, in this case, many of the existing markers had been turned to face in odd directions, like the work of vandals.

In fact, I have often found myself playing roles in a courtroom drama—alternating as judge, peer, attorney, witness. Despite my basic theoretical commitment to a *multinarrative* approach, the strong emotions attached to this case and the passage of half a century's time have forced me into a familiar judicial dilemma. "What is at stake here," as Alessandro Portelli writes in another context, "is, in fact, the [very] *definition* of [the] 'event.'"[21]

But having in effect chosen a side, as I try to ascertain motivation and meaning by reconstructing the plots of the stories that admittedly, only *selected* groups of collective actors *think* they're telling about this conflict, I reproduce my informants' testimonies as often as possible to allow the reader to see what it is I thought I heard and why and to emphasize my own strong faith in the integrity of my informants and deep admiration for their courage, not so much in "coming forward" as in having survived some horrible times with humor and dignity. With little previous scholarly work to build upon regarding the dynamics of inclusion and exclusion in the Greek resistance movement, I have tried to synthesize my own blend from a range of literatures and analogies to similar aspects of other cases. This means that I refute various other views of

---

[20] For a brief summary of this historiographic dilemma, see Iatrides 1981, 195.

[21] Portelli 1991, 25, my italics. Portelli writes: "Luigi Trastulli, a 21-year-old steel worker from Terni, an industrial town in Umbria, central Italy, died in a clash with the police on 17 March 1949 as workers walked out of the factory to attend a rally against the signing of the North Atlantic Treaty by the Italian government. The walkout, the clash, and the killing of Trastulli lasted less than thirty minutes; but, from that moment on, the memory of this brief episode has exerted a shaping influence on the town's identity and culture" (1). Portelli presents various versions of the story of this event, each with its own adherents, emotional charge, and symbolic potential.

this conflict, presenting an account that those convinced by a different set of narratives will always find unpersuasive.

I want to reflect briefly on what is essentially a moral vision. In the tradition of C. Wright Mills, I see my words as expressions of a political, even "civilizing" agenda. Acknowledging this mission is particularly tricky in view of the negative effects of imperialist discourses on two of the communities comprised in my own identity: my "original" people, a *divers* black people, and now my adopted people, participants in the progressive Greek national resistance struggle—a group of which I have declared myself a member by virtue of my emotional attachment.

Sanctimony has created at least as many problems as it has solved for many groups, and taking the part of the narrator who points out the moral at the end puts me in the company of sincere educators *and* pedants. On the one hand, I am very much aware of the importance of tone and its underlying moral agendas, which may never realistically be divested of ego and claims to superior knowledge/power. On the other, I am driven by the visceral concerns behind the genre Thomas Laqueur calls "humanitarian narrative," characterized by the "reliance on [*narrative*] detail as the sign of truth" and "on the personal body [the *body politic*], not only as the locus of pain but also as the common bond between those who suffer and those who would help and as the object of the scientific discourse through which the causal links between an evil, a victim, and a benefactor are forged. . . . Ownership is for [David] Hume the most obvious way for this to happen, and 'humanitarians' do implicitly claim a proprietary interest in those whom they aid. They speak more authoritatively for the sufferings of the wronged than those who suffer can speak themselves. But, more generally, Hume is suggesting that moral concern and action are engendered not by the logic of the relationship between human beings but by the pain of a stranger crying out—as if the pain were one's own or that of someone near" (1989, 177–80). I have felt the need to share "ownership" of my perceived version of this story with a larger audience.

One reason this case has obsessed me has been my aspiration—humanist that I remain—to say, if we know about these successes, they can surely happen again in other contexts, and if we know about these sufferings, we'll be less careless about leaving incendiary social bombs lying around. Perhaps through creative analogy across time and space we might begin to draw ideas from alternative sites for the possible reversal of negative trends and for empowerment, using a bolder range of "case studies." Fluid boundaries are indeed critical to our quest for solutions, simply because there is no strategy without theory or indeed without comparative history. I cannot be alone in wishing that the initial surges of popular unity, enthusiasm, and conceptual fertility typical of emergency mobilizations and fresh republics could be skimmed off and put to everyday use.

Contemplating the possibilities, I look to the traditional use of the storytelling mode as a vehicle for pragmatic socialization in the greater black imagined community. In Greece and other cultures in which oral communication plays a central role, this pedagogical method has proven convincing and effective. Whether or not the original incidents can actually be verified is less important than the trust placed in the narrator and the narrator's ability to persuade the listener to alter or disavow certain behaviors at critical stages in life. For many African Americans, parabolic messages have been passed along in church; for most, lessons have been woven into the fabric of everyday life, voiced by parents and other elders. Yet the basic form and ideological content (broadly about maintaining "dignity," an inherently political notion if there ever was one in a subaltern context) have varied less across class and region than many realize. Spreading cultural messages of resistance, preaching about political realities, imparting information vital to survival—such modes of socialization are common to many diasporic "imagined communities." These are the threads of a rope holding many households together in the sense that Benedict Anderson means when he writes that "the members of even the smallest nation will never know most of their fellow-members, meet them, or even hear of them, yet in the minds of each lives the image of their communion" (1983, 15).

Subconsciously, and if necessary consciously, fragmentary synopses of family *cum* diasporic folklore are with me always, even as (since these lessons are not just for children) I add to my store with each fresh encounter with my relatives.

"We took you kinds to a playground in New Orleans and they told us to leave, that it was for whites only, and that was the last straw. We knew we had to move."

"I don't know *what* got into my brother Vance, your great-uncle, but he gave away *two hundred dollars* to *Marcus Garvey*! And we needed that money, too." (Later, after learning more about the Universal Negro Improvement Association and the Black Star Line in Afro-American History class, I was less moved by the family's financial problems in New Orleans in the 1920s than I was thrilled to be related to a follower of Marcus Garvey.)

"Now A.P., his mother was a chef-cook, and all of his people, that is the women in the family, thought there was nobody, and I mean this *very sincerely,* they didn't think there was *anybody* in the whole wide world who could cook, or plan meal, like Mother Richardson. Nobody but Mother Richardson and her two daughters could do it! So, that was funny to me, and insofar as I was concerned, I agreed. Well, that was the fun I had with the other daughter-in-laws, well they wanted to match their wits with these Richardson women. And then the youngest, her name was Grace, the youngest of the daughter-in-laws that was married to the youngest boy, she just couldn't cook *period*! She couldn't even do as well as I could! (laughing) And I just tried to get Grace to accept Mother Richardson and her cooking. I couldn't see why she let that worry her. I said, 'Grace, when Mother Richardson comes to my house, the kitchen belongs to her!" And I said, 'Grace, I'm so glad to get rid of that kitchen! And if that's what she wants, and I tell her, I know you want to fix some of those so-good meals for your son, and I am buying out! Here is the kitchen, you cook anything in the world. And if you don't find it in there, I'll send A.P. to get anything, or you can send him yourself!' And I was glad to walk out of that kitchen and eat Mother Richardson's so-good meals, because they *were* good, and I couldn't come within ten miles of what she was doing, so why should I bother?"[22]

"Mr. B. always wore a carnation in his lapel. It was always white, except on Thursdays, when he would wear a pink one. He refused to tell anyone why the pink one on Thursdays. People would always try to get him to tell. He took that secret with him to his grave."

"Since they were sisters, you could tell, they resembled just a little bit, she and Erminie, but Irene walked like she *owned* the world! She held her head just like that. She couldn't hold it any other way. It was just automatically thrown back."

"They wouldn't let your father enroll in the school. So Erminie, your grandmother, marched into that man's office and told him that Edward belonged in that class!"

"My father always said to me, 'If you want to have an easy life, *do* nothing and *say* nothing!'

These passages would be recounted as fables, or as the punchlines of fables meant to emphasize the kind of performance in which anyone could justly take pride.

If we accept the concept of shared appeal and responsibility on which the fable—the story with a moral—is based, then it is as immaterial that the metanarrative of this book occurred in Greece as it is that the Holocaust had its roots on German soil, that biblical narratives happened many centuries ago in what is now the Middle East, or that an African American woman became committed to a study of Panhellenic resistance. Consider, then, these sorts of anecdotes, told to me by informants, which have obsessed me and have taught me a great deal more than I knew before about politics and power.

> I can tell you that then [during the war] we women were, socially, in a better position, at a higher level than now. Even though now we have made certain advances in terms of knowledge and education, etc. But our organization and our own government [of the mountains] gave so many rights to women that only much later, decades later we were given. That is, we girls would sometimes be away from our houses for whole days on end, and no one would say much. That is, we gained these rights, by our-

[22] Oral history with my great aunt Lida Hart Richardson, Thanksgiving 1986.

selves. We voted after the age of eighteen. We voted, we women, at a
time when . . . [women didn't vote]. We did theater productions; we
would go a little way out of town and would put on various performances. And I, as a public employee and as an EPONitissa, many EP-
ONitisses, we would take part in plays both in the mountains and in the
cities. This happened after liberation but also during the occupation in
places that had been liberated. We had a lot of such places in the area
around Elassona; practically all the province was liberated. Only in the
town of Elassona, where there were first the Italians and afterward the
Germans, only there in the town of Elassona there wasn't. . . . And many
times, battles would take place right in Elassona. The Andartes, the partisans, would come and they would even strike at the Germans when they
would come in to get grapes out of the vineyards; they would strike them
so hard. So that along with the resistance and as a result of Free Greece,
women gained many things. . . . Yes, out of necessity, out of necessity
and because the opportunity presented itself, circumstances were created
in which the man could no longer stand in the way, and there was a
desperate need—the need for the woman to help as a nurse, as a partisan,
as a soldier, to help in the soup kitchens. Children were dying; there was
no other way. That is that same need, more generally, but also in her
home, every day she fought to go out to work, to be included in propaganda, in the army, to go anywhere she wished. And they never said to
you, "Oh, you're a woman, you can't possibly understand." . . . And if
some of them said it . . . how can I tell you? The woman basically took
this right with the sword. Eh, of course, there were a number of cases,
but slowly, even they began to believe that things couldn't happen any
other way. There were however, situations in which women simply outvoted the men. They outvoted them—that is to say, they didn't pay any
attention to them. How can I tell you? The woman was freed; she "unfolded"; she became "unbuttoned" [*ksedhiplothike avti i yineka, ksekoum-
bothike*]. Women became less afraid. . . . Many of these ties to the old
ways were dissolved, the constrictions were loosened, the difficulties were
surpassed, they were overcome.

And two later scenarios:

So as I said, I was on death row for eight years. And even when they announced that they were suspending the executions, we had no way of knowing that they wouldn't resume them some day. They kept the cell of death
through the fifties [*to kelli ton mellothanaton*]. But we all lived with the
thought of death, and if we were chosen, that would be that. It was really no
big deal. We got used to the idea, because we felt that we were upholding our
ideals. You know when a person really believes something, they'll gladly die

for it, and that's how we felt. And so they would come take girls away, and we lived through it. Because under those circumstances, when you have said to yourself, "I believe in this, and I'm going to die for it," every day that you live comes to you like a gift, you understand? (laughing). It's like being given a gift.

I remember a girl, Elli Svorou; she was from Mitillini. She was twenty-two or twenty-three years old then. She was engaged. And when they came to get her . . . they would come and get them at night and put them in solitary confinement. In the morning they would be put before the firing squad. And she followed the guard out of the cell, with her jacket slung over her arm . . . and it was as though she was going on an excursion, on a picnic! You see, we all had decided that if they came to take one of us, we would never show how afraid we were, to give courage to those who were left. So Elli, she bounded cheerfully down the stairs after him, and then suddenly she came back and called to us: "Oh, no! Silly me! I forgot my little pillow! Hand me my pillow, would you? How in the world am I going to sleep tonight?!" So we threw her the pillow, and she bounced back out of the room. And the next morning. . . . [Elli Svorou, a dressmaker, was executed on 16 June 1949.]

Consider this passage from a letter written in 1988:

One of my husband's sisters, quite severely crippled, was extremely active in EPON, and clearly found tremendous release of energy and potential from being accepted as a valued member of a committed group as opposed to being despised as an "unmarriageable cripple" in her village. After the civil war, she was imprisoned for a time, like so many of the cases you mention. But what is interesting is that when she was released, she did not change her values: she worked as a tailor in Larissa for fifteen years; she fiercely defended her right to have men friends as she chose (despite the strong disapproval of her family); and, although some people gossiped against her, she had many more loyal friends. Today she is married to another ex-Resistance fighter who was twenty-one years in prison, and although politically somewhat disillusioned (mainly as a result of the factionalism rampant in the KKE), they have not lost their "vision" (I can't think of a better word). They devote their whole time and energy to looking after my handicapped (autistic) son. I mention this case not because of its personal relevance to me but as strong evidence that the "reconstruction" of gender roles during the Resistance *has* left a permanent mark on Greek society, and this change needs to be fully taken account of by the Greek women's movement today.[23]

23 Regarding Katina Kapsali, letter from Meg Alexiou, George Seferis Chair of Modern Greek Studies, Department of Classics, Harvard University, 12 June 1988.

Finally, I return to Alice Walker:

> Because of the Movement, because of an awakened faith in the newness and imagination of the human spirit, because of "black and white together"—for the first time in our history in some human relationship on and off TV— because of the beatings, the arrests, the hell of battle during the past years, I have fought harder for my life and for a chance to be myself, to be something more than a shadow or a number, than I had ever done before in my life. Before, there had seemed to be no real reason for struggling beyond the effort for daily bread. Now there was a chance at that other that Jesus meant when He said we could not live by bread alone. (1983, 125)

Anaïs Nin once wrote, echoing Talmudic lore, "We don't see things as they are, we see them as *we* are." The people who gave me their eyewitness accounts certainly joined the EAM not because they were coerced at gunpoint, as critics of the organization claim, but because they saw it as they were then and as they needed to be in the 1940s. Recalling their experiences years later, most find that what the organization meant to them then in retrospect still registers with their current circumstances and convictions, with who they are now. But also, finally, if a song is as much about the lyricist as it is about its dramatis personae or its listeners, what follows is a very long and personal allegorical ode to political possibility.

CHAPTER I

Protean Modernism and
Narrative Identity

To set the stage for my analysis of the resistance movement as a political phenomenon, I begin with a historical overview of events in the Greek political world between 1941 and 1964. My basic critical tool is the *culture of modernity*, which constituted a vital framework for social movements of the epoch. It is here that we must turn first to comprehend the political fantasies of a generation of leaders and legislators. Later, I theorize a *narrative approach* to modern social and political transformations and then discuss case-specific narratives generated by movement authorities. Participants in the resistance came to accept and deploy such stories to justify deeds beyond the usual scope of their imaginations.

Indeed, this book raises critical questions about the realm of the social imaginary that energizes human behavior. What caused this particular kind of movement and why did it occur when it did? Why was it conceived as a broad popular movement with ramifications for larger political processes and memberships, instead of a more limited military defense of Greek sovereign territory against Axis invaders? How might we explain the drive to alter the orientations of sizable numbers of people with no previous record of participation in politics? With an eye toward answering such questions, I devote the first part of the book to isolating the *social texts* or *narratives* behind the extraordinary events that transpired in the 1940s in Greece—as John Iatrides aptly calls it, "a nation in crisis."

It is clear that the stories social movement leaders tell to bring adherents into the fold have consequences. Equally significant, these stories also have *histories*. In what follows I consider both preconditions and consequences in a case that for various reasons has been bypassed in world history and often misconstrued in Greek history. That the Greek resistance movement has been so negatively painted by its critics is surprising in view of the enthusiasm evident in the accounts of a substantial portion of its protagonists, among them the women I interviewed. Moreover, much of the material used in these reconstructions comes from oral histories conducted a good four decades after the events, evidence that the legitimating narratives maintained their hold on popular emotions years later.

Historical Background, 1941–1964

Axis troops invaded Greece on 7 April 1941, following the country's defeat in the war begun the previous year with Italian forces in Albania. The government and royal family left the country for the Middle East on the 27th of the same month. The government-in-exile, operating out of Cairo for the duration of the war, consisted of the king, a group of politicians from the pre-war political parties, and a number of British advisors. At home, the resulting political vacuum would eventually be filled by the two major resistance organizations, EAM-ELAS (Ethniko Apeleftherotiko Metopo, National Liberation Front–Ethnikos Laikos Apeleftherotikos Stratos, National People's Liberation Army) and EDES (Ethnikos Demokratikos Ellinikos Syndhesmos, National Republican Greek League), along with several smaller, Athens-based groups. After its defeat by the Axis, Greece was divided into a tripartite regional occupation under German, Italian, and Bulgarian control, in a Nazi-dominated coalition.

When the first resistance organizations were formed, the Pindos mountain women who carried supplies loaded on their backs to Greek forces in Albania had already become legendary in the popular press. Similarly, women played a well-publicized role in the Battle of Crete (April–May 1941), with Cretan regulars caught on the mainland while being evacuated from the Albanian front. During the winter of 1941–1942, an estimated 300,000 Greek citizens starved to death due to food shortages caused by requisitioning on behalf of occupying forces. At the local level, women organized the soup kitchens that kept the death toll from rising higher. Throughout this earlier period, women were active primarily through traditional support functions such as cooking, cleaning, and sheltering (commonwealth troops). These traditional roles were adapted and extended only when the men were absent. But as the war progressed, and with the advent of an organized resistance, women and girls began to undertake more radical activities. They were recruited into specific organizations and began to commit acts of sabotage that were punishable by death or imprisonment. In Athens, this was particularly true of the youth organizations EPON and PEAN (Panellinia Enosi Aghonizomenon Neon, the Panhellenic Union of Fighting Youth). In the countryside, where the EAM had recruited whole villages, married, widowed, and elderly women also engaged in a wider range of activities, at greater personal risk and increasingly, based on a corporate rationale. Thus, although statistics are unreliable, by 1944, a significant percentage of women had engaged in some kind of resistance activity.[1]

In the beginning, the goals of the resistance organizations were fairly straightforward. They were to liberate the country and to coordinate the scattered exploits of ordinary citizens, such as exploding two Bulgarian ships in the Piraeus harbor, sabotaging a munitions dump in Salonika and demonstrating against newly endowed chairs in German Language and Literature by students at the University of Athens (Hondros 1983, 96–97). One such act that had considerable symbolic impact occurred on 30 May 1941 when two students, Manolis Glezos and Apostolos (Lakis) Santas, ripped down the Nazi flag flying over the Acropolis.[2] With both the government and the national army in Egypt, however, such efforts remained small-scale and relatively ineffective. In the fall of 1941, the first ELAS units were formed in the mountains of Roumeli, a legacy of the old Klephtic guerilla fighting bands, which were part of a tradition dating back to the resistance against Turkish occupation. In the major cities and in some villages, the EAM began to organize workers, young people, and medical personnel into coordinated resistance teams. As noted earlier, the EAM leadership consisted mainly of activists from the prewar Greek Communist party cadres. Nearly all had recently survived sojourns in jails and exile camps under the fascist regime of General Ioannis Metaxas, which ruled Greece between August 1936 and April 1941.[3] The "movement within a movement" was born, as the EAM began working to restructure

---

[1] Here, I include any sort of insubordination that defied the rules of the occupation and for which imprisonment or death were the cost of discovery. Such acts included owning or using a radio; participating in neighborhood soup kitchens; breaking curfew for any reason; knitting socks or supplying any kind of food or shelter to victims of the occupation. Numbers of official participants are very difficult if not impossible to obtain. Membership data are generally not available. According to L. S. Stavrianos, the combined strength of EAM-ELAS has been estimated at between 1.5 million and 2 million members out of a population of 7.5 million. It is not possible to pin down the actual numbers of women in the organization. As Stavrianos comments, "The fact of the matter is that accurate statistics could not be compiled under occupation conditions. Members drifted in and out of the various organizations, depending on the pressures of the given moment, and the distinction between intermittent support and actual membership was always difficult to define" (Stavrianos 1952, 44).

[2] This incident has been widely cited in the secondary literature, irrespective of the authors' political positions. For example, see Woodhouse 1976, 21; Clogg 1979, 139; M. Sarafis 1980, xc; Hondros 1981, 38; Vlavianos 1989, 169.

[3] Throughout the period, Constantine Maniadakis, the minister of public security, showed great efficiency in targeting and detaining nearly all the important KKE leaders. He also established a fraudulent parallel Communist party, which issued deceptive copies of documents and of the party's daily newspaper *Rizospastis*. Maniadakis is also known for contriving various mental and physical tortures. See Chapter 3 and Vlavianos 1989, 163–64.

Greek political culture while operating as a resistance movement mobilized to dismantle the Nazi occupation.

Soon after the resistance organizations were inaugurated, forces from EAM-ELAS and EDES began to engage in localized clashes, predating the Civil War (1946–1949) by several years. The organizations quickly became entangled in a struggle between Left and Right, which had been the hallmark of Greek politics since the early part of the century, as governments alternated unpredictably throughout the 1920s and 1930s. In November 1942, EAM-ELAS, EDES, and members of a British envoy collaborated in sabotaging the Gorgopotamos Bridge. However, after the bridge was successfully blown up, EAM and EDES did not cooperate in any further operations. A brief initial period of reciprocity gave way to more acrid encounters and the two sides spent the rest of the war as adversaries, a situation that would later develop into civil war.

A significant development, from a military and state-building standpoint, was the surrender and evacuation of Italian troops in September 1943. This allowed for the creation of a large zone in the middle region of the mainland known as Free Greece (Eleftheri Ellada) and led to the official instatement, on 10 March 1944, of the provisional "Government of the Mountains," administered by the Politiki Epitropi Ethnikis Apeleftherosis (PEEA), the Political Committee for National Liberation. Alexandros Svolos, professor of constitutional law at the University of Athens, was elected president on 20 April. In May, PEEA presided over the election of a 250-member national council with representatives from both free and occupied Greece. As a quasi-political party supervising a Panhellenic "parliament," which, according to its literature, would stand until free elections could be held, PEEA was both an expression and a persuasive source of popular legitimacy for the EAM.[4] We will return to the state-building aspect of EAM shortly.

On the subject of gender equality, the July 30 issue of the PEEA Bulletin of Actions and Decisions reported that on May 27, the first Greek equal rights

---

[4] See Hondros 1983, 121, 189. The desire for free elections and a popular plebiscite on the future of the Greek monarchy was first expressed in the pamphlet, *Ti einai kai ti thelei to Ethniko Apeleftherotiko Metopo* (What is EAM and what does it want?), published and distributed in September 1942. Its author was Dimitrios Glinos, who had been an active member of the KKE since its inception and who figures prominently in our story. Glinos served as EAM's leading ideologist. Like Bukharin in *The ABC of Communism*, Glinos tried to lay out an ideological plan that would arouse a commitment to the goals of the organization in "ordinary" people. His death coincided with the creation of PEEA, and he was eulogized (a fate different from Bukharin's) at the 21 May 1944 meeting of the newly elected national council. The pamphlet was mined in the process of formulating legislation announced in PEEA's *Dheltio prakseon kai apofaseon* (Bulletin of acts and decisions); and its influence is also strongly evident in articles appearing in the KKE's *Kommounistiki epitheorisi* (Communist review), and the Free Greece newspaper, *Kodhika poseidhona* (The Poseidon codes) edited by Yiorgoulis Beikos. It was reissued in Athens in November 1944 by Rigas Press.

clause was put to a vote and approved. According to Article 5 of the PEEA constitution, "All Greeks, men and women, have equal political and civil rights." This declaration allowed women to vote for the first time in Greek history. A number of women deputies were elected, including Fotini Filippidi from Larissa, Kaiti Zevgou from Athens, Mahi Mavroeidi from Kalamata, and Maria Svolou from Athens.

Other significant events followed PEEA's initial creation. On 31 March 1944, Greek army personnel stationed in the Middle East and supporters of the liberal politician Eleftherios Venizelos, mutinied in support of the PEEA government, touching off a crisis that continued into April and was repressed by British and Greek authorities by the end of the month. Key participants were sent to the North African prison camp of El Daba (Fleischer 1978). PEEA ministers attended various plenary conferences called by the Allies during the latter part of the war, in Lebanon (May 1944), Caserta (September 1944), Varkiza (February 1945), and elsewhere, with mixed outcomes. These negotiations significantly reduced the PEEA's autonomy—a major aim of British and Greek authorities in exile. There was considerable consternation among rank-and-file members of EAM-ELAS, who later accused their representatives of selling out the cause and of failing to ensure adequate protection from the growing right-wing backlash. Between 1943 and 1944, the "White Terror," aimed at Communists and former partisans began. As a result, many EAM leaders, members, and their relatives were arrested and sent to jails and concentration camps or were pursued by extreme right-wing terrorist bands throughout the 1940s and 1950s.[5]

German troops left Greece in October 1944. The government-in-exile returned. However, the situation worsened with the "Dhekemvriana" (December Events), a series of street battles between ELAS, the Athens police, and the British, which continued through 1945. From 1946 to 1949 the Democratic Army, made up of former EAM-ELAS members, and the National Army, supported by the British and the Americans, fought a bitter civil war. A critical factor in prolonging the conflict, often cited by commentators, was EAM's decision to abstain from the March 1946 general elections. Widespread support garnered during the resistance virtually assured a sweeping victory for the Left. Two reasons have been identified for the decision to abstain, despite the probability of electoral success: first, strategists viewed the repressive climate as a clear and present danger to EAM campaigners and supporters and, second, EAM was now under the directorship of prewar KKE leader Nikos Zachariades, who had begun to steer the organization away from its former commitment to bourgeois democracy or, more accurately, popular democracy. Thus a raging campaign of terror, the EAM's own questionable policy choices,

[5] For a discussion of the legal ramifications of the White Terror during the civil war years, see Alivizatos 1981.

and massive vote falsification despite the presence of AMFOGE (American Mission for Observing Greek Elections) combined to produce an overwhelming victory for the monarchist Right, and the political violence continued unchecked.[6] On 16 October 1949 the Democratic Army announced a cease-fire. Its remaining forces, said to include many women and adolescents,[7] were defeated in the Grammos and Vitsi mountain region near the Yugoslavian border.

The resistance movement was thus demobilized by state and parastate repression during the late 1940s and throughout the 1950s. Among the casualties of this countermovement were the newly emancipated women who had taken part in the resistance, along with the female relatives of EAM members. Rapes and killings were common features of the postwar reign of terror. By 1964, as a result of less stringent regimes, most of the political prisoners engendered by the resistance had been released. Although the number of left activists in general and activist women in particular fell dramatically, the resistance left an important ideological impression on the political system. For instance, in 1952 the constitution was amended to give women the vote. This move was by all means politically expedient for the reigning government and the extent to which it was meant to advance the cause of women's rights and status is certainly debatable. Nevertheless, the new policy showed that women had now been discerned as a mass political force and the resistance, together with such other factors as prewar feminism and developments in other countries, had generated certain expectations in the voting public. In view of its many ramifications beyond the vote, the resistance can be seen in an international context as a modern historical moment that endeavored to fix a national consciousness in people's minds. Those invested in the ways of the old regime did not resign themselves to the brief but definitive insertion of mass elements into politics. In one way or another, a good part of the rest of the century would be spent "neutralizing the ghost of EAM," in the words of one observer (Constantine Tsoucalas, in Iatrides, 327) and dismantling its claims to sovereignty. Let us, then, turn our attention to the longer "durée," and the ways in which the culture of modernity shaded and gave meaning to the picture.

Modernism, Postmodernism, and "Crisis of Innocence"

In the freshness of the revolution and its goals, the Fourteenth of July always infuses a new life and a human face, even after and without the Bastille. The light of 1789

---

6 See M. Sarafis 1994; Mavrogordatos 1981.

7 See Eudes 1972, esp. 326–39. For a literary account of this battle, see Stratis Haviaras's novel, *The Heroic Age*.

persists everywhere: like the Ninth Symphony, which is so close to the citizen, it
cannot be taken back.

—Bloch, *Natural Law and Human Dignity*

Can we confine the production of images, symbols and legends solely to the realm of
ideology and see their controversies as no more than a "deliberate political mystifica-
tion"? Or should we enter into the sensibility and the collective mentalities of the
activists in order to uncover the meaning and the power of the "legend"?

—Haupt 1986, 47

In the late 1980s, references to the terms "modern" and "postmodern"
began to appear with increasing frequency in the discourses of a range of
academic disciplines. The literature generally locates the French Enlightenment as the key historical conjuncture that produced the combination of
intellectual forces and political proclivities known as "modernism."[8] The
modernist cultural pattern began to develop during the eighteenth century
and intensified between 1870 and as late as 1970, by some counts. The 1970s
and especially the 1980s saw the introduction of postmodern styles of social
interaction and expression.

In spite of their ever more frequent mention in contemporary texts, these
concepts have been underutilized as formulae for understanding empirical
aspects of social, historical, and especially *political* developments, partly because in the late 20th-century we remain unclear about the nature of changes
in prevailing governing structures, whether established or transitional, liberal
democratic, former colonial, or socialist leaning. With fresh information constantly destabilizing our "truths," we will no doubt continue to ponder how
postmodern democracies, postmodern political movements, postmodern legal
structures, or postauthoritarian redemocratization differ from earlier, more
recognizable forms of social and political activity; and to consider how continuities from the past might render novel categories unnecessary.

The culture of modernity has been depicted in various literatures in ways
that suggest its tremendous transformative power: as a "global" phenomenon,
a "break with the feudal past," "a time of excitement and new freedoms" (B.
K. Scott 1990, 6) a "revolutionary force" (Jacques Derrida in Patterson 1989,
85). The modernist mentality, according to theorists, can be recognized by its
attraction to universal laws and immutable standards of conduct. During the
modern era, considerable time was devoted to constituting and reconstituting

[8] For example, see Caplan 1989; and Patterson 1989. General essays on the topic are R.
Williams 1989; Habermas 1981 and comment by Giddens; Tyler 1986; and Marcus 1986. Marcus
and Fischer 1986, esp. 67–73, 157–62 specifically compare modernism and postmodernism.
Specific modernist moments are explored in Burke 1978; Jelavich 1982; Jusdanis 1991; Pollock
1988; Hobsbawm 1987; Hobsbawm and Ranger 1983; Wohl 1979. Perry Anderson (1988) warns
against a too casual use of key analytic terms.

the broad tenets of human "decency," unwavering "standards of excellence," determinants of "quality"—all words whose definitions of course very much depended on who spoke them and in what context. There was also a tendency to acknowledge only the most obvious and unequivocal differences, whether in art, scholarship, state building, or insurgency. Thus, on the whole, the modernist horizon was limited to fixed conceptual categories conceived to maximize the predictability of any given social interaction. During this period, neat taxonomies circumscribing rights, duties, and deviance and equated with "woman," "citizen," "worker," "respectability," and so on were encoded and internalized in the public mind.[9] One hallmark of modernity was the normative consciousness that all members of a given category ought somehow to be constituted as the same or roughly equivalent, based on a "totalizing" paradigm. Diversity and failure to assimilate were often read as "chaotic" or even more fraught, as "anarchic"—in other words, as dangerous impediments to the engineering necessary to social order.

From a social movement standpoint, the culture of modernity encouraged relatively intransigent notions of what it meant to be liberated from oppression. Modernist movements tended to strategize capturing or neutralizing "large" centers of power: the State, the Party, the Union, the Class. The pursuit of universal truths and common ground created the psychological basis for movement solidarity that was crucial to the "fight." Monoculturalism rather than multiculturalism gave modernism the emotional charge needed for collective action. Whatever multiple hegemonies existed in any given society, movement organizers tended to target one or two around which to rally their counterhegemonic forces. But undoubtedly generalizations about modernism need to be tempered with several further points.

First, whether or not its cultures were willing to tolerate diversity, the basic zeal to erase differences meant that modernism was both troubled by the existence of variations and contained many, especially as new groups and ideas burst onto the public scene. In art and literature, difference may have posed fewer problems and found more ready acceptance than in formal institutional politics, where higher stakes, competing forces, and the urgent need for action created powerful tensions. Modernism as a problem of political economy centered primarily around "modernization" processes. At issue was how to move away from the "backward" and the "traditional" as efficiently as possible, a goal that partly entailed denying or finding a way to control existing differences.

Second, although predicated on the idea that certain characteristics were the "foundation" of singular identities, for their duration modern movements

---

[9] Critical legal studies scholars have noted parallels in modern jurisprudence. See Kelman 1987; Gordon 1988, 1981.

were constantly in flux, since modernity, as Perry Anderson writes, "flowered in the space between a still usable classical past, a still indeterminate technical present, and a still unpredictable political future" (1986, 326). Shifting expectations and the need to respond to unintended consequences meant that though built around universal tenets, modernist social movements were essentially construction projects, whose outcomes often surprised even their contractors. Modernism was not a static division but rather an orientation whose content was continually changing.

Third, although modernist art and literature addressed the subject of social alienation, especially during the 1920s and 1930s, its fundamental project cannot really be considered "fragmentary" in the postmodern sense, because modernism was so clearly tied to underlying myths and hopeful truths about social processes. At its core modernism was a "larger emancipatory project." Today, many agree with Regenia Gagnier that "we need the postmodern equivalents of the . . . stories that provided slogans that incited action" (1990, 30; and see Hart 1992).

A product of late twentieth-century capitalism, *postmodernity* has generated new cultural dynamics and new perceptions of personal and collective identities. Jane Flax writes:

> The meanings—or even existence—of concepts essential to all forms of Enlightenment metanarrative (reason, history, science, self, knowledge, power, gender, and the inherent superiority of Western culture) have been subjected to increasingly corrosive attacks. . . . The "essential contestability" . . . of the constituting notions of Enlightenment metanarratives [has] been exposed. This creates a *crisis of innocence,* since these notions then become mere artifacts that humans have created and for whose effects and consequences we alone are responsible. It is difficult for humans to live without secure grounds below and ontological or transcendental guarantees from above. (1990, 450–51)

Postmodern or "new" social movements, in contrast to their modern counterparts, are now said to center on more local, personal concerns, styles of expression, ways of living, and cultural interactions among increasingly multi-identified communities.[10] Yet despite its emphasis on "healthy" self-exploration, the multicultural postmodern world has not generally been successful in producing the peaceful coexistence among societal groups that many have hoped for. Instead, the resulting "identity politics" have tended to create centrifugal forces that confound cultural critics and policy makers alike. Despite widespread agreement in a range of disciplines that significant qualitative differences exist between the two eras, there is still disagreement as to

---

[10] For example, see Barbara Epstein's 1991 treatment of "direct action."

whether the contemporary human condition is wholly postmodernist or an amalgam of modernist holdovers and postmodern zeitgeists. For example, the sociologist Anthony Giddens (1990) maintains that the current era is not so much one of postmodernity as "high-modernity" in which the resonances and repercussions of the modern period are still quite profound.[11]

Political Modernism: A Profile

As a foundation for analysis, modernism has often been associated with the aesthetic realm. In the European art world of the 1880s, for example, a search for self-regarding "truth" in the work of postimpressionists such as Paul Gauguin, began to replace the dreamy recumbent visions of Georges Seurat. Later, during the interwar period, the Russian constructivists and the Dada movement called older artistic conceptions into question.

With notable exceptions the modernist concept has only secondarily and fairly vaguely been used to illuminate historic developments in institutional politics and economic systems.[12] During the years when the terms "progressive" and "avant-garde" came into popular currency, however, politics, art, social science, and social engineering were without a doubt connected, somewhat ambiguously, as what Raymond Williams calls "a whole cultural movement and moment" (1989, 48).

From a comparative political perspective, if the Greek resistance were to be considered the smallest of a set of concentric circles, with each new circle adding elements of a larger contextual universe, the circle with the farthest, most meaningful reach would be the modernist mentality. Having said this, I intend to isolate what I find serviceable about the concept and then to narrow my discussion directly back to the case at hand, which ought to be appreciated for its own internal consistencies, particularly inasmuch as modernism as an

[11] In social movement terms, using the American Civil Rights movement as a yardstick, the modernist phase would have ended around 1970, when the language of struggle for "rights," "justice," and "freedom" was replaced by less unitary goals such as ending the Vietnam War and radically restructuring the American economic system, and when disparate tendencies, including cultural nationalism, proliferated in the movement. Yet the difficulty of precise historical periodization is demonstrated in the Afrocentrism movement of the 1980s and 1990s, itself a product of cultural nationalism, but based on modernist premises in that its goal is to project an image of unity and essentialized identity. The postmodern phase of the women's movement might be pegged as beginning either with the cultural feminist debates of the 1980s or with the Anita Hill–Clarence Thomas hearings and the so-called "Third Wave," on which see Walker 1992.

[12] On modernist politics, see Chatterjee 1993a and b, 1989; and the range of contributions in Lash and Friedman 1992. Hobsbawm 1987 and Hobsbawm and Ranger 1983 combine specific periodization (1870–1914) and a multifaceted exploration of the quintessentially modernist trait of mass incorporation. Also see Mouffe 1990, 1991, on modernism and democratic philosophy; and Z. Bauman 1992.

analytic code has been used far too superficially in the past. In the broad sense in which I use the term, fascists, black cultural and political nationalists such as W. E. B. Du Bois and Marcus Garvey, Weimar republicans, Victorian suffragettes, plus a wide range of other unlikely bedfellows were driven by what I am calling the "modernist mentality." This might make the concept too broad to be meaningful. My point however, is that the terms of public debate, the rules for engagement, and the emotional playing field were the same even if the goals of certain groups were different and fascism was by any standard morally reprehensible.[13] Hence, for the moment the methodological imperative of precise classification and periodization normally subscribed to will be left aside. As a distinctive ideological factor motivating behavior, the modernist *problématique* cannot be fastened to a specific decade, since versions that, for example, appeared in the nineteenth century were influential well into the twentieth. In presenting a diverse assortment of examples, I assemble a "collage" of modernist thinking, sometimes at the cost of contextual specificity.

One of the most significant social changes of the modernist period was the introduction of various categories of latent citizens into politics. As Charles Tilly notes, "The nineteenth century . . . saw the rise of the social movement in the sense of a set of people who voluntarily and deliberately commit themselves to a shared identity, a unifying belief, a common program, and a collective struggle to realize that program" (1984, 303). With this point in mind, I want to set Greece in its widest international context and explore the ways in which the politics of the Greek resistance movement represented a local instance that incorporated certain features of this more universal trend. In many respects the Greek resistance *cum* social movement typified the drive toward unmitigated idealism. Its shifting nature had more to do with the nature of political process than with any lack of fixed referents seen to typify postmodern "new social movements." Analytically, my aim is to take into account those aspects of social and political deconstruction which postmodern approaches have made it a point to emphasize, but also to give full weight to those aspects of the modernist imagination that plausibly steered the EAM movement, as a child of its times, in certain directions. Indeed, from a comparative perspective, EAM's social revolutionary and state-building efforts were not fully spontaneous or completely anomalous and local, but instead were the conscious products of modernist thinking.

During what we now conceive of as the late modern era, and reflecting nineteenth- and earlier twentieth-century ideologies, the interwar period saw a renaissance of political and cultural debate and a quest for solutions to crises of social inequality in Harlem, Barcelona, Paris, Weimar, and points in between.

---

[13] For example, see R. Williams 1989; and P. Anderson 1988.

Take, for example, the common ground beneath various twentieth-century constructions of black consciousness. Of the uptown literary generation of the 1920s, Henry Louis Gates Jr. writes: "The confusion of realms was complete: the critic became social reformer, and literature became an instrument for the social and ethical betterment of the black person" (1987, 30).[14] Earlier, in 1906, Maggie Lena Walker of the Order of Saint Luke, a branch of the Negro Independence movement in Richmond, Virginia, called upon black men in her community to "record [yourselves] as . . . the strong race men of our city. . . . I am asking each man in this audience to go forth from this building, determined to do valiant deeds for the Negro Women of Richmond." In 1933, after more than twenty-five years of advocacy, Walker called for struggle, "first by practice and then by precept" (quoted in Brown 1990, 217, 218).

Marcus Garvey offered as remedy "the dream of a Negro Empire," stating that "It is only a question of a few more years when Africa will be completely colonized by Negroes, as Europe is by the white race. What we want is an independent African nationality. . . . Everybody knows that there is absolutely no difference between the native African and the American and West Indian Negroes, in that we are descendants from one common family stock. . . . It is only a matter of accident that we have been divided and kept apart for over three hundred years, but it is felt that when the time has come for us to get back together, we shall do so in the spirit of brotherly love" (Jacques-Garvey 1969, 70–71).[15] Garvey's wife and co-worker, Amy Jacques-Garvey, wrote: "The women of the East, both yellow and black, are slowly, but surely imitating the women of the Western world, and as the white women are bolstering up a decaying white civilization, even so women of the darker races are sallying forth to help their men establish a civilization according to their own standards, and to strive for world leadership" (quoted in hooks 1981, 174).

The modernist critiques of previous cultural habits and expressive styles that arose in different environments shared a common philosophical stance and in some instances were interactive and contagious, even when some branches of modernism conflicted with others. For example, Garvey's movement argued for separate social, economic, and political spheres, and in any case, most direct black-white alliances, real or imagined, would have been invalidated by the conscious and unconscious racism of the era.[16] The "New Negro" campaign generally opposed both Garveyism and radical socialism (see, e.g., Locke 1992, xxxi). The "New Woman" movement was the essence of modernist

---

[14] Also see Huggins 1971; and Locke 1992.

[15] In spite of interpersonal tensions and interpretive disagreement, Garvey and W. E. B. Du Bois both subscribed to a modernist code. See Cedric Robinson 1990, 45.

[16] The literature on nineteenth- and twentieth-century racism is of course vast. On racism and racial stereotyping in cosmopolitan Weimar Germany, see Bathrick 1990.

discontinuity with the past, but the backlash against it from across the political spectrum was equally modern.[17] Although the connections between modernist schools were not always direct and were sometimes controversial, there were often cross-regional similarities and in some cases, engagement. Thus, as Peter Gay notes, "just as the Weimar style was older than the Weimar Republic, so was it larger than Germany. Both in the Empire and in the Republic, German painters, poets, playwrights, psychologists, philosophers, composers, architects, even humorists were engaged in a free international commerce of ideas; they were part of a Western community on which they drew and which, in turn, they fed; chauvinism was not merely offensive to the Weimar style, it would have been fatal" (1988, 6).

What were some of the guiding principles of the modernist moment? In what ways did modernism constitute a coherent political debate? Several aspects of the modernist problematic are relevant. Eric Hobsbawm (1987, 3–5) persuasively demonstrates that many of the guiding lights of twentieth-century politics were the intellectual offspring of the formative years between 1870 and 1914. In fact, the hallmark of this generation was as much formation as transformation, involving an increasingly public (hence Jürgen Habermas's focus on the establishment of a relatively novel public sphere in the nineteenth century) and at times transcontinental struggle over questions of identity, hierarchy, and the fundamental construction and survival of whole societies. In Greece and elsewhere prominent leaders were literate and audience to new communications media. Conceivably, these leaders were exposed to some of the same contested events and exchanges: the French Revolution, the consequences of 1815 and 1848; the Crimean War, the first to be covered by foreign correspondents; nineteenth-century banking and imperialism; the incorporation of new mass publics such as the propertyless and women into political activity; battles over cultural-territorial unification and infrastructural development; the genesis of state-administered welfare systems and controversies about their viability; labor unionism; the Paris Commune and Franco-Prussian War; the Great Depression of the 1890s; the Dreyfus affair; the Russian Revolutions of 1905 and 1917; and World War I and the growth of fascism. Politics, like aesthetics, are inspired by creative as well as strategic considerations. The interplay between advocacy and culture that characterized the modernist period fostered a certain collective "mood" as many a minority ancien régime found itself forced to make way for popular social actors.

Top on the list of constituent elements of this mood of controversy and reconstitution of older values labeled modernist should be, *first*, utopian and universalist impulses. Idealism prevailed in academic and popular political discourse. Earl Lewis, for instance, notes the framing by black residents of

---

[17] See Smith-Rosenberg 1989; Bridenthal et al. 1984; McCormick 1993; Lavin 1992.

Norfolk, Virginia, in 1865 of the *Equal Suffrage Address,* which "highlighted America's democratic promise and celebrated the role of Afro-Americans in the preservation of national independence. Independence and liberty were important symbols and cherished rights, and blacks therefore defined freedom to mean the full enjoyment of equal economic, social, and political rights, the full guarantee of independence and liberty" (1991, 11).[18]

On the European political stage, we can see in Nietzsche's nihilism and in his "will to power"; in Freud's "unconscious"; in Marxist dialectics; in Croce's intellectual engagement with Vico and Gramsci's with Croce; in Sorel's radical syndicalism; and in Weber, Durkheim, and, more obliquely, in Georg Simmel's discussions of exchange and interaction; the fantasy of potential improvement and progressive modification. The modern era was also marked by the growth and articulation of the Enlightenment-based doctrine of legal positivism, which held that systems of jurisprudence could be structured so as to affirm certain "objective" norms and procedures based on a code of "fairness" and enforced by state officials (see Schmitt 1990). Nietzsche, in fact, is one of the major modern philosophers and in spite of his trademark pessimism, Robert B. Pippin remarks, in characterizing "the modern moral problem tends to highlight such things as liberal-progressivism, romanticism, Christian humanism, socialism and egalitarianism as prototypical of modernity" (1991, 91). Ortega y Gasset's 1933 comment, though he seeks to mark out a new rhetorical path, remains profoundly modernist and further demonstrates its code of instrumental faith and innocence: "There exist, in effect, many reasons for presuming that European man is lifting his tents off that modern soil where he has camped for three centuries and is beginning a new exodus toward another historic ambit, toward another mode of existence" (quoted in Wohl 1979, 122). Thus, despite its strong antagonisms, modernism involved a religious belief in the idea of improved and universal outcomes, to be expected if a broad metanarrative plan were followed. In the long term modernism relied on an ethic of postponement and delayed fulfillment that was intrinsically utopian since it was not at all clear what national fates would be or where "the new devices and inventions were going to lead," as Perry Anderson says. "It was precisely this ambiguity—an *openness* of horizon, where the shapes of the future could alternatively assume the shifting forms of either a new type of capitalism or the eruption of socialism—that was constitutive of so much of the original sensibility of what had come to be called 'modernism'" (1988, 325, 329).

This brings us to a second modernist theme. For many, especially the avant-garde, modernism was about discontinuity and self-assertion. It aimed for

---

[18] Lewis notes that echoes of this document could still be heard in political polemics as late as 1910 (17). Modernist issues of "respectability," "race-consciousness," and community politics are discussed in Evelyn Brooks Higginbotham's fascinating account (1993).

conscious and deliberate disruption. Although received tradition was detectable in modernist reasoning, the core of its politics derived from tendentiousness and the ability to shock with its ambitions for social change. Aspirations to challenge or replace comfortable ways of doing things combined with the kind of melodrama often used to preach to the unconverted. Modernism constituted a youthful dialogue with absolute patriarchal authority, in Mikhail Bakhtin's terms "a conscious relationship with . . . normal language and its belief system . . . [but] in fact set against them, and set against them *dialogically:* one point of view opposed to another, one evaluation opposed to another, one accent opposed to another" (1981, 314). Modernism was youthful not only because many of its exponents were chronologically young but also in its inclination to drop strange animals at its father's feet. Attention to youth, vigor, revitalization, and self-declaration manifested itself, for example, in advertising and popular iconography.

A third theme, related in its search for identity, was the more formal political side of modernism, which involved an emotionally charged conversation—at times violent argument—between insurgents of diverse class origins, ruling bourgeois factions, and state authority. In retrospect, a major participant and theorist of these issues was Antonio Gramsci, whose writings about the genesis of civil society and the role of state actors in its creation, about conflicts over hegemonic dominance and control over outcomes, and about political development in general were classically modernist. These struggles are particularly interesting because of the paradoxical connection between elite and proletariat at the level of organic leadership.

In popular aesthetics and in the political construction of bourgeois democracy, so-called high and low cultures and indeed homogeneity and heterogeneity have long been mutually constitutive through constant reaction and counterreaction. Despite its historic relationship with the *lumpen*, however, high culture, with its claims of homogenetic "purity," has been reluctant to admit any formal connection.[19] Modernist ethics were not successful in soothing or resolving this tense relationship, but to a novel extent, new interactive channels were nonetheless established and dialogues begun. The whole question of mimesis was brought to the fore in both art and politics, especially in the industrial and late modern periods through the 1930s,[20] particularly if we accept Fredric Jameson's description of mimesis as "the ways in which the pedagogical figure, by his own praxis, shows the disciple what else you can think and how much further you can go with the thoughts you already have . . . free[ing] you from the taboos and constraints of forms learnt by rote and assumed to be inscribed in the nature of things" (1990, 52).

[19] See Stallybrass and White 1986; and Stallybrass 1990.
[20] For example, see Zukin 1977. Also Auerbach 1953.

Types of influence on a continuum from mimicry to coercion were at the heart of the normative debates of the period. The complex exchange between bottom-up and top-down socialization was apparent in a number of areas from literature to film to statecraft.[21] Oppositional modernists were of several minds about appropriate modes of influence. Among the alternatives was, first, enlightenment by the benevolent powerful either through deliberate instruction or trickle-down processes. Exchanges of this type would require deference on the part of those of "lower" status or "falser" consciousness, an option relevant across the political spectrum and rooted in the evolutionist paradigm of Hobsbawm's (1987) "age of empire." This legacy and its Eurocentrism were strongly and in some sense counterintuitively apparent in Marx and Engels's discussions of "the national question."[22] Another route was the radical separation between "high" and "low," a philosophy adopted by the Frankfurt School, which held that from a cultural-cum-political point of view, popularization naturally diminished quality.

Another alternative for powerholders was actually to accede to demands for autonomy from the increasingly confident margins. These attitudes were often blended in the ideas of national leadership strata, reflecting their ambivalence about what Gramsci called the "national-popular," or the culture of ordinary people, which he felt had revolutionary potential when guided by a vanguard party (see Forgacs 1984). In many cases, a basic distrust of the "mass" and a fear of collective action as a license for unbridled behavior if "the crowd" was left to its own devices shared emotional space with a sincere respect for mass potential, a desire to improve the world, and the hope of "rationalizing" social change. This ambivalence partly resulted from new forms of upward mobility, distancing the era from the "age of absolutism" and engendering compound loyalties in national elites. Through relatively more democratic educational systems, dispersed modes of business transaction and domination in colonial and neocolonial frameworks, changing sexual mores, foreign travel, and access to a more extensive and widely available popular press, organic intellectuals might now straddle certain ideological fences due to a mixed cultural exposure.[23] Mohandas Gandhi, founder of the Indian Nationalist movement and, as we shall see, Dimitris Glinos and Stefanos Sarafis in the Greek resistance context, are examples of leaders whose multidimensional backgrounds may have led them to conceive broad-gauged policies. Whereas these policies were basically inclusive and expansive, their authors plainly had not reconciled themselves to the notion that the "national-popular" might be capable of enlightened political action when not guided by those better educated and more experienced.

[21] For an intricate theoretical discussion of related questions, see R. Williams 1977.
[22] See Nimni 1989; and Traverso and Lowy 1990.
[23] B. Anderson 1983 makes this point. Also see Nairn 1977; and Eley 1981.

A fourth theme came from the need to construct an effective response to the virulent new ideology of fascism. The official fear of revolution was among the factors behind fascism and can be traced back to Metternich's "dissolution complex." The fear that revolutionary forces would destroy all that "rational souls" held dear had been building among state makers throughout the nineteenth century, climaxing with the infamous local insurgencies in 1848 and 1870. For communist parties, after 1920 and 1934 respectively, the fantasy of an exploding series of national versions of October 17 and the Comintern's Third Period dogmatism were transformed—reluctantly in some quarters—into more pragmatic expectations and solutions (see Hobsbawm 1976). Generally, after 1930 "left" modernists grew anxious to find ways to counter fascism as an extreme variant of the fear of revolution, seeking to withstand the assault on Enlightenment ideals by fascist "modernists."[24]

For a cross-cultural community, two events foregrounded the need for immediate action: the 1933 German Reichstag fire with its show trials well publicized in the international news media and the Spanish Civil War, 1936–1939. As the decade progressed, the Comintern directed national communist parties to form popular and national fronts until the threat became less menacing. At the official announcement of the new popular front strategy during the Seventh Congress in 1935, for example, General Secretary George Dimitrov announced that the primary goal was to "find a common language with the broadest masses for the purposes of struggling against the class enemy, to find ways of finally overcoming the isolation of the revolutionary vanguard from the masses of the proletariat and all other toilers, as well as overcoming the fatal isolation of the working class itself from its natural allies in the struggle against the bourgeoisie, against fascism."[25] For a wider European reading public, the novels, essays, and short stories of Heinrich Mann, Aldous Huxley, George Orwell, and Nikos Kazantzakis, the historical and sociological work of Karl Mannheim, and even Marc Bloch—to identify only a few—explored the roots of fascism and speculated about its unchecked expansion.[26]

[24] As I have maintained, fascism, though distinctly *anti*modernist in some respects, was also part of the "modernist moment," particularly in its conceptualization of ready and powerful solutions to social problems.

[25] Quoted in Hobsbawm 1987, 224. Bulgarian George Dimitrov, who gained widespread international prestige as an antifascist leader within the communist movement following his acquittal at the Reichstag fire trials, was highly regarded on the Greek Left. As was typical in the popular front period, at first the bourgeoisie and fascism were constructed as equivalent; this aspect of left ideology was reexamined and to some extent adjusted with the advent of war and the even more urgent need for coalition building.

[26] The changing political views of Kazantzakis, one of the most influential modernist writers in Greece, are discussed in Bien 1989. Famous works by Kazantzakis include *Zorba the Greek* and *The Last Temptation of Christ*. Marc Bloch's *Strange Defeat*, written in the fall of 1940, was a timely reaction to the problem of fascism, although it was not publicly available until after the war.

One of the larger issues at stake in the fascist crisis was the question of alliance building. Who were the highest-yield, lowest-risk, most morally sound allies? How much *difference* could an alliance tolerate? When did an alliance become unholy in the sense that it compromised the basic collective values of the parties involved? As the modern era progressed, European leftists augmented the symbol of the Paris Commune with more recent archetypes of workable coalitions, such as Leon Blum's Popular Front, and they reinterpreted these lessons before, during, and after the Second World War.[27]

As a template for political behavior and a backdrop for twentieth-century thought, modernism has some of the same limitations as other frameworks for understanding cultural dispositions: too liberal periodization, an impressionistic view of motivation, and not enough differentiation among diverse elements. The modernist "style" is akin to what Raymond Williams calls "structures of feeling," for as a processual form of consciousness, it has remained partially submerged and partially visible, both to historic actors themselves and to historians of political culture (1977, 131). Pierre Bourdieu's notion of "habitus" or Foucault's "regimes of truth" are also germane but, similarly, more as a source of interesting questions than as explanation of how collective consciousness orders individual perceptions and precipitates action in specific cases.

Like any cultural system, modernism contained silences, blind spots, vanities, conflicts, hypocrisies. It was paradoxical in striving simultaneously for both freedom *and* limitation. Ironically, it was accused of being too revolutionary by the orthodox and not revolutionary enough by its various hardliners (see Dolar 1991). Uncritical conceptions of gender, race, class, and the meaning of power took their toll. Like its Enlightenment model, the Eurocentric, androcentric, modernist impulse sometimes actually thwarted the advance of those it might logically have united with.[28] Through neglect, snobbery, bigotry or even ruthlessness, it sometimes based its actions on discriminatory moral "imperatives."[29] Driven by a philosophy of manifest destiny, it was often motivated by self-interest, sanctimony, and the desire to dominate rather than the avowed altruism.[30] Who the beneficiaries of modernism actually were and its underlying moral positions were often complicated by issues of protection and control (see, e.g., L. Gordon 1990). Nevertheless, the method behind what was frequently called madness must be

[27] See Haupt 1986, 23–47; and Wall 1986.

[28] For examples of myopias and injustices, see Kennedy 1987; Gates 1986; Z. Bauman 1989; Gibson 1990. Specific asymmetries of the Enlightenment and French Revolution are the theme of Landes 1988; and Melzer and Rabine 1991.

[29] This point is emphasized in Mosse 1985. Also see Mazrui 1991.

[30] See Newton 1987, 133–34. From a different angle, the potential for contradiction and hypocrisy in the narratives of suffragists and pioneering women of the era is raised in Burton 1991; and Birkett and Wheelwright 1990.

portrayed, even in its sketchiest terms, in light of the central role modernism has played in nineteenth- and twentieth-century politics.[31]

Narrative Analysis, Identity Formation, and the Shifting Fortunes of the Rules

Social construction is central to my interpretations. In accordance with recent trends in social history, I have concluded that it is neither possible nor desirable to try and "prove the truth" about this case, especially given the dearth of so-called hard data about sometimes clandestine revolutionary activities. Furthermore, since objective truth cannot exist unmediated by factors such as informants' biases and my own, the passage of time, and contemporary politics, I find the narratological approach the best way to piece together the components of a collective consciousness far removed from where I sit today. In addition to presenting relevant historical details, therefore, I also rely on the hermeneutical device of narrative, examining these events as a collection of stories. Using a range of sources and my own historical imagination, I infer the stories that developed over the course of leaders' political lifetimes and took shape more clearly and urgently with the advent of a crisis. In telling these crucial stories about the Greek past, present, and future, leaders created policies that made sense to them, as Gramsci would say, under concrete historical conditions. The resulting morality tales were relayed to members to be accepted or somehow transformed by the act of participation itself. In summary, it is difficult to understand this case and others like it as a set of unvarnished "facts" or, in an older narrative style, simply as a chain of events. My view of political mobilization and demobilization also depends on my interpretation of the suasive social texts that these particular circumstances produced.

Later, I consider the significance of crises as vehicles for political development, as well as the content of this particular crisis. For now, I want to focus my attention on narrative as a formula for expressing substantive changes in personal and group identities. The contours of specific narratives are especially pronounced during crises, when emotions are running high and participants are constantly reinterpreting and trying to find meaning in unfolding situational dramas.

By now it has become fairly commonplace to recognize that crises are not caused by mass psychological deviance, nor are they lacking in internal logic, as asserted by the "classical" collective behavior school (see McAdam 1982, 5–

---

[31] On the problem of historiographic and related theoretical absences with regard to the modern period, see Pollock 1988, 50. David William Cohen (1985) examines the modernist-related biases of African history.

19). Traditionally, narrative has been defined as the straight sequential detailing of events, a linear presentation of the "truth" with little or no theoretical or normative structure to interfere. The kind of narrative I envision, however, is actually a fusion that is oxymoronic in conventional social science terms: *narrative analysis,* a way of mining "social texts" connected to the larger field of "narratology."[32] The method blends the stories of individual social actors about personal experiences, popular mythologies, and macrocausal explanations and uses them to account for the course of events in particular cases. Identity change is reflected in the types of stories the researcher, as collaborator, "hears" participants telling about "the way things happened" and "the way things are now."

If informants cite their membership in specific social categories to account for their experiences, broader generalizations can begin to be made. The more the same story is heard, the more confident we can be about how representative it is. Daniel Bertaux, and other proponents of qualitative measures, refer to this phase as the "saturation point." Based on his study of French bakers, regarding this crucial concept, Bertaux comments, "The first life story taught us a great deal; so did the second and the third. By the fifteenth we had begun to understand the pattern of sociostructural relations which makes up the life of a bakery worker. By the twenty-fifth, adding the knowledge we had from life stories of bakers, we knew we had it: a clear picture of this structural pattern and of its recent transformations. New life stories only confirmed what we had understood, adding slight individual variations. We stopped at thirty: there was no point in going further. We knew already what we wanted to know. Thus we went through a process of saturation of knowledge" (1981, 37–38).

The problem of representativeness can also be addressed through "triangulation," or using the widest possible array of methods and data sources. It is an approach that no social historian, especially one faced as I have been with a highly politicized historiographic data base, can afford not to employ (see, e.g., Denzin 1989, 92–94). The narrative alternative combines mythical influences on expressions of human consciousness and perceived reality with a commitment to understanding the material, complexly contingent bases of political actions. In narrative methodological logic, it is impossible to fully "certify" claims made since these data derive from the representations conceived in the minds of human subjects rather than from a more traditional collecting of "facts" for analysis. That various versions often compete with

---

[32] Renato Rosaldo's *Culture and Truth: The Remaking of Social Analysis* has been a significant source for me in thinking about how to identify and make sense of social narratives. My use of the term "narrative analysis" must be credited to his chapter (127–43). Also see the two-volume special issue of *Social Science History* (1992) on narrative analysis; Bal 1985; and analyses of oral historical data from an essentially narratological perspective in Passerini 1988; and Portelli 1991.

"the official story" squares with Gramsci's comment: "One could say this about the authority of thinkers and experts: it is very important among the people, but the fact remains that every conception has its thinkers and experts to put forward, and authority does not belong to one side; further, with every thinker it is possible to make distinctions, to cast doubt on whether he really said such and such a thing, etc." (1971, 338). Moreover, as I said earlier, in narrative analysis the values of the author are viewed as essential to the production of the work as a whole insofar as the writer's vision stands as a kind of morality tale in progress. Even so, for the sake of clarity, it is in the reader's interest that this presence, once acknowledged, be kept off center stage.

The Uses of Narrative Analysis

What is narrative analysis and how can it be used to understand processes of identity transformation? How is identity change more intelligible during periods of dramatic national upheaval when seen as a collection of narratives? A review of such linkages is key to understanding our case. The type of narrative most relevant to social historical analysis is parallel to its more common humanities' usage: a story with a beginning, middle, and end; with a plot; with main characters, scoundrels, and paragons; with background settings. Incidents are placed in some meaningful context, and it is possible to analyze relationships among key elements of the story or, in Mieke Bal's words, the "series of logically and chronologically related events that are caused or experienced by actors," called the fabula (1985, 5). Thus, the most important element in the construction and deconstruction of narratives is *emplotment*. Emplotment, Hayden White says, entails "providing the 'meaning' of a story by identifying the *kind of story* that has been told." Emplotment is a type of explanation. It "is the way by which a sequence of events fashioned into a story is gradually revealed to be a story of a particular kind" (1973, 7).

Attempting to make sense of the message behind the words of subjects in the search for operative social patterns is more a matter of interpretation than of "science." The social historian is called upon to conceptualize a broad story line and to draw logical conclusions about those sections of the story where the evidence is either deficient or indefinite. Narrative interpretive history can be contrasted with an older, more mechanical style of narrative in which the content is not accorded any special symbolic meanings and the author—as chronicler—strives only to produce faithful notations about the past. Although very much concerned with establishing causality, this type of interpretive history is also different from the conventional positivism that insists on "scientific" proof of assumptions about the relationships among historical actors. Narrative analysis relies on anecdotal evidence, traditionally derided by practitioners of more orthodox methodologies because it can never be reliably proven "true." As an interpretive rather than a scientific approach, theory is both deduced from and applied to social processes by isolating central themes and metaphors that motivate collective behaviors. But it is vital to note that both the beginning-middle-end schema and the fabula are ultimately conceits of the social historian, which exist only as a matter of translation and are in no way ironclad. The method rests on the proposition that through a kind of second- or even third-party *Verstehen*, it is possible for a self-appointed authority to gauge what could have been going on in the head of another person during or with regard to an earlier era. By the same token, evidence does not simply emerge from the data. As in research of any style, the selection of key informants and their rank ordering are the author's responsibility and ultimately assert a personal agenda.

Integral to narrative analysis is the perspective that the authors of narratives frequently are, *but need not be,* intellectuals in the strict sense. The participants in historical events are authors, too, comparable to novelists, poets, and social theorists.[33] Like witnesses in a court of law, any and all participants and informants who are touched by the events and whose experiences can be shaped into testimonial evidence achieve the status of author. Whether projecting into the future or explaining the past, participant-authors order events into parables whose message might be considered a reflection of what C. Wright Mills calls the "major issues and key troubles" of individuals and communities.[34]

Here we might return for a moment to the issue of how the concept of "experience" is understood and used. The recent debate in feminist scholarship has, I think, needlessly dichotomized "experience" and "social construction." This debate takes place on a battlefield already considerably worn down by mainstream social theory's earlier stand against phenomenology, which had been touted as a radical approach to understanding social problems. In that round, phenomenology was critiqued for its failure to organize experiential data theoretically. It seems to me that one unfortunate effect of the more recent polarization of positions is that those who address "women's history," building at least some of their arguments around the emancipatory or brutal aspects of women's historical experience, are characterized as naive, whereas those who explore "gender history" are seen as engaged in more complex

---

[33] Regarding the narratives of classical social theorists and writers of literary texts, respectively, see White 1973; and Jameson, 1981.

[34] "What are the major issues for publics and the key troubles of private individuals in our time?" Mills asks. "To formulate issues and troubles, we must ask what values are cherished yet threatened, and what values are cherished and supported, by the characterizing trends of our period. In the case both of threat and of support we must ask what salient contradictions of structure may be involved" (1959 11).

readings of their material.[35] Joan Scott's interventions have been central to scholarly debate about experience. While I agree with Scott that it is useless to separate "experience" from its historical and cultural context, at the same time, I believe it is not really possible to measure or contain the self-serving and possibly exclusionary aspects of the re-creation of experience. Any testimony about personal experience may include elements of fantasy, inaccuracy, self-aggrandizement, opportunism, even questionable claims. The question is not so much how or whether scholarly mediation is possible but rather what mix of circumstances have produced any intrinsically "fictional" narrative in the first place. Seen in this light, an individual narrative is simply one version among many of a multifaceted story that we may or may not choose to hear or take into account, and we should not view its lack of "mediation" as a deterrent (see Scott 1991). In modern Greek scholarship, the "experience" controversy arose after a conference held at Cornell University entitled "Voices of Greek Women." Here, the debate centered around a set of issues partly touched off by my own contribution. Gail Holst-Warhaft reports: "Some felt that even the title was problematic and others that certain participants overemphasized their personal experience of Greece. The lively correspondence that extended the controversy beyond the conference itself has made some of us wonder whether the use of one's own or other people's stories in an academic discourse is a form of appropriation fraught with too many problems, or whether, on the contrary, being emotionally affected by personal stories is acceptable even in the halls of academe, where impersonal objectivity is normally prized" (1991, 143). As a conciliatory move, I want to suggest that what is important here is *both* how social historians "naturalize" experience to create ways of modeling social and political trends; *and* how subjects themselves, not just singularly but in significant numbers, naturalize their experiences and then derive certain conclusions and behaviors from foundational assertions.

Ontological and Mobilizational Narrative

The narratives of participant-authors or historical protagonists can be divided into two interrelated spheres: the *ontological* or subjective, that is, the internalized stories that combine received historical, psychological, and cultural messages, subsequently transposed into particular behaviors; and the *mobilizational* or intersubjective, designed by their authors to establish and support collective values and to encourage solidarity.

[35] For example, see the especially useful summaries of the epistemological controversy in the *Journal of Women's History* 2 (Winter 1991), especially the articles by Louise M. Newman, Joan C. Williams, and Lise Vogel.

The relevance of ontologies is insightfully addressed by Agnes Hankiss, who notes:

> The image of the self is never just a simple reflection of the experiences related to the self: it always includes a specific response to the "Why" of the development of the self. Everyone builds his or her own theory about the history and the course of his or her life by attempting to classify his or her particular successes and fortunes, gifts and choices, favourable and unfavourable elements of his or her fate according to a coherent, explanatory principle and to incorporate them within a *historical unit*. In other words, everybody tries, in one way or another, to build up his or her own ontology. *Specific mechanisms* are involved in this building process. Human memory selects, emphasizes, rearranges and gives new colour to everything that happened in reality; and, more important, it endows certain fundamental episodes with a symbolic meaning, often to the point of turning them almost into myths, by locating them at a focal point of the explanatory system of the self. (1981, 203)

Thus ontological narratives unite the psychological need Hankiss identifies for "structuring of the image of the self," elements of a weltanschauung or world view, and actors' collective interests, whatever they may be. Jo Freeman makes a related point when she writes about reference groups. "Although a reference group is not always a group, it is a standard against which people compare themselves in order to judge their behavior and attitudes. This well-established concept in social psychology is not one that has been used to analyze social movements," she notes, "but it has a great deal of explanatory power." Freeman gives an example:

> When I first watched and read about Weatherman's "Days of Rage" and other low-key terrorist tactics, I found myself puzzled by what seemed to be a totally unrealistic assessment of potential support from the American public. Only after I had read extensively in Weatherman literature and about the group did they begin to make sense. I realized that many of them had spent the preceding years visiting international revolutionaries, largely Cubans and North Vietnamese, outside the United States or had talked to those who had. These revolutionaries in effect became their reference group. From them they acquired the idea that the true revolutionary is one who is not afraid to strike a blow in "the belly of the monster" (i.e. the United States), even if the blow was suicidal. I suspect that Weatherman tactics were calculated not to gain support, or even attention, from the American public but to gain a sense of having met revolutionary standards. (1983, 201–2)

Similarly, participant-authors might title their ontological narratives or salient metathemes in them "Striking a Blow in the Belly of the Monster" or

"Out of Poverty" or "I Have Always Tried to Be Accommodating to Others" or "How I Overcame My Setback" or "X-Relative's Illness (Seeing So-and-so Killed; My Arrest and Torture; Finding Religion) Changed My Life Forever" or "I Am . . . (a Prodigy; a Particular Historical Figure; a Friend to the Downtrodden; Just Like My Namesake; the First Person in a Given Category to Accomplish a Certain Thing)." Such titles do not so much posit a single theme or story in the life experience of a social protagonist or superimpose cogency in cases where none exists, as suggest a way to summarize narratives that are central to self-definition and, ultimately, to political identity and choice. Sherry Ortner makes the point especially effectively in her discussion of the cultural schemata of Sherpa Buddhist monks that the tone of stories narrated by their protagonists (as opposed to sifted out of a broader range of evidence by a historian) is frequently triumphant, and failing that, one of victimization by circumstances beyond the control of the protagonist. This is not to discount the possibility that narrated events actually occurred in the way in which narrators claim, though it is impossible to know for sure. At the same time, it is important to remember how rare it is for protagonists to blame themselves or admit to humiliations, defaulted opportunities, or personal shortcomings in their accounts. Survivors, almost by definition, rarely want to appear in anything other than the best light, either to themselves or to a wider audience. This is particularly true of revolutionaries imbued, sometimes years later, with spiritual belief and the desire to promote their cause. If, however, such tendencies are kept in perspective, they should not necessarily take away from the usefulness of narrative data.

What makes narratives politically significant is that they are at least partially externalized during periods of social unrest. In other words, the ideologies subsumed in informants' versions of stories about what happened or is happening have public consequences precisely because they don't remain private but are in some sense acted out by participant-authors anxious to find solutions to current problems. We might envision titles for such "circumstantial" dramaturgical stories, or mobilizational narratives: "Why My Family Joined the Mau Mau Rebellion," "Why I Chose to Ignore My Family's Disapproval and Donate My Savings to Marcus Garvey in the 1920s" (a story that my late Uncle Vance could have told), or as in a recent book written by a Yugoslavian partisan commander which happens to be about the Greek Resistance, "How and Why the People's Liberation Struggle of Greece Met with Defeat" (Vukmanovic 1985). Implicit in these titles is a collectivization of individual experience and the metaphorical proposition that others, faced with similar situations, might conduct themselves according to an analogous logic or face similar results. The narratives facilitate a process of identification with the speaker's portrayal.

The two kinds of narrative are so interconnected as to make hard-and-fast conceptual binarisms untenable. The semantic distinction is between the *diachronicity* of ontological and the *synchronicity* of mobilizational stories. Ontological narratives incorporate key phases in the life course of an individual upon which behavior during particular episodes is contingent. Such narratives usually unfold in a broadly linear way. Strewn through the otherwise hazy period between early childhood and death are significant occurrences such as wars, famines, floods, relocations, divorces, deaths, plagues, scandals. These events, separate from the mundane and everyday are recalled more vividly and given special weight by participants and observers alike. Moreover, cultural phenomena are by nature speculative, and teleologies exist mainly in the imagination and are open to reconstruction at any point. Although the exact order of events might not always be clear and may never be solidly confirmed, an ontological narrative implicitly or explicitly purports, "First *this* happened, which seems to be why subsequently *that* happened."

In contrast, mobilizational narratives are more situational and synchronous in nature and origin, tending to take shape in response to present circumstances and to be deployed for specific strategic reasons, even though their content is often laced with references to the past. The basic purpose is persuasion in the context of crisis, urgent because time is at a premium: divergent tendencies must be unified before oppositional forces gain the upper hand. Selective versions must be propagated.

Again, ontological and mobilizational narratives often coexist in a symbiotic relationship and are not always clearly distinguishable. Still, a deliberate effort to separate them is a worthwhile prerequisite to further generalization. In the case of the Greek resistance movement, to the extent that the rather patchy data permit and the ontological dimension can be excavated and "imagined" by researcher and reader, attention to the ontological dimension of narrative is vital to understanding why the leaders of a Gramscian "historic bloc" would initiate and guide a certain kind of movement and what motivated sometimes unlikely players to join. How did the movement facilitate participation by the "national-popular," and what attracted ordinary people to the prospect of social transformation? Ontological and mobilizational narratives are a critical resource for discerning the core problems that produced a movement of distinctive character and appeal.

CHAPTER 2

Crisis and Transformation: A Gramscian Approach

European resistance movements have generally been interpreted in Western popular culture as a combination of military history and secular iconography, and justifiably so. Death and annihilation were ubiquitous. Many survivors persevered only through tenacity, design, or luck, making for drama of mythological proportions. Decisions to defy the Nazi war machine and follow the dictates of conscience deserve continual revisiting as matters of collective responsibility and inspiration. If the familiar litany of survivors— "Never again"—is to be taken seriously, then the *idea* of resistance should remain an icon of valor and ethical practice.

Yet the political value of remembering the resistance has to a large extent been distorted by the agendas and fantasies of a contemporary generation.[1] Throughout the postwar era images of street battles, of careful timing in the face of frightening odds, of rescues and destroyed bridges, have surfaced in films and been used by European politicians to promote popular unity, to gain pensioners' votes, or to make austerity measures more appealing to constituents.

Resistance movements also signaled broader, often painful, national transformations with lasting consequences. In this sense, resistance movements have become a political lesson manqué. Conjointly with their military dimensions, resistance movements devolved into battlefields where fundamental conflicts of modern state and identity formation were fought. The events of the Greek resistance were particularly tragic on these grounds, touching off waves of unresolved friction. The impact of that earlier turmoil helps account

---

[1] Although not expressly about the resistance, an exception is the more careful debate about moral accountability within the radical democratic Left in Germany in the middle to late 1980s, known as the *Historikerstreit*. The specifics of this case are addressed in Eley 1988.

for the conspicuous silence about the era in many textbooks and contemporary political analyses.

Even in nations where the resistance is remembered with official fondness, a reluctance to revisit and understand these struggles for their larger political significance has left new mutations of conflict as a legacy, and the trials and tribulations of the former Yugoslavia are a prime example. Keeping such evasions in mind, I intend this book as more than a collection of anecdotes featuring death, danger, and narrow escapes, even though the drama and brutality of the Nazi period are vital components of the story. By investigating the unprecedented involvement of women in the Greek effort to resist the Nazi occupation, my purpose has been to discover a more comprehensive political meaning in their mobilization into the resistance movement and in their participation in later struggles against authorities' attempts to dismantle the Greek Left.

It is no particular revelation that women played a subordinate role in the public sphere during the first three decades of the twentieth century. The restrictions on their public activities and their generally greater association with the domestic sphere in most geographical and historical contexts have been well documented.[2] Although some maintain that for both sexes private and public are enmeshed in experience and consciousness and that historically women have played a crucial "shadow" role in war, business, and politics, documented examples of gender symmetry in the public domain remain scarce or mythic.[3] Channels have sometimes existed for women to participate equally in traditionally male-dominated activities but not on a large scale and not often. Along the same lines, anthropologists working in rural villages and urban neighborhoods in Greece note the consistently low and clearly demarcated profile of women in public life.[4] Historically the public-man/private-woman dyad noted by Jean Bethke Elshtain and others has been widely accepted, nonnegotiable, and relentlessly enforced by social sanctions.

[2] For example, Reiter 1975; Herzfeld 1985; Brandes 1985; Alexander 1994; Eley 1994.

[3] See M. Rosaldo 1980. Gerda Lerner (1986) traces the "social fact" of female subordination back three thousand years. For an early hagiographic treatment, see J. J. Bachofen 1967. As a matter of fact, Bachofen's work was read and cited polemically by turn-of-the-century Greek feminist contributors to the journal *Efimeridos ton Kyrion*. Their main point—that, despite strong counterevidence from the ancient world, contemporary society had failed to appreciate women's true capacities—provoked a reaction from several male readers. A controversy that mirrored the international debate about women's equality raged in subsequent issues of the journal. Avdela and Psarra 1985. For a balanced reconsideration of the issue, see Pomeroy 1976. For the mythic dimension, also see such celebrations of matriarchy and women's spirituality as Christ 1980, 1979.

[4] For example, Friedl 1962, 1986; Campbell 1964, 1983; Du Boulay 1974; Hirschon 1983; Skouteri-Didaskalou 1984; Cowan 1990; Stewart 1991, esp. 49–51.

Much of the literature on women in war reaches a gloomy conclusion about the potential for change in the legitimate parameters of women's behavior during national mobilizations (e.g., McClintock [n.d.]). "Although most of the combatant nations had experienced some form of feminist mobilization prior to both wars," Margaret Higonnet and her colleagues note, "the organic discourse of wartime patriotism, with its emphasis on national solidarity, discouraged expressions of women's rights and needs, labelling them selfish, divisive, or even treasonous" (1987, 7).[5] I do not entirely disagree with this "strong" interpretation of female experience in war; nevertheless, the mass participation of women in the Greek resistance does contradict this dreary premise. Despite male leaders' obvious distrust of feminist discourse if "taken too far," women clearly experienced significant qualitative change in the short term and, it can be argued, in the long term as well. The profoundly gendered behavioral codes of early twentieth-century Greece, when prospective partici-pants were growing up and learning what society would expect of them, made the conscious, future-oriented choice to enter the male-dominated realms of politics and even war unusual. If, in fact, significant numbers of Greek women managed to defy the rigid standards of conduct that the highly patriarchal sociopolitical structure of Greece in the 1940s demanded of them and if, more surprising, they were officially encouraged to do so, then it is plausible that factors more complex than military expediency explain such unprecedented action. If we keep in mind that public and private interact in a complementary way at particular historical junctures, the evidence suggests that during the 1940s in Greece, some of the same young women previously excluded from the political system emerged from their homes to actively participate in a military resistance struggle and were able to gain new political rights and social prestige.

My main objectives in the first part of this book are to determine, first, what led Greek leaders to attempt to mobilize women into political activity in a more than cursory way, and second, what led such a large cross-section of women to join the fight for a cause not exclusively related to their traditional lack of power. Significantly, the purpose of this movement was not, as it was for an earlier branch of Greek feminism, to awaken a distinctly *feminist* consciousness.[6]

The answer to the first question can be found partly in the social imagination

[5] The transience of women's political gains in war and revolution has also been raised with regard to the French Revolution. For example, see Landes 1988; Offen 1990.

[6] See Avdela and Psarra 1985, especially regarding women's suffrage and legislation for work-ing women. An excellent discussion of the development of turn-of-the-century Greek feminism within the *messaia stromata,* or "middle classes," is Varika 1987. These books explore the collective consciousness and internecine struggles of the small but vocal, mainly bourgeois Greek feminist movement and also, though not explicitly, suggest links to the EAM platform on the subject of women's emancipation (*hirafetisi ton yinekon*).

of movement leaders. Like many of their political contemporaries, for the men in question a major motivation behind efforts to construct new political traditions and institutions was the desire to create the "proper" conditions for nation-state building.[7] The new traditions and institutions were products of their personal experiences and understandings of "our social question," in the words of turn-of-the-century theorist George Skliros.[8] Although not always recognized as such, to a significant degree these novel policy measures also derived from tacit conversations with European nations to the north, the former Ottoman Empire, the United States, and the Soviet Union. Furthermore, favorable policies toward women in the movement can also be construed as a matter of "masculinity construction" for elites, who sought collective validation according to prevailing images of modern statehood and leadership. That modernist leaders qua men *cared* how others perceived them had global consequences. We will explore some of the discourses relevant to Greek policy innovations of the 1940s shortly.

The answer to the second question, that is, what motivated the women themselves to join up, cannot be gleaned solely from the motivations of founding members. Here, responses of women and girls to the movement's novel appeal are crucial, both in terms of their active participation and in some cases insofar as they pushed for change and a recognition of feminist goals in the organizations which they belonged to. For many of the women I spoke with, the processes of participation and radicalization continued well into the postwar era, challenging the conservative social and legal structures reasserted in Greek culture during the 1950s. My understanding of that version of the story derives from my interviews with survivors.

In view of certain geopolitical and historical factors, Antonio Gramsci's work on popular responses to fascism forms the theoretical skeleton around which I assemble my contribution. While the philosophy of this Italian Communist leader does not explain every aspect of the resistance, it does help to locate this case study in a comparative framework. But first we must review the history of the Greek Communist Party (KKE), in order to lay the groundwork for our subsequent discussion of relevant Gramscian themes.

Interwar Greek Communism

The process of tracing EAM genealogy must start with Communist—originally Socialist—party history. As Robin D. G. Kelley comments about black radicals in 1930s Alabama, "Local Communists cried out for direction,

[7] See Wohl 1979; Grimshaw 1992; and Hobsbawm 1989.
[8] Perhaps the most influential text for Greek leaders of the late nineteenth and early twentieth century generation was George Skliros, *To koinonikon mas zitima* (Our social question), written in Germany and first published in Athens in 1907.

especially after wrestling with vague theoretical treatises on capital's crisis or on the growing specter of fascism" (1990, xiii). In these and in a number of other cases, the interwar period fostered the critical lesson that success was more likely when a balance was struck between external direction and internal development. Communist parties worked hard to maintain conformity with the larger cause, and to preserve national credibility among a community of peers. Such ambitions were sometimes as much a matter of image management as actual policy, and the desire for Comintern recognition often competed with regional considerations. Keeping these formative elements in mind, a brief review of inter-war period and its radical dilemmas is necessary background to understanding how EAM originated.

The Sosialistikon Ergatikon Komma Ellados (SEKE), or Socialist Labor Party of Greece, was founded on 10 November 1918 by a small group of adherents, including trade unionists, intellectuals, workers, and members of regional political organizations. After the Third International, or Comintern, was established in March 1919, the executive council of the SEKE voted at its May 1919 meeting to break officially with the Second International, which had "betrayed the socialist ideology," and to work toward a radical transformation of organizational goals in keeping with the Comintern's bolshevization drive. At its Second Congress, convened on 5 April 1920, the SEKE adopted several important measures. First, the organization voted to accept all future principles and resolutions emanating from the Third International; second, it opted to join the Balkan Communist Federation linking the Bulgarian, Greek, and Serbian parties under the Comintern umbrella; and finally, it added the word "communist" (*kommounistikon*) to its title in brackets. At its Third Extraordinary Congress in 1924, the SEKE officially changed its name to the Kommounistiko Komma tis Ellados or Communist Party of Greece, and it reconfirmed its allegiance to all Comintern principles.[9]

According to official KKE documents, from 1918 to 1934, Comintern representatives were present on numerous occasions (see, e.g., Loulis 1982, 28). Among other things, this "tutelage" enabled the Greek party to affirm its acceptance of the Twenty-one Conditions for Comintern membership in no uncertain terms. The rigidity of Comintern policy and the restricted nature of debate, especially from 1918 to 1921 and from 1928 to 1934, are well documented; as is the fact that an authoritative tone was seen as a necessary antidote to the failures of the Second International and the supposed laxness of the United Front period. On 7 August 1920, at the Second World Congress, Zinoviev issued his famous warning: "Just as it is not easy for a camel to pass through the eye of a needle so, I hope, it will not be easy for the adherents of the centre to slip through the 21 conditions. They are put forward to make

---

[9] Vlavianos 1992, 7–8. Also see Leon 1976 for a history of Greek socialism through 1918.

clear to the workers in the USPD and in the Italian and French Socialist Parties, and to all organised workers, what the general staff of the proletarian revolution demands of them."[10] This stern dictum made the intended impression on Greek Communists, contributing to the triumph of the pro-Comintern faction.

Some Communists, however, harbored skepticism about international alignment and on this issue, Greece was not alone. As the historian L. S. Stavrianos writes: "The Comintern was able to keep most of its followers in line in the Balkans as elsewhere in the world. But a few refused to accept the argument that the international revolutionary cause required acceptance of dictation from Moscow. Pouliopoulos, a Greek leader who later became a prominent Trotskyite, challenged the very principle of Comintern domination. 'It is inadmissible that any international commando should autocratically decree that other Communist Parties should promulgate principles incompatible with the objective conditions of their countries'" (1958, 615). Majority adherence to the Comintern's stringent contract was among the factors that limited the size of the party's ranks in the 1920s.[11] Dogmatism continued to obstruct a more broadly based political discourse until the Popular Front directive of 1935.

In fact, throughout much of the 1920s and 1930s, the KKE was plagued by several kinds of adversity. Its weak position in the Greek political world during the interwar period depended as much on factors internal to the party as those external. These factors included, for example, its small size (only fifteen hundred members by 1933) (Loulis 1982, table 1); internecine leadership struggles that continued well into the 1930s; a refusal by those in command to target the peasantry and petty bourgeois sectors as the party's clearest potential constituency given the structure of the Greek economy; and a related insistence on a "workerist" vision of Greek radicalism advanced by a Comintern mindful of other contexts. The last was a corollary of the announced intention of the Fifth Congress in 1924 to "bolshevize" member parties, that is, to work toward a peasant-worker alliance and toward proletarian hegemony.[12] Although the

[10] Degras 1971, 1:167, and see "Conditions of Admission to the Communist International Approved by the Second Comintern Congress," 6 August 1920, 168–72.

[11] It should be noted that Greek resistance to the actions of the Balkan Federation, headquartered in Moscow as of 1924, is also recorded. These sometimes bitter disputes mostly centered around Balkan territorial issues (i.e., Bulgaria, Macedonia, Thrace). Greek Communist protests to the Comintern executive committee are noted in Degras 1971, 2:157, 185. The Italians, for their part, vigorously objected to Zinoviev's solution to the "Italian question": a fusion of the Communist and Socialist parties. Under pressure from the Comintern the attempt was made, but as Joseph Buttigieg reports, "the whole effort fell apart within a few months; the leading members of both parties could hardly function as they faced arrest, exile, or constant harassment by the Fascists" (1992, 78).

[12] Buttigieg 1992, 81; Sassoon 1980, 80.

Comintern formulation included peasants, in Greece (and in Italy) no serious effort was made to recruit in the countryside. Furthermore, at that juncture the number of Greeks who could be classified as industrial proletarians was negligible, especially compared to shopkeepers and merchants. But to be fair, any attempt to mobilize the petty bourgeoisie for communism would have jeopardized the Greek reputation within the Comintern, and leaders were understandably not willing to take that risk. The increasing threat and incidents of government repression in both countries also deterred peasant mobilization.[13]

The tendency to invest confidence in foreign models for radical action while ignoring discrepant local realities was not unusual but was certainly problematic. Not only did such factors handicap the mass appeal of the KKE before the war and deeply influence its earlier character, these elements probably also gave rise to the EAM's remedial efforts after 1941. In addition to the crucial variable of new Comintern directives during the 1930s, especially the Popular Front announced by the much-admired Bulgarian figure and Comintern leader Dimitrov, recognition of the consequences of prior formulations encouraged party representatives to seize upon the resistance as an opportunity to strategize a popular-democratic alternative more convincing to a mass audience than had been possible in the past.

A dramatic turnaround in party fortunes occurred between 1934 and 1936 when membership rose from six thousand to fourteen thousand (Loulis 1982, table 1). This increase stands as one of the key accomplishments of Nikos Zachariades' reign as KKE general secretary, even though the Civil War period (1946–1949) and the 1950s would mark him more as a divisive than a unifying force for the party. Unlike his predecessors, Zachariades was able to cut through what he called the chronic "factionalist struggle without principles" to organize a solid party structure with more effective channels for recruitment and characterized by much greater cohesiveness. Growth in the KKE ranks and increased labor unrest were among the factors leading to the 1936 putsch by General Ioannis Metaxas. Communist success in the 1936 elections put the KKE in a position to wield a crucial swing vote. As John Loulis notes: "The 1936 elections actually provided the communists with considerable power to influence political developments in Greece as neither of the two major parties, the Liberal and the People's Party, could now govern without the support of the fifteen communist M.P.s in Parliament. It was exactly in that year that General Metaxas with King George's support, staged a coup on August 4 and established a dictatorship" (1982, 4). After the coup, writes Hans Vlavianos, "a police state soon began to impose a carefully controlled reign of terror directed primarily against the Communists, trade unionists, intellectuals, and others

---

[13] Important variables affecting the fate of Greek communism during this period are reviewed in Vlavianos 1992, 8–11.

known for their strong republican leanings" (1992, 15). Phillip Minehan observes,

> On August 4, 1936, Metaxas declared a dictatorship with the justification of combating the general strike threat, which was allegedly geared to "overthrow the legal, political and social system of the country." What kind of threat did the ruling system in Greece actually face? Despite the claim by Metaxas, and the KKE's warning of a "popular volcano," there were neither the developed social conditions nor any serious plans for a social revolution in Greece. . . . The situation verged neither on a conspiratorial nor a popular uprising. The strikers demonstrated against particular conditions—low wage levels, newly-imposed restrictions on trade union activity, and the holding of political prisoners. But the state system against which the demonstrations were directed was plagued with ruthless interparty rivalries, debt and revenue crises, and an inability to adjust structurally to the newly-emerging social conditions. (1983, 25)

Between 1936 and 1940, nearly all prominent KKE leaders were either jailed or sent to island exile camps for political crimes against the state. Tortures and other deprogramming tactics conceived by the notorious minister of public security Constantine Maniadakis to some extent successfully disrupted KKE's newfound party unity. However by the spring of 1941, remnants of the party had begun to form secret organizations with the intention of resisting the Occupation begun in April, and by September, a reconstituted central committee had convened to create the EAM (see Vlavianos 1992, esp. 15–24).

Modern Cultural Politics and Ordine Nuovo

A key aspect of the resistance as a popular revolution was the way in which the EAM organization tried to reconstruct political culture, particularly its stance on the question of citizenship. The writings of Antonio Gramsci provide an especially incisive theoretical framework for interpreting the evolving ideology and structure of the movement. One reason Gramscian thought is useful for this case is that historical data about the backgrounds, comings, goings, and analyses of Greek Communists are difficult to find because of official repression of the movement following the war and because scholarly attention has been scarce. There are some risks in using Gramscian thought to make sense of activities at a geographical remove from the Italian scene that gave rise to these theories. Perhaps the main risk is a kind of intellectual colonization that devalues indigenous factors. The approach, however, would be more accurately described as analogic in that my goal is to highlight parallel ideological developments among Greek and Italian state builders rather than to compare the national histories of Italy and Greece. There are resemblances and differences in how agents of social change processed conditions and events in the two countries. The combination helps me to answer puzzling questions, to construct a conceptual framework, and to fill in certain informational lacunae. From this perspective, the marriage of Greece and Italy during the modern period offers a valid "context of discovery." What such metaphorical risk taking can contribute as a means of deducing the logic of this particular movement and of organizing more general knowledge about contentious political culture and modern social change seems to me to outweigh its injustices.

Inasmuch as leaders in both the Italian Communist Party (PCI) and the KKE were involved with the Comintern during the twenties, it is not entirely implausible that Antonio Gramsci or others within his sphere of influence had at some time met and held conversations with the Greek Communists who would later shape the content and form of the EAM's state-building efforts. Though Gramsci makes no mention of actual contacts in his writings, historical convergences are possible. Somewhat earlier, Greek socialists, like their Italian counterparts, were involved in pan-European debates about the proper socialist position on the Great War.[14] As members of a larger, cosmopolitan group, Greek civil servants, intellectuals, and politicos often traveled abroad for education or conferences. Several prominent Greek socialists spent time in Moscow studying Marxist doctrine, possibly during Gramsci's own stint (1922–1923), offering opportunities for dialogue.[15] Intriguingly, a small community of Italian descent lived on the island of Corfu, the site of some of the earliest syndicalist activity. Finally, on an ideological plane, during the 1930s Greek political prisoners in island exile camps, many of whom would later join the resistance, formed study groups in Marxist Leninist theory.[16] Did the

[14] At issue was whether the war only served the interests of global capitalism or whether national territorial integrity was actually at stake. See Judt 1986; and Goldberg 1962. For an account of the complexities of the Greek case, see Leon 1976. This debate continued to resonate even after the war. For example, Nikolai Bukharin and Evgeny Preobrazhensky published *The ABC of Communism: A Popular Explanation of the Program of the Communist Party of Russia* in 1919, and though I have been unable to ascertain the publishing history of this volume in Greece, it appears to have been translated and in circulation fairly quickly after its release in the USSR.

[15] Greek names appear only twice on the Comintern rosters, however: Dimitros, as a member of the fourth congress "with a consultative voice," and Syphneios as a member of the Comintern of the sixth congress (Degras 1971, 1:454–55, 2:575). Furthermore, Gramsci seems to have kept a relatively low profile during this time, partly because of illness and partly because of events in his personal life such as meeting and marrying Julia Schucht.

[16] See Kenna 1991, esp. n. 6; M. Sarafis 1990, 20; Loulis 1982, 5, 6, 39, 59, on the significant concentration of Communists in the island exile camp of Akronauplia (approximately 630). Though Loulis is well-versed in the documents and technical details of the period, his

tutors convening these sessions, cognizant of Comintern debates, ever mention the 1920s Italian Communist gloss on revolutionary epistemologies? In light of the international political identity crisis occasioned by the Great War, Greek attendance at Comintern-sponsored events, and the presence of Comintern delegates at local meetings, the possibility of meaningful and substantive contact cannot be ruled out entirely.

In my own historical imagination, discussions transpire between Greek Communists and Gramsci, Palmiro Togliatti, and others who shared a certain outlook on social policy questions during the formative period following World War I. At the Athens offices of the Greek Communist newspaper *Rizospastis* (The radical) or those of the *Ordine nuovo* on Turin's Via dell'Arcivescovado, at a Vienna workers' cafe or at a Comintern world congress, insights are traded about the special dilemmas of political power in a Mediterranean or Balkan, as opposed to an Anglo-Saxon, context. A participant in the Factory Council movement (the precursor of Gramsci's later conceptions about the role of education in popular mobilization) passes through Patras or Salonika and gives a speech at local party headquarters, or is sufficiently impressed by the social analysis of a Greek comrade to carry the news back to Italy.

Evidence of such exchanges has yet to surface. Presently, we can only speculate that at some point paths may have crossed either literally or philosophically. Gramsci's newspaper articles were obviously available to Italian speakers and travelers to Italy around the time they were written, though fascist censors later cut the flow. Gramsci's prison writings were not available in Italy until 1947, when the first edition of the *Lettere dal carcere* (Prison letters) was brought out. The final tome of the six-volume original set of the *Quaderni del carcere* (*Prison Notebooks*) appeared in 1951 (Buttigieg 1992, 40–41). It was only during the Colonels' dictatorship, some forty years after Gramsci's death, that the first selections of his work were translated into Greek by a jailed communist whose prison guards appear to have had no concept of the extent of their captive's subversion (see Van Dyck 1989).

For our purposes, whether there was ever any direct contact is probably immaterial. As a philosophical system, Gramscian thought can serve us well in analyzing the political significance of events in wartime Greece. First, whether

---

witheringly anticommunist tone detracts from his argument. So anxious is he to prove his "sinister plot" thesis that he completely discounts the possibility that many of his subjects were, like others of their generation, trying to find intelligent solutions to the problem of fascism, rather than perpetuating an elaborate hoax on the Greek people. Loulis exhibits what Heinz Richter calls the "myth of the communist danger" ("o mithos tou kommounistiko kindhinou"), which has had significant mobilizational potential in Greek society since 1917 and which has also dominated much of the existing scholarship on Greek communism. See Richter 1975, 55–56. A more balanced, "humanistic" but nonhagiographic study of the personalities and politics of the prewar KKE has yet to be published.

or not conversations between influential leaders took place which somehow facilitated the actual cross-fertilization of ideas, the geopolitical "context of discovery" in which antifascist political activists operated—the European semiperiphery—was similar in a number of important ways. Broadly speaking, during the 1920s and 1930s, the southern European Left responded to many of the same critical dilemmas of state building, class formation, mass political mobilization, capitalist contradiction, and national autonomy.[17] In answer to the classic epistemological question "What is this case a case of?" Gramscian thought helps to demonstrate that the case was indeed a case of international scope.

The case is also a case of how political development occurs at the national level. Gramsci's principles of popular organization can introduce the Greek case by helping us understand how the social engineers of a certain generation and region steered the movement in a distinctive direction. In the spirit of more recent strategists such as Saul Alinsky and Paulo Freire, we can comprehend the logic behind particular movement phases and tactics.[18] Just as Gramsci admonished Italian political actors to be as concerned with the concrete as the theoretical, the Greek leaders brought to their project an organic knowledge of their cultural environment. Their pragmatic solutions are a striking match to Gramsci's propositions in style and tone.

Finally, Gramsci was a nationalist at heart. His life's work involved the search for egalitarian solutions to the problems of the Italian nation-state at a time when capitalism was demonstrably there to stay but also open to restructuring and permutation. He never authored a book; his writings were produced under difficult conditions of physical illness, disability, and after 1926, imprisonment. Gramsci's theories were incoherent in places and in retrospect belied many unrealistic expectations. Here he had much company. One can argue that much social movement activity of the era was shaped by utopian visions, and that these visions were not always well conceived or attentive to all

[17] Gramsci frequently employed cross-national examples in his analysis of political trends, and the Greek case appears in several places in the *Prison Notebooks*. For example, see his use of Spain and Greece to illustrate points about military intervention in "State and Civil Society" (1971, 215–16).

[18] Legacies of the New Left movement, among the most widely known cultural guides to radical popular action in the American context are Freire 1992 and Alinsky 1989, 1972. These manuals, like Lenin's *What Is to Be Done?*, Bukharin's *ABC of Communism*, and Glinos's *Ti einai kai ti thelei to Ethniko Apeleftherotiko Metopo* (What is EAM and what does it want?), are part of a genre that forms the backbone of mobilizational narrative, combining plain speech, social analysis, strategic planning, and preemptive and prescriptive suggestions for a popular audience. Such texts describe the general ideological terrain on which "combatants" will be operating, what participants can expect to accomplish if they adhere to certain principles, and how they should behave in order to maximize the chances of movement success. These monographs are useful guides to the value systems that social movements hope to substitute for traditional modes of participation, and to the value systems behind existing political attitudes.

angles of social problems. Idiosyncratic and personal considerations aside, Gramsci shared with many of the EAM's founders an imagined mandate to reconstruct his own native state along more equitable lines. This desire was like any "successful political discourse," writes Renata Salecl, "a symbolic space, a point of view from which we can appear likable to ourselves . . . a space open to be filled by images of our ideal ego" (1992, 57). The cynicism of hindsight shouldn't obscure the romanticism behind the sort of reconstructive project evident in such works as Lenin's influential *State and Revolution,* a representative piece not only in content but in style. Since my purpose is to uncover the strong emotions and changing languages that made certain political convictions possible, one way to start to understand the psychology and vision of the modernist founders of the Greek movement is to examine the reasoning process of their Italian contemporary.

The best place to begin is with Gramsci's uniquely inclusive vision of politics. Simply put, politics in any form concern the negotiation of social power. A crucial element is the capacity to establish and maintain some degree of control over one's own or others' behavior in the short run and in the long run to ensure continuity, since fundamentally political control aims to reproduce itself. Conventionally, the term "political" is defined as "of, pertaining to, or dealing with the study, structure, or affairs of government or institutions of the state" (*American Heritage Dictionary* 1985). Thus, formal institutional politics involve various elected and appointed government posts, courts, and parliaments. This is what Gramsci calls "political society," which he contrasts to "civil society."[19]

The type of politics that occurs in political society is distinctive in that it depends on the concentration of coercive forces in the hands of the state. It is the tangible instruments of domination such as legal regulations, government bureaucracies, police forces, and armies, combined with the spectre of domination that secure the cooperation of the governed. In other words, the formal infrastructure is maintained by the popular expectation that deviations will elicit sanctions from authorities.

Often, the formal political system is conceptualized as the only site of power struggle. As Michel Foucault stresses, however, "One impoverishes the question of power if one poses it solely in terms of legislation and constitution, in terms solely of the state and the state apparatus. Power is quite different from and more complicated, dense and pervasive than a set of laws or a state apparatus" (1980, 158). According to Gramsci, equally deserving of attention are politics in a second sense, at the level of broader social discourse, or *cultural*

---

[19] Perry Anderson (1976–77) notes the conceptual slippage in Gramsci's writings regarding these and other terms. At this point, I leave aside Gramsci's blending of the political and the civil in his theory of the state and the "philosophy of praxis," which takes Marx several steps further into concrete action.

politics. Although Gramsci's actual use of this term is sparse, it is at the heart of even his earliest writings on the Sardinian tragedy and on the human condition. A gloomy twenty-year-old Gramsci writes that universal history is marked by "an insatiable greed shared by all men to fleece their fellows, to take from them what little they have been able to put aside through privations" (quoted in Nairn 1982, 160). Four years later, his newfound socialism had strengthened his faith in political possibility:

> Culture is something quite different. It is organization, discipline of one's inner self, a coming to terms with one's own personality; it is the attainment of a higher awareness, with the aid of which one succeeds in understanding one's own historical value, one's own function in life, one's own rights and obligations. . . . This means that every revolution has been preceded by an intense labour of criticism, by the diffusion of culture and the spread of ideas amongst the masses of men who are at first resistant, and think only of solving their own immediate economic and political problems for themselves, who have no ties of solidarity with others in the same condition.[20]

These and other youthful writings contain the seeds of Gramsci's sociocultural view of politics, developed more fully in the *Prison Notebooks.*[21]

Throughout large portions of his prison manuscript Gramsci sees cultural politics as an epiphenomenon of civil society. He was by no means the first to factor a conception of civil society into his discussion. The concept had also appeared in much less precise terms in the works of Kant, Rousseau, and Locke, among others.[22] Gramsci acknowledged his engagement with Hegel (who used the concept in connection with the dialectical method), as well as with Marx and Benedetto Croce, in theorizing civil society in relation to the state. He was among the first, however, to isolate civil society as not only a constructed but also an open and reconstructible terrain for political activity, in contrast to other more mechanistic views. In discussing the role of intellectuals in the "world of production," he makes his famous distinction: "What we can do, for the moment, is to fix two major superstructural 'levels': the one that can be called 'civil society,' that is the ensemble of organisms commonly called 'private', and that of 'political society,' or 'the State'" (1971, 12).

By drawing attention to civil society as a site with reconstitutive potential, Gramsci developed the cognitive alternative Geoff Eley and Keith Nield describe as a uniquely "de-institutionalized understanding of politics, in which

---

[20] Antonio Gramsci (signed Alpha Gamma), "Socialism and Culture," *Il grido del popolo,* 29 January 1916, in Gramsci 1990, 1:11–12. Specialists cite this portion of the essay as one of Gramsci's key engagements with the concept of culture.

[21] Also see Fiori 1973; and Davidson 1977.

[22] See Bobbio 1988; and Williams 1983, 57–60.

the possible sources of working-class oppositional impulse are displaced from the recognized media of political parties and trade unions into a variety of non-institutional settings, embracing behaviour previously regarded as 'non-political'" (1980, 267). Thus, Gramsci's "cultural politics" were embedded not just in formal political structures and processes but also in folk traditions, leisure activities, social conventions, and educational curricula. Politics of the cultural realm only *seemed* innocuous; taken seriously, they contained critical lessons about how to immunize formal political institutions against reactionary forces and still allow the democratic process to survive, despite fascism's already considerable advance. It was no accident, Gramsci felt, that fascism and Mussolini owed much success to a resolute, though often superficial strategy in the cultural area.[23] A key example was the much-touted "Gentile Reforms" drafted by Mussolini's minister of education in collaboration with Croce, the idealist philosopher. These were the Italian government's first major educational reforms since Unification. Gramsci felt that their persuasive language, emphasizing "active" as opposed to rote learning, couched an entirely different agenda, and one that was thoroughly in keeping with the fascist program (see 1971, 24–43, "On Education").

Gramsci links cultural politics to the concept of "hegemony." As with "civil society," Gramsci did not originate the term, but he extended its meaning to encompass a broader range of political and sociological phenomena. In contemporary scholarship and postwar left politics, "hegemony" has often been overused, the implication being that this was Gramsci's only theoretical contribution. Nevertheless, the concept is a central one, and Gramsci's spin on it original.

In Gramsci's view, the legitimacy of the formal institutional politics usually associated with the state does not rest entirely on coercive domination. As an economic-corporative structure, the state is also maintained by a field of cultural belief cultivated to the point where the rightful dominance of the ruling class is unquestioned. The ruling class, Gramsci observed, also rules by "hegemony." Thus it is not always necessary for the dominant bourgeois class to wield its authority directly. Its dominant position depends on the passive consent of the majority of the population, which does not have the social resources necessary to challenge its own lack of power. A subtler form of power than coercive domination, ruling-class hegemony infiltrates multiple domains, from "artistic" and "popular" literature,[24] advertising, drama, and visual art, to journalism, partisan campaigns, and customs that, in the words of Marc Bloch, are "so ingrained, so much part of a fully articulated system at once legal and material, that they [are] accepted as belonging to the nature of things"

---

[23] On the ambiguities of cultural mobilization under Italian fascism, see De Grazia 1992.

[24] On literature, see Antonio Gramsci, "The Concept of the National-Popular," in Forgacs 1988, 364–78.

(1966, 177). Political passivity leaves the subaltern classes vulnerable to "Caesarism," Gramsci's generic term for fascism.

Passive consent and internalized domination allow the hegemonic class to direct, rather than force, an exclusionary program. In other words, a status quo of privilege and oblique domination permeates fundamental cultural institutions, naturalizing a particular configuration of power relations. But the status quo can be subverted and eventually superseded by subaltern rule. In contrast to "false consciousness," which implies stasis, Gramsci's hegemony could be reconstructed and made to work for social change in the hands of a political elite sensitive to the expressed concerns of people living in "concrete historical conditions."

It is important to note that despite his preoccupation with the concrete, Gramsci, like most Marxists of his generation, set his sights on a utopian vision that caused him to imagine "reality" in a particular way. Clearly influenced by Lenin's arguments in *State and Revolution*, Gramsci's utopian narrative held that one day "a regulated society" constructed around governing coalitions of proletarian allies would replace the stranglehold of state domination and ruling-class hegemony. These allies would have synchronized goals and would benefit from their ability to "listen" to and continually enlighten the body politic. The state would become obsolete and, in classic Leninist terms, would wither away. Achieving a proletarian telos[25] would not, however, come without cost, since, Gramsci explains, "creating a group of independent intellectuals is not an easy thing; it requires a long process, with actions and reactions, coming together and drifting apart and the growth of very numerous and complex new formations" (1971, 395–96).

But with the right blend of analysis and pedagogy, a progressive hegemony predicated on active, informed consent might eventually replace the political sleepwalking so pervasive among popular segments with no better guide to action than their "common sense." Like "hegemony," for Gramsci, "common sense" had both negative and positive connotations, depending on which class is dominant. Under bourgeois hegemony, commonsense assumptions contribute to a mentality of ignorance and fear among the subaltern. On the other hand, the function of proletarian hegemony would be to implant more enlightened popular "instincts," so that "good sense" and "a new culture" could prevail. For Gramsci, hegemony is both the prize to be captured through revolutionary strategy and the adversary that makes radical action necessary in the first place.

Gramsci's aspirations to "applied research" can be traced from his early political tracts (1910–1926) through to the prison writings (1929–1935). "Interpretations of the past," he wrote, "when one seeks the deficiencies and the

---

[25] This term is used by Adamson 1980, 151.

errors from the past itself, are not 'history' but present-day politics" (quoted in Sassoon 1987a, 205). The dilemmas of "present-day politics" to which Gramsci refers cut across national lines and baffled much of his generation. Political leaders grappled, writes Showstack Sassoon, with the "changing relationship between State and society in the period of monopoly capitalism, a relationship intensified and modified by the First World War, and the new international reality created by the Russian Revolution" (1987a, 16). Gramsci argued forcefully that political leaders would need to confront these burning issues of present-day politics with a sensitivity to local circumstances. Geopolitical conditions outside the Soviet Union, notably where advanced capitalism had taken hold, must be accounted for in building a socialist state. Capitalism had proven more resilient than Marxist thinkers originally predicted and the "crisis theory" of its inevitable downfall, which would pave the way for proletarian revolution, became an ephemeral hope when the 1929–1930 stock market crash did not prove fatal. Moreover, the quick spread of fascism throughout various socioeconomic sectors demonstrated that no national public was equipped to recognize its dangerous implications without the proper political guidance and education. In short, it was Gramsci's attention to the concrete— what it would take to offset ingrained political mentalities—that set him apart from Bukharin and Trotsky, "ideologues" he criticized for failing to appreciate what a transition to socialism would actually require.[26] Gramsci, by contrast, was willing to tackle the issues of political citizenship that the modern era had given rise to from the perspective of the "common people," however "common"; although his prescription in some ways remained more theoretical than practical, a function of his modernist idealism. The movement, he felt, could

[26] For an evaluation of Bukharin, see Gramsci 1971, 376 ("The Study of Philosophy"), and 419–72 ("The Problems of Marxism"), for critiques of Trotsky, 236–56 ("State and Civil Society"), and 301–2 ("Americanism and Fordism"). Gramsci exempted Lenin from this indictment. He admired and was greatly influenced by Lenin during the formative period between 1917 and his tenure as PCI Comintern representative in Moscow and Vienna (1922–24). For example, see the article written in 1917 for the newspaper *Il grido del popolo* titled "The Russian Maximalists" (1990, 1:31–33). There, in a quixotic style common to an international generation of young socialists excited by the revolutionary events in Russia, Sassoon says, "Gramsci considers Lenin and his companions as revolutionaries who went beyond an evolutionary view of history because they did not wait for the revolution to occur automatically but had awakened and conquered the conscience of the people" (1987a, 28). In effect, says Adamson, Gramsci had created the Lenin he needed at that time, "a most libertarian Lenin, a democrat, an organizer of soviets, and a leader of a mass-based party conscious of the need for the political education and cultural autonomy of the proletariat" (1980, 49). After 1923, Gramsci saw himself as continuing to build on the propositions advanced in *What Is to Be Done?* and *State and Revolution*. Despite strong similarities in their positions on vanguardism and radical voluntarism, however, Gramsci goes beyond Lenin to offer a more sophisticated analysis, one tailored to conditions outside the Soviet Union, of the role of intellectuals, the nature of their relationship to state and society, their contributions to revolutionary mobilization, and the means by which the masses might absorb their message.

not afford to presume that socialism would triumph over fascism without constant communication between the "leaders and the led."

Gramsci espoused extending Marx's "philosophy of praxis," a method for reading workers' substantive concerns and behaviors as a way of achieving empathy with the popular stratum. He recommended that "the conception of ethico-political history" be adopted as an "empirical tool" for historical research, to be "constantly . . . borne in mind in examining and understanding historical development, if the aim is that of producing integral history and not partial and extrinsic history (history of economic forces as such etc.)" (Forgacs 1988, 195). "This," he wrote, "is the central nexus of the philosophy of praxis, the point at which it becomes actual and lives historically (that is, socially and no longer just in the brains of individuals), when it ceases to be arbitrary and becomes necessary—rational—real" (1971, 369).

Data culled from such readings could then be used to chart a more sensitive mobilizational course. Attention to this level of analysis would yield a better payoff than the demagogic solution of superimposing rigid party doctrine on a pliable public, which he felt lay behind Bukharin's exhortations in the *Popular Manual*.[27] Without the kind of elite intervention in civil society which took account of the actual structure of popular political culture and praxis, he reasoned, the mass of the population would remain limited by mundane expectations or, worse still, fall victim to a Mussolini or some other form of authoritarian rule. This "subaltern social group" he described as "deprived of historical initiative, in continuous but disorganic expansion, unable to go beyond a certain qualitative level, which still remains below the level of the possession of the state and of the real exercise of hegemony over the whole of society" (Forgacs 1988, 351).

Theorizing how to begin to combat this situation, Gramsci proposed that "the attitude to be taken up before the formation of the new state can only be critico-polemical, never dogmatic; it must be a romantic attitude, but of a romanticism which is consciously aspiring to its classical composure" (Forgacs 1988, 353). Thus, it is the attention Gramsci paid to politics-from-above, directed and controlled by those who are, in the best Machiavellian sense, "in the know" (1971, 135), *and to* politics-from-below, predicated on education and measured feedback, which makes what he had to say relevant to a reconstitutive national movement like the Greek resistance. With care, we can connect Gramsci's philosophical tenets to the modernizing objectives of Greek leaders who, cognizant of the power of cultural politics, arrived at similar conclusions about revolutionary change and the forging of a new "State spirit," as Gramsci called it (1971, 146). For example, the January 1944 issue of *Nea Ellada* (New Greece), which eulogizes the EAM strategist Dimitris Glinos (1882–1943), expresses comparable positions:

[27] See Bukharin and Preobrazhensky 1988; and Bukharin 1969.

(Among other efforts) the monthly periodical *Anayennisi* (Renaissance) which [Glinos] founded in 1926 and edited until August of 1928, were not only valuable contributions to Greek thought but also reflected the development of his own personal thinking . . . [Glinos decided] that the only sure way to overcome a backward educational system was a very broad struggle for the redemption and triumph of the people. This he initiated in the pages of *Anayennisi* . . . In May of 1929 he characterized the role the periodical had played at that phase of revolutionary development: '*Anayennisi*,' he wrote, 'devoted two years to its struggle, not only without retreating from the road that it hoped to open among educated Greeks but also by marking out in everyday life clearer routes TOWARD THE OPEN HORIZON OF SOCIALIST CULTURE [SOSIALISTIKOU POLITISMOU].[28]

Creative History: Interpellating the "National Collective Will"

> As a first formulation I shall say: *all ideology hails or interpellates concrete individuals as concrete subjects.* . . . ideology "acts" or "functions" in such a way that it "recruits" subjects among the individuals (it recruits them all), or "transforms" the individuals into subjects (it transforms them all) by that very precise operation which I have called *interpellation* or hailing, and which can be imagined along the lines of the most commonplace everyday police (or other) hailing: "Hey, you there!"
> —Althusser 1971, 173–74, "Ideology and the State"

Forty years earlier, Gramsci focused his attention on the phenomenon that Althusser would call "interpellation." How was it that so many people could now be "hailed" as fascists or, equally disturbing, as radical democrats in name only? What philosophical lacunae had the European Left failed to address that had allowed fascism to flourish? In fact, much of the fuel for Gramsci's prison writings came from his desire to account for and suggest ways to ameliorate fascism as "politics gone bad," and to historicize the lost opportunities that might have contributed to Left decline. By the period of the *Notebooks* (1929–1935) and fascism's successful rise, a combination of personal experiences and empirical developments led Gramsci to theorize cultural politics as integral to a program of social change. These factors are germane to the Greek situation because, as we know, there a history of elite-dominated politics and effective mass disfranchisement also culminated in a fascist regime in the 1930s. What could the working class or, in more general terms, the subaltern learn from the political configurations of the past? Gramsci found the roots of twentieth-century asymmetries in nineteenth-century political culture but also in the

---

[28] "Dimitris Glinos: Enas protagonistis tou laou" (Dimitris Glinos: A champion of the people), *Nea Ellada*, monthly publication of Free Greece, no. 5, Athens (January 1944): 3, courtesy of the Lagoudakis Collection, Mugar Library, Boston University. Capitalization appears in the original text.

outmoded assumptions behind Left party politics in the 1920s. It is his reading
of Italian history as stories of political exclusion and opportunity that interests
me here as an analogy to the Greek case.

As a modernist, Gramsci found his theoretical flashpoint in the standards of
universal political participation derived from the Enlightenment and the
French Revolution. The nineteenth century generated a range of movements
and countermovements that built on the Enlightenment debate about
democracy, citizenship, and civil rights. News of these collective actions spread
through innovations in the communications media.[29] At both the national
and international levels, a newly mobile modernizing elite disseminated narratives about mass prerogatives. The story of the struggle for Italian unification
(the Risorgimento), a movement heralded as a success in the folklore of the
liberal state, typified such a narrative. But in Gramsci's view, most nineteenth-
century "mass" reform movements had proven deficient because they embodied what he called *passive revolution*. Although the reforms of these revolutions
were lauded as progressive and appeared to be a step in the right direction,
Gramsci, deconstructing their social meaning from a universalist perspective,
saw them as mixed blessings. He argued that nineteenth-century revolutions
across Europe were partial transformations that merely added a bourgeois
dimension to the ruling class and left the feudal aristocracy largely intact. True,
the old estate system had been replaced by associational politics, but participation was still far from universal. The danger was that subordinate groups had
been led to believe that they counted. However, this attested more to the
power of symbols manipulated by politicians than to what had actually
transpired.

Gramsci focused primarily on the successes and failures of the major players
in the Italian "revolution from above": the "moderates" led by Cavour and the
Action party of Mazzini and Garibaldi. The moderates won the contest to
control Italian political society. The Action party, more expressly concerned
with political action at the mass level and at certain points spectacularly successful, deteriorated after a series of factional disputes and abortive uprisings
and faded from the scene. Neither group had any success in mobilizing widespread popular support; both had begun their campaigns as elite formations
and barely managed to scratch the surface of mass participation. Although the
moderates attained a position of political leadership, their base of support
continued to be thin. On the failure of the Italian bourgeoisie in the midst of
success, Gramsci remarked:

> The merit of an educated class, because it is its historical function, is to lead
> the popular masses and develop their progressive elements. . . . Those men in

[29] See Anderson 1983 for a now-classic discussion of the socializing role of the print media in
the nineteenth century, a development which was significant on an international scale.

effect were not capable of leading the people, were not capable of arousing their enthusiasm and their passion. . . . Did they at least attain the end which they set themselves? They said that they were aiming at the creation of a modern State in Italy, and they in fact produced a bastard. They aimed at stimulating the formation of an extensive and energetic ruling class, and they did not succeed; at integrating the people into the framework of the new State, and they did not succeed. (1971, 90, "Notes on Italian History")

Gramsci's primary concern was political change that went beyond the window dressing of state structures. Politics was not therefore crassly synonymous with the state. For genuine political change to occur, it was necessary to address the moral and cultural foundations of society directly and to replace the feudalistic collection of corporate groups with a more universal distribution and understanding of power. Thus, "the interests of the subordinate groups must have some concrete and not simply ideological weight; otherwise the interests of the dominant class would be merely economic-corporative. The definition of the highest development of a class consists in its ability to represent universal interests"(quoted in Sassoon 1987a, 119). Whereas the bourgeois state had so far presented a paper image of universality, the proletarian state promised to "create the conditions" for authentic popular participation, based on local circumstances.

The Greek Revolution of 1821 and its aftermath provides an excellent example of "passive revolution." Ultimately the beneficiaries of the 1821 struggle were the national bourgeoisie and an international aristocracy, both with limited mass contacts. The founders of the revolution, which was initiated by an intensely patriotic intelligentsia, had managed to instill a broader national consciousness, but this noesis was largely confined to questions of Greek territorial integrity and colonial liberation. Issues of mass education and participation were left for a triumphant future, and although rooted in Enlightenment philosophy, remained nebulous. As with many revolutionary offshoots of the French experience, the printed word was crucial to the spread of revolutionary fervor both in Greece and abroad. This factor alone served to confine those mobilizations with future consequences to the literate (and largely male) public, a pattern reinforced by other characteristics such as the exclusive membership of the Filiki Etairia, or Friendly Society, a primary instigator of anti-Ottoman activity, which remained influential throughout the conflict (see Clogg 1979, esp. 47–50). To be sure, the ancien régime had in no uncertain terms been destabilized. Nevertheless, after 1832, the popular groundswell that helped to win the revolution was fairly rapidly excluded from the political process with the establishment of a foreign constitutional monarchy supported by an elite parliament, its elected representatives in office only by the grace of personalistic and clientelist modes of participation. This pattern subsequently repeated itself in the small labor movement largely dominated by people of privilege and learning through the 1930s. The configuration was not unusual in countries of the European periphery and semiperiphery (see Jayawardena 1989). Echoing Gramsci, EAM propagandist Glinos called for the critical, selective use of historical example in rectifying the nation's stagnant past, a fight to be spearheaded by a Jacobin force cognizant of the power of past distortions (Glinos 1971a).

A second set of lessons from Italian history provide helpful background to our case. Gramsci wanted to propose an alternative to the strict economism and false universalism which had in his view unproductively enveloped Comintern analyses since the organization's inception in 1918. All too often, the Comintern set a doctrinaire example that Gramsci, virtually from the beginning of his involvement, had found difficult to reconcile with struggles closer to the ground. Furthermore, although he felt that the Comintern should formulate international guidelines and standards, at the same time he and a number of his colleagues also felt that a whole range of local problems specific to national Communist parties needed to be considered when implementing policies set in Moscow or Vienna (see, e.g., 1990, 1:79–82). "We are defending the future of the Italian revolution," wrote Gramsci in 1923 (1990, 2:155). The detailed "Notes on Italian History" in the *Prison Notebooks* (44–120) exemplify his desire to see close attention paid to contingent regional developments. "Gramsci's chief concern," observes Showstack Sassoon, "was to improve the ability of the party to intervene in a specific national context" (1987a, 66). A 1943 Greek resistance pamphlet titled *Laokratia kai sosialismos* (Popular democracy and socialism) bespeaks parallel sentiments: "We need to proceed by examining contemporary Greek problems [*neoellinikon provlimaton*] in order to confirm for ourselves not only that 'socialist' declarations may be deceptive, but also that they don't automatically correspond to today's level of development and to the needs of the region. Our immediate problems are different" (11). The tenor of the rest of the pamphlet is clearly not to negate the socialist enterprise or even to advise defecting from an international arena of cooperation but rather to warn against mechanistic solutions to local dilemmas.

Redirecting the National Collective Will

In addition to his Sardinian experiences, the early years Gramsci spent in Turin as a student and political activist had convinced him that a strategy that did not synthesize the aspirations of "the leaders" with those of "the led" was inherently unworkable. Opening the channels of political and cultural communication was key. The working-class masses were much discussed but not always actually listened to by the Communist parties that were their supposed representatives. Slighting popular concerns and failing to extend opportunities to learn and participate to the working-class and peasant foot soldiers of the coming revolution would result in a top-heavy authority structure that stunted personal and collective growth. Gramsci felt that the movement would be poorer for it. The value of proletarian input should not be underestimated, since eventually, if properly prepared, that group could replace the present rulers as the hegemonic force. That eventuality would be possible only if a victorious revolutionary movement was able "to prevent the central nucleus of the party from being submerged and fragmented by the mighty new [mass] wave . . . without political preparation" (Gramsci 1990, 2:286). In other words, only a combination of education and strategy would allow effective participation on such a scale. Furthermore, the party must not attempt to "lead the working class through an external imposition of authority. . . . Every tendency to separate oneself off from the life of those organizations, whatever they may be, in which it is possible to make contact with the working masses, is to be combated as a dangerous deviation, indicating pessimism and generating passivity" (2:368). Leadership should continually strive for political *Verstehen* in relation to those masses.

Here again, Gramsci's approach to political construction and the logic and context of modernist political transformations makes sense in relation to events in occupied Greece. Especially germane is Gramsci's metaphorical use of the concepts, in this case corresponding not coincidentally to the actual thing, of the "wars" of movement and position. The *war of movement* Gramsci equates with the Russian Revolution, the sudden relatively cataclysmic overthrow of one regime and its replacement with another. The *war of position* is the steadier, more gradual confrontation with the structures of psychological and material domination which have been erected on all societal levels. This kind of studied confrontation is necessary, Gramsci thought, to institutionalize "real" changes in the everyday lives of "real" people in the future and for progressive forces to triumph over fascist ideology. The essence of a war of position as a political process is the transvaluation of mass belief systems or the strategic reconstruction and resocialization of key communities operating in the public sphere, so that after a time political and civil society constitute a reasonably well integrated whole (see Bobbio 1988). This "integral state" then forms the basis of a new hegemonic order.

The Greek war of movement occurred almost gratuitously and minus the characteristic bloodshed of October 1917, when the monarchy and older politicians relocated to Cairo and set up a government-in-exile in concert with the British in the spring of 1941, leaving a power vacuum that the EAM had filled within six months. As ephemeral as this state of affairs turned out to be, in retrospect it contained the seeds of lasting change, and perhaps more significantly as the months went by, came to be seen as an important *opportunity* by key players in the conflict. The rather dramatic, though somewhat inadvertent, victory of "movement" in 1941 set the stage for a more deliberate war of position in which the EAM took the main initiative in reconstructing popular notions of Greek citizenship.

To conclude: in the foregoing discussion I have argued that while Gramsci's theoretical approach emanated mainly from Italian political history, its basic concepts have a wider resonance. Exploring Gramsci's reasoning is therefore useful for the present case because his views took shape in the course of international conversations that other communist nationals involved themselves in either directly or indirectly. Gramsci's ideas about collective action, political socialization, and the ingredients of enlightened leadership grew in response to a range of debates blowing in the political wind of the 1920s and 1930s. The wider applicability of his work is perhaps no better illustrated than in Gramsci's consideration of the question of the revolutionary party, which, adapting Machiavelli, he called "The Modern Prince."

From a literal standpoint, the EAM cannot be conflated with a Bolshevik party given the scope of its activities, nor would we want to characterize its membership as strictly proletarian. But I would "analogously infer" certain structures and processes from Gramscian philosophy and from the Italian case that informed it. Thus, while neither "bolshevik" nor "proletarian," the EAM functioned as a quasi-political revolutionary party both during and after the resistance period, profoundly changing the lives of subaltern groups and generating intense loyalties. In the space of four years, the EAM leadership inaugurated a change in the Greek system of government from an elite-based network to a mass political phenomenon that even managed to take on a life of its own. Clearly, argument by analogy raises questions that can never really be answered and hypotheses that can never be "proven true." But what this approach does inspire, it seems to me, is creative reflection about the kinds of icons that may have influenced political behaviors during critical conjunctures.

As in the situation of the Italian communists, for EAM's founders, debates both in and out of the Comintern informed crucial decisions. Methods of state building and the negotiation of political power were of primary concern, as was the potential reconstitution of civil society—all points taken up by Gramsci and various of his contemporaries. Furthermore, the types of human resources available (such as, workers, peasants, the petty bourgeoisie, youth, international allies, etc.) and strategic opportunities (autonomy, alliances, dependency, etc.) were comparable at major turning points, and lessons gleaned from discussions of the Twenty-one Conditions (1920–1921), the United Front (post-1921), the Bolshevization campaign (1924), the Third Period (1928–1934), the Popular Front and other milestones undoubtedly affected subsequent policy choices, even if not always consciously. The national and international spheres moved together in an elaborate "interactive dance."[30]

There is also an important argument to be made concerning popular cosmologies about communist party conduct, and not just in the relatively high heat of historical debate during the Cold War period. As a result of the recent eastern bloc collapses and "failures," communists and their motives have been discredited anew. Yet villainization provides only a partial and needlessly unimaginative view of events. Historicizing social movements of the modernist era deserves a far more complicated reading than is allowed for within a prevailing post–Cold War "structure of feeling," if for no other reason than that the situations themselves and the stock of ideas available to communists were more complex than such caricatures permit. Thus, Gramsci's programmatic solutions and predictions (and, as we will see in subsequent chapters, those of Dimitris Glinos, Stefanos Sarafis, and George Siantos) are especially relevant if we concede certain conceptual points regarding the forces behind many communist-led movements of the modernist era. These movements tackled such unprecedented social problems as creating civic identities out of whole cloth, attempting to rectify distortions in the distribution of political power, and fortifying national political cultures against fascist rule. The convenient but rather exaggerated view that local movements were necessarily propelled by the desire to reproduce themselves as obedient Soviet progeny or to diabolically corrupt liberal systems of government, needs reexamining.

In many cases, these men (and some women were also leading figures), as *nationalists,* simply thought they could "do better" than the regimes in power. As fascism became a less distant possibility, their exertions took on a new urgency. After 1919, the Comintern was one of several *contexts,* but of course not the only *site* of the acquisition of political consciousness. Aside from conformist rhetoric and what Gramsci calls an "internationalist spirit" (1990, 2:361), for many the Soviet Communist party provided an exploitable wellhead of ideas and should not be seen as a kind of monitor of cyborg parties powerless to construct their own identities and solutions. In Chapter 3, I examine the various sources of behavior that shaped the organization of the EAM movement.

---

[30] I owe this phrase to Zald and Useem 1987.

Harnessing Popular Enthusiasm: Tales from the Greek Resistance

Wars, crises, natural disasters, and the like have been described as breaks in the political opportunity structure. "The point is," writes Doug McAdam, "that *any* event or broad social process that serves to undermine the calculations and assumptions on which the political establishment is structured occasions a shift in political opportunities. Among the events and processes likely to prove disruptive of the political status quo are wars, industrialization, international political realignments, prolonged unemployment, and wide-spread demographic changes" (1982, 41). In the midst of such metabolic shifts, new political agendas are considered, and political cultures, institutions, and processes are open to restructuring.

Crises are significant not only because they may involve societal groups in a series of violent encounters with each other and with authorities. Crises are also significant because they create what has been termed "political space," making new resources, information, and ideological support from strategically placed allies available to groups who want to change their positions in the political hierarchy or to gain access to the political system for the first time. Whether or not groups fully achieve their potential, political space makes the acquisition of power and prestige *possible*. Different ways of doing things are now conceivable to policy makers and to the public. An unintended consequence of war as a crisis signaling "dangers that threaten the identity of a society" (Habermas 1975, 25) may be the introduction of revised narratives. In other words, wars and other apparent disasters may in retrospect provide a *narrative* opening for the political system: an opportunity for new political stories to be told, featuring new plots and nontraditional characters acting in hitherto inconceivable settings. I do, however, want to emphasize the importance of connections between crisis situations and everyday life under non-emergency conditions, and in particular how movements tap into everyday understandings when mobilizing participants. At the same time, it is important not to conflate the two, and judge what goes on during a crisis using the same terms that we would to analyze everyday life, the domain of "normalized" ways of living. What concerns me in this chapter is how leaders seized the wartime opportunity to direct changes that were expressed in forms the public could recognize and accept. I am also interested in the possible ways in which the resistance may have represented a missed opportunity.

We have already noted that the Greek resistance movement which formed after the Nazi invasion of 1941 occasioned a structural opening for the country's political system, with the EAM playing a major role in formulating and spreading the narratives that characterized the movement. During the occupation period, from 1941 to 1944, the EAM managed both to function as a popular front movement at the leadership level and to initiate a populist movement at the base. In addition to coordinating military maneuvers, the organization worked to alter traditional participatory structures and to recast popular definitions of Greek nationhood in the context of its wartime mobilizations.

What political stories fall under the rubric of the Greek resistance? My aim will be to analyze resistance testimonies and popular culture for the stories that in taking part in the resistance, participants thought they were telling about themselves, about the Greek past, and about the country's future prospects. With mass consistency, groups with heretofore limited public voices, such as youth and women, now had roughly similar stories to tell not only about the course of the war but also about their role in politics. Nationalism was the overall theme of these stories and the rallying cry that gave the EAM, as even a conservative critic admitted, "control of almost the whole country" by the end of the war (Woodhouse 1985, 146). These stories were an amalgam of continuous and discontinuous themes that acknowledged the past glories of ancient times and the Revolution of 1821; added current events such as the Greek successes on the Albanian front in 1940 and the Nazi atrocities against civilians, and advocated, for the future, full citizenship rights for all Greeks qua Greeks. The story entitled "The Greek Resistance" that leaders and members of the EAM were telling can be seen as nationalist in two senses: first, that one of its major goals was national autonomy and self-determination (*ethniki aftodhikisi*) of which the slogan "Greece for the Greeks" was emblematic; and second, that it was a popular plebiscite in favor of "the empowerment of subordinate classes [through] the transformation of conditions within civil society" (Keane 1988, 23), and the expansion of citizenship rights to include traditionally subaltern groups. EAM was the organizational expression of a consensus that the political code built upon clientelist structures and political exclusion was open to question as never before. Based on a reinterpretation of available documentary evidence, I assert that this complex of stories may be contrasted with the oversimplified version enshrined in traditional histo-riographic accounts entitled "The Stalinist Insurgency."

Narrative Approaches to the Greek Resistance

It is perhaps not widely known that the events in Greece during the 1940s remain controversial and emotionally charged. Represented among the characters in this ongoing and in many ways still unresolved controversy are the forces of resistance, collaboration, and subsistence, as well as participants in older, unconnected feuds that erupted during this period of tremendous dislocation. Over subsequent decades a legacy of clashes typical of wartime combined with a bitter civil war, which followed almost immediately on the heels of the German evacuation. From a symbolic and affective point of view, the country continued to fight related battles well into the 1970s, and strongly held beliefs about the resistance period remain a feature of the contemporary political landscape.[1] As noted earlier, that authors on different sides of the conflict take issue with one another's stories, giving rise to controversies that may stretch across generations, introduces a fundamental epistemological challenge for narrative analysis that remains to be reconciled. My point, though, is that one way to get at motivation is to try to reconstruct the plots of the stories that various collective actors *think* they're telling, a multinarra-tive approach, which hopefully makes theoretical overdetermination less likely.

A further, equally important, and perhaps by now obvious point is that what I summarized in Chapter I as "historical background" is not and can never be "objective" history, because there is no such thing. What I have presented here is my own narrative rendering which has led me to structure the text according to my personal view of what happened, based on the pockets of evidence I have been able to uncover. It is no exaggeration to say that there are those who, upon reading this account, would become apoplectic. Contrary to stan-dard postwar historical texts and also to a segment of popular belief, I have painted the EAM movement more as victim than victimizer. In so doing, I support the allegorical position, shared by some scholars[2] and not others, that what we think we know about this movement has gotten tangled in Cold War rhetoric, leaving little room for a fair reading of its popular political and psychological dimensions. While I acknowledge such negative factors as occa-sional violent episodes during which innocent people were accused of col-

---

[1] For a brief summary, see Iatrides 1981, 195.

[2] See, for example, the essays by Svoronos, Petropoulos, Hondros, Richter, Alivizatos, and Tsoucalas, among others in Iatrides, *Greece in the 1940s*.

laboration, at times sloppily defined (which were not, I would argue, emblematic); the sinister (but again, in my opinion, atypical) role prewar KKE leader Nikos Zachariades played in fomenting conflict within the party and attacks against it upon his return from Dachau in 1945; and the general confusion regarding long- and short-term goals, common to hastily conceived populist coalitions, which was evident in various contradictory policies from 1943 to 1949—my account features an essentially pro-EAM subtext that laments the idea that a nascent popular democracy was crushed during an uncritically repressive era. Consequently, the best way to approach my narration (and all others, I would argue) is as a plausible model rather than a scientific proof which asserts a decisive, universal truth (see Mink 1978). But this caveat in no way lessens my belief in the accuracy of my narrative analysis.

It would of course be impossible to give a full account of all the personal anecdotes to come out of the Greek resistance. Instead, I begin by sketching the broad outlines of an especially salient metanarrative that has what Hayden White calls the "capacity to unite all of the individual stories" belonging to a particular perspective (1987, 148). The textual interpretation favored by a broad range of resistance participant-authors is a story of the resistance movement as the embodiment of redemptive, Panhellenic *nationalism*. I offer a few illustrations of the apparent power of this motif as a means employed by the organization to engender a new collective Greek political identity and as an incentive to potential participants in the resistance-cum-social revolution that the EAM represented. My examples come from the oral histories I conducted with Greek partisans and from resistance songs, secondary sources, and other published materials, such as pamphlets, bulletins, posters, and newspapers. The range of sources in which I detect the same story will hopefully provide a kind of reality check and grounds for assuming some degree of reliability in my interpretation.

Cracking the Political Code: Clientelism and Populism

During the twentieth century, Greek politics have been dominated by political clientelism. Patronage is a prominent feature of politics in general, but patron-client exchange networks are more central to some systems than to others (Mouzelis 1978). Clientelism is a vertical mode of political linkage whereby citizens promise politicians loyalty and support in exchange for protection and the provision of goods and services. Voters' contacts with the state, therefore, are through complicated, personalistic networks rather than through more mass-based political associations, which, at least theoretically, equalize public access to the halls of government. The primacy of political clientelism in Greece meant that certain groups were excluded from participation. This method of political exchange excluded those not in a position to seek favors or to accrue the political currency necessary to make their voices heard. Included in the ranks of the disfranchised in these terms, either de facto or de jure, were peasants, the elderly, many young people both male and female, refugees from Asia Minor, and adult women.

A perceived political antidote to clientelism, and often a dramatic public-relations success, is populism.[3] Working "from above," charismatic leaders or social movements seek to mobilize the political participation of strategic groups—some of them latent—in the society. The attempted incorporation of new groups represents a direct challenge to the status quo as new participatory opportunities are extended and, with varying degrees of success, a new weltanschauung is constructed which takes as its guiding ideological theme the inherent right of the people, as opposed to the traditional politicians, to rule. The definition of the "people," or those who deserve to rule, varies from case to case, but possibilities include women, workers, youth, peasants, the middle classes, intellectuals, economic collectivities, and various ethnic groups.

As a people-based philosophy, political populism is generally ideologically linked by its exponents to nationalist appeals. But the concept of the nation is purposely kept indeterminate. Leaders creatively employ history and pithy cultural symbols to construct narrative frames that attract a cross section of the population, while seeking to divert attention away from particularistic identities such as class, gender, region, ethnic group, or religion. Paradoxically, then, at the same time that influential "authors" are emplotting narratives based on inclusionary principles, localized concerns are viewed with suspicion. The generic "progressive" is oriented in the collective imagination toward a slightly blurry utopian future. The conglomerate nature of populist ideology means that frameworks designed to explain cases where mobilization is based on more unitary concerns or where it is in support of single issues, are inappropriate tools of analysis. Movements linked to populism often confound researchers because by nature they rest on ideological patchwork. But it seems to me that it is worth rising to the challenge if the ultimate goal is to be theory-building informed by historically specific empirical cases.

In summary, the mobilizing narratives of populist movements by definition may address diverse class, national, ethnic, and gendered themes. In the detective work required to understand populist movements, therefore, it is advisable to remain open to a range of possibilities regarding the ideological makeup of these social formations when constructing one's own narrative account. Accordingly, in the case of the Greek resistance, the mobilizing narratives of the

---

[3] As Nicos Mouzelis (1985) points out, populism can also be a rightist political phenomenon. On this point, also see Eley 1991.

EAM movement represented a number of distinct but by no means incompatible tendencies. Contrary to the totalizing biases of certain segments of the social movement literature, the fact that class, popular nationalism, clientelistic paternalism, and mass organization shared political space in Greece in the 1940s does not make that movement unique in its complexity. Instead I would argue that in broad theoretical terms, the EAM ought to be seen as adhering to a norm for populist movements; the problem, which is not small, is how to map the contours of populism in particular settings.

Greece in a Balkan Context

Nikos Mouzelis offers a definition of political populism which, although he doesn't apply it to the Greek resistance, is useful in conceiving of the EAM as a social movement:

Political populism involves drawing into the political arena people hitherto excluded from it or admitted to it only marginally. This type of political mobilization entails a radical restructuring of the prevailing relations of domination, without a concomitant radical transformation of the prevailing relations of production. This definition of political populism excludes revolutionary movements (like those of Russia, China, and Cuba) where popular mobilization [sought] an overall restructuring of both relations of domination *and* relations of production. (1985, 344)

Similarly, the EAM viewed itself as confronting the forces of domination, ambiguously defined. In resistance popular culture, classical themes are privileged over those of class; patriotism and the "nation" are stressed, either as parental or Titan figures; and generally the resistance qua nation is cast in a morality play in which good is forecasted to prevail over evil. "Voice of the people—voice of God," begins one marching song, equating citizenry and deity, "the enemy hears and trembles" (*To andartiko traghoudhi* 1979, 58). History is put to "safe" allegorical use, to emphasize the glorious classical past or the role of the nineteenth-century revolutionary hero(in)es in the war against the Turkish occupation. The future is also used as a rationale for taking risks in the name of the nation: "We fight for the right of our generation, to see what kind of government we prefer!" goes a stanza, repeated once sotto voce, of one song (cassette, *PEAEA Songs from Magnesia*).

In part the EAM's reluctance as a mass organization to narrate its claim to political sovereignty in strictly orthodox communist terms is attributable to the idiosyncracies of Greek class structure. From the late nineteenth century, the Greek economy had been dominated by a petty bourgeoisie rather than a significant industrial working class or landless peasants in the mood to revolt. For example, comparing the situation of Greek and Bulgarian peasants during the interwar years, Mouzelis concludes that "the only Balkan country which did not experience a strong peasant movement was Greece" (1976, 85). To account for the apparent quiescence of peasant sharecroppers, Mouzelis cites the neutralizing role of foreign labor migration; return flows of foreign currency from emigrants; and the depoliticizing effects of the Metaxas dictatorship from 1936 to 1941. The result was a decreasing gap between urban and rural elites.

Class-based ideologies were a less compelling reason for collective action than cultural nationalism, modeled after previous struggles against foreign powers. Late nineteenth century Greeks had a strong collective memory of colonial domination, incompetent foreign rule, and outside intervention, from the Ottoman Turks to a four-year allied British, French, and Turkish occupation during and after the Crimean War (1853–1857), to the Othonian dynasty, which fell to rebellious forces in 1862 (see Clogg 1979). Following the Russo-Turkish War (1877–1878) the Russians sought, unsuccessfully, to include most of Macedonia in a pan-Bulgarian state. In response to this move and the establishment of a number of Bulgarian churches and schools throughout the region, in the 1880s Greek nationalists redoubled their efforts to counteract a chronic, undisguised territorial interest on the part of the country's northern neighbor. Thus, although after 1917 many occasionally admired ideas generated by the "Great Bear" (*I Arkoudha*), they were not especially inclined to adopt unfamiliar symbols or to conceive of themselves as provincial extensions of the Soviet Union. With the exception of the relatively small community of socialist, communist, and pacifist thinkers, notions of national self-determination and irredentism (such as the Megali Idea to recapture Byzantium, disastrously attempted in 1897 and 1921) were more appealing to potential adherents than dialectical materialist proposals formulated elsewhere.[4]

The character of the EAM is perhaps best contrasted with that of its closest spiritual sibling, Yugoslavia's Antifascist Council of People's Liberation (AV-NOJ).[5] Although the two movements shared populist narrative tendencies, their orientations were strikingly different. In Yugoslavia hints of the 1948 split with Moscow were present as early as 1941, evident in miscellaneous defiant acts on the part of Tito and other Communist party leaders. Nevertheless, as Ivo Banac points out, "Tito's group, which for years had carefully educated party members to exult in the example of the USSR and to revere Stalin as its

[4] Accounts of formative events in nineteenth- and early twentieth-century Greek history are in Augustinos 1977, esp. 20–24; and Clogg 1979, 70–132. Many leading intellectuals were critical of irredentism, but it had been so widely appropriated as the symbol and narrative of nationalism in Greece at the time that strong and open opposition was decidedly controversial.

[5] Djilas 1977; Dunn 1989, 96–120; Wheeler 1989; Jancar 1981.

leader, now had an opportunity to extol Stalin's cult among new recruits to the resistance, men and women who often had no previous exposure to Communist rites." Accordingly, most Yugoslavian recruiting propaganda sought to create "the impression . . . that Stalin was the only antifascist leader and that Tito was his Yugoslav interpreter" (1988, 7). An additional factor was Yugoslavia's ethnic heterogeneity. In order to forge a union of diverse groups, Tito was obliged to employ relatively "neutral" rhetoric, choosing symbols that could be used to promote wholesale allegiances because they were not part of any particular group's repertoire. Ironically, just how fragile the Yugoslavian resistance coalition was has been shown in the tragic civil war of recent years.

A deeper structural reading of the evidence in the Greek case suggests an inverse scenario. Not only was there infrequent contact between the Soviet and Greek resistance leaders during the war, unlike the ongoing dialogue in the Yugoslavian case, it is also evident that the EAM tried to encourage neither allegiance to the Soviet Union nor solidarity with other communist states in a direct assault against capitalism. Still, once in a while class or Soviet themes surface in resistance discourse, such as, for example, in the opening stanza of one song: "Black crows with their hooked claws, fell upon the working-class; wildly squawking and aiming to draw blood, they wanted to see Dimitrov hang along with Danev and Popov, Thaelmann and the other antifascist leaders . . . and . . . they're still killing the heroic proletariat." However, the song also calls upon "workers, peasants, soldiers, people" to "move forward together in the fight against fascism" (*To andartiko traghoudhi* 1979, 66).[6] Classical communist motifs are also evident in the last words of a political prisoner executed in July 1949. Before she was shot, Lambrini Kaplani, a factory worker from Ikaria, announced: "I am a worker. And I am proud that I did not betray the working class. I fought so that better days would come for all working people as well as for those of you who are killing me. You are all my brothers. Long live freedom! Goodbye!"[7]

But despite their power, such words were not, as far as I can tell, a common feature in resistance narratives. Significantly, when they do appear, they are often tempered by broader populist ideological constructions. A pamphlet published by the EAM Central Committee intended to mobilize women from all walks of life begins its categorical review with "the woman worker"

[6] Dimitrov was a prominent Bulgarian Communist leader, Thaelmann a martyred German Communist leader, and Popov the head of the Soviet Military Mission to ELAS. The song was possibly sung in conjunction with the visit of delegates stationed in Yugoslavia in July 1944 to the ELAS general headquarters. Sarafis describes this visit, 1990, 351–55.

[7] Recording, Olympia Papadouka, *I yineka stin andistasi: Traghoudhia tis filakis* (Women in the resistance: Prison songs). It was first issued in France in 1977 after permission was denied by Greek authorities, who felt, according to the record jacket, that it would "stir up memories of the past" (*tha anamohleuvei to parelthon*).

(*ergatria*), noting that "the factory is the most important battlefront of an enslaved people. That is where fighters will be forged; there they will act systematically and persistently and from there they will rush forward unbridled toward the final victory." The monograph continues in an inclusive vein, describing how the movement will gain equally from the participation of the peasant, the teacher, the public employee, the housewife/mother, the young student, and finally, from the "anonymous masses . . . who have but one thing in common, the decision to sacrifice themselves for a greater cause: *their freedom*" (*Pos prepei na dhoulevei i yinaika*, 5, 39–40).

A number of factors can account for the absence of solidly "red" narratives. Communist leaders wanted to play down potentially incendiary motifs, feeling that the goals of mobilizing large numbers of people would be undercut by mass perceptions about "bolshevism." Also, many felt that they could afford to be patient, since they saw themselves as adhering to the Comintern's call for a preparatory bourgeois social revolution. Moreover, communist leaders were fairly well educated, often with middle- or upper-middle-class origins; some had grown up in what could broadly be called bourgeois households. Lacking prior experience with mass organizing, they were not entirely sure how once instituted, socialist praxis might actually function on the ground and so tended to keep to a fairly shallow dialogue regarding the new and improved state. Some, like Dimitris Glinos, had begun their political lives in the liberal camp— not at all uncommon for communist leaders—and, having boarded the train fairly late, may have retained room for interpretation and compromise. In any event, the mobilizing text of the Greek resistance greatly underplayed materialist and internationalist themes and sought instead to reconstruct politics using populist rhetoric tailored specifically to the Greek historical and political context.

Resistance Narratives

As I suggested earlier, the EAM's conception of nationalism had two facets. The first, which I have elsewhere called "defensive nationalism," concerned the defense of national borders and took as its primary objective the expulsion of Axis invaders (Hart 1990). The second, "political nationalism," involved the extension of citizenship rights to marginalized or disfranchised groups.[8] In the Greek case, the need for defensive nationalist solutions made it possible to address simultaneously the issue of nationalism as citizenship.

The coexistence of these two types of nationalism is not unique to Greece in the 1940s. Over the years many revolutions and resistance movements have

[8] For an especially helpful discussion of nationalism which influenced my thinking on this point, see Eley 1981.

blended the same two definitions of "the problem," although it remains to be seen whether this particular pattern belongs exclusively to the modern past and its foundational growing pains. What is most suggestive is that although the two types are conceptually separate and might be expected to lead to different sets of mobilizing activities, in resistance movements they have often been intertwined in the minds of leaders and followers and have worked to drive one another forward. Furthermore, the two kinds of nationalism have together provided a compelling rationale for collective action by heterogeneous groups of people. As key elements in an epic trope defining the Greek movement as progressive and reconstructive, the two types of nationalism were unselfconsciously woven together into a collective participant narrativization of the event. Based on my reading of the figurative significance of nationalism, I have extracted two versions of "The Story of EAM" as authored by its members.

Defensive nationalism. It is 1940 on the Albanian front. Greek forces are pushing the Italians back to Italy and making a fool out of *koroido* Mussolini— Mussolini the laughingstock. The joke is circulating, "If you want to visit Italy, join the Greek army." Each new victory at the front brings people out of their homes and sets them cheering and congratulating one another. But eventually the Greek army begins to suffer dramatic reversals, culminating in a series of humiliating defeats and Hitler's decision to invade Greece in April 1941. With so many men caught on the mainland in the process of evacuation from Albania, women, children, and elderly people fight with sticks and stones against the Luftwaffe in the Battle of Crete (May–June 1941). Greece is divided into a tripartite occupation by Germany; Bulgaria, a longtime enemy; and especially galling after heady victories, Italy. Yolonda, the daughter of a bank executive from a wealthy suburb of Athens, recalls:

> The Greek resistance was one of the most spontaneous; that is, it wasn't necessary for someone to tell us, "Come join this organization to fight the Germans," but by ourselves, as soon as we saw the Germans were coming down, we experienced a *shock* because, *we* were the winners, and that played a large role; that is, if the Greeks in Albania hadn't won against the Italians, we might have been otherwise. But since we felt so proud of winning, so. . . . The feeling in the souls [*o palmos mesa stin psihi mas*] of the young people in Greece and of others, of everyone, was so enormous because of the victory of the Greeks up in the mountains of Ipirus and in Albania, where they pushed the Italians out, abruptly, and without any declaration of war. *That* came later when they had crossed our border. The enthusiasm of the Greeks at that time was such that, and so great the heroism of the boys that were constantly leaving for the Albanian mountains to confront the enemy that had so underhandedly [*ipoula*] tried to cross the border. And in Athens, every Greek

victory was something . . . very triumphant. They would beat the drums, and there would be shouts of joy. Everyone came out into the streets . . . yelling and celebrating. It was absolutely divine! [*Itan kati to thespesio!*] And suddenly, we, the victors, had become slaves to a much greater power, the Germans. . . .

Suddenly, we found ourselves faced with a conqueror [*kataktitis*] that we had already won against, because the Germans had brought in the Italians . . . that is, Italian orders on the walls, *kommandatoura*, blockades. . . . For instance, to go from Filothei, where we lived, by bus [with the very rare buses then] the Italians would make checks [*sou kanane elengho oi Italoi*]. At a stop, they would board the bus, searching around, yelling, "Madonna," . . . and we *despised* them. The Germans we hated, but we just couldn't *believe* that now we were faced with the Italians in this way. . . .[9]

We never expected the occupation to last so long. That is, if anyone were to read the diaries that we kept as children . . . the first year, for example, my sister writes, "So many days of war, but it won't last the year," and she says here, "288 days of war, 107 of slavery." Every day she would write how many days had passed. Here she says: "281 days of war [on 4 August 1941], 100 days of slavery, but it won't last out the year. September is coming and with it, freedom." That is, every day we lived with these thoughts. *Na,* here she says, "110 days of slavery. *Po, po, po* . . . what a horror. Today we got 30 grams of bread. People are beside themselves [*o kosmos exallos*]."

Soon after their arrival, the Germans plant a Nazi flag on the Acropolis. On 30 May 1941, students Manolis Glezos and Lakis Santas rip it down. Their heroic deed is well publicized. Later that year, Axis troops are shocked to discover that cheering Athenians have not come out of their homes to welcome their heroic Aryan conquerors, as expected, but rather in support of the commonwealth prisoners of war, now chained to one another in carts being escorted through the streets. Especially harsh and gruesome conditions ensue. During the winter of 1941–42, an estimated 300,000 Greeks starve to death because of Axis requisitioning of supplies. Children are heard moaning, *pinao,* "I'm hungry." Whole villages are executed. Curfews are enforced. People are shot for having radios or for stealing potatoes.

The EAM is organized in 1941. Among its first activities in Athens is to help coordinate soup kitchens to keep the population from starving to death. "The first goal EAM had set," says Anthoula, twelve years old at the time and from

---

[9] It is important to note here that along with this kind of anti-Italian sentiment there was also the feeling that of the three occupying forces, the Italians were the lesser evil and behaved relatively more humanely than did the Germans or Bulgarians.

the middle-class Athens suburb of Kypseli, "was the fight for life—against hunger. The first song that was heard was [starts to sing] 'For life and for freedom, bread for our people! The old, women, men and children, for our beloved country.' That was the first hymn of the EAM that was heard around the city. It was sung to an old island tune and it went, 'Brothers and sisters, we who are faced with starvation and slavery; we will fight with all our hearts and our strength; for life and for freedom, so that our people might have bread.' That was our first song."

In 1942, the poet Kostas Palamas dies. Huge crowds defy patrolling soldiers to attend his funeral and shout allegorical slogans about bondage. Throughout 1943, the EAM organizes strikes of public employees in Athens to protest their unwilling role in helping the occupation to function. Responding to mass demonstrations organized by the EAM, the Nazis rescind the orders for *epistratevsi,* or the transporting of Greek workers to munitions factories in Germany. The organization constantly recruits new members and trains them in clandestine work. In the mountains, its military wing, ELAS, is a cross between a guerrilla and a tactical army and engages regularly in battle with the armies of the Axis. Joining the EAM is viewed as an opportunity to rid the country of the despised fascists and to help change the course of the war.

To summarize, the hero(ine) in the defensive nationalist story is Greece in contest with, in a phrase common to many resistance songs, "blackest [sic] fascism." (*o mavros fasismos*)[10] The enemy is the Axis menace that has overrun the country and is rationing food, performing executions, and shouting orders at innocent people in the square. The struggle takes the form of an epic drama in which sacrifice is for a righteous cause, harking back in the popular imagination to the ancient wars against the Persians, the 1821 War of Independence, and the more recent war in Albania. The story ends with the occupation a shambles since "Greece cannot be enslaved by the Bulgaro-Germans" (*To andartiko traghoudhi* 1979, 36). The Axis "dogs" slink away humiliated and Greece is free of all foreign domination, prepared for a future of national self-determination (*ethniki aftodhiikisi*).[11]

Nationalism as citizenship. The year is 1938. Greece is under the stifling dictatorship of General Metaxas. People are disappearing daily into jails and prison camps in which tortures such as the infamous *retsinolado* are prac-

---

[10] In the defensive nationalist narrative, fascism is an evil external force, equated with the Nazi war machine. From the standpoint of political nationalism, fascism is indigenous, associated with the Metaxas dictatorship. But as stated above, the two conceptions probably constituted an interlocking sphere in the popular mind.

[11] The Nazis are often referred to as dogs (*skiloi*) in the Greek resistance songs. In the popular "St'armata st'armata" (To arms, to arms) the "foreign wolves" are made to "shut up and shrink back trembling" (*loufazoun endhromoi oi xenoi oi likoi*).

ticed.[12] The designation "political prisoner" takes on a new meaning. For example:

> I'll start with the story of my father, so you can understand one of the reasons I became so active in the resistance against the Germans. At the time, my father was a builder, but he was a master craftsman and he worked and made quite a bit of money. We didn't go hungry at all—that is, until we were forced to fight against what Metaxas was doing, against Maniadakis, who gave the *retsinolado* and who started putting people into falange units. My father had read a pamphlet, and at the time he had said, "It says words of great beauty, like those of Christ." And the person who had given him the pamphlet had been a plant and betrayed him to the authorities. They arrested him and gave him forty days in jail. I was very young then, nine years old. In jail they hung him upside down and they beat him on his feet and he suffered internal hemorrhaging. When I saw this, I asked my father, Why? because I was afraid that he had done something bad. I didn't know that in jail . . . I thought they only put murderers in jail, or robbers. I didn't know there was such a thing as political prisoners. But my father said, "Because I don't want there to be any poor people," when I asked him, when he got out of jail. And that's how it happened, originally. So when the Germans came into Greece I was in my first year of high school and I knew what fascism meant. I knew very well what fascism was, from that previous experience of my father. There weren't any organizations right in the beginning. But as soon as EPON started, I joined.

Students are organized into mandatory falange units called Metaxas Youth, which are modeled after Hitler's youth organizations. Political organizations not controlled by the dictatorship are outlawed. In the period before the coup in 1936, the country has seen a number of government changes and highly unstable political conditions. For the most part, these short-lived regimes have alternated between coalitions of liberal democrats headed by the republican leader Eleftherios Venizelos and right-wing coalitions supported by the monarchy.

Women have no formal political rights. Political parties are built on clientelist networks rather than on mass participation. In the 1920s, Mouzelis reports, Venizelos had "tried several . . . times to create modern party structures [but when] faced with the adamant opposition of strong clientelist elements, [he]

[12] *Retsinolado* is a kind of resinated oil that was given to prisoners to make them vomit blood once their stomachs were empty of food. Often they would be given *retsinolado* in addition to being made to lie naked on ice (another type of torture associated in popular memory with the Metaxas period) in order to force admissions of usually spurious political crimes.

had to give up his attempts at party reforms." Thus, the last time a populist solution was tried, even at a time when the franchise belonged solely to men, it failed due to "the threat of dissatisfied local factions walking out en masse . . . [since] Venizelos . . . could not so easily bypass their authority and appeal directly to the people" (1985, 336, 337).

The EAM is formed in September 1941. Although its leadership coalition is dominated by party members and its initial organizing strategies influenced by cell-structure methods, its fundamentally communist origins are not widely known until well into the war (see, e.g., Hondros 1983). A significant number of members come from the ranks or are the children of the middle classes, civil servants, intellectuals, wealthy peasants, and the petty bourgeoisie.[13] Thus, seeing others of the same class participate and motivated by patriotism, upper- and middle-class members come to view the EAM as a legitimate form of resistance.

Young people are particularly disenchanted with patriarchal restrictions, as well as with the lack of political alternatives during the 1930s. Characteristically motivated by idealism, they join and participate enthusiastically in EPON, the youth organization created in 1943. An EPON poster shows a group of young people holding a banner that says, "Long live freedom." The caption proclaims, "Youth always march forward. Pure and incorruptible, with the heroic spirit shining from within, properly enlightened, they perform miracles." Tasia, from a moderately prosperous peasant background on Crete recollects:

> If the resistance hadn't come along, I and a lot of men and women—I
> don't know, of course. It's hard to tell how the conditions of life would
> have been and how much it woke us up [*mas ksipnouse*], but I'm fairly

[13] For example, Hondros's 1983 study concluded: "The GFP [German Field Police] and Wehrmacht Ic [Intelligence Branch of the German Army] reports sometimes included captured resistance documents. A September 9, 1943, GFP report on EAM/ELAS in the Peloponnese listed fifty-two names and thirty-four occupations of the region's EAM/ELAS. According to this report, the EAM/ELAS leadership in the area included seven teachers, six students, six self-employed individuals (merchants or shopkeepers), five lawyers, four skilled laborers, two former Greek Army officers, two medical doctors, two civil servants, two police officials, and one bookseller. . . . These figures reaffirm the broad national and social basis of EAM/ELAS as emphasized by L. S. Stavrianos, who listed sixteen generals, thirty-four colonels, and 1,500 commissioned officers of the prewar Greek army in ELAS. There were also six Orthodox bishops, many labor leaders, thirty professors from the University of Athens, and two members of the Academy of Athens in EAM/ELAS. . . . A noncommunist source inside of Greece in 1943 reported that EAM/ELAS was strongest among civil servants, white collar workers, merchants, shopkeepers and professionals in the urban areas and among wealthy peasants in the countryside. Artisans who were members were judged to be above average in number of years of education. Leadership positions went to professional classes and merchants who were motivated by patriotism. EAM/ELAS was indeed a bourgeois movement that brought a new administration to Greece" (119–20). Also see Stavrianos 1952.

Resistance poster by Vasso Katraki. The caption reads: "Youth always march forward. Pure and incorruptible, with the heroic spirit shining from within, properly enlightened, they perform miracles." Courtesy Mariana Katraki Despotidi

certain that the war woke us up a lot more intensely, and if it hadn't happened, I doubt we would have been woken up so easily. Our political education up until that time, we had the Metaxas dictatorship and the kind of regime that didn't politicize us correctly. It led us astray. [*dhen mas provlimatize sosta. Mas paraplanouse*]. Whereas the war was a lesson for all of us. And especially for us women. That was when the woman began to understand that she also needed to participate in politics and to follow what was going on politically. Before the war, the society was very conservative. We couldn't go around freely, and we didn't really know much about politics. Before the war, I was in the Metaxas Youth Group, EON. I went to a high school, and they had organized us all into the youth group. And once Queen Frederika came here to Rethymno and I cried. . . . I saw her and I was moved to tears! She was our queen! That's how I felt then. That was all we knew. Later on, in the resistance, I learned who the queen was, what kind of role she had played. Slowly I learned these things. And I saw them. Later on, in the war, I saw what fascism was and that the youth group I had been in was a fascist organization, and I was very ashamed. I was very sorry that I had participated, but I just didn't know. How could I? And that's why I became such a loyal member of EPON. I believed in the cause of EPON very much. Partly to purge myself from having been in that youth group! [laughing] But I didn't know.[14]

One of the responsibilities of EPON was to shout messages about resistance activities through bullhorns (*honakia*) to keep the population informed. For example, Anthoula says, "I was out early the morning of 25 March [National Independence Day], writing on the walls. I spoke into the horn. I still remember it like it was yesterday, what I said. 'People of Athens! The Voice of EPON is speaking to you! Tomorrow is a day of national joy, of national freedom! No one is to go into the center of the city! No one is to take part in the parade planned by the Germans! Everyone in the neighborhoods, in the churches, in the squares, together with EAM and ELAS, we will celebrate the 25th of March together!'"[15]

A fictional narrative based on the notes of Themos Kornaros, and published under the title "Andreas Lykourinos" in the PEEA newspaper, *Eleftheri Ellada*, 6 May 1945, expresses adolescent wartime "structures of feeling." Given its publication date, it can also be seen as a justification for the movement, a declaration that the defensive nationalist cause is a legitimate reason to

[14] A good account of EON in the Greek schools is in an autobiographical novel by Alki Zei, *Wildcat under Glass* (1969).
[15] Also see Myrsiades 1977, 101.

transcend parental and other forms of domination, as a prelude to political nationalism:

"Why were you late again, my son?" Andreas's mother knew that times were hard and that human life had been reduced to the cheapest possible commodity. Armed squads of Germans and Italians patrolled the streets of Athens and needed no pretext whatsoever to open fire on innocent passersby. It was best to return from errands as soon as possible and to remain inside until dawn, when life under this evil would no doubt bring new challenges. . . .
Andreas knew all this very well; he'd been given the same advice over and over. But now another voice had found a place in his heart. He had heard it around midnight one night during the winter of 1943. It seemed to come from a height, from somewhere up on Philopappou Hill and it spoke, it said, for an organization. The voice urged Greeks to take up arms and fight in order to rid the country of the occupying forces. That night Andreas had gone up on the roof to sleep and it was almost morning by the time he was able to shut his eyes. The words he had heard made a great impression on him. Who could they be, these people who shouted into the darkness, fearing neither the occupation forces nor their collaborators? How could one join this struggle for freedom? In the morning he asked his father what was this EPON, this voice he heard in the night, and how could one find this group that was appealing to people to help in any way they could? His father replied tersely, advising him instead to concentrate on his studies, especially this year, so that he could enter the gymnasium and eventually earn a decent living. His father hoped Andreas would strive hard to succeed as he had.
But Andreas wasn't a kid who was easily silenced. He asked other kids in his neighborhood if they had also heard the voice in the night. On his own, he went to some of his classmates whom he knew he could trust to find out if they knew anything. And little by little he learned that this organization was created especially for young people. And so with patience and persistence, eventually he was able to contact some of the leaders [*ipefthinous*]. And he learned then how the organization had launched a fierce struggle to rout the oppressor. . . . And so Andreas made his decision. . . . Of course he was young; he was barely twelve. (From Sakellariou 1984, 9–11)

The EAM offers an organizational alternative for political participation, in many ways modeling itself after a mass party and in some respects taking on de facto the duties of civil administration normally reserved for governments. It provides an appropriate organizational category for virtually every member of the family. Here, the famous quote by C. M. Woodhouse, the conservative commander of the Allied Military Mission in Greece during the war and generally critical of EAM/ELAS, is apropos: "[The organization] had acquired control of almost the whole country, except the principal communications used by the Germans, [and] they had given it things that it had never known before. Communications in the mountains, by wireless, courier, and telephone have never been so good before or since; even motor roads were mended and used by EAM-ELAS. . . . The benefits of civilization and culture trickled into the mountains for the first time. Schools, local government, law courts, factories, parliamentary assemblies began for the first time. Communal life was organised [for] the Greek peasant. His child was dragooned into EPON, his nest egg levied into EA, his caique (boat) commandeered to equip ELAN" (1985, 146).

The institution of the *ipefthinos,* or "responsible one," at the regional, neighborhood, and village levels helps to ensure that the decentralized administrative apparatus functions smoothly and with some sensitivity to local issues. The ipefthinos, Philip Minnehan notes, "was the key local EAM/ELAS recruiting agent and the person through whom the district's EAM superiors would execute their policies" (1983, 28; and see Stavrianos 1952). "People's Courts" are set up to adjudicate cases in remote areas. The system is implemented more fully in 1943 when the Italians evacuate Greece and a provisional government called Free Greece is set up in Roumeli province. For example, the official resistance photographer Spiros Melitzis says, "One time me and a friend were walking up the hill and we got hungry. We passed a cherry tree, and I said, 'Let's take some cherries.' And my friend said, 'We'd better not, because if someone sees us, they could turn us in to the Popular Court and we would be in big trouble.' Who dared to violate the law? You just didn't dare. But it wasn't only fear. Something had been awakened, not fear but some kind of consciousness. It just was wrong morally. So I went and knocked on the door, the owner of the orchard came to the door. We went inside and asked him, 'Do you mind if we have some of your cherries?' He said, 'Fine, take some,' and that's the way we had to do it." Literacy classes are held for those who have never learned to read or write. For the first time, women are officially given the vote in the spring of 1944 under the PEEA government. Early in the war, proto-organizations are set up for girls, to teach the social and political skills necessary to subsequent citizenship. In Athens,

I must say that, before the war, women who had a greater politicization [*politikopoiisi*], etc. were ridiculed, they were the objects of a lot of joking [*itan san andikeimena ironeias*]. Therefore, about that kind of thing, we were—that is, I'm talking about my generation now, and the girls in my circle—we would go to school, and we thought that—that is, it made us. . . . We were exasperated by the joking, but I believe that we weren't ready to do a lot of things to break through this irony because we also had accepted, we had somehow internalized the ridicule. It wasn't something that we were in any way ready to fight. But after the war, after the occupation, when we entered the organizations, there wasn't the same problem. There, we fought because we were many together and we had conscious goals [*sinidhitous stohous*]. We knew what we wanted. And it was something else. But at first, it was all kind of hazy.

Later on, when girls were organized to take part in the national resistance struggle, in demonstrations, and they were killed on the streets and I don't know what else—all that changed the mentality in Greece. That is, there, where they would make fun of women, they would laugh at them, when we talked, they began to see things differently. And in the organizations, the mentality changed. Whereas in the beginning they would say, "Ach, she's a girl, she'll never be able to do it," afterward they said, "So-and-so did that, and she did it very well," or, "She organized that assembly; she organized that operation; and maybe she did it better than such-and-such man would have." So we took on more responsibility.

In a model girls' unit in the mountains near Karpenissi:

One thing I want to point out is that even though I was used to a very different life . . . my father was a wealthy merchant, he was in charge of dispensing fish for the region around Missolonghi . . . and because in my family I was the youngest and the most catered to and very spoiled—that is, to the point where when my mother washed my hair, her big concern was that she couldn't let any soap get in my eyes. . . . In spite of that, I must say that I adjusted pretty well to the *andartiko,* to the life of a partisan, and I wasn't bad, in calisthenics, or whatever. I was very disciplined, I took part in all the activities and did whatever they told me to do. Remember, Maria, how many illiterate girls we had? There were quite a lot. I remember one, when we were having a geography lesson, the teacher, Captain Ilias, put her on the spot and asked about a particular term. What was her name, the girl with the sort of hooked nose?

Athanasia.

Right. And she said, "I don't bone it," meaning, "I don't understand it [*dhen to kokiazo*]." And I burst out laughing, because it seemed so hilarious, because we don't use that word where I'm from. Then I realized that she didn't understand, and that's why she didn't answer. And because I laughed, I remember it very well, Captain Ilias got angry and said to me, "*You* tell the class." And I said the word. I said it and he asked her, "Now, do you understand?" and she nodded her head that she did. Because she was one of the girls who was completely illiterate [*dhen iksere katholou grammata*].

Thus, by filling the vacuum left by the government-in-exile and by reaching out to "the people" in unprecedented ways, the EAM offers a means of participating in politics never before available to the masses of Greeks. "Woman's time has come!" claims a song. "She must throw herself into the struggle and fight like a man! Nothing—not mother, not house, not husband and children—should deter her; her single goal should be—Freedom or death!" (*To andartiko traghoudhi* 1979, 55). In attempting to fulfill military goals, many, it could be said, were also now newly exposed to visions of political freedom and political death.

To summarize: The hero(ine) of the story of nationalism as citizenship is the Greek people enlightened by the EAM. The enemies are fascists such as General Metaxas and those who would limit political participation to elites. The form the struggle takes is as a populist social revolution working to create a mass parliamentary democracy. The story ends with the much-disliked royal family remaining in exile, and free democratic elections being held as soon as the occupation is terminated. The chorus of the song "We Are of the New Generation" is representative: "O Sweet Greece, people's democracy, o sweet Greece, we don't want the king" (*Traghoudhia* 1975, 27).

Organic Intellectuals and Socializing Movements

A good way to approach certain kinds of deep structural collective actions, extending the term for organized, extra-institutional challenges to the political status quo, is through the concept that I have called "socializing movements." Socializing movements teach new political values to members of a particular target group and also attempt to recondition political attitudes within civil society regarding what kinds of groups may legitimately exist in relationship to state structures. Seen in this light, socializing movements perform exactly the same pedagogical function as such traditional agents of moral and political instruction as families, schools, labor unions, and political parties. In the absence of narrative modes of persuasion, it is as hard to imagine an effective socializing movement as it is to imagine early childhood education without stories. For example: "There comes a time that people get tired," says Martin Luther King in his Monday night speech to bus boycotters in Montgomery. "We are here this evening to say to those who have mistreated us so long that we are tired—tired of being segregated and humiliated; tired of being kicked about by the brutal feet of oppression." Thus, life for southern blacks is identified as constituting a narrative of oppression. Behind King's statement is a loaded morality tale: history is reviewed; the enemy and grievance are identi-

fied; common people are dignified as martyrs; links to more universal structures are made; the signal is given that it is now valid to act.[16]

At the heart of socializing movements is an attempt to reconstruct civil
society through deliberate (though sometimes informal) pedagogical means.
The central role played by radical organizations in promoting civil reconstitution as a "cause" distinguishes socializing movements such as the EAM or the
American Civil Rights movement from more frontal, protest-centered forms
of collective action, intended to produce immediate outcomes. Hence it is no
accident that socializing movements devote considerable time and attention
to youthful and otherwise "prepolitical" segments of the population and in
turn draw significant support from latent constituents. In this process, basic
traditional curricula combined with normative messages about what qualifies
as legitimate public-sphere behavior, are vital strategic resources. As Gramsci
points out to justify "wars of position" waged by revolutionary parties, success
in the fight against hegemonic structures depends on effective modes of
countersocialization.

Earlier, I asserted that a combination of psychological antecedents (private
ontological narratives) and dramaturgical factors (public mobilizational narratives) cause leaders to push movements in particular directions. Given that
many national-level movements are initiated "from above," rather than mate-
rializing spontaneously from a discontented rank and file, it strikes me as
difficult to fully comprehend the narrative emplotment of specific "big" events
without paying close attention to the development of leadership consciousness, an idea that I continually revisit in this book. Gramsci underscores the
importance of the concept of the "organic intellectuals," distinguishing this
group as "in general the entire social stratum which exercises an organizational
function in the wide sense—whether in the field of production, or in that of
culture, or in that of political administration" (1971, 97). As Gramsci's editors
note, the organic intellectuals play a preeminent role "in directing the ideas
and aspirations of the class [socioeconomic or political] to which they
organically belong" (Hoare and Nowell-Smith in Gramsci 1971, 3). For Gramsci, the organic intellectuals constitute a resource pool from which the leadership of any movement is likely to emerge. Broadly speaking, the organic
intellectuals can be understood as a cohort that shares a common exposure to a
range of cultural influences. In delineating this category, Gramsci makes the
point that those who engage in the intellectual work of strategizing and forcing social change include both the more traditional type (i.e., disgruntled
academics and political leaders) as well as teachers, local party and labor union
personnel, priests, and others who come to play an authoritative role.

[16] J. Williams 1987, 76. Interesting discussions of the authoritative construction of childhood
can be found in the essays by Gil Frith, Carolyn Steedman, and Valerie Walkerdine in Steedman
et al. 1985; and in Lurie 1990.

The leadership of the EAM was a short-lived but stable coalition of organic intellectuals from particular social classes and ideological schools, whose different political conceptions, as Eley says, "were . . . combined in the same political movement, and even in the ideas of the same person" (1981, 87). Although dominated by members of the Communist party, the EAM ruling council was a popular front comprising the major nineteenth- and early twentieth-century tendencies—communist, social democratic, nationalist, and liberal. To a politically significant extent, the coalition shared an intellectual history and a consensus regarding the desirability of movement goals. Under emergency conditions, leadership of the EAM movement was a necessarily cooperative enterprise and rank-and-file members were mobilized based on a program condensed from several ideological tendencies. The EAM, as a social actor, sought to define the boundaries and content of Greek nationalism in a way that was congruent with the value systems and political histories of its leadership. Resistance ideology as translated into policy, therefore, bore the various stamps of its leaders' formative experiences.

Needless to say, a functional consensus was required to direct the grass-roots national movement under emergency conditions. Later, this spirit of compromise began to give way to a more tenuous understanding and then to outright internecine conflict, especially as the movement was suppressed more emphatically during the White Terror of the mid- and late 1940s. The prewar general secretary of the Communist party, Nikos Zachariades, returned from a German concentration camp in 1945 and resumed leadership from the generally less-dogmatic George Siantos. As the Civil War progressed, the wartime populist coalition, with its expedient tendency toward defactionalization, deteriorated. Among other anticonsensual elements was Zachariades' vision of himself—his psychological referent, in Jo Freeman's terms—as the Greek Stalin. This self-conception led to his support of Stalin over Tito in 1948 and ultimately to Yugoslavia's decision to close its borders to escaping Democratic Army partisans in 1949, thus bringing about a particularly bitter end to the civil war. Vlavianos has commented: "Zachariades had dismissed the notion that peaceful evolution in Greece was possible by the time of the Second Plenum, and now led his party to the disaster that the abstention [from the 1946 parliamentary elections] was supposed to have prevented. . . . As Zachariades himself admitted after the defeat of the KKE in the civil war, the decision to boycott the election was also taken on the grounds that the boycott 'would prepare the people better for the new armed confrontation.' It is not difficult to imagine what this 'better' meant. Blinded by his revolutionary illusions and following textbook instructions, Zachariades became a prisoner of his own ideology" (1989, 196).

As we have seen, the KKE was never very prominent in Stalin's own referent narrative. Soviet disinterest in Greek events can be contrasted with Churchill's more blatant regard for Greece as a salient figure in his own allegories of receivership and even classical grandeur, as well as his long-term allegiance to the idea of the Greek king as a cornerstone of British Mediterranean policy (see, e.g., Richter 1986, 119). The course of the movement, like most, was largely determined by the ontological and mobilizational narratives of the organic intellectuals who initiated and directed it, interacting at various junctures with those of key international actors, and circumscribed by various structural constraints.

Of course, the character of the movement was also contingent upon how administrative policies were absorbed into everyday practice by the membership. It is not uncommon for assorted popular reinterpretations to take on lives of their own, yielding unanticipated consequences. Space does not permit a full exploration of this aspect, but it is nevertheless an important consideration in assessing the trajectories of social movements. In this case, however, I would argue that, owing to the relatively hierarchical structure of social authority in Greece, the membership was not inclined to deviate too widely from policy initiatives set at the top. Thus, an understanding of the "human element," or the reasons behind the authoritative decisions of the organic intellectuals who defined the character and direction of the movement, is crucial to an empirical grasp of the Greek resistance as an event. Approaching political developments in this way makes it harder to hang one's argument on uncomplicated models that posit a false uniformity of psychological referents among leaders ("communists had only one thing in mind in mobilizing popular movements and bourgeois liberals another"). In the next chapter, I take a closer look at the "organizers of the collective will" in the Greek war of position.

CHAPTER 4

Prosopography, Gender Politics, and the War of Position

One key to the direction and character of the EAM lies in the backgrounds and goals of its leaders, who represent a local version of a broader modern nationalist narrative. At the root of the EAM as a "dual" movement were a series of experiential and philosophical developments that shaped the political ontologies of members of the Greek intelligentsia and led them to construct mobilizational narratives designed to effect change. It is now well established that nineteenth- and early twentieth-century nationalisms were the constructs of state builders who, acting on behalf of their nations, were anxious to distance themselves from "premodern" *ancien régimes,* to prove their "modern" credentials within the larger international community, and to establish "rational" secular states. I have already reviewed KKE history and have raised the issue of Comintern influences. I now want to extend my analysis to consider the origins and constitution of other components of Greek nationalist ideology. To make sense of the Greek resistance as a quintessentially national movement, it is necessary to examine how it was piloted from a "prosopographic" point of view. Lawrence Stone describes this approach as "a tool with which to attack two of the most basic problems in history. The first concerns the roots of political action: the uncovering of the deeper interests that are thought to lie beneath the rhetoric of politics; the analysis of the social and economic affiliations of political groupings; the exposure of the workings of a political machine; and the identification of those who pull the levers. The second concerns social structure and social mobility: one set of problems involves analysis of the role in society, and especially the changes in that role over time, of specific (usually elite) status groups, holders of titles, members of professional associations, officeholders, occupational groups, or economic classes; another set is concerned with the determination of the degree of social mobility at certain levels by a study of the family origins, social and geograph-

ical, of recruits to a certain political status or occupational position, the significance of that position in a career, and the effect of holding that position upon
the fortunes of the family; a third set struggles with the correlation of intellectual or religious movements with social, geographical, occupational, or other
factors. Thus, in the eyes of its exponents, the purpose of prosopography is to
make sense of political action, to help explain ideological or cultural change, to
identify social reality, and to describe and analyze with precision the structure
of society and the degree and the nature of the movements within it." (1987,
45–46)

Ontological narrative is similar to Stone's prosopographic approach, although it includes a literary dimension that goes beyond externally observable
traits to extrapolate subjective identities from the raw materials of unconscious
thought, self-image, and imagination. Analyzing the transformation of leadership narratives can help to explain why history unfolds in particular ways at
particular junctures. For the moment I will leave aside the question of how
narratives emanating from the subaltern may force a reckoning with certain
neglected issues, and come to challenge, subvert, and transform leaders' understandings of critical "social facts."

One of the major components of the EAM's social justice agenda and
indeed one of the movement's main identifying characteristics was the push
for gender equality, as part of the process of recasting the meaning of nation
and citizenship. As Sonya O. Rose writes in her pathbreaking book, "Recent
scholarship has turned to the place of family, work, and community in the
construction of masculinity. As long as scholarship focused on women or
remained centered on the differences between women's and men's work, our
understandings about economic and social transformation could be broad-
ened but not undermined. Recent attention to men as gendered beings and to
men's work as having something to do with men as men has been a vital step in
undermining gender-neutral accounts of industrial transformation and class
formation" (1992, 3).

The same, of course, may be said for the study of political participation. The
social construction of gender—what it meant to be a political man, a political
woman, and to belong to a community of citizens—were essential components of the mass incorporation linked to modern political development. Ultimately, the gendering of citizenship cannot be separated from images of
honor, morality, sexuality. Citizenship as a social concept always contains visions of maleness and femaleness, in effect theorizing such things as inclusion,
exclusion, and correct and necessary behavior. These ideas are the products of
power holders' personal experiences, which find expression as mobilizational
narratives when the right opportunity comes along. This is especially true of
socializing movements, as compared to more spontaneous forms of collective
action.

The social movement within the Greek resistance originated among a relatively small group of Communist leaders but was soon enlarged to include a broader spectrum of other participants. The male-dominated social structure up to the outbreak of war had significantly constrained women's demands, making allies among the male leadership essential to meaningful change. The point is not that every leader was an enabling force or that there was no foot-dragging or outright hostility from those invested in the status quo. Nor would I want to caricature Greek men solely as active initiators and Greek women as mere passive victims, or the one-dimensional recipients of male generosity during this era. Yet a recognition of the *periodization of the possible*—a temporalization of Foucault's notion of governing as the capacity "to structure the field of the eventual actions of others" is crucial here (quoted in Hoy 1986, 135). Since in 1940 "politics" fell within what was considered to be the male domain, few Greek women would have been in a position to demand substantial political power or to function freely in that male reserve. A small, dedicated band of Greek feminists was active before the war, but for the vast majority of Greek women, any attempt to emancipate themselves or women in general from sex-role restrictions would have met considerable family and public ridicule.

The ontological narratives of male leaders of the EAM unfolded in a certain way based on developing images of their own masculinity, the meaning of male authority in national and international political arenas, and concerns about how they (and Greece) might be judged by others and by history. The ontological narratives of the smaller number of female leaders were likewise influenced by transformative negotiations beginning before the war, regarding how gender categories ought to be reconstructed and more generally about the components of a wider social justice agenda.[1] But like most social movements, certainly during the modern period, the EAM was an essentially masculine construction. Unquestionably, Kaiti Zevgou, Rosa Imvrioti, Chrisa Hatzivasileou, and other prominent women served as role models in certain circles, and their writings in movement bulletins were influential, especially among the literate. Nevertheless, hegemony clearly rested with male leaders such as Stefanos Sarafis, Aris Velouchiotis, George Siantos, Andreas Tzimas, Dimitris Glinos, and Alexandros Svolos. Consequently the extent to which policies favorable to women's interests were instituted in "their" movement depended on how amenable key male figures were to lending their authority

---

[1] Unfortunately I have not been able to conduct close ontological readings of top women leaders' backgrounds, due partly to a lack of information. I have not been able to obtain biographical material on the few women in the top ranks, although some does undoubtedly exist in Greek. Excellent studies of feminist activists before the war are Avdela and Psarra 1985 and Varika 1987. It is interesting but not really surprising that prewar feminism tended to be underplayed in EAM "feminist" texts in favor of themes of national unity.

to give voice to agendas they found personally compelling. We must also remember that any male authority figure advocating radical changes in gender relations still faced the strategic problem of persuading other men with more traditional views without causing undue alarm and thereby ruining any chance of actualization. Indeed, the deeply felt urgency to reconstruct and "modernize" national culture, a discourse that envisaged moving the nation away from chronic backwardness and into an enlightened future, often involved subtle negotiations within the boundaries of otherwise shared territory.

One way to explore how the Greek resistance combined readings of past lessons with present realities and future visions is to focus on the backgrounds and political scripts of critical leaders. Dimitris Glinos, intellectual architect of the EAM and author of the highly influential popular manual that framed organizational goals, is a pivotal case. His ideas converge with Gramsci's in interesting ways, demonstrating a confluence of thought quite in the absence of direct personal contact. Both Gramsci and Glinos dedicated their efforts to waging a war of position aimed at reframing and reconstituting national political culture as a prerequisite to a new hegemonic order. By examining the basic values, beliefs, and strategies that in their minds defined the terms of counterhegemonic struggle, we can gain some understanding of the various dimensions of the Greek movement's attempts to incorporate women and girls.

Dimitris Glinos

The corpus of material produced during Gramsci's internment in Mussolini's jails—the purpose of which was to, in the words of the prosecutor, "prevent this brain from functioning for twenty years"—represents the most suggestive stage of Gramsci's enterprise. "Gramsci and the prosecutor at his trial understood one another very well;" writes Joseph Buttigieg, "they both appreciated, each in his own fashion, the extreme political efficacy of intellectual labor" (1992, 16). The same could also be said of Dimitris Glinos, whose intellectual labor centered on concerns often remarkably similar to Gramsci's. Glinos and Gramsci had read some of the same authors, including Marx, Hegel, and Lenin, and thought deeply about them in their own cultural contexts. Glinos, however, unlike Gramsci, spent considerable intellectual energy on the "woman question," and was more actively engaged in the pursuit of solutions.[2] His exposure to local feminist praxis, and his engagement with theorists of gender are readily apparent in the prewar writings that he would eventually transpose into wartime policy.

[2] As I mentioned earlier, gender equality barely appears in Gramsci's writings. Showstack Sassoon, Patricia Hill Collins, and others, however, have shown that the underpinnings of Gramscian philosophy are relevant across cases. See Sassoon 1987b, 18–19; Collins 1991.

Unlike Gramsci, Glinos is barely known outside of Greek intellectual circles. His work has not, to my knowledge, been translated into English. Like the movement he helped to found with the writing of *What Is the National Liberation Front (EAM) and What Does It Want?*, he has generally been relegated to historical obscurity, rarely cited in the few existing works on this period in Greek history. Indeed, more often than not, books and articles on modern Greek history are written as though the 1940s never occurred, and Glinos, as a major leftist figure, has floated ghostlike amid this silence, except among a limited audience.[3] Glinos, as the casualty of a profound historical schism in Greece, can be contrasted to Gramsci, who achieved a far greater renown in the postwar Italian Left and in international circles and whose popularity continues to grow.

Given the less-celebrated nature of his oeuvre, a biography/ontological narrative will help uncover some of the roots of Glinos's efforts to process and manufacture ideas for broader public consumption. Especially important was Glinos's early participation in the nationalist demotic movement, formed to advance the cause of a popular form of modern Greek language over the more formal *katharevousa*. Known for its stilted style and elements of ancient and byzantine ecclesiastical Greek, *katharevousa* was familiar only to an educated elite. At issue, notes Gerasimos Augustinos, "was the unification of the nation's culture through the use of one form of Greek. Literary works during the first half of the nineteenth century were written in the *katharevousa* with very few exceptions. . . . By the end of the century practically all significant poets were writing in [demotic] and an increasing number of prose authors had turned to it also. . . . Demoticism was the answer for those such as Palamas and Dragoumis who were seeking a Greek way" (1977, 32–33).

Augustinos describes a typical early organization, the Society for the Spread of Useful Books, which "endeavored to supply suitable reading material for the people in the countryside. The society or *Syllogos*, as it was called, and its activities were imbued with the values of its members who were merchants, businessmen, professionals and teachers. Numerous titles were published covering everything from beekeeping to world history. The little red books were sold at a small price, which was within the means of most everyone. The importance of these works to the reading public in the provinces is noteworthy since they were practically the only books to be found in village bookshops along with translations of 'bad French novels' as one traveler observed. The language of these books was not the demotic that most people learned from childhood, but rather the *katharevousa*. Those who directed the society were

---

[3] I understand that in Greece Glinos's work is better known in the educational field. Two volumes that I make extensive use of here are Tomeas Filosophia, Filosophikis Skolis Pan/miou Ioanninon 1983; and Kokkini 1989. I am grateful to Penny Katsika for obtaining these volumes for me.

interested in enlightening their countrymen but obviously along lines that reflected their outlook and position in life" (31).

As we shall see, the demotic movement embraced participants from across the political spectrum, from socialists of varying stripes to conservatives. One segment of the movement, including Glinos and the well-known educationalist Penelope Delta, devoted its energies to creating a public educational system essentially "from scratch," writing textbooks and manuals designed to socialize generations of Greek citizens while neutralizing, it was hoped, the chaotic effects of poverty, ignorance, and imperialism. A good example of this kind of resocialization aimed at the Greek mother is Delta's 1912 pamphlet *Stohasmoi: Peri tis anatrofis ton paidhion mas* (Reflections on the upbringing of our children), which applauds the extraordinary tenderness and maternal affection toward children sanctified by the culture but is highly critical on questions of discipline and education within the home and worries about standards which fall short of the criteria necessary to meet the demands of modern life.

Next to the Communist popular front, demoticism was perhaps the most significant precursor of the EAM in its synthesis of ideological tendencies. Glinos would essentially be won over to the Communist cause by 1930, formally joining in 1936. However, his convictions about the importance of transforming national consciousness through language and education continued despite his changed political affiliation and in fact formed the basis of his call for political revolution among what Gramsci termed the "national-popular."

Glinos's main occupations and preoccupations were teaching, public education, and journalism, the last a subject which not coincidentally, Gramsci would also explore in his cultural and political writings (e.g., 1985, 386–425, "Journalism"). Glinos was born in Smyrna, Turkey, in 1882. Several times his family's precarious financial situation forced him to interrupt his university career in Athens to work as a teacher, first at the Kasaba School in Asia Minor in 1901 and later as director of the civil academy on Lemnos from 1903 to 1904.[4] His first published piece was a letter to the editor expressing concern about the use of foreign words in demotic Greek. Influenced by his acquaintance with demoticist Manolis Triandafilidi, in 1904 he joined the short-lived local chapter of the organization Our National Language (I Ethniki mas Glossa), the brainchild of Kostas Palamas, Andonis Delmouzos, Kostas Hatzopoulos, and other national figures.[5] In 1905 he received his degree "with distinction" and was appointed director of the Anahagoreio School (1905–1906) and then professor at the Greek-German High School in Smyrna

[4] The material for this section is mostly taken from Evangelia Kokkini's (1989) short and very helpful study of Glinos's life and times.

[5] See Kokkini 1989. It is unclear to me whether this is the same as the National Language Society, whose formation Augustinos (1977, 34) dates to 1907.

(1906–1909). Evangelia Kokkini notes that "during that time, he confronted virtually alone the wave of conservative pro-katharevousa feeling in the Greek community of Smyrna, submitting articles in philosophical and educational newspapers and literary journals, arguing in favor of 'the ideology' of demotic Greek as a mainstay of the educational curriculum" (1989, 12–13).

In 1908 Glinos married Anna Kroni and began graduate study in the German city of Jena and later in nearby Leipzig (1908–1911), concentrating on philosophy and child and experimental psychology. It was in Jena that he first came into contact with the influential Greek Marxist writer George Skliros, author of *To koinonikon mas zitima* (Our social question). As a result, Glinos was inspired to form a society of Greek students with socialist tendencies in 1909 and to write a study of the Young Turk rebellion. Nineteen hundred and nine was also the year of the Goudi insurgency, the officer's coup that brought liberal politician Eleftherios Venizelos to power for the first time and initiated a protracted series of regime shifts which would continue into the 1930s. The Young Turk rebellion had, in fact, served as an example for the conspirators, who drafted an open letter to the king, the government, and the Greek people outlining demands for military reforms, including the ouster of the crown prince and other royal family members from the armed forces (Clogg 1979, 98–99). This event and Venizelos's ascendancy as prime minister in 1910 on a platform of constitutional reform renewed hope in a number of centrist and left-leaning circles about the possibility of liberal democracy as part of a general political renaissance taking root in Greece .

Clearly the goals of the Venizelist movement were bourgeois democratic: capitalist development, national integration, and moral and intellectual renewal (Kokkini 1989, 14). Glinos's attitude was marked by a willingness to collaborate with and learn from a range of political positions in pursuit of nationalist aims, from the Second International socialism of Skliros to the bourgeois liberalism of the Venizelists, however indefensible such concessions may have seemed to any given side. Prompted perhaps by Goudi and the ensuing talk of republics, in 1910 Glinos entered a writing contest sponsored by the University of Athens with a submission entitled "On the Moral Philosophy of Plato." In 1911 he returned from Germany to become a teacher of early childhood education and in 1912 became director of an Athens academy for middle school teachers.

It was at the 1910 conjuncture that Glinos's pet cause, the demotic movement, really began to gel as a movement to redefine national citizenship. In May 1910 the Educational Society (Ekpaidheftiko Omilo) of the movement was formed and continued to function until 1927. Represented within the society were a range of political persuasions from the upper- and middle-class ranks. The common goal was to institute an educational system in Greece better suited to the requirements of a truly modern state and based, according to its statutes, on "ideas taken from Greek life." Its constitution announced: "Genuine modern Greek reality and ideals are manifested in the neo-Hellenic tradition, folk songs, folk tales, legends, proverbs, customs, and the varied ways of life . . . and above all in the living language and creative literature. This unadulterated modern Greek world must become the basis of our education" (both quoted in Augustinos 1977, 35). The society decided to establish a model school in Athens, and it sent out a circular to all interested parties, which declared: "We have decided to recruit students and inaugurate a school that will, using methods most appropriate to the needs of young Greek children, give our country a model curriculum, including a model instructional ABC, model textbooks, and teacher's manuals, with the ultimate aim being to produce graduates of enlightened character and knowledge, of great appetite and energy for learning, because it is only through their mother tongue that they will find sufficient means to advance" (Kokkini 1989, 14). Imbued with the desire to "catch up" to a perceived "European" standard and be vindicated among a community of nations, as Augustinos rightly notes, "The Society was not . . . chauvinist. Its members tried to place Greek civilization in the perspective of world civilization as a whole" (1977, 35). This stance, progressive as it was no doubt construed, also points to an ongoing national ambivalence about Greek identity and status in the world community. The underlying orientalist subtext—wanting to secure honorable membership among the "enlightened" nations of Europe rather than allow Greece to languish shamefully among less "Aryan," more "backward" groups—can also be distinguished at points in the popular recruiting manual Glinos wrote for the EAM.

The school was never actually established, mainly because conservative academics would not support it. Nevertheless, the plan represented the society's first concerted effort to reform Greek education along demotic lines and it set the tone for future ventures. The responses to the model school initiative were, in fact, typical of reactions to the organization's reformism and to the conception of national citizenship congruent with the demoticist cause. Objections from conservative *katharevousiani* would repeatedly kill the organization's legislative initiatives for educational reform, many of which were authored by Glinos after he formally joined the Society in 1916. During the same year, he entered Venizelos's Ministry of Education. This transition marked the beginning of a series of political struggles on behalf of popular education, linked to the chaotic fate of a regime that was in power one minute and out the next, and also to conflicts within the organization.

The external threat to educational reform and the goals of the Educational Society came primarily from conservative reaction to the socialist cast of demoticism. Whenever the Venizelos government fell from power, Glinos was arrested along with other members of Venizelos's staff. On at least two occasions, Glinos was charged with "insulting the monarchy" because of his sponsorship of parliamentary bills favoring demotic educational policy and his authorship of various newspaper and journal articles and textbooks. In 1920, for example, as general secretary of education under Venizelos, he headed the team charged with revising the early childhood educational texts—not an especially safe or neutral undertaking in the prevailing political climate.

Within the Society, members disagreed about the role of politics and political reform, as opposed to purely literary and linguistic agendas. Meanwhile, Glinos underwent a growing radicalization and came to see social reform in Greece as intimately tied to political advocacy and the radical redistribution of power. This brings us to four aspects in Glinos's ontological narrative relevant to subsequent EAM ideology.

The first requires a closer examination of the split within the organization that culminated in its final dissolution. This split stemmed partly from the same kind of coalitional problems common to many "catch-all" alliances and social movements, problems that would one day also begin to undermine the EAM's unity of purpose. Through its spokesperson Andonis Delmouzos, the conservative wing of the Society expressed strong opposition to the idea of tying the educational question to the need for broader social change. The radical wing took the position that the deformities of the Greek educational system were causally linked to imbalances inherent in the social hierarchy. After heated discussion the conservatives put two related proposals on the table for a vote:

a) on issues of religious training and national political socialization, the Educational Society should continue to follow a neutral path;
b) the Society is an educational, not a political, body and it does not concern itself with nor does it work for any specific political party or social class; but instead represents the educational interests of the whole society (Kokkini 1989, 21).

Glinos countered with a quintessentially left-modernist response, reaffirming the need to separate faith from reason but also emphasizing a goal-oriented politics and championing the subaltern against entrenched interests. Kokkini summarizes Glinos's rebuttal:

a) The Educational Society is not a political body. It is concerned with the careful study of the educational problems and general societal enlightenment on such topics, and consequently, stakes out and exercises the kind of educational politics necessary to fulfill its aims.
b) Each systematic social, not to mention educational, reform takes place within the boundaries of the class struggle. The Greek bourgeois class, in the experience of the Educational Society, cannot remove itself from this social

reality but must take a direct part in the social struggle if it hopes to effect fundamental popular educational reform. For this reason the Educational Society believes that true popular educational reform can be accomplished only by taking up the burden of social defense on behalf of those classes who, because of their long-standing subordination, consciously understand vital social problems and are willing to fight for the realization of social reforms, thus forcing the ruling class to restructure and improve its legal and civil institutions.

c) The Educational Society has never addressed the question of religious instruction. Since, however, it has repeatedly had to defend itself against charges of atheism, anti-religious sentiment, and antagonism toward religion, etc., the Society feels obligated to declare that it considers the religious question to be above all a question of freedom of conscience and therefore it does not consider religious training an appropriate part of the public school curriculum. (Kokkini 1989, 21–22)

The left wing of the society, including Rosa Imvrioti, an early feminist and resistance participant, and her husband, thus sought to represent "the new social forces, which even though as yet immature, nevertheless were at the forefront of critical social struggles, and [to] give them guidance, after a fashion" (Kokkini 1989, 22). The conservative branch took a different direction, and by March 1927 the Society had essentially disbanded. Glinos construed the outcome as a victory for the Left: "The principles and causes of the socialist demotic current today constitute the program of the Educational Society" (quoted in Kokkini 1989, 23).

A second noteworthy conjuncture involves Glinos's interest in women's education. From 1920 to 1922 he worked toward establishing the Women's School of Higher Education (Anotera Yinekeia Skoli), a kind of popular university meant to compensate women for the inadequacies of the state system, both in terms of curriculum and the limited access afforded female students. Originally, Glinos and Delmouzos planned to start a free university, and a proposal was drawn up and sent to Venizelos in Paris for approval. When they got no response, Glinos decided to proceed with the plan anyway but on a smaller scale, making it a female-only academy. Its purpose, summarized in his opening speech on 11 October 1921, was "to allow the woman to take her place in accordance with her true worth in the highest manifestations of social life" (1971b, 36).

The inaugural message deserves close consideration for what it reveals about the scope of Glinos's own reading and thinking as well as his explorations on the topic with leading feminist and demoticist activists. Glinos opened with powerful imagery:

Ladies and Gentlemen: If I wanted to follow the method of those silent Eastern philosophers, who with a nod of the head or with one word could express whole worlds of thought, I could today demonstrate to you quite dramatically the purpose of the Women's School of Higher Education. Perhaps it would be enough for me to ascend the podium to show you in very clear terms not the program or the lessons that will be taught here or even what they will be called. I would only have to show you the list of the professors' names. Then you would see that of the twelve individuals on that list, eleven are men. And the antinomy [*andinomia*] would be completely obvious to you. (1971b, 36)

Greek society had, to its detriment, said Glinos, limited itself to subservient female stereotypes. The modest, helpful, supportive Navsika; the patient, loyal, resourceful Penelope; the seductive Afroditi; and the celebrated hetaerae Aspasia and Phryne were all animated by "the need to please," Glinos said, "to please the man." Moreover, "we also have the doll woman, creature of today's high society, the 'femme chic,' the Parisian Femina. The slim-figured, fragrantly perfumed flower, the ethereal butterfly, shining with color, happy-spirited and shallow" (1971b, 42).

Glinos rhetorically bracketed this point with quotations from two of the most notorious sexists of the philosophical tradition, framed in this speech as major narratological villains: "And then along comes a Rousseau, who gives the age-old stamp of approval to this model. 'La femme est faite spécialement pour plaire à l'homme.' This is woman's destiny. Decorative object in life, with the secondary role of mother. But another philosopher places his age-old stamp on another type of mother-woman. 'The woman is an enigma, whose solution is called motherhood,' said Nietzsche, and elsewhere he asks: 'Woman? A cat, a bird, and in the best instance, a wet-nurse'" (1971b, 42).

From a global perspective, Glinos reviewed the historical contingencies that fostered the growth of mass education, citing economic and political shifts engendered by capitalist development, greater attention to moral, intellectual, and social progress, and revolutionary demands for popular voice; changes that gave more men their rights while most women were left behind to fulfill the traditional roles assigned to them in a patriarchal context. Yet a variety of forces in the nineteenth and twentieth centuries, including war and economic necessity, had had the liberating effect of forcing many women out of their homes and into the light of progress, initiating an important trend. By the end of the nineteenth century, "in America, in France, England, Germany, with certain parallels and gradations, they had begun to put the new demands for women's education into practice." Glinos reassured his audience that the issue was not the masculinization of women and the emasculation of men. Rather, the ideal of women's humanism would only benefit society, generating a far deeper and more comprehensive transformation that would lead to much healthier social relations and to a stronger nation operating at full capacity. Reviewing the history of women's education, Glinos concluded that serious and fundamental reform must bring women's education into line with that afforded to men. Female suffrage would be a boon neither to the Greek woman nor to Greek society as long as the mass of women remained in their present intellectual and psychological state.

Like other nations, Greece suffers from a debilitating backwardness (*ka-thisterisi*) compared to "Western" societies, Glinos said, which is perfectly understandable given historical patterns. Greece in fact exhibits a mixture of the good and bad effects of global capitalism. Yet it is exceptionally backward in the development and functioning of its cognitive resources, which should be enhanced and supported by the intellectual sector. Something must be done to restore the resolve to provide that crucial social guidance now missing from the traditional intellectual stratum.

Glinos praised women's work inside, but especially outside, the home and posited the woman worker as a true heroine. Though the illiteracy rate among women had declined from 82 percent in 1907 to 60 percent in 1921, it was still unacceptable for a democratic citizenry. Only after 1917 did changes in state policy permit special schools and gymnasia to be set up for girls in Greece, and these institutions of middle education, trade schools, and indeed schools at all levels were flooded with female pupils. Thus, despite the state's indifference toward female education and its incompetence in providing it, Greek girls had vigorously pursued educational opportunities, forging their own heroic way into the previously male domain. "Now," said Glinos in closing, "is exactly the right moment. Now that the postwar humanist ferment has created a longing for a better future and has yielded a more enlightened consciousness of human ideals, now that the woman of the civilized world marches decisively and assuredly forward to win her own humanism, now that in Greece some small and fruitful beginnings of a new life for women have taken place" (1971b, 59).

As this speech makes clear, Glinos was an eager participant in the revolving conversation that included, among others, 19th- and 20th-century Greek feminists, Clara Zetkin, August Bebel, Friedrich Engels, Mary Wollstonecraft, Harriet Taylor, John Stuart Mill, and other prominent figures, who polemicized and puzzled out loud about "the woman question." Glinos taught at the academy for two years, along with several of his colleagues from the Educational Society. There can be little doubt that the educational policy for women and girls stressed in the resistance partly originated in this project.

A third factor to be considered is Glinos's role as founder and editor of the scholarly cum popular journal *Anayennisi* (Renaissance) from 1926 to 1928. Here we can see the position on intellectual activism so reminiscent of Gramsci's.[6] For example, Glinos admonishes Greek scholars to "live among your people and unite with them, in order to guide them!" In the May–June 1927 issue, he declares, "*Anayennisi* has made progress on the problem of diglossia. Up to now it has published its articles in an everyday demotic language, featuring studies on various subjects, such as philosophy, psychology, sociology, fine arts and art history, education, law, physiology. Greek intellectuals, write your work in demotic [so that it is accessible]. Liberate your people from diglossia."[7]

Many of the burning debates of the time, both domestic and international, appeared in the pages of the journal. As Anna Frangoudaki writes, "It is clear from the various selections, both original articles and translations, that the purpose of *Anayennisi* was both to cultivate in its readers a Marxist perspective and to make a more general educational intervention in the social realm. . . . Perhaps the most important thing of all is that in the space of its two-year life *Anayennisi* tackled all the new currents of opinion, the new social scientific theories and intellectual tendencies of the times. Its pieces were all directed toward the common reader, indirectly propounding Glinos's pet theme: Greek intellectuals, help to enlighten and guide your people" (Frangoudaki, 80).

Glinos's explicit goal was to provide a public forum for even the stickiest issues of the day—in some ways, the more controversial the better, though, as Peter Bien says, "subjectivism and partisan rhetoric were excluded. Glinos's dream was to raise the level of intellectual debate in Greece in order to encourage those ideas that showed the way to a 'radical regeneration of contemporary civilization' at home and abroad" (1989, 105–6). Articles bore such diverse titles as "Beethoven's compositions as a social phenomenon"; "The development of the concept of private property in contemporary law"; "Contemporary philosophical thought in France"; "Einstein's theory of relativity"; "The feminist movement"; "Critical observations on contemporary feminism"; "The Greek working woman in today's society"; and "Women and politics." Commentary on Freudian theory and selections from Bernard Russell's *Icarus on the Future of Science* and *What I Believe* translated into Greek appeared also. Significantly for the future, a majority of the authors of these articles were women (Frangoudaki, 80).

Finally, a fourth path that would lead Glinos from socialist sympathies to the position of intellectual strategist for the EAM was the Communist party. As we have seen, Glinos was attracted by the social commentary of the Marxist thinker George Skliros, long before the decline of the Educational Society.

---

6 For an explicit comparison of Glinos and Gramsci on the topic of Latin instruction in the schools, see Bobis Noutsos, "O Glinos, o Gramsi kai ta Latinika" (Glinos, Gramsci, and Latin), in Tomeas Filosofias 1983, 82–96.

7 Glinos quoted in Anna Frangoudaki, "O Glinos kai i paidheia" (Glinos and Education), ibid, 77–78.

Increasingly, Glinos began to question just how dedicated the local bourgeoisie was to solving the glaring social problems of Greece and its lack of mass political and economic integration. By 1930 Glinos had squarely rejected bourgeois ideology in favor of Marxism, although for several years he remained critical of KKE intransigence and its apparent weddedness, pre-1934, to a strict interpretation of Comintern policy. His grave doubts about the sincerity of the ruling classes were, as usual, expressed in terms of the problems posed for education. In a characteristically Gramscian statement, he addressed the subject of ruling-class hegemony, noting that "education was in all epochs and it is today in all countries of the earth without any exception the tool for the imposition of ruling-class values. Everywhere and always . . . the ruling class seeks to impose and inflict on children values that support its own interests" (quoted in Kokkini 1989, 23).

In 1932, before joining the KKE, Glinos began to collaborate with *Rizospastis*, the Communist party organ, and with its youth paper, *Neoi protoporoi* (Young pioneers), writing extensively on Communist theory. Highlights of this period were an essay on Hegelian philosophy in 1932 and an article devoted to youth entitled "Poioi dhromoi anoigoun brosta mas" (Which roads stretch before us). In 1934 he was invited to the Soviet Union along with the poet Kostas Varnalis for a conference on Soviet journalism, and he published his impressions in a series of articles in the newspaper *Neos kosmos*. His first political incarceration came in 1935 when he was sent to the prison camp of Agios Evstratios. After the coup of 4 August, like nearly all leading Communists, he began a round of prison stays and transfers, from Anafi to Akronavplias to Santorini. While imprisoned, Glinos was integrally involved in inmate education, helping to organize classes on such subjects as Marxist philosophy, economics, history, and ancient literature. "According to fellow inmates," Kokkini notes, "Dimitris Glinos was a dynamic presence, not only in the people's movement but also in the hearts of all prisoners, because of his exemplary conduct. As a national leader, he took the job of raising their consciousness very seriously" (1989, 24).

After his release in 1940 Glinos pioneered a technological innovation in classical studies, creating an original philosophical-demotic grammar intended for use in what he termed "creative history" (*dhimiourgikos istorismos*), whereby antiquarian life and philosophy could be mined for their contemporary value. Starting in the spring of 1941, Glinos devoted his energy exclusively to EAM's genesis, and was put in charge of the effort to recruit traditional republican leaders to the resistance cause. The goal was to widen the scope of the organization to create a national front, an offer most of the targeted leaders refused. In 1942 Glinos wrote the EAM guide. In December of the same year, he took part in the Panhellenic conference of the KKE and was elected to the central committee. Not surprisingly, in view of his background, Glinos took a particularly energetic interest in creating educational structures and policies for the movement. Citing his failing health, he declined the nomination for president of the PEEA government of the mountains, and died in 1943 at the age of sixty-one.

On Reframing National Culture: State and Civil Society

> If the State represents the coercive and punitive force of juridical regulation of a country, the parties—representing the spontaneous adhesion of an elite to such a regulation, considered as a type of collective society to which the entire mass must be educated—must show in their specific internal life that they have assimilated as principles of moral conduct those rules which in the State are legal obligations. . . . From this point of view the parties can be considered as schools of State life. Elements of party life: character (resistance to the pressures of surpassed cultures), honour (fearless will in maintaining the new type of culture and life), dignity (awareness of operating for a higher end), etc.
>
> —Gramsci 1971, 267–68

Gramsci's war of position, we recall, is linked to the concept of hegemony, or the underlying regime of cultural power that facilitates ruling-class domination but which can also be developed to serve oppositional interests. For Gramsci, the problem is not only how power is created and wielded but also how power can be recognized and challenged. He distinguishes two types of national revolutionary activity, for which he employs military analogies: the "war of movement," or a tumultuous governmental overthrow, and the "war of position," which involves more subtle maneuvering. As I have said, a war of movement took place when Nazi forces invaded Greece and a substantial power vacuum was created when government personnel and the monarchy evacuated to Cairo. To be sure, battles in the war of position had already begun before the Nazi invasion, fought out in the demotic movement and elsewhere. However, given the new "structure of opportunity" occasioned by war (in its commonly understood sense), how and why was this particular "war of position" waged?

Assessed jointly, Gramsci and Glinos made their most significant intellectual contributions on questions of political process. The "evolutionary" legacy of the Second International and the static and mechanistic currents in the Communist world in the twenties and early thirties had left large theoretical and practical gaps. This sometimes meant that when parties were confronted with the exigencies of counterfascist struggle, their strategies and tactics proved woefully inadequate. For example, Ernst Bloch and others took Kautskyan Marxism to task for its stubborn refusal to adequately theorize and offer sufficiently attractive and concrete alternatives to the Nazi appeal—that is, to actually "listen" and respond to the histories and habits of mass publics. It was through a blend of social and historical analysis, an interest in grass-roots activism, a sensitivity to the requirements of "cultural politics" and metaphysical argumentation, that Gramsci and Glinos made their political contributions.

According to Gramsci, among the most effective weapons in a war of position (or the process of altering the balance of power between dominant and subaltern political forces and ultimately creating a more responsive and responsible State), are the party and the educational system. These should be administered by, in Gramsci's words, "organisers of confidence," enlightened intellectuals who operate analogously to capitalist entrepreneurs. "It should be noted that the entrepreneur himself represents a higher level of social elaboration, already characterised by a certain directive (*dirigente*) and technical (i.e. intellectual) capacity: he must have a certain technical capacity, not only in the limited sphere of his activity and initiative but in other spheres as well, at least in those which are closest to economic production. He must be an organiser of masses of men; he must be an organiser of the 'confidence' of investors in his business, of the customers for his product, etc." (1971, 5, "The Intellectuals").

Glinos very much shared this orientation. A few examples of their congruent positions regarding the dominant forces in society, the intellectuals, education and the revolutionary party will suffice to make my point; keeping in mind of course, that there are also numerous differences between the two men, as well as further root similarities—such as their readings of Hegel, thoughts on public education, ideas about the political significance of language—which I am not able to explore here. One point I do want to emphasize is that the quintessentially modernist ambivalence about the masses when left to their own devices, is strongly evident in the words below. Note that in the Greek case, I view the EAM as a type of "revolutionary party" in the sense that Gramsci envisions it and, as such, a culmination of Glinos's previous "researches" on social change.

Back in November 1910, Glinos wrote to Ion Dragoumis that "Of course none of us believes that language is everything, that it is enough to get rid of katharevousa and to replace it with demotic to revolutionize today's souls and to energize their characters. . . . The educational reform that the Greek race needs today is that which will become a channel for intellectual, psychic, social, and political renewal. . . . educational reform must be the organ of a new ideology."[8]

Glinos' and Gramsci shared similar views on the role of the intellectual in this process. For example, Gramsci states that

The position of the philosophy of praxis is the antithesis of the Catholic. The philosophy of praxis does not tend to leave the "simple" in their primitive

[8] Phillipos Iliou, "Apo ton Mistrioti ston Lenin" (From Mistrioti to Lenin), Tomeas Filosofias 1983, 15.

philosophy of common sense, but rather to lead them to a higher conception of life. It affirms the need for contact between intellectuals and simple it is, not in order to restrict scientific activity and preserve unity at the low level of the masses, but precisely in order to construct an intellectual-moral bloc which can make politically possible the intellectual progress of the mass and not only of small intellectual groups.

Critical self-consciousness means, historically and politically, the creation of an *elite* of intellectuals. A human mass does not "distinguish" itself, does not become independent in its own right without, in the widest sense, organising itself; and there is no organisation without intellectuals, that is without organisers and leaders, in other words, without the theoretical aspect of the theory-practice nexus being distinguished concretely by the existence of a group of people "specialised" in conceptual and philosophical elaboration of ideas. . . . innovation cannot come from the mass, at least at the beginning, except through the mediation of an elite for whom the conception implicit in human activity has already become to a certain degree a coherent and system-atic ever-present awareness and a precise and decisive will. (1971, 332–33, 334–35, "The Study of Philosophy")

Gramsci's "elite," as Quintin Hoare and Geoffrey Nowell Smith rightly note, is the revolutionary vanguard of a social class in constant contact with its political and intellectual base (Gramsci 1971, 334). Compare this with Glinos's statement in the February 1933 issue of *Neoi protoporoi* that progressive intel-lectuals "have the obligation to organize into an ideological front, to hold high the light of dialectical materialism, and to maintain *constant contact with the fighting proletariat* in order to assist their struggle with all our might, sinking the first stones of the foundation of socialist culture in our country."[9]

The party is crucial, Gramsci says: "The modern Prince must be and cannot but be the proclaimer and organiser of an intellectual and moral reform, which also means creating the terrain for a subsequent development of the national-popular collective will towards the realisation of a superior, total form of modern civilisation" (1971, 132–33, "The Modern Prince"). He recommends the mobilizational techniques of religion:

Specific necessities can be deduced . . . for any cultural movement which aimed to replace common sense and old conceptions of the world in general:
    1. Never to tire of repeating its own arguments. . . . repetition is the best didactic means for working on the popular mentality.

---

[9] Evtihis I. Bitsakis, "Dimitris Glinos: Apo Ton Astiko, Sto Socialistiko Anthropismo" (Dimitris Glinos: From bourgeois to socialist humanism), Tomeas Filosofias 1983, 33.

2. To work incessantly to raise the intellectual level of ever-growing strata of the populace, in other words, to give a personality to the amorphous mass element. This means working to produce *elites* of intellectuals of a new type which arise directly out of the masses, but remain in contact with them to become, as it were, the whalebone in the corset. (1971, 340, "The Study of Philosophy")

Arguably, Glinos's most important work is the pamphlet *Ti einai kai ti thelei to Ethniko Apeleftherotiko Metopo?* That document demonstrates the scope of the EAM's authoritative message and helps to explain the striking homogeneity of purpose exhibited in the personal testimonies I have gathered and in other popularly disseminated materials. The work is organized into seven chapters, each weaving in a successive strand of resistance narrative: "Darkest slavery" (Mavri sklavia); "The collaborators and the jackals" (I prodhotes kai ta tsakalia); "A people's fight" (I agonia enos laou); "The creeds of the national liberation struggle" (Ta sinthimata tou ethnikoapeleftherotiko aghona); "The people search for their leaders" (O laos anazitei tous arhighous tou); "The organization of the struggle" (I organosi tou aghona); and "Forms of the struggle" (I morfes tis palis). A close reading of this as-yet-untranslated document would be extremely fruitful for any student of social movements interested in mobilizational tactics and frame alignment or how movements create meaning for recruits by linking their activities and goals to familiar and compelling symbols. The project of transforming the boundaries of national moral and political culture in the course of popular struggle is strongly evident, especially in the last four chapters. Here again are echoes of Gramsci on the function of organic intellectuals and the broader contours of the counterhegemonic project:

This struggle emerges out of the contemporary objective reality and from the current mood of the entire people. In order to succeed, it must correspond both with the practical needs and with the true disposition of the people. This struggle must be deeply rooted in the concrete, rooted in our earth, to embrace the unconquerable need of the people for their freedom. This is why it is necessary that its features and its goals and creeds come from the actual needs and passions of the people. Only then can we proceed down the right road toward its organization. What, then, does the struggle consist of?

The people's struggle of today can only be liberational. We must gain our freedom, expel the foreign invaders from our country, and safeguard our rights in life, politics, and society. We must clear the road for a free, civilized, and happy Greece. . . . The struggle can only include all the people, embrace all levels of society, the worker, the aristocrat, the farmer, and the intellectual. . . . Such a struggle, in order to get results, more than anything and above all, calls for *unity*. . . . This duty falls upon all who, regardless of their station in life, their work, their mission, or their personality, consider themselves and are the moral guides of the people: their intellectuals, their journalists, artists, poets, teachers, priests, judges, doctors, lawyers, mechanics, etc. Today, more than ever, the people must feel their moral and intellectual guides are close to them, they must see them in the front lines of the struggle and in the front lines of sacrifice, even where the people may not yet perceive how much they need their intellectual leaders by their side, their moral guidance. (Glinos 1944, 38–44)

Gramsci sounds the final note:

Divergence, in the meantime, between political intuition and aesthetic, lyric or artistic intuition; only by metaphor does one speak of the art of politics. Political intuition is not expressed through the artist, but through the "leader"; and "intuition" must be understood to mean not "knowledge of men," but swiftness in connecting seemingly disparate facts, and in conceiving the means adequate to particular ends—thus discovering the interests involved, and arousing the passions of men and directing them towards a particular action. . . . the "leader" in politics may be an individual, but also be a more or less numerous political body: in the latter case, unity of purpose will be achieved by an individual (or by a small inner group, and within that small group by an individual) who may change from time to time even though the group remains united and consistent in its on-going activity. (1971, 252, "State and Civil Society")

Rethinking Traditional Models and Core Values

There is no doubt that the Greek Communist party dominated the EAM leadership stratum. The assumptions commonly accepted in postwar historiography, however—that the movement was administered from Moscow or that its social and political goals were insincere—are not justified. The widely accepted, cynical interpretation is represented in Peter Stavrakis's 1989 account, which discounts the thesis that the KKE was Moscow directed but eagerly participates in the Cold War–style demonization of the EAM (citing, incidentally, the not-unbiased Office of Strategic Services and U.S. State Department reports of 1944). Stavrakis writes:

Supposedly EAM gave expression to the Greek people's desire for national liberation, which allowed it to serve as a political front for KKE; the Communists could act through EAM and appear to represent the great majority of the

Greek people. . . . By 1943 . . . ELAS was large enough for the KKE to contemplate the elimination of all rivals. With an independent base of military power, an effective mouthpiece for the expression of popular sentiment, and an efficient clandestine organization throughout Greece, the KKE was in an excellent position to pursue its own interests. One final attribute of the KKE is of crucial importance to this study: regardless of circumstances, the Greek Communist leadership remained overwhelmingly faithful to the Soviet Union and respectful of its position as the homeland of communist revolution. This pro-Soviet orientation had its basis in the KKE's fidelity to the ideology of Marxism-Leninism as developed under Stalin. The Greek Communists looked to Russia for guidance and advice, as is evidenced by their continuous attempts to reestablish direct radio contact during the war and their requests for more Greek-language broadcasts from the Soviet Union. Everything Russian was idolized by the KKE; ELAS general Stefanos Sarafis has described the adulation accorded the Russian Military Mission's members when they arrived in the mountains of Greece. (1989, 11–12)[10]

This portrayal does not square with my reading of primary and secondary literature or with what I believe myself to have heard from informants and participants. Yet the narrative of the EAM as a sinister, Soviet-worshiping menace remains dominant in the current literature, and is very much part of a larger metanarrative and morality tale. Because this story has played such a crucial part in shaping postwar historiography and practice, its Greek incarnation bears closer scrutiny. Any changes in the national cultural treatment of "the woman question" must be seen in a much broader social policy context, one with mixed antecedents.

Expanding on points made earlier in this text, there are several reasons to reexamine critically this Cold War metanarrative and its especially insistent Greek version. First, the EAM and the KKE were not wholly synonymous, even though EAM has been habitually referred to as "The Communists" even in the scholarly literature. The EAM leadership actually comprised a coalition that in fact included two prominent social democrats from the Union for Popular Democracy party: Alexander Svolos, a professor of constitutional law at the University of Athens, and Dimitrios Tsirimokos; together with Dimitrios Stratis of the Socialist party; Dimitrios Asimakes from the United Socialist party; and Constantinos Gavrilides from the tiny Agrarian party. These participants were drawn in from the early coalition-building efforts of EAM founders in an initiative, mentioned earlier, that was spearheaded by Glinos. Later, General Stefanos Sarafis joined the coalition. Sarafis had been a

---

[10] The subtext of Stavrakis's book is as distrustful of the EAM as mine is favorable. Another example of this type of account, referred to as "the Chatham House Version" by Elie Kedourie, is Edgar O'Ballance, *The Greek Civil War, 1944–49*, (1966).

colonel in the Greek army and a prominent supporter of Venizelos's Liberal party before the War and was sent to the mountains on a mission to negotiate with ELAS. Seeing what the organization had accomplished in terms of social policy, he agreed to become the strategic commander of the ELAS forces in 1942. Soon he joined the KKE as well. His widow, Marion Sarafis, later commented on interparty relations during the resistance:

> EAM practice . . . was to promote unity in the liberation struggle by not overstressing party political identities. Everyone was first and foremost a member of EAM, whether on an individual basis or as a member of one of the EAM parties was to be of no significance. . . . In relation to his general way of thinking there was nothing problematic about his membership so long as KKE was prepared to accommodate—as apparently it was—his personal, distinctly Utopian version of communism. (1990, lvi–lvii)

At the time of EAM's inauguration, its leading Communist was George Siantos, who, more in the style of Gramsci or Togliatti than Stalin, decided the best way to establish legitimacy for the new organization was to pursue a popular front strategy that would include representatives from all interested political parties and would emphasize mass mobilization. Apparently, this decision was not disputed within the top ranks of the party. In 1943 the KKE publicly announced that it would follow parliamentary methods to achieve political power, thereby formalizing an earlier policy direction (see Hondros 1982, 111–12). Surely the communist members of the EAM also hoped that these strategies would help the KKE achieve power in the postwar era. But this hope does not signify a priori that its communist leaders were driven solely by political mercantilism or by the clearly dreadful and, even at the time, dreaded Stalinism. It is more probable that the Greek leaders, like other twentieth-century communists, were motivated to blend principles of democracy, nationalism, and citizenship, taking their own *terza via*.[11]

Second, on the eve of the war the KKE was small and relatively weak compared, for example, to its counterpart in Yugoslavia, which was at the highest point of its power since its inception in 1918 in terms of both membership and charismatic leadership.[12] In the years just prior to the Metaxas dictatorship, the KKE had had modest success, compared to Venizelos's liberal democrats, in transforming itself into something other than a party of notables (Vlavianos 1989, 159–60). During the late 1930s, however, most of its members were out of circulation in the jails of the Metaxas regime. Opposition to the regime was defined broadly and men from a variety of backgrounds were

---

[11] For example, see Szporluk, 1988; and an interview with Giorgio Amendola, "The Italian Road to Socialism," *New Left Review* 106 (1977): 39–49.

[12] See Johnson 1962, esp. 164–67; and Denitch 1976.

arrested and presumably politicized in jail, but the party remained small and not in any position to pursue ambitiously communist goals among the Greek mass public. Moreover, despite the influence of Comintern debates and certain Marxist texts, actual ties to the Soviet Union were not particularly robust. Glinos and others managed to give inmates secret lessons in Marxist theory (M. Sarafis 1990, xlvi), but prison censors were particularly vigilant about "subversive" written material, and it might be fair to assume that those who were exposed to Marxist thought for the first time did not feel it necessary to pledge formal allegiance to the cause under clandestine circumstances. It is true that party head Zachariades had been able to increase Communist party ranks to unprecedented numbers in the year prior to Metaxas's August 4th coup. But it is also important to remember that the debates over policy and courses of action that occurred in most communist parties of the era, with certain tendencies at times purged or out of favor, also occurred within the Greek party. In other words, like most, the Greek party could not really enforce a monolithic ideology any more than any other political party of the era, nor could it "will" for itself a mass support base.

On a global dimension, prison terms kept Greek communists from joining their comrades from other countries in the Spanish Civil War. For other communists of the 1930s generation, Spanish terrain served as a proving ground and a place of socialization through international contacts. Elsewhere the solidarity forged in Spain had fostered a resilient collective identity, albeit sometimes on a relatively uncritical ideological basis,[13] and had attracted new party recruits. In other countries, national party leaders could buttress their legitimating narratives about Marxist ideology with the allegory of the Spanish republican cause. Because ordinary people could readily identify with this fable of good overwhelmed by fascist evil, the Spanish example strengthened communist parties and bolstered the confidence of their leaders in settings far from Barcelona.

Furthermore, and perhaps most important, those prewar KKE leaders who were versed in the tenets of Marxism and had followed and participated in the Comintern debates during the 1920s and 1930s took the popular front directives of the Third International seriously, interpreting the inclusiveness instituted during the resistance as both justifiable compliance and an expedient course given a still uninitiated mass base (Vlavianos 1989). Stefanos Sarafis described a meeting with KKE leaders in Athens in the spring of 1943, before he joined the party ranks:

The Communist leaders explained their view that, irrespective of the Party's ideology and long-term objectives, they believed that in Greece the bourgeois

[13] See, for example, Horn 1990; Johnson 1962.

revolution had not solved all the bourgeois-democratic problems, and the conditions had not been created in which a socialist programme could be implemented. Consequently, they were aiming at popular democracy which would solve the outstanding bourgeois-democratic problems and prepare the ground for socialism. To arrive at popular democracy with free expression of the popular will, in accordance with EAM's programme, we needed to fight at the side of the allies to achieve liberation and secure our liberties. (1990, 97)[14]

Third, in some cases the bourgeois and petty bourgeois social backgrounds of EAM's KKE leadership may have contributed to their willingness to play down the idea of proletarian revolution and support parliamentary strategies. Glinos is a prime example, as are other participants in the demotic movement. The social origins of demotic leadership were mixed, but in any case exemplified an elite, distinct in trajectory from the segment of the population Augustinos describes, who "generally knew only their local Greek dialect, dressed in the native attire of the area and cared little for the frills of Western civilization" (1977, 11).[15] Instead, these were Fanariot and middle-class Levantine Greeks from Constantinople and Alexandria, former trade union members, wealthy peasants, free-lance merchants and small business owners, civil servants, and lawyers, whose shared perspectives and educational priorities may have contributed to a propensity to form alliances with non-communists in pursuit of nationalist goals and made them, in Tom Nairn's terms, "a restless middle-class and intellectual leadership trying to stir up and channel popular class energies into support for new states." For, as Nairn notes, "Nationalism is always the joint product of external pressures and an internal balance of class forces. Most typically it has arisen in societies confronting a dilemma of uneven development—'backwardness' or colonization—where conscious, middle-class elites have sought massive popular mobilization to right the balance" (1977, 41–42).

Given this shared weltanschauung, the rationale for cooperation among communist and non-communist leaders alike was a strong but typically vague populist nationalism, which welded together a heterogeneous base during the resistance. For example, the non-communist leaders Svolos and Tsirimokos did not leave the ruling council until 1945, perhaps only then responding to destabilizing tendencies that are said to have surfaced somewhat before the

---

[14] A bit further on Sarafis adds: "At the end of this discussion I had complete faith in the sincerity of EAM and the Communist Party. I asked them to help me meet certain politicians and military leaders so that I could give them a picture of the situation and try to persuade them to co-operate with EAM" (98).

[15] Augustinos is describing Greeks of the period around the 1821 uprising against Turkish rule, but his remark is relevant into the late nineteenth and early twentieth centuries.

German evacuation.[16] Prior to their departure, however these men actively advocated the EAM position at the strategically important wartime conferences in Cairo, Caserta, and Lebanon in 1944.

Fourth, throughout the war, the lack of either Soviet or British sympathy with the EAM as a political organization made alliance seeking a particularly attractive alternative to almost guaranteed marginalization. As Iatrides observes, "On important Balkan issues . . . the Kremlin could be counted on to advocate positions that would benefit the Bulgarian comrades and embarrass the Greeks" (1981, 208). Stalin clearly considered the Greeks too nationalist. At the Moscow conference in October 1944, Stalin's stance toward the Greek communists in the EAM became even clearer. At that time, a famous redline bargain was struck in which Stalin joined Churchill in a crude imperialism that did not augur well for international communist cooperation. Europe was divided into territorial jurisdictions, with 90 percent of Greece bestowed on Britain. Churchill's famous comment at the time was, "It's a pity God did not seek our opinion when he built the world," to which Stalin replied "*This* was God's first mistake." Churchill's well-known conflation of EAM goals with those of "rabid communism," as well as his desire to counteract the organization's popularity as a threat to his support of the Greek monarchy, ruled the British out as potential allies. Faced with rejection by representatives of the traditional parties, for organizational strategists movement success was predicated on a more conciliatory position regarding broad participation.[17]

Finally, the EAM's success in mass organizing reinforced its tendency toward inclusiveness. From 1942 to 1944, encouraged by favorable outcomes in remote villages and the results of PEEA's efforts, national leaders and local ipefthinoi began to take an even less restricted position on membership. The civic enthusiasm evident in areas dominated by the EAM inspired a vision of populism which, perhaps naively, allowed some potentially incompatible bedfellows. After all, the EAM had accomplished what the nineteenth-century parties had not: it had proven, John A. Petropoulos says, "unstoppable in its

[16] George M. Alexander, for example, noting that "the details . . . are still shrouded in mystery," holds that the Communists actually provoked the anti-EAM backlash and that "public disorders orchestrated by the communists much perturbed the socialists in EAM, who were anxious that Greece should enjoy a peaceful political future." Dimitrios Stratis, he says, told a British intelligence informant that he "still believed that the communists wished to cooperate with democratic parties, and he described their acts of violence as designed solely to counteract any right-wing effort to seize power. But he acknowledged that communist excesses, particularly in the countryside, were producing exactly that which he believed they were supposed to prevent: 'The danger of a rightist coup,' he observed, 'becomes greater by the very excesses . . . of EAM itself'" (1981, 158). A rough content analysis of the KKE journal directed toward a general party audience, *Kommounistiki epitheorisi* (Communist review), from 1944 to 1947 does show a greater usage of such terms as "working class" and "proletariat" after 1945 when the mantle of leadership passed from Siantos to Zachariades.

[17] For example, see Svoronos 1981, 11; and Petropoulos 1981, 34–35.

enterprise of mass mobilization and in its ability to establish structures of effective control, even in areas still under direct German military occupation. KKE and EAM had far outpaced the traditional parties in the art of mass mobilization, showed tremendous potential for power or political predominance through the peaceful democratic process, and therefore threatened to relegate the traditional parties to permanent obsolescence with an effectiveness that the king and Metaxas had failed to achieve" (1981, 34).

Like all ontological narratives, those associated with the EAM leadership were shaped by a range of correlated political, cultural, and social/psychological influences. I have already noted some of the main components of the communist experience and speculated about some of the reasons behind that party's conciliatory tendencies during the resistance. The range of communist opinion, as elsewhere, was wide—with tendencies from strict materialism and constitutionalism to idealism and integrationism represented in the small but growing KKE. Throughout the 1920s and 1930s, when the party was rocked by factional disputes and with faithful adherence to principle detracting from the party's mass appeal, the very existence of sectarianism is an indication that communist doctrine was a work in progress, and the party, like its counterparts in other lands, was buffeted by shifting visions of the future and of what constituted true democratic praxis. In this regard we might say that confident modernist determinism and reductionism struggled with the disorderly diversity now generally associated with the tentativeness of postmodern social transformations. As the 1930s progressed, the Greek communist and noncommunist Left had in the final analysis steered a relatively moderate course, dedicating itself more to a nationalist than a reverently Soviet Communist party [CPSU] lineage. A KKE-EAM pamphlet published in 1943 entitled "Our national problem and the Communist Party of Greece" briefly reviews the history of Marxism and cites the central practical role of the October Revolution before proceeding to engage the more pressing problems of fascism and the local economic and political legacies of capitalism. Significantly, the monograph confines its praise of the Soviet Union to the "brave struggles of the Russian people against tsarism and against fascism"; and at no point does the pamphlet applaud the Soviet system itself.[18]

The writer Nikos Kazantzakis provides a good example of an idiosyncratic conscience butting against the wall of modernist unitary consciousness. His developing "meta-communism" combined an initial enthusiasm after the Bolshevik victory with elements of Henri Bergson (his revered professor during graduate studies in Paris), mysticism, orthodox religion, ancient ritual, and ample poetic license. Kazantzakis's public visibility as a contemporary figure, role model, and referent meant that his foundational contribution to the

---

[18] *To ethniko mas provlima kai to kommounistiko komma tis Elladas*, Ekdhosi KOMEP (1943; Athens: Mnimi Press, 1985).

debate did not go unnoticed. Partly, this stemmed from his popularity as a writer. But his notoriety was also in large measure derived from the fact that many of his most controversial moves, contentious articles, and disputed creative works had been featured in Glinos's *Anayennisi* and were thus hotly contested in cafes and meeting halls around Athens.[19] "Meta-communism" irritated many on the Left who found its antinomies unsettling and even dangerous. Its existence, however, does raise the possibility that Kazantzakis was not alone in tailoring his ideological beliefs to fit his own multiple outlooks and needs. The indignant reaction from many quarters underscores the unitary aspirations and basic conformism endemic to political modernism, even while some used their imaginations more than others.

In summary, it is important to keep several things in mind. First, the language and logic of coalitional politics greatly affected public behavior, especially after 1935 but also to a significant degree before. The coalition was based on the consensus conveniently provided by the common enemies of internal and external fascism and by the passionately shared goal of introducing a "modernizing" agenda into Greek social and political life. This pact was possible, in Greece as elsewhere, because of a Wittgensteinian "family resemblance" among believers in the ecumenical modernist ethic (see Card 1993, 253).

Second, we must remember that communism itself was never really synonymous with hard-core Stalinism. This point would almost seem too self-evident to bother making were it not that an incredibly tragic and sour note in socialist history has consistently been conflated with the full complement of factions, contested issues, complex philosophical bases, and conflicting interpretations represented in nearly all local parties during the protracted foundational identity crisis of the 1920s, 1930s and 1940s. The more plausible common denominator, if one existed, was a loosely construed Leninism, with its counterhegemonic, reconstitutive, nation-building cast, combined with various other sources of inspiration and programmatic solutions. When tempted to stereotype communist thought, we need only remember Lenin's own consternation and doomsday warnings about a CPSU commandeered by Stalin, whom he increasingly perceived as capable of the most desperate of acts and as fairly deranged.

Influences on Leadership Narratives

> As bilingual intelligentsias . . . and above all as early twentieth-century intelligentsias,
> they had access, inside the classroom and outside, to models of nation, nation-ness,
> and nationalism distilled from the turbulent, chaotic experiences of more than a

---

[19] See Bien 1989, especially about the so-called Alhambra Incident and the publication of excerpts from the book *Askitiki*.

century of American and European history. These models, in turn, helped to give shape to a thousand inchoate dreams.

—Anderson 1983, 128

Before concluding, I want to construct a brief (and necessarily speculative) synopsis of ontologies which, in addition to that of Glinos, the 1940s Greek organic intellectuals would translate into the EAM's mobilizational narratives. This is undertaken more to delineate an approach than as an encyclopedic portrayal. What were some of the relevant political, psychological and intellectual reference groups for EAM leaders? How would these leaders emplot their stories about their prewar past? What narrative aspects—main characters, timing of entrances, salient role models and incidents, to name a few possibilities—could be traced to resistance social policy? In short, what sorts of factors account for the transformation of these individuals as an age cohort—"born at a similar time . . . [and] destined to experience a particular set of meaningful events at the same stage of life-cycle development" (Braungart and Braungart 1986, 215)—into a political generation which, through its reformist aspirations and despite its rather dramatic failure, altered the course of Greek social history?

I have devoted considerable attention to the case of Dimitris Glinos. The case of Stefanos Sarafis, a major figure and influence on resistance social policy, is also illuminating. His prior political history is noteworthy and very much in keeping with the ontological patterns identified so far. Born in 1890, Sarafis was old enough to remember the national humiliation following the 1897 defeat of irredentist forces attempting to recover Byzantine Empire lands from Turkey. Soon after hostilities broke out, on Easter, the Sarafis family fled Trikala to settle temporarily in a nearby village. Sarafis's narrative features his encounter with partisans in the mountains of Thessaly at that time. He recalled: "One day I saw some men armed with rifles and crossed cartridge-belts. They had long beards and wore shaggy coats, black tunics and *foustanellas*. They told us they were guerillas with Capetan Arkouda and had come from Mouzaki to stop the Turks from reaching the mountains. They made a great impression on me and I couldn't take my eyes off them" (quoted in M. Sarafis 1989, xvii). One might speculate that these partisans struck a romantic chord in Sarafis and later inspired his penchant for soldiering in the service of national mythology.

A further formative influence was the failure of his father's various business ventures. Eventually, the family fell into poverty, which, in a society influenced by relatively unforgiving codes of public honor and shame was, his widow writes "concealed as far as possible from the mocking eyes of a gossip-ridden provincial town. . . . he began to think that a world in which this could happen to his honourable and kindly father and in which some of those who had contributed to his ruin could flourish like the green bay tree was a world without justice. From now on, when he was asked the question usually put to small boys, 'What would you like to be when you grow up?' he would reply rather threateningly that he would be a judge and see justice done" (1980, xvii–xviii). In fact, Sarafis did go on to study law before becoming an army officer and Greek military attaché in Paris during the 1930s.

The prewar years were crucial antecedents to the subsequent decision to join the EAM and assume commandership of ELAS forces, and also gave rise to his ardent commitment to the cause of popular democracy in Greece. In an excellent biographical essay and introduction to his memoir about the history and overall meaning of ELAS, Marion Sarafis details critical events at greater length than is possible here. Several episodes deserve mention, however, for what they reveal about Sarafis's radicalization in the context of his times, as he grappled with key incidents and matters of conscience. Primarily these involve his experiences as an army officer and his 1935 induction into the league of political prisoners produced by the contradictions of the Greek political system throughout the 1930s and '40s. For example, he sat for the entrance examination to the military academy in Athens in 1912 and was informed beforehand that his strong application file, even if coupled with a brilliant performance on the test, would not affect his chances, since it had been agreed in advance that no noncommissioned officer would pass. In effect, all places had been reserved for students from military and aristocratic families with connections. Later, assuming the post of assistant director of the academy in 1927, Sarafis attempted to shake up such established hierarchies. "Remembering what had happened when he himself sat the entrance examination," writes Marion Sarafis, "he came in as the newest of new brooms, determined to make a clean sweep of abuses. He reformed the educational programme, hitherto almost entirely theoretical, adding practical instruction so that an officer would be able not only to command but to do. He followed the lessons in the classrooms and any cadet who did not make the grade was kept back to repeat his year. For the duration of his tenure he was successful in putting down the traditional ritual bullying of juniors by seniors and of new entrants by everyone. . . . But the crunch came with his entrance examinations. He was determined that results would be strictly in accordance with merit and announced that any attempt to operate the patronage network would automatically disqualify" (1980, xxxvi).

As sergeant major during the Balkan Wars (1912–1913) Sarafis marshaled his battalion in much the same way that he would similar brigades during the resistance. Marion Sarafis describes the scene: "He found himself with a battalion of bored and homesick men in a rest-camp on an isolated upland plain. So he organized athletics for them, working up to a battalion Olympiad with prizes. This, he thought, would not only be good for physique and morale but would enable him to teach these men—most of whom had had only minimal schooling—about an ancient Greek tradition and so send them back to their villages prouder and better Greeks. Such attention to welfare was innovatory for the Greek Army of that date and he began to acquire the ambivalent reputation which attaches to innovators in a hierarchic structure. He saw it as service to the conscript, to the citizen in arms" (1980, xxii).

On the subject of citizenship, an intriguing incident in 1919 during the Asia Minor campaign offers a somewhat paradoxical variant of feminist advocacy:

> In the area assigned to his battalion there were no civil authorities functioning except for the basic village communes and he found himself necessarily replacing the civil administration—a valuable experience. In one instance, he even functioned as an ecclesiastical court, hearing a divorce case brought by a Greek peasant against his otherwise exemplary wife for disobedience because she refused to use the scythe, maintaining that this was men's work and the sickle was for women. He found for the wife and reconciled the couple. (M. Sarafis 1980, xxix)

In 1935 Sarafis was arrested and tried for his participation in the Venizelist officers' coup aimed at overthrowing the Metaxas regime. He had been part of the group that volunteered to seize the Makryianni barracks in central Athens. At the trial, the statement he made in his own "defense"—"I know you and you know me. Judge me"—greatly enhanced his public popularity and rendered his execution a chance the government could not afford to take. He was sentenced instead to political exile on the island of Aegina, where "he found what seemed to him a splendid opportunity. There was a group of communist prisoners (the net of 1935 arrests had swept wide) and, since they included intellectuals and trained Marxists, they had organized themselves into the traditional prison university, each member lecturing on a subject within his competence. Prominent in this group was Lefteris Apostolou, later to be the first General-Secretary of the EAM Resistance movement. Alone of the republican prisoners, Sarafis applied to follow the lectures and, thus, for the first time became acquainted with Marxist philosophy and a Marxist interpretation of history and even of ancient and modern Greek literature" (M. Sarafis 1980, xlvi).

Sarafis was later transferred to Milos, where he met his wife, an English student of classical archaeology at Oxford researching the ruins. On issues of democratic practice, "the Makryianni experience had shown him," his wife would later write, "that the rising in defence of the republic and democracy had seemed so alien to the ordinary soldier in the barracks that most of these had taken refuge in the basements rather than risk involvement. He could now see that the revolution which was needed in Greece to make a clean sweep of kings and *coups* and capitalists, could never be imposed from on top, by politicians and serving officers in the absence of the people. It must come from the people themselves. Later, in Crete where he went after being amnestied, when he was not permitted to live in Athens, he would speak in village cafes about the need to create 'a more popular democracy.' He confessed to me that he did not then know exactly what he meant by this, only that it must be a movement based on the people, from which they were not absent as they had been in 1935. He was to find this 'popular democracy' again as the basis of EAM's liberation programme" (1990, xiv–lxvi).

In 1946, after a six-month stint hiding underground in Athens, Sarafis was arrested for his resistance activities and began the rounds of exile camps and prisons including Ikaria, Serifos, Vourla in Piraeus, Makronisos, and finally Ai-Strati. He was released in 1951 following his absentee election to parliament as a candidate from the EDA party. Among the other candidates on the slate were Manolis Glezos, whom readers will remember had torn down the swastika from the Acropolis as a young man, and Tony Ambatielos, leader of the seamen's union.

On Sarafis's continuing preoccupation with social justice and inclusive policy, Marion Sarafis commented in a preface to *Rigas dedigi* (What Rigas said) by Mihri Belli (a Turk, the only non-Greek to have fought in the Democratic Army during the civil war):

> Bulgarians, Albanians, Armenians, Greeks,
> black and white, let us belt the sword
> all together in a surge for freedom,
> so the world will know that we are the brave

How often, nearly thirty years ago in Greece, I have awoken to the sound of these strains! . . . in the whole of this war-song by his 18th century Thessalian compatriot (widely sung in the resistance) his favorite verses were those which called for a common Balkan struggle. Already at our first meeting in 1938 when he was in deportation on the island of Milos under the Metaxas dictatorship, he had spoken to me of Balkan brotherhood and solidarity. This made a deep impression because it was the first time that I had heard such thoughts in Greece. Any mention of other Balkan countries had seemed guarantied to produce stories of "Bulgar-slaying" and "Turk-eating" heroes. I had already realised that the man I had met on Milos would one day do something important for his country. He thought deeply and with constructive originality about his country's problems. He had understood this need for brotherhood from his first army days as an NCO and then as a junior officer. . . . as his thinking matured, he realised that such Balkan quarrels served only the interests of those Great Power "protectors" who were fighting out their differences

with Balkan pawns. When in discussions with friends the subject of Turkey or
of the "northern neighbors" came up, I would hear him say, "They've got us
all boiling in the same pot," and the implication was clear: it was the Great
Powers that were the cooks. (Belli 1984, 165–66)

The above passages suggest that O Stratigos (the General), as Sarafis was
called, was in some respects unique, but we should not underestimate his
desire to reform the behavior of his associates or his considerable reputation
and influence over EAM policy. It is also significant that, as part of a cohort
that came of political age during the post-1897 era, Sarafis was accustomed to
periods of systemic crisis followed by national self-critique. In this sense, he
and the other leaders can be placed in a larger late nineteenth- and early
twentieth-century context. Globally, rapid and often sudden social changes,
public-sphere power struggles, and debates over collective identities and mass
political processes were common in this period, shaded of course with the
specifics of various national histories and environmental contingencies.

In Greece as elsewhere, the typical aftermath of a political crisis was marked
by much heated debate in the popular press about how state-society relations
were to be structured and broader questions of nation building resolved.
These episodes often turned polemical, with the sides glaring at one another
across an ideological divide made less bridgeable by a cultural fixation with
demonstrating honor (*timi*)—or perhaps *dignity* is a better word here—and
avoiding shame and public ridicule (*dhropi*). Here, I lapse momentarily into
the terms anthropology has traditionally applied to such cultures (and like so
many social typologies, the honor-shame classification has recently come under fire as part of a broader questioning of the inherent value and political
ramifications of categories).[20] This mode of self-consciousness pertained not
so much to issues of sexuality as to questions of national image and gender.
The "honor-shame complex," if by that we mean that "social acceptance is
impossible in the absence of unspoiled honour" (Safilios-Rothschild 1969,
205) was often a central subtext in any popular intellectual forum, especially
when larger questions of national identity were being contested. This was
never more true than in the post-1897 crisis, when a decisive setback for the
irredentist solution to problems of national integration caused a round of soul-
searching. For a sizable segment of nationalists concerned with issues of statecraft and the instrumental reform of civil society, a significant preoccupation
during this period of self-exploration was the "face" Greece was showing to
the world. I should also note parenthetically that "face" and fear of humiliation have been driving forces behind *most* public discourse in all regions and at
all levels, even though in some cultures it is a more explicit part of the prevail-

[20] See, for example, Loizos and Papataxiarchis 1991; Herzfeld 1987.

ing sociolegal code and carries a particularly stinging and overt emotional charge.

Again, not atypically for aspiring nineteenth- and twentieth-century nationalists from noncore states, the "West" had been constructed as an exemplar of Cartesian rationality and a standard by which "progress," or the lack thereof, was measured.[21] Greek self-criticism, at times submerged and at times openly communal, took place on a number of dimensions: the merit of existing economic structures, the persistence of "folkloric" culture, popular educational attainment, "balance" in political institutions and activities. Even how people looked and dressed were matters for symbolic concern in the midst of the nineteenth-century European imperialist/orientalist overlay. As was the case more generally in western and eastern Europe and the Balkans, at the same time that romanticists were recapturing indigenous folkloric traditions and celebrating them as valuable popular cultural expressions, some viewed these traditions as alarmingly parochial. In the wake of the 1897 defeat, to those nationalists distressed by a perceived "backwardness" that continually seemed to obstruct the path of civil society toward Enlightenment goals, augmented by general anxiety about exposure to world ridicule based on various stereotypes and "deficiencies," the notion that Greece might visibly fail in both the international and domestic arenas seemed an affront to the national self-image and code of honor.

As a nation at a geographical and historical crossroads, Greece had a binary orientation toward "East" and "West" which was definitive and yet difficult to reconcile. Clearly, Greek national identity was double sided; on the one hand, the Egyptian, Byzantine, Orthodox, Ottoman legacy was a source of both pride and contempt; on the other, a European connection among intellectuals combined a keen interest in the ideas of the *philosophes* with the repackaging and reimportation of the idea, as Augustinos says, that "the ancestors of the modern Greeks possessed those characteristics of perfection in thought, art and literature which were so highly prized at the time. It mattered not if the picture of the classical age that Europeans created for themselves was faulted by time and their own contemporary views. The images were satisfying and the form well set by the time the modern Greeks began to make use of these notions for their own purposes" (1977, 7). This view of the Greeks as the original, undiluted Europeans, which Martin Bernal (1987) has called the "Aryan model," provided a powerful symbol for Greeks and philhellenes alike.

The political significance of this dualist *mentalité* for Greek organic intellectuals throughout the modern period cannot be underestimated, whether com-

---

[21] The "yardstick" impulse was not of course unique to Greece. For example, the Young Ottoman and Greek nationalist debates were symbiotic. See Taner Timur, "The Ottoman Heritage," in Schick and Tonak 1987, 3–26. The cross-cultural relevance of this type of relativism in a world system context is evident in Irokawa 1985.

munists, socialists, liberals, centrists, or conservatives. The works of certain figures caught the attention and imagination of educated Greeks across the political spectrum and helped to define the terms of this Janus-faced discourse. Vital antecedents in this dialogue were Rigas Velestinlis (1757–1798), author of Sarafis's favorite war song; Adamantios Koraes (1748–1833), who from Parisian exile, Augustinos says, "edited the Greek classics in a series called the *Greek Library,* prefacing them with critical introductions, which he hoped would give his countrymen a proper understanding of their classical heritage" (1977, 9), and Dionysos Solomos, poet of the revolution who wrote the lyrics for the Greek national anthem. Subsequent historical narrators to which twentieth-century organic intellectuals had varying degrees of exposure were the nationalists Ion Dragoumis and Perikles Giannopoulos; and Iannis Psiharis, George Skliros, Penelope Delta, Alexander Delmouzos, Kostas Palamas, and of course Dimitris Glinos. As I have already claimed, in my estimation the latter group, salient figures in the demotic movement, had the most directly traceable effect on the intellectual proclivities of the EAM leadership as a whole.

Whereas irredentist nationalism and its converse, defensive nationalism, were linked in different ways to external aggression, the demotic movement, like the political nationalism into which, I contend, it devolved during the resistance, focused its energies on a domestic agenda. Externally and internally oriented nationalisms had been complementary elements in the minds of influential reformers long before the Nazi occupation. As Iannis Psiharis, a leader of the demotic movement, commented, "A nation, in order to become a nation needs two things; its frontiers must be expanded and it must produce its own literature" (quoted in Augustinos 1977, 22).[22] Thus, the other historically significant dualism, in addition to the East-West dichotomy, was ostensibly linguistic but in fact concerned the politics of exclusion and inclusion, as a dialogic interaction between elite and subaltern. As we have seen, demoticists believed that what united a nation was its language and this should be the language spoken by "the people."

Much of the controversy surrounding the language question was played out on the pages of the journal *O Noumas,* read by most politically active individuals, as well as in popular newspapers. Sarafis, for example, was an avid reader in his youth. The point is that these debates occurred at a formative stage in the political thinking of the EAM leadership. Debate in *Noumas* was open to supporters of the demoticist cause regardless of political persuasion. "Bourgeois nationalists" like Dragoumis and socialists like George Skliros, who felt that demoticist doctrine could serve the needs of the working class, participated in defining the movement's positions. Much of the EAM educational

[22] Also see the pathbreaking work of Gregory Jusdanis (1991).

policy and the decision to institute demotic as the official resistance language, to be used in all communications, can be traced to the participation of demoticists in the EAM. Leaders of diverse political stripes were able to agree so easily on radical social policies in large part because of this early inclusive intellectual "collaboration." Not accidentally, one of the most cohesive incidents of the resistance period was the death of the demoticist poet Kostas Palamas in 1943. Huge crowds turned out on the streets of Athens for his funeral in covert support of the EAM. Palamas's belief that art and poetry could be used constructively to ignite national pride and spirit was very much in keeping with both an ancient narrative tradition and the socializing goals of the EAM. The use of mobilizing narratives to convey a social message of inclusion is expressed in the work—turned into organizing song lyrics—of such poets as Sofia Mavroeidi-Papadaki and Vassilis Rotas, PEEA minister of culture and director of the Resistance Theater. What we now must explore is how the rank-and-file participant-authors might have heard and identified with these narratives.

CHAPTER 5

Issues in Mobilization

Movement within a Movement: Mobilizing for Change

Movements within movements have not received a great deal of scholarly attention as a *type* of political event, despite several noteworthy exceptions. The English revolution of the mid-1600s, for example, generated various radical sects including the Ranters, whose protest methods have been incorporated into popular metaphor (see J. C. Davis 1986). Clearly, the women's movement that was launched within the context of the New Left is also an instance of a movement within a movement (see Evans 1979).[1] Nancy Bermeo (1986) characterizes the workers' mobilization in rural Portugal as an insurgency that occurred while a more comprehensive uprising was under way and added a new dimension to the revolutionary agenda. These cases, however, involved active protest by the groups involved. Campaigns were formulated around demands for recognition within the movements in question and for the assimilation of particular values into the list of movement goals. As grievances became more salient, disassociation from the movement provided activists with an additional bargaining tool, and they were able to draw upon their anger and collective interpretations in publicizing the significance of their struggle to potential members and to relevant communities at large.

What distinguished the revolution within a revolution that I focus on here from these cases and from far more common single-issue mobilizations[2] is the

---

[1] Todd Gitlin (1987) also discusses this phenomenon from his own perspective as a New Left participant.

[2] Such as abortion campaigns around the 1989 reversal of the Roe v. Wade case in the U.S. Supreme Court; or, the "Anti-US Brutality" march organized by Chinese students in 1947 to protest the rape of a Beijing University student by U.S. marines (see Wasserstrom and Xinyong 1989). In these cases, protests were part of a much wider range of concerns, but in the short term, activists unified around one particular issue or incident.

proactive role the Greek resistance played in shaping the collective consciousness of its women members; and the way in which mobilization was directly linked to nationalism and state-building. Traditional Greek culture framed the debate about women in strict terms (see Laitin 1988, 590). For the most part, the time that women spent in the public sphere had to be accounted for, either as an extension of private-sphere activities, such as errands for family maintenance, or in very circumscribed areas of the labor force. Even when working, women had to behave in a manner considered above reproach to avoid punitive social sanctions.

Perhaps the most significant type of public sphere activity closed to women was formal political activity. The stringency of this cultural code can best be understood in terms of the small range of life choices open to adolescent girls in contrast to their male counterparts. Young adults were socialized into civil society according to a fixed set of rules. Girls learned humility and domestic efficiency and not to venture into the places where politics were conducted, such as the village or neighborhood *kafeneion* or political party headquarters. Boys learned that men were responsible for, among other things, enhancing the family socioeconomic status in the public world, whether through farming, commerce, or educational achievement. Elementary education was generally viewed as acceptable, if unnecessary, for girls whose families could afford it. Some upper-class women pursued more extensive academic training, but Glinos's efforts on this score testify to how precarious this possibility actually was. The small but active prewar feminist movement was an outgrowth of this educated stratum, many of whom had received their training abroad. Their activities in many ways paralleled those of other nineteenth-century women's organizations in Europe and the Third World, and they maintained links with international organizations and with their national counterparts.[3]

Traditional and legal sanctions against women's activities in the public sphere, combined with women's lack of political rights, meant that the Greek resistance movement's chances of mobilizing any substantial number of young women depended on its ability to cast its challenge to the political status quo in terms deemed legitimate by the wider Greek society. Indeed, popular legitimacy is essential to any process that seeks change at the mass level. Proposals for change that aspire to be both effective and noncoercive must be framed in such a way that they do not clash with cherished cultural tenets. A successful social movement, as Roberta Sigel notes, must "accomplish more than resocializing movement followers. It also has to raise the consciousness of a

---

[3] An example of a prewar organization dedicated to the cause of women's emancipation through education and, to a lesser extent, suffrage was the Union for Women's Education founded in 1872. See also Avdela and Psarra 1985; Varika 1987. Discussions of similar developments can be found in Lovenduski 1986; and Jayawardena 1989.

sufficient number of noninvolved people,, i.e., it has to aim for large-scale popular resocialization" (1989, 268).

So intransigent were traditional sex-role constraints that something rather unusual would have to appear on the horizon to transform or extend them. Proposals for change would have to speak to the latent political desires of the Greek population and be composed in a way that would not jar or fly directly in the face of tradition. EAM strategists proposed youth-oriented sex role changes and placed great emphasis on chastity and parental consent for girls, honesty and respect for boys, liberal education, and nonexploitative relations between the sexes. Glinos presented a strong message of inclusion in his programmatic pamphlet (What Is the National Liberation Front and What Does It Want?:

> Just as the national struggle cannot happen without unity at the leadership level, neither can it occur without unity within the organization. The struggle will include all social strata among the people, from the worker to the aristo-crat and from the poorest farmer to the propertied. It will include boys and girls, women in the factories and in the public offices and banks and house-wives in the suburbs and apartment buildings. (1944, 51)

In the interest of mass political mobilization, the EAM made a concerted effort to educate and empower women with limited political experience and to radically reconstruct public moral codes. What I earlier called defensive na-tionalism cut across class and gender barriers and gave the EAM leaders the opportunity to alter communal beliefs regarding women's participation in the public sphere.

The development of the nation-state in various regions of the world has often been preceded by a revolution, a concept which Theda Skocpol notes was once reserved for astronomical cycles but with the advent of the French revolution "came to connote a sudden, fundamental, and innovative departure in a nation's social and political life" (1989, 53). It is not unusual for political revolutions to be linked in some way to the concept of nationalism in the minds of revolutionaries. Calls for radical social changes to revitalize or define the limits of the nation have provided the philosophical justification for many types of revolutions. Students, bank clerks, peasants, and pensioners may throw themselves in front of rolling tanks in the name what Benedict Anderson has called the imagined community, "*imagined* because the members of even the smallest nation will never know most of their fellow-members, meet them, or even hear of them, yet in the minds of each lives the image of their commu-nion" (1983, 15). Anderson captures the intersubjective nature of nationalist sentiment and its mobilizing potential, but he does not directly address the process by which ordinary and even relatively powerless individuals reach the point where they might "not so much kill, as willingly die for such limited imaginings" (1983, 16). This is indeed a very helpful way to begin to think about the question of motivation: a dynamic conception of the ideological bases of social change also needs to emphasize development over time and the contingencies of the mobilization process. Nationalism is a variable form of identity, and the transformation of collective consciousness a central goal of revolutionaries qua social movement leaders which also bears examining.

How do nationalisms fueled by a modernizing rationale—something that people must *learn* that they are ready to die for—develop? The source of political nationalism is an empirical question to be investigated in particular national contexts and in relation to movements as agents of political change. For example, the American Civil Rights movement, Aldon Morris and his colleagues state "was a tool of political socialization. Its mass tactics required people to learn and execute new forms of political behavior" (Morris, Hatchett, and Brown 1989, 284). It is this type that I distinguished earlier as a socializing movement. To grasp the radicalizing potential of the sort of nationalism which seeks to increase political participation, it is necessary to study the social movements that have made it their goal to include groups left out of the political system. Here the social movement organizations, which include indigenous revolutionary fronts, play a direct and causal role through their mobilizing activities.[4] For example, one of the ways in which social movement organizations create new political identities is by tapping into already extant "sentiment pools" and convincing prospective members that their "individual interests, values and beliefs and [movement] activities, goals, and ideology are congruent and complementary"—a process called *frame alignment*.[5] The power of successful frame alignment is brought home to me when I assign Saul Alinsky's *Reveille for Radicals* in my social movements classes and observe how his chapter "What Is a Radical?" still, nearly fifty years after it was written, creates in students the desire to be a "radical." Alinsky's rhetorical skill lies in his ability to spin a mobilizational narrative that casts a positive aura around radicalism and convincingly makes nonradicals seem unholy and highly defective.

Another processual concept, by now perhaps somewhat overused, is *political empowerment*. Yet it is difficult to understand how socializing movements operate or how any sustained radical action is possible without paying close attention to processes of political empowerment, a type of social change that involves increasing the capacity of the weak to recognize and act in their own

---

[4] "A *social movement organization* (SMO) is a complex, or formal, organization that identifies its goals with the preferences of a social movement or a countermovement and attempts to implement those goals" (McCarthy and Zald 1987, 20).

[5] For a fuller treatment of the term originally inspired by Goffman 1986, see Snow et al. 1986, quotation on 464. On "sentiment pools," see McCarthy and Zald 1987; Snow and Benford 1988; Snow et al. 1986.

individual and collective interests, and by definition what social movements do. New experiences or special challenges often serve to empower participants, so that the very act of participating engenders personal transformation. Narratives of empowerment that identify a process of mobility from one form of consciousness to another are a common feature of the testimonies of participants in social movements and especially *socializing* movements, across cultures. Bui Thi Me, vice-president of the Women's Union for the Liberation of South Vietnam, for example, describes the conscious resocialization of women during the 1950s:

> When women stayed home all the time, they lost touch with society. Their isolation bred insecurity and, after a while, shyness and passivity seemed like women's "natural qualities." The ideology of feudalism became internalized in this way. We work to overcome this problem by struggling against feudalism. . . . We also think it is important to struggle everyday with shyness. . . . We use political courses to help overcome shyness. When the shy ones mingle with women who are confident, little by little they overcome their passivity. (Eisen 1984, 122)

The didactic value of social movements stems from the exchange relationship whereby the movement gains adherents and the politically inexperienced become less vulnerable to "learned helplessness," to use Elizabeth Janeway's term, by which "the creature, whatever it is, is educated into a belief in its own absolute impotence" (1981, 207). In defining a related process, which they call "transvaluation," Frances Fox Piven and Richard Cloward stress the acquisition of "a new sense of efficacy: people who ordinarily consider themselves helpless come to believe that they have some capacity to alter their lot" (1977, 4). In addition to a new sense of efficacy, political empowerment also entails an expanded sense of community and new expectations about skills, civil rights, and horizontal contact with other political organizations. One now belongs not just to a family, neighborhood, town, or village, but to a *political class,* however inchoate. Members of the new political class now not only see themselves reflected more favorably in their own fantasies about the future but also insist more audibly on access to "power and knowledge" in the public domain, or truth, in Foucault's sense:

> Each society has its regime of truth, its "general politics" of truth: that is, the types of discourse which it accepts and makes function as true; the mechanisms and instances which enable one to distinguish true and false statements, the means by which each is sanctioned; the techniques and procedures accorded value in the acquisition of truth; the status of those who are charged with saying what counts as true. (1980, 131)

The emotional charge of "belonging" is, of course, far more familiar to established activists. By contrast, empowerment for latent groups whose restricted conceptual frame has been widened in accordance with the hopes and dreams of the movement is euphoric. Empowerment can also be stubbornly uncritical, although the kind of "critical consciousness" that Paulo Freire (1992) calls "conscientization" is also possible. Testimonies of the recently empowered, faced with a new range of choices, a new conception of their abilities, a new understanding of their possible contribution to contemporary discourse, have in common a tone of wonderment. Thus, the comment of a Mississippi Freedom School volunteer reflects the mutual empowerment that was a key feature of the summer of 1964:

> Every class is beautiful. The girls respond, respond, respond. And they disagree among themselves. I have no doubt that soon they will be disagreeing with me. At least this is one thing that I am working towards. They know that they have been cheated and they want anything and everything that we can give them. I feel inadequate to the task of teaching them but I keep saying to myself that as long as I continue to feel humble there is a chance that we might all learn a whole lot together. (McAdam 1988, 86)

In an entirely different setting, "the driver of a three-ton truck," a member of the women's Auxiliary Territorial Service in England during World War II exclaims: "I loved it. People said women hated to be in uniform, that they missed their party dresses. Balls! It was lovely, all that way from home and boarding schools, with no one knowing who you were. The uniform took away your identity and gave you freedom—even if it was just to do something like have a pint of beer in a pub" (Saywell 1985, 15).

For a vague sense of discomfort with the prevailing system to be transformed into political empowerment, the desire for change must take root at the individual psychological level and be felt by enough people within a roughly similar time frame. Atomized grievances are likely to reach a critical threshold when a favorable structure of political opportunities enables separate spheres of discontent to be bridged by movement organizations or creates situations that bring isolated individuals into contact with one another, such as the work place or wartime affiliations. "The micro-mobilization context," Doug McAdam insists, is key. "Movements may occur in a broad macro context, but their actual development clearly depends on a series of more specific dynamics operating at the micro level. . . . A micro-mobilization context can be defined as that small group setting in which processes of collective attribution are combined with rudimentary forms of organization to produce mobilization for collective action" (1982, 127, 134–35).

McAdam cites several examples of the micromobilization context, from the preexistent political groups such as unions, which organized pro–Vietnam War "hardhat marches" of construction workers; to the Greensboro A & T students who began their assault on Woolworth's and other segregated lunch counters after dorm-room planning sessions; to the black churches that served as rallying points for various strikes and demonstrations during the Civil Rights movement. Similarly, it would be virtually impossible to make sense of the South African antiapartheid movement without examining the effects of the different contexts in which mobilization took place: the schools and jails of Soweto, local branches of the black miners' union, and women's groups such as the Domestic Workers Association and the African National Congress Women's League.

Thus, the micromobilization context is where prospective participants initially experience empowerment. Here, the critical mass of individuals who fall between the cracks of the system and remain either uninformed or hesitant, may become convinced, first, that a movement offers a possible solution to the problem; second, that the movement has a chance to succeed; and third, that significant others—friends, relatives, mentors, people whom they have come to respect—also think the movement is a good idea. Microlevel empowerment is as important to social movement analysis as the more easily measured success at the institutional level. One possible outcome of political empowerment is that individual changes in consciousness may gain enough momentum to be translated into sustained collective action. The involvement of women in resistance and war often represents an opening in the political system, an opportunity for women to become a conscious political class with new access to the public sphere and all its attendant power structures. The possibility of a reversal of fortune is, however, embedded in any "opening." Thus, in the Greek case, we see that during the Civil War (1946–49) and the 1950s, members of the EAM were marked and many of its social gains discredited. In the last part of the book, I discuss how and why newly empowered women were demobilized as a part of the return to exclusionary politics after the war, which were accompanied by a change in the wartime ideology favorable to women's empowerment and participation. Nationalism and national interest were now diametrically interpreted. To have been in the resistance, whose stated goals had been "national self-determination" (*ethniki avtodhikisi*] and "people's power" (*laokratia*) was now to be officially reclassified as "antinational" (*anti-ethnikofrosin*). To have been a woman in the resistance and thus to have been exposed to hubristic notions of female personal and political power was now to inhabit the realm of the morally suspect.

Nevertheless, the effects of a more active role for women in political life were never completely erased, because of the way in which the EAM mobilized women during a period when the central political institutions of the country were particularly vulnerable to change.[6] Moreover, the women and girls who either joined or had some contact with the resistance say that the lessons in confidence and personal power it provided were invaluable. Especially strong traces of the reorienting influence of the resistance can be found in the life histories of those women who became political prisoners during the Civil War.

Resistance and the Woman Question

Films, novels, and plays dramatizing the sordid events of the Nazi era have had perennial popular appeal. Exploring themes of injustice, military pageantry, love among the ruins, and the triumph of good over evil, tales of defiance of Nazi terrorism in the occupied territories of Europe have been of intrinsic interest to mass publics throughout the postwar era. In the symbolic realm, memorials have been erected to those who gave up their futures to contest fascism. Political speeches have made frequent mention of the lives lost in this costly struggle. Critical reviews of elite responses to Nazism have also occurred periodically. The Nuremberg trials in the late 1940s, the Claus Barbie case in France, and the debate surrounding Kurt Waldheim's election in Austria have shown that responses to domination varied along a continuum from collaboration to passivity to resistance. Limited attention, as I argued earlier, has been paid to resistance movements for what they can tell us about core principles of social organization and how these movements might have reflected the popular political will as it seeped through the cracks of the fascist ruling structures of Europe in the 1930s. Instead, treatments of wartime resistance movements have most often dealt with instances of individual or collective bravery rather than the consequences of their formation for the polities that produced them.

The tendency to emphasize heroism also extends to treatments of women in the resistance. Thus, despite evidence that women enlisted enthusiastically and participated gladly, their willingness to serve is not sufficient to make the Greek case *politically* interesting. The simple fact that they participated in the traditionally male-dominated areas of resistance and war during the Nazi occupation is not surprising. Wars often occasion social upheaval and shifts in gender norms. We know that long-standing conflicts and hierarchies are often ignored, as societies pull together to face external threat. At such times, it is not

[6] In a "three-wave panel study of young adults surveyed in 1965, 1973, and 1982 to test the theory [of political generations] with respect to the Vietnam era protest movement," M. Kent Jennings discovered "very strong continuities . . . for attitudes associated with the protestors'political baptism" (1987, 374). The participants in the Freedom Summer of 1964 provide another illustration of the potential for the effects of social movement activity to linger in protest cohorts. "The long-term effects are remarkable," writes James Fendrich, summarizing McAdam's findings. "Next to their counterparts, the activists remain further to the left, are more active in conventional and movement politics, and have avoided traditional careers and family commitments" (1988, 227).

unusual for women to be recruited into military struggles and even, in some cases, to trespass into male territory by operating tanks and shouldering machine guns.

Two schemata of women's mobilization should be considered here, which I label enemy assault mobilization and theoretical mobilization. According to the enemy assault model, women are mobilized *solely* for war, to help repel the enemy as efficiently as possible through their contributions in the military and economic realms. British women, for example, were recruited as pilots during World War II, but few remained in the Royal Air Force (RAF)—and indeed it was never part of the stated plan that they should. In the United States, Rosie the Riveter was urged to become a machinist and play her part in the war, but by 1945, the message had changed and the factory again became a male preserve. In Iran, women were mobilized through mosque networks, and in their fervor played a key role in the demonstrations that led to the Shah's downfall. But Shi'ite mullahs clearly did not envision a role for women in Iranian politics once the Khomeini regime had come to power.

According to the theoretical model of women's mobilization, by contrast, extensive and quite impressive theoretical claims are made by movements, organizations, or governments. Utopian visions of postmovement equality are discussed in clandestine meetings. Yet no concrete steps are taken to ensure that these revolutionary theories are actualized and that women are in fact integrated into the society at the mass level. This type of mobilization can be clearly seen in the case of the Spanish anarchists in the late nineteenth and early twentieth centuries. The official narrative deemed full sexual equality a necessary and desirable part of the postrevolutionary phase of the movement. Yet anarchist leaders also attacked and sought to destroy the two institutions that were most central to Spanish women's lives—the family and the church. Furthermore, male anarchists made no effort to train or educate women to assume roles in the one institution they planned as a viable substitute—the workers' syndicate. Nor was any effort made to prepare male skilled and unskilled workers to labor alongside female comrades—a situation with no precedent in Spanish society (Kaplan 1977, 402–3).

These archetypes, then, lead us to expect outcomes that fall considerably short of societal transformation. Although British and American women were involved in the war economy to an unprecedented extent, and the experience could not fail to leave an indelible mark on many personal identities, their recruitment was clearly for military expediency. Supervisors had no particular interest in empowering women per se or in challenging the status quo after the war. As soon as the Shah fell, Iranian women were summarily stripped of previously held rights (although Western biases in assessing this situation have been problematized and the literature on normative consequences presents a mixed picture). The Spanish anarchists, in spite of their idealism, appear to have had no immediate plans to incorporate women into the political system or the economy once broader revolutionary aims were fulfilled, something that in any case the cultural rules would have prevented women from doing without the support of male allies.

Thus we can see the danger of associating military participation a priori with women's political emancipation. This point is illustrated by Juliette Minces, who introduces her case study of women in the Algerian resistance to French colonization with a critique of a commonly held expectation about women in nationalist movements:

> In *A Dying Colonialism* Frantz Fanon affirmed that through violence and armed struggle, the condition of women in Algeria, like that of young people, was undergoing a revolutionary mutation. . . . The very fact of taking up arms, of participating in a violent action, he argued, would lead women to realize their own alienation and, consequently, would lead them to emancipate themselves. As for men, finally convinced, probably, of the injustice of the condition in which they had until then kept women, they would support women's claims in greater and greater numbers. In other words, according to Fanon, armed struggle with no other purpose than national independence should by itself modify mentalities in an irreversible fashion and, in consequence, change the status of women. (1978, 159)

On the one hand, Fanon's logic seems impeccable. But on the other, when revolutionary optimism met impossible-to-ignore cultural factors, the outcomes were decidedly not reflexive or involuntary. The way in which the Algerian movement defined nationalism and the steps taken to transform women into politically active citizens in the postrevolutionary phase of the struggle were, according to Minces and other students of the case, based on a constricted estimation of women's capabilities and a mobilizing narrative characterized by limited goals (see, e.g., Knauss 1987). Reconstructing, historicizing, and linking gender bias to other kinds of oppression were not salient parts of the revolutionary narrative. Nationalism was never officially tied in with social policy, nor were even the bare outlines of such themes as literacy, political education, or empowerment ever broached.

In summary, the Greek case presents a more ambivalent narrative of women and national liberation. As in the first "enemy assault" scenario, the male modernists in charge of the movement were anxious to involve women in the struggle against fascist tyranny, using all necessary means. This narrative was common to the largest number of participants, male and female, at all levels of the encounter. A smaller group adhered to the second scenario, a narrative which featured women as part of a theoretical *analysis* combining, among other things, a reconstituted ideal of Greek democracy (definitely on a scale unrecognizable to the ancients) to which modern liberal and Marxist tenets of liberty and equality were added. These protagonists agreed in basic discursive terms in a way that was logically prior to any possible changes. Finally, the smallest but perhaps most willful group of all believed Greece to be disgracefully backward concerning "the woman question" and were in a position to do something practical about it. Carrying, perhaps, images of the unjust fate of mothers, sisters, daughters, and selves, these men applauded the new scenario placed before them for consideration. Among all groups there was definite variability as to how far along the road to true integration women should be encouraged to travel. The point here is that any movement has a basic directional impetus, and this one was no exception. Yet it is also important to remember that despite unitary rhetoric designed to center and consolidate, all movements are in an important sense prismatic fields of contest, on gender as on other matters.

Emplotting the Greek Case

It is time to turn our attention from theoretical issues to the logistical aspects of my research. I formally interviewed forty-four women who were members of one or more of the following resistance organizations: EAM, ELAS, EPON, EA (Ethniki Allilengii, National Solidarity, the welfare organization), EDES, RAN (Roumeli-Avlon-Nisi), PEAN, and a British liaison group. I talked informally with twenty-seven other resistance participants, thirteen of them men. I have also used secondary histories, personal accounts (usually published by vanity presses), and archival records in search of women's motivations for participation. Initially, a major priority was to include members of all key resistance organizations across the political spectrum, although it turned out that the smaller right-leaning organizations, because they had not given any special priority to "the woman question," had fewer female members. Those who belonged to organizations other than the EAM generally joined for individual reasons, rather than as part of any concerted plan.

To learn if specific demographic attributes led to participation, I contacted interviewees with other general characteristics in mind—namely, age, marital status, and place of residence in 1941 when war was declared. These characteristics included urban vs. rural, and the particular region, e.g. Roumeli, Thessaly, the Peloponnese, the islands. In fact, some areas of Greece saw more resistance activity than others. Most of the interviews were conducted in Athens, although many of the interviewees lived in other parts of Greece during the occupation. The justification for the disproportionately large number of interviewees in the sample currently residing in Athens is that in the postwar period, Greece experienced a mass exodus from the villages to the capital city and migration to larger regional towns, such as Volos and Kavalla.

Other social variations with conceivable relevance to the case at hand included previous membership in a women's organization or in the Greek Communist party, previous work in a factory, study at a university, economic status, and whether the subject was a refugee from Asia Minor. Names were brought to my attention by word of mouth, through my own personal social contacts (the greengrocer's aunt, the cabdriver's mother, the friend of a cocktail party introduction) and through contacts with the major resistance survivor organizations with national offices and regional affiliates. In addition to the forty-four full oral histories with women, I conducted fourteen partial ones. Many of those sessions produced fairly extensive and important statements, but for one reason or another interviewees were not asked the complete roster of questions tracing their political lives from adolescence until later adulthood in 1985. Some interviews, for example, had to be cut short because of time considerations, and sometimes the subject was too painful for the person to talk about for very long, as in the case of one woman whose favorite brother was beheaded during the Civil War and another who was raped by a terrorist gang in 1946. In the mountains of Crete, some of the women hesitated to talk freely with men around, and in those cases, an assortment of brothers-in-law, husbands, and uncles who had been in the resistance and were anxious to have their own heroic deeds known, would take over the conversation and intimidate the women. Several informants insisted on group interviews, believing that I would learn more from listening to collective memories in a more interactive setting.

Some of the thirteen men were the husbands of the female interviewees. From the EAM-ELAS organization, I spoke with Spiros Meletzis, the official resistance photographer; Dr. Andonis Floutzis, Haidari prison doctor; Yiorgos K., a Cretan mayor (who could not complete the interview because he became upset over the loss of his sister, a teacher and EAM member beheaded during the Civil War); Dinos R., a journalist; Vangelis P., an Athens attorney;[7] Constantine Z., ELAS regional captain in Thessaly; Alekos M. and Stavros V., local Cretan *kapetanoi;* and Yiorgos S., ELAS captain from Kaissariani.

Of the forty-four women, twenty-seven had been in the EPON, the most common organizational affiliation. Most of the rest were either in EPON-ELAS units or the EA. Several gave multiple organizational identities. Four were from non-EAM organizations: RAN, EDES (her brother was a well-known resistance journalist executed at Haidari Prison in 1944), PEAN, the Athens youth group, and a British Special Operations Executive spy network.

[7] This interview was conducted for me by his son, Adrian.

In addition, I had a long telephone conversation with Evanthia Zervas, niece of General Napoleon Zervas, military head of the EDES.

Fifteen of the women were from districts in Athens; three were from Salonika; five were from Chania, Crete; five were from Rethymno and villages in the Cretan mountains; the rest were variously from Thebes; a mountain village between Karpenissi and Lamia; Kilkis and Serres in Macedonia; Kalamata, Githio, Messinia, Parnitsa in the Peloponnese; Elassona; Siatista; Messolonghi; the island of Zakinthos; Volos; Patras; Kozani; Larissa; Evoea Island. The average age when the Nazis invaded Greece was seventeen, with the youngest participant ten at the time and the oldest, thirty-seven.

In the customary language of sociological method, the reader should be alerted to several sampling biases in these data. First, because potential interviewees had to have been young enough at the time to be alive to talk about the experience today, undoubtedly there is overrepresentation of members with youthful perspectives on the resistance, or an age bias. But, in many ways the EAM was indeed a youth movement, whose participants were guided from above toward a comprehensive socialization that included preparation for adulthood as well as for national citizenship.

Second, the material contains a class bias. In order to talk to me, interviewees had to have survived the inordinate repression of the postwar era. Many peasant women were executed on the spot when arrested or were subsequently shot in local prisons; or, having been forced to flee into the Democratic Army which fought government troops during the Civil War, were killed in battle, especially during the final stages in the Grammos and Vitsi Mountains in 1949. Girls from wealthier backgrounds sometimes managed to escape authorities during the repression of the postwar years through family contacts. Their relatives were more likely to have had the means to pay lawyers, allowing them to buy time and keep their cases pending in the court system, or they were better connected through standard clientelist networks. This survival bias suggests that the EAM may have been more broadly based in class terms than my information about it reflects.

Third, the material is to an extent politically biased. Interviewees were overwhelmingly from the EAM, since rightist organizations did not recruit women on a mass scale. My assertion that the EAM was a populist movement in contrast to those in which women members were exceptions to the rule is supported by my inability to find women from other organizations to interview. Lastly, those women who joined the resistance from rural areas and who also survived the postwar repression are not well represented in the sample, partly, as mentioned, because their families lacked the resources to pay lawyers or the means to help them escape to other parts of Greece after the war. Many active peasant women were killed or silenced during the period when resistance participation became official anathema. They are also underrepresented because traveling into the mountain villages to do interviews is both time-consuming and methodologically problematic. In many areas public opinion is still deeply divided on the subject of the Civil War. The lack of anonymity afforded respondents thus would have affected the data in difficult-to-assess ways, as interviewees might be inclined to "fight the Civil War all over again." Thus, for pragmatic reasons, a slate of rural villages was not included on my interview schedule.

Family socioeconomic class and political orientation deserve special mention, since they contradict some of the usual expectations and support others. Only the relatively few women in the rightist organizations came from a unitary class background. In my sample, all were from the upper class. As Linda Reif (1986) claims for some Latin American resistance movements, the class base of the women in the EAM was not always predictable. Some could be called working class, but there was also a significant upper-class presence. Most of my EAM informants, as noted, were from the middle and professional classes. It is also important to keep in mind that Greek class structure differs somewhat from West European, peasant-subsistence, or even other Balkan formations. The petty bourgeoisie, consisting of small shopkeepers and merchants, is overrepresented in the Greek economy, and remittances from abroad have long played a major role in keeping the domestic economy afloat. The industrial sector has remained small and weak, and the economy has traditionally been supported by a large number of middlemen and tradesmen. "My father was a merchant," *emboros,* was the phrase I heard most often when I asked about fathers' occupations. *Emboros* can mean shopkeeper, merchant, traveling salesman, tradesman, middleman. Other common occupations of fathers were building contractor, civil servant, bank president or employee, and farmer.

Moreover, because clientelism functions in a depoliticizing way, self-interest should have made these groups the least likely to be spurred to protest by economic dissatisfaction. In fact, according to Gramsci and other observers of the social bases of fascism, the middle bourgeoisie proved especially vulnerable to fascist appeals in Germany, Italy, and indeed throughout Europe. Their presence in the resistance also counters the notion that peasants, the "have-nots," are the group most likely to revolt to protest unfair conditions. As Joel Migdal observes, "The participation of peasants in revolutionary organizations is preceded by the development of an organizational superstructure by students, intellectuals, and disaffected members of the middle class" (1974, 232).

On the issue of political exposure, Donatella della Porta (1988) and others have found that young participants in such movements are often from families that have exhibited a consistent political orientation, usually communist or leftist. Although della Porta's work concerns a more recent era, her claim is logically relevant to past as well as present examples. Evidence from the oral histories of participants in this movement, however, is paradoxical on this question. First, for the women I talked to, membership in the EAM was almost always the first independent political activity, besides voting, undertaken by any member of the family, including prior Communist party affiliation. Exceptions were one woman whose father was active in the tobacco workers' union in Kavalla; two painters who had moved to Athens from their villages and had joined the party before the war, one as a university student, the other as a bank employee; and one woman from Thebes whose older brothers had joined a Communist party labor union in Athens. This finding is in keeping with Hondros's estimation that

> the KKE's control of EAM/ELAS was played down and not generally known inside Greece until the spring of 1943. As late as March 23, the SOE reported to London that, although the KKE dominated EAM/ELAS, the rank and file were not communist. . . . The actual number of Communists in EAM/ELAS is in dispute. Those who argued that the actual power of the KKE was limited, claiming that the Communists made up an insignificant total of the overall membership, have found support in the German records. . . . The GFP claimed that only twelve of . . . fifty-two [members of an EAM group in the Peloponnese belonged to] the KKE, a low estimate when one remembers that the Germans labeled as a communist anyone who opposed them. This analysis indicates that approximately twenty-five percent of the leadership in the Peloponnese was communist. (1983, 119)

A second puzzle contained in this sample is the mixed political background of the female participants in the EAM. Parents were as often staunch monarchists as republicans or Venizelists. Quite a few of the women were from politically "mixed" marriages, in which the mother's background was royalist and archconservative and the father voted liberal; or the mother's background was Venizelist and the father supported the conservatives or the fascist regime. Fathers were often labeled "progressive" (*prodheftikos*) by their daughters. In such cases, progressive could have several meanings: progressive when it came to the value of education and to the role of women in society; progressive politically, by this the former EAM members obviously meant "leftist" (but possibly conservative to reactionary about what girls should do in life); or that as teenagers the women felt especially close to and emotionally supported by their fathers.

The testimonies show that parents were usually not members of the organizations, although some helped in neighborhood soup kitchens. Apparently many parents were inspired by their children's resistance work, however. Respondents frequently claimed that during the course of the war their parents "became more leftist than us" or otherwise changed their more conventional orientations.

All respondents felt that resistance activity changed their lives. This apparent congruity seems to show that in the Greek context the resistance, at least among my sample, was in fact a vehicle for change in women's perceptions of themselves. Not only was the EAM the largest organization, but it had also made the mobilization and consciousness-raising of women part of its formal strategy, evident in the strikingly national level of coordination, recruitment, and member socialization. Validation for the claim that the resistance was a movement whose aim was to introduce Greek society to the phenomenon of women's political participation, and confirmation that a more general revolution in social values was under way, lies in assessing the experiences of EAM's female membership.

Women and the EAM

Four questions organize my analysis. First, what was the initial starting point in terms of women's status in Greek society? It is, I think, quite possible to generalize about the political climate for women during the decade preceding the German invasion in 1941. Through oral histories and secondary anthropological evidence, we can speculate about the kind of life girls born in the 1930s might have looked forward to as adolescents, teenagers, and adults had it not been for this cataclysmic event.

Second, based on my sample, who were the women and girls taking part in the resistance, and how did they join? As might be expected, family reaction to the initial decision to join was often negative. Parents, especially, tended to greet the prospect with great trepidation. As the resistance progressed, however, the testimonies indicate that parents displayed some variability on this issue.

Third, why were large numbers of women mobilized? The three explanatory dimensions that have emerged from the oral histories are organization, timing, and the ideological antecedents of the key players in the drama: the last encompassing the EAM leadership versus that of the smaller rightist organizations; parents and their capacity to change; and, not least, the then young women, now in their sixties and seventies, who were the most active.

Finally, what were the discernible results? As Bert Klandermans and Sidney Tarrow note, "In the formation of mobilization potentials, movement organizations must win attitudinal and ideological support. . . . In arousing motivations to participate, they must favorably influence the decisions of people who are reached by a mobilization attempt. In removing barriers, they must increase the probability that people who are motivated will eventually participate" (1988, 10). To what degree can it be said that the resistance fulfilled its mobilization potential? Often, women's mobilization into resistance movements, war, and revolution is viewed pessimistically. Women are seen as pawns in a game that they have no hope of winning once the state of emergency is over. According to this view, male dominance is so firmly entrenched in the structure of politics and society that even if women join the fight, suffer along with the men, and sacrifice enthusiastically, ultimately their participation wins them no concessions and their spirits are destroyed by the backlash.

However valid their claims, such analyses run the risk of ignoring the voices of the women themselves, failing to allow participants to contribute to the discourse about participation based on their own experiences.[8] Unless we discount the concept of articulated experience entirely or accept a notion of false consciousness, my interviews raise the possibility that despite the pervasiveness of patriarchy, women do not always believe they are, so to speak, mobilized in vain. The women I spoke with experienced profound alterations in their self-perceptions and, in many cases, their life courses. Unfailingly, I emerged from the interviews deeply moved by the powerful and irreversible impression that the resistance had left on each woman's life. Thus, as a young writer friend of French intellectual Henri Massis summarized the effect of World War I on his own "sacrificed generation," the women that I interviewed would surely all have concluded that "We shall live our entire lives with what we have done during this war" (Wohl 1979, 17).

What Will People Say?: The Social and Institutional Contexts

> The moment the Germans left Vaphe with our operator, Elpida quickly took the wireless and the other incriminating things a little way off, and hid them; conducting herself, although she was a woman, with all the sense and coolness of a brave man.

> But the one he had most enjoyed writing, he said, was an anti-feminist poem satirizing the women who, during the previous particularly bitter winter, had worn men's trousers to protect themselves from the cold when engaged in olive picking in the fields.
>
> —Psychoundakis 1955, 91, 7

The essential features of the sociopolitical environment for women at the beginning of the war can, I think, be made plain by means of the Weberian device of ideal-typical description. As Max Weber himself pointed out, to describe what is typical is not to deny "real-life" exceptions. Certainly there were Greek women and girls who for some reason were exempted from the stylized rules of conduct, but exceptions were relatively few in number. Most Greeks born female in the early twentieth century shared a texture of experi-

[8] See personal testimonies in Randall 1981; Gluck 1987; Rossiter 1986; Saywell 1985; Laska 1983.

ence which cut across major social divisions such as region and socioeconomic class. Pushed too far, the concept of the ideal-type tends to caricature complex reality, but it is nonetheless useful in capturing salient features of the landscape that will later on explain so much. I suggest regarding the ideal-type as a culturally shared *narrative* relevant for significant numbers of people. In the domain of collective memory, then, the idea is that when asked to tell a tale of their life circumstances, many emplot their story in the following way.

Before 1940 a plurality of Greek women were effectively confined to the domestic sphere. The dominant narrative has the Greek woman spending most of her time in the house, preparing meals, watching children, cleaning, and supervising young family members as they scrub various parts of the house. A clean house was particularly important. Neighbors, friends, and in-laws would judge wifely success on how clean the house was should they have reason to visit. Failure as a homemaker would elicit gossip and reflect badly on husbands and on all who carried the family name.

The scenarios that would legitimately allow a woman to spend any significant time in public were limited. Thus, a female person could be sighted in Habermas's "realm of our social life in which something approaching public opinion can be formed" (1974, 49) when:

(1) helping in the family fields or the family store. It was very much in her interest to be cautious with male fieldworkers or customers unless related by blood, for any hint of flirting or misconduct could elicit gossip and lead to the possible ruination of the family. Trifling with the family reputation and honor were the suicidal prerequisites to sure tragedy.

(2) engaged in specific duties required to sustain the family, such as taking food to be baked in the public oven, going to the neighborhood well, or buying bread. During the course of these errands, behavior that might be deemed as "loitering" was not tolerated. "Unmarried girls on an errand," writes John Campbell, "should walk briskly. Those who habitually loiter on corners, and look around, endanger their reputations" (1983, 201).

(3) chaperoned by a male member of the immediate household. For girls, the sole chartered path ran from the school to the house. Brothers and fathers with any self-respect or sense of duty knew that it was their job to accompany girls of marriageable age, whose most valuable resource and ergo their greatest vulnerability lay in their reputations. A tarnished reputation could easily render meaningless the worth of any dowry.

To be sure, exceptions to this stringent moral code of honor did exist. For example, there were women teachers before the war. This profession, however, did not guarantee a warm reception when a woman crossed over into the public realm. One observer tells of overhearing a man refer to teachers traveling on a train in the 1930s as *adhespota koritsia* (masterless girls), employing the same adjective applied to stray dogs. This derisive term for women who were morally out-of-bounds was well precedented and indicative of the chilling atmosphere for those venturing freely into the public sphere.

When, in April 1941, Axis troops invaded Greece, Greek women had virtually no citizenship rights. They could not vote. Only a small percentage of girls expected to finish secondary school, to attend a university, or to take a job. Moreover, in the countryside, where nearly three-fourths of the population lived at the time, many women (and men) were illiterate. Consistently, women and girls were isolated by an intense system of social control which, as mentioned earlier, seldom allowed them to venture outside their homes unchaperoned and without a specific mission duly sanctioned by custom. Under a classical patriarchal arrangement, which held sway in urban neighborhoods and rural villages alike, the father was legal and customary head of the household and had the authority to rule the premises like a king. On the subject of paternal rule, for example, Marion Sarafis comments that "Sarafis told me that in his youth in Trikala a man was acquitted of raping a girl because she was illegitimate, in other words, 'no man's property.'"

Nuclear family males—brothers and fathers—were in charge of protecting a girl's honor in the community by judiciously keeping her from falling prey to her "baser instincts" and by helping to amass a dowry sufficient to relieve the family of one of its most serious burdens. Widows and women without a man were treated as pariahs, to be avoided and pitied. Gossip and family reputation were highly effective social sanctions in the Greek context. These weapons could be wielded viciously and produce serious consequences. The words *Ti tha pei o kosmos?* (What will people say?) still govern social interactions in many settings and inspire fear. In the 1930s these social regulations were far less flexible than they are today, and were fairly uniform from Athens and Salonika to Sparta and Lamia to the tiny mountain villages of Roumeli and Thessaly. Equally plain is the social fact that no protest movement of any magnitude had materialized.

If the male-dominated social and legal systems excluded women, so too did the political system. On a structural level, women's political exclusion was perfectly obvious. But, just as important, on an ideological level, women were politically discounted. The Greek political system was based on well-entrenched clientelism.[9] Patron-client networks not only supplemented the more formal institutional structures, they also replaced them in remote areas of the country. This method of political exchange excluded those not in a position to grant or to seek favors, or to accrue the political "currency" necessary for participation. As a system of barter between politicians and families, clientelism made politics an almost exclusively male domain, since only the head of

[9] See Tarrow 1967; Weingrod 1968; Lemarchand and Legg 1972; Kaufman 1974; Mouzelis 1978.

the family, a man, could represent it in the political arena. For one thing, it was necessary to command sufficient respect in the community to give weight to promises and threats. This premise was related to the concept of "*timi*," or honor, which had culturally different expressions for men and women. Men displayed their inherent *timi* or *filotimo* (uncompromising loyalty to close friends and family) by the manner in which they represented their families in the outside society.[10] Thus, men were judged by their external conduct. Women's *timi*, on the other hand, was directed inward and depended on how roles were fulfilled within the family. A woman venturing out in public was expected to conduct herself with *dhropi* (shame) and *semnotita* (modesty), so as not to invite the "derision by society of the males (of the extended family), who (were) incapable of controlling her" (Pollis 1980, 10).[11] Thus, feminine honor, as defined by society, did a woman no good outside the home.

Furthermore, the places where politics were conducted were off limits to women. For example, many political deals were concluded in the kafeneion, or neighborhood coffeehouse, where women were tacitly forbidden to set foot. Other connections were made through the schools, but girls, especially in rural areas, often stayed in school only as long as the family thought necessary, and secondary schools were not coeducational until years after the war. Men made vital contacts in the workplace too. Women employed in the large number of family-run businesses were usually not salaried per se, and industrial working women were not the politically significant (or potentially threatening) force they had long been in other countries such as Germany or Britain.

As stated earlier, there was a profound adherence in Greek society to maintaining the honorable public image that would check the possibility of humili-

---

[10] " 'Timi' expresses the idea of worth," says Campbell, "whether this is an economic value in a market, or social worth evaluated in a complex of competing groups and individuals" (1964, 268). Also see Du Boulay 1974; and for a notably complex interpretation, Herzfeld 1983. Adamantia Pollis defines *filotimo* as "the dominant Greek value; it integrates all other values and norms, defines appropriate behaviour both toward other group members and toward foreigners (*kseni*). . . . Functionally, *filotimo* and individual integrity are comparable. Whereas in the West individuals are evaluated as to whether they possess integrity, in Greece they are judged as to whether they possess *filotimo*. The difference lies in that integrity refers to the consistency of an individual's behaviour with his self-definition as an autonomous individual, whereas *filotimo* refers to the consistency of an individual's behaviour with his assigned role as an integral part of a greater entity, and with the preservation of the public image this demands. Behaviour which violates *filotimo* brings shame upon the individual and hence upon his membership groups" (1965, 34–35).

[11] See the now-controversial Peristiany 1965. Also see the very interesting Safilios-Rothschild 1968. Jane Schneider writes: "The repository of family and lineage honor, the focus of common interest among the men of the family or lineage, is its women. A woman's status defines the status of all the men who are related to her in determinate ways. These men share the consequences of what happens to her, and share therefore the commitment to protect her virtue. She is part of their patrimony" (1971, 18). This general cultural schema was certainly resonant during the modern period, even if postmodern culture has brought with it new wrinkles.

ating ostracism. Community memory was extremely long. This meant that women's behavior was organized around a set of closely enforced ethical standards. Actual breaches of proper behavior were dangerous in their own right, but the most serious offenses were those that became known to the immediate community and thus gave members of the out-group—especially those who were not part of the immediate family—an opportunity to publicly mock that individual and by extension, the entire family. Shame, as Constantina Safilios-Rothschild points out, is the obverse of honor, the sanction for its loss: "Honour, as the core of one's essence representing one's masculine or feminine integrity, is the prevalent value. . . . Closely connected with honour is the concept of shame: an individual usually feels ashamed when [she or he] is dishonoured in the eyes of . . . friends and the community at large" (1969, 205).

Safilios-Rothschild also argued that the class dimension was salient in that "member(s) of the upper class or the power echelons of the society" were to a degree exempted from having to conform to the so-called honor-shame behavioral code. Using a sample of 197 cases from the newspaper *Kathimerini*, she posited that those most likely to engage in crimes of honor came from lower-middle and peasant strata. While bourgeois women probably had other channels available to redress their grievances, my oral histories nevertheless reveal that earlier in the century women from a variety of circumstances, including the upper and middle classes, oriented their lives around *timi* in its feminine expression and appeared to feel the ubiquity of social confinement and powerlessness. Moreover, vulnerability to problems of health and sexuality, arbitrary suppression by fathers and brothers, and relentless social restrictions were recurrent themes in many of the women's life histories when they talked about the time before and just after the German invasion. And as we shall see, in some worlds honor killings were an accepted way of adjudicating moral and legal problems.

The most vivid accounts of what life was like for Greek women and girls during the pre-war period are those expressed in their own words. For example, Despina, who grew up in a mountain village between Karpenissi and Lamia in central Greece, organized the young women in her village into an EPON unit and coordinated support services for the ELAS partisans fighting in the area. She describes the atmosphere for women through a series of anecdotes:

> One time in the village, a kid from our village married a girl from another village. We went to the wedding. He received all the goods that were coming to him—sheep, cash, dowry, five or six mules and horses loaded with wool clothing, with place-settings, everything. . . . Eh, we danced and celebrated until the morning and the next day we learned that the marriage had been

dissolved. Why was it dissolved? Because the groom didn't find "proof of virginity." In those days, the first night that the couple slept together, the woman would wear a gown that went from her chin to her ankles. . . . with the first contact, there is supposed to be blood, right? If the garment isn't stained, that meant the girl wasn't O.K. The next morning, the bride was supposed to bring the gown to her mother-in-law, to show her that all was well. If there was no such proof, the bride wasn't honorable [*timia*]. That's what honor [*timiotita*] was, it wasn't what she had or hadn't done! So the next morning, they threw the girl out and her clothes behind her, they sent her back to the village.

Now, I'm telling you this so we can see the development [*i ekseliksi*) that occurred. Another girl, very beautiful, a village girl, she lived in the village with her mother and brother. . . . her father had gone to America, as used to happen then, for "better fortune" [*kaliteri tihi*]. Another family, cattle breeding, with two boys. The one worked on the farm; the other was very clever and they sent him to study law. He was a wonderful boy, clever, handsome. . . . he and she fell in love, had an affair, everyone in the village knew it . . . but when he finished his studies, to get his diploma he needed some money, and suddenly he became engaged to another girl, a higher-class family, that is, not a local peasant girl like Evanthia was, with her kerchief on her head and her hair in a bun. . . . so, after about a month, one evening, Evanthia . . . as the lawyer was sitting in the square with his friends, under the plane tree . . . there was a road that went up from the school to the back of the square and Evanthia slowly crept up it and BAM! killed the lawyer. Of course, there was a funeral. Like a dream I remember it. They threw his books on top of his coffin and everyone cried because he was such a popular boy, but no one blamed Evanthia at all.[12] Because, I mean, the girl was ruined; if she hadn't killed him, no other man would've married her and she would've been considered unfit, tainted. She had to establish her honor [*i timi tis*] somehow, you see? For ethical reasons, reasons of honor. She was sentenced to three to four years in jail; of course, someone else had given her the pistol she used, a relative, and no attempt was made to hide that. She stayed five or six years in jail, got out, and got married, a nice guy, he had good circumstances in life, had studied, etc. If she hadn't killed the other one, no one else would've come along and married her. Do you see how things were then, the question of morals? So that's why I say, it was very difficult to organize the women in the villages, all those things existed and were very real, customs, superstitions, "preventions" [*prolipseis*], prejudices [*prokatalipseis*].

---

[12] Safilios-Rothschild mentions that "a woman killing her lover because he broke his marriage promise and abandoned her after having sexual relations is usually acquitted" (1969, 215).

Despina's mother had eight children, four of whom perished at birth. She gave a grisly account of the death of one of her siblings in 1915, which happened, she felt, "because of women's condition then":

I'll tell you about a situation my mother experienced. It was the season when they sowed the wheat fields. My mother was in her last month of pregnancy. The fields they were working in were about an hour and a half to two hours away. They loaded up a pair of mules with feed and also food for themselves because they would have to spend about a week out there. So, they left. They had a shelter, a little hut where they stored their things. They worked the next day, my father with the pair of mules and my mother following behind, gathering up the wheat. They were working the next day when it started to rain, in the afternoon. They ran for the shelter. It was fairly crude, not really waterproof, so that they got soaking wet. My mothers labor pains started. Night fell. They were forced to make a decision. They lit a small fire, and tried to dry their feet, they took off the clogs they were wearing, and their socks and tried somehow to dry off. But finally they decided to leave and try to make it back to the village. They were on the road back and the weather had cleared a bit (it was still raining but not as hard) and suddenly the baby dropped. At that time, people wore clogs, not the kind made of wood, but the sort made of pig hide. When they slaughtered the pigs, they would dry the hides and make them into rough shoes. So what with going up and down hills and the rain, it was very slippery and they struggled on their way, falling and sliding. Of course on some of the steep hills it was even worse for a woman about to give birth with her fallen stomach in front of her. They arrived back at the house around midnight. My grandmother got up, lit the lamps, and sent someone to fetch the midwife. So the midwife arrived, and the baby began to come, but feet first, in a breech position. Outside it was raining, pitch-dark, how were you going to find a doctor, or even a friend to help out in this emergency under those conditions? So the midwife had to deliver the baby. So she was slowly pulling the baby out by the feet and it got up to the neck and got stuck. My father was holding on to my mother from the top end and the midwife was tugging at the baby, trying to get it out from the bottom. You can imagine the torturous pain my mother was in. The situation really called for a doctor. Finally, from all the strain of pulling, the body became detached from the head, that is, the baby's body fell out and the head stayed in the stomach. And we children witnessed the whole thing, because we were older. It was very scary. Of course she was weak from the pain, she was covered in blood, and suffered so much. It was a terrible experience, but the sort of thing that happened to women then. They were helpless. That is, this was the kind of tragic situation many women found themselves in at that time, that is, around the time of World War I, 1915, 1918, 1920. So in some way or another four died, as I told you, the one that way, another right after birth, two others born dead.

On a lighter note, Despina recalled the political atmosphere during her childhood and remembers with humor overhearing a conversation between her father and a neighbor:

After around 1918, 1920, people started to get a better perspective [*o kosmos arhize kapos na vlepei pio makria*]. That is, when I say people, I mean some of the men, who were literate [*pou'kseran opos ipame pende grammata*]. For instance, some of them had gone into the army and there they heard various things about the world, you know, within the confines of the army and all. What I mean to say is that after the revolution that occurred in the Soviet Union and the first socialist state was created, some people started to view the future differently, let's say, to understand their place in society. I mean some of the people in the villages (who ordinarily wouldn't have been exposed to such things). I'm telling you this as an example of what you were asking me about the political position of women.

I remember an example. Once, as a little girl, I was on my way back from school one afternoon, and my father was mending shoes in a corner shed next to our house. He was sitting there at the little bench—it was wintertime—and one of our neighbors was keeping him company. They were sitting there, and the neighbor said to my father, "Eh, Thanassi, I—what can I do, I have four daughters, how am I going to marry them off when they grow up?" (They used to say "you have two daughters and two children" if you had two girls and two boys. Girls didn't count as children.) And you know how kids always have big ears when grown-ups are talking. They're always trying to listen in on adult conversations! [laughing] And my father said to him, "Listen, Panayioti, don't worry. When your daughters are grown, things will have changed. The [Soviet] 'bear' will come down from above and change things and you won't need to make dowries for them anymore." And I thought to myself, "How strange. Who is this bear, and why won't there be dowries anymore?" [laughing] So after the neighbor had left, I asked my father, "Father, why did you say to Barba that a bear would come? What bear?" And he said, "You have no business hiding, listening in on grown-up conversations. You're little and you should study. When you grow up, you'll learn and then you'll understand. Now you're little." And as I grew up, I thought more about it all and was able to figure it out from talking to my brothers, who didn't live in the village, the one was a shoemaker but he was very clever, and the other even managed to finish high school, so they knew a thing or two; so, from various conversations with my brothers and cousins, whatever, eventually I figured out who the bear was and why she would abolish dowries! [laughing]

As an adolescent, Maria was a founding member of an EPON unit and later spent fourteen years in jail for her part in the resistance. She was from the medium-sized town of Kozani, considered the "capital" of western Macedonia because of its strategic position as the major railway stop in that region on the route to Salonika. Regarding the status of women, she commented,

> In the old days in the villages, it was considered shameful [*itan dhropi*] for a woman to work. They would say to you, "You don't have any money to live and that's why you put your daughter to work!" It was an embarrassment. And besides that, for the most part they never sent them to school. You would know how to read, count, and write, and that was enough. Then they'd say, "Get back in the house, to wash the dishes and sweep the floor." That was the role of the woman.

Lilika, the daughter of a tailor from Chania, Crete, and former member of an EPON unit, described the bounded world of an average Greek girl:

> At that time there wasn't . . . women couldn't really go outside much, we couldn't be out at night, no, no . . . but after the resistance, and with what it had created, the woman came out of her house. That is, before, in the house, you had to always be in the house; for girls, our path ran only between school and the house. If we were going somewhere, we would go with our father, with our brother; we weren't even allowed to go anywhere in a group, do you understand? And the married woman: in the house. Neither work nor any wandering around was tolerated. There were women who were teachers, but they were few before the occupation.

Tasoula's family was originally from Izmir (then Smyrna), Turkey. She grew up in a neighborhood largely inhabited by Asia Minor refugees in Greece's second largest city, Salonika (Thessaloniki). According to her, "My mother wasn't like my father. The one I really feared was my father, because our taboos [*ta tabou mas*] still basically meant that they didn't let girls go around freely, unchaperoned, especially in the evenings. It was very conservative." Tasoula participated in a EPON-sponsored theater group right after liberation. Her answer to the question of whether there were girls in the group sheds light both on the politics of immigration and of gender in the prewar period:

> Yes, yes, our parents let us because they were all progressive. They were all among those who had come as refugees and they were very progressive peo-

ple, the refugees [*oi prosfeeges*].[13] They could all read and write, whereas when they came here they found the people much more backward, you understand? They were all very broad-minded; they enjoyed cultural pursuits and other progressive things; they thought learning was important. But they couldn't do much about the various taboos that already existed; they were forced to go along with what everyone else wanted and expected and that meant, and I'm ashamed to admit it, the gossip that was common in smaller areas. You know, that the daughter of so-and-so was no good anymore because she did something she shouldn't have. And the worst part of it was that they didn't really have any idea what morality was, what was ethical and what wasn't. They thought that when a girl went with a boy, that it was unethical. If that girl stole something, it wasn't unethical. If she told a lie, if someone committed a crime, it wasn't considered unethical. If the person was able to hide what they did, it was best and they weren't punished for it. And the girls weren't allowed to go outside. Even the girl who had a bit of freedom, like me, . . . would have problems, because, for example, I was a swimmer, I was something of an athlete. I even placed first in a contest. I hid the newspaper because they wrote something about me and I was afraid my parents would see it and punish me for embarrassing the family.

Eleni was raised in a small village outside of Githio in the Laconia region of the Peloponnese, and later became an EPON regional representative. Since there was no high school in her village, her mother braved the reactions of her husband and the other villagers and rented a room in Githio so that Eleni could attend high school. When asked about the response to this unconventional arrangement, she commented:

Look, my father was quite progressive in his views, that is, his ideas were progressive in a general sense. Because inside the house he was a very bad husband, a tyrant. My mother lived a very tortured existence, that is, oppressed. He beat her; he abused her; he drank. He was a very clever man, but he was frustrated. And since he wasn't able to accomplish what he wanted and was capable of in life, like, I don't know what, studying, or whatever, he took the easiest way out, that is, pounding on my mother [*na kopanaei ti mana mou*], and he would take his disappointments out on her. So, from one standpoint, my father was very progressive. He was an atheist, for example. In that sense he had very liberal views. But from another point of view, my

---

[13] In 1922 a population exchange was arranged with Turkey and approximately a million and a half ethnic Greek refugees residing in Asia Minor were repatriated. The Asia Minor refugees were said to be a "cut above average" in education and cosmopolitan taste. The issue of the refugees was a very loaded one and the source of ongoing, but for the most part nonviolent, communal conflict.

mother, because she herself was a very intelligent woman, she didn't want me to have go through the torment that she experienced, especially since I was the only girl (I had four younger brothers). So because of all that, with a thousand tribulations, with a thousand deprivations, with her working night and day, not even having shoes to wear sometimes, she sent me to school, to the *gymnasio* in town, because it was really a big thing then, a girl going to school, and the villagers, the other villagers would laugh and would say to her, "You have no brains, you fool [*dhen eheis mialo*], that you want to send your daughter to school." Because the high school wasn't even in the village; it was three hours away, in Githio, and so we rented a place and I stayed there with my mother coming and going and two of my brothers. But the point is that my mother so believed in the cause, that is, that I shouldn't be subjected to the same kind of existence, she said to herself, "I'll go through anything so that my daughter won't have to live the same life as I did." So for us, there were those two types of influences coming from home.

Eleni also discussed the status of women in rural Greece in more general terms,

I was born in a village in the Mani [southwestern Peleponnese] where the moral standards [*ta ithi*] were very severe. Of course, all over Greece the position of women was desperate and hopeless [*i thesi tis yinekas itan ap-elpistiki*], but in the Mani the situation was really terrible. We had honor killings; that is, they would actually kill girls who were not virgins, who had had extramarital or premarital sexual relations. Oh yes, definitely. It was a special problem in areas like the Mani. Women had no say on family matters and even inside the house. The husband was the boss.

It is often assumed that the urban environment afforded women and girls more freedom of movement than village life. In many ways, however, city neighborhoods functioned in much the same way as villages, with the fundamental mechanisms of social control embodied in the dreaded phrase "What will people say?"[14] Anna was from a wealthy family. "My father was one of the most well known merchants in Piraeus," she said. As a teenager she smuggled weapons for the tiny right-wing resistance organization RAN.

[14] Supplementing the legal and social constraints on women were a number of cultural notions originating from a mixture of mythology, tradition, and Orthodox religion, some of which were long-entrenched features of social and political discourse about women. Accordingly, women were seen as unreliable, irresponsible, and like Eve, easily seduced if left to their own devices. Females were thought to be most efficient and trustworthy when fulfilling their responsibilities within the home, in spite of evidence that in many rural areas, women labored under the "double burden" of maintaining both the house and the family fields. See Friedl 1962; Du Boulay 1974; Dubisch 1986. For an interesting comparison, see "On More Responsibilities for Women," Athens, fourth century B.C., Plato, *Republic* 5, and "Men and Women Should be Treated Alike," Plato, *Laws* 6, in Lefkowitz and Fant 1982, 66–75.

My parents didn't know about my activity, and I hid all my documents in my grandmother's drawer under her underwear. She was blind, and couldn't hear too well and my parents almost never checked her room. My parents often said, "A girl should be tended like a hothouse flower," and that's exactly how I felt, because in the beginning they wouldn't let the girls in our school go out into the yard. They had us on a veranda which was surrounded by glass and we weren't allowed to leave this enclosure. So for me it was an extension of what my parents always said, that I really was locked in this protected little green-house, on the veranda with glass! I think now, looking back, that my greatest resistance was not on the streets of Athens, but at home.

These passages reveal that Greek women of various backgrounds faced a dearth of choices in life under the patriarchal ancien régime that modernist reformers hoped to challenge and restructure. Under the circumstances, to defy the social order would have amounted to a highly irrational act for most girls and women, and in fact, in only a few families was participation in any organized feminist activity possible at all. Thus, it becomes clearer why the nationalist resistance movement was able to provide an alternative and why so many girls were receptive to its appeals.

Enlisting, Reactions, and the Scope of Activities

Recruitment

As we have seen, women's primary allegiance was to the family as embedded in a more extensive system of social control existing in villages and neighbor-hoods all over Greece. In this regard the public and the private spheres func-tioned in tandem to define the boundaries of suitable behavior. Indeed, women had few other countervailing sources of moral authority in the prewar period. To the extent that the legal system dealt with women at all, it rein-forced this informal, yet universally understood code of law by transposing everyday conduct into practices acceptable to the very harshest critics, the neighbors and *o kosmos*. How, then, did the women and girls whose lives were so circumscribed before the war come to join the resistance? How did their families, as the standard-bearers of patriarchal ethics, react? Finally, what kinds of things did women actually do in the resistance?

Female members of social movement organizations are generally recruited in two ways. In her study on the recruitment of Italian terrorists, Donatella della Porta has demonstrated that members of the extremist brigades, espe-cially women, are linked by strong previous affective ties to neighbors, family members, or school friends (1988, 158). Affective recruitment was relatively common in Greece, too, partly because resistance organizations are by nature subversive and engage in clandestine activities.

Martien Briet, Bert Klandermans, and Frederike Kroon (1987) point out another plausible scenario. They say that the women who became involved in the feminist movement in the Netherlands in the 1970s frequently joined through the organizations formed by the political parties or the labor unions to which these women belonged. They also emphasize the importance of face-to-face contacts and the expansion of what Luther Gerlach and Virginia Hine call a "fishnet structure" arising from smaller, private meetings in women's homes and women's groups within community centers, as sites of micro-mobilization. Although these authors are directly concerned with movements that grew out of the second wave of the women's movement in the late 1960s, the patterns they isolate are also relevant to the case of the women who joined the Greek resistance and to women who became active in other "old social movements" such as the labor movements in various countries.

Essentially women and girls joined the EAM in two ways. Some were recruited through contacts originating in the private sphere, through the kinds of relations cited by della Porta and others. Yet, in the kind of modern party system the EAM meant to create (as we can see from Glinos's pamphlet), personal contacts were not the only route to participation. Some women were directly recruited by the organization itself, at public meetings or other gatherings arranged specifically to attract members to the *aghona* (the struggle). These kinds of meetings were a more common method of recruitment among peasant women, and in the countryside tended to occur when ELAS (the resistance army), EA (the relief organization) or the Theater of the Mountains passed through the village or neighborhood. The local EAM representative would often sign up whole families, giving some legitimacy to the idea that female family members might participate if their male relatives also participated. In addition, some rural widows, like Kazantzakis's tormented character in *Zorba the Greek,* as well as other "low-status" individuals, would unilaterally join the organization to escape pervasive ridicule and economic strife.

Examples of typical recruitment methods can be seen in the following interview passages.

Athens (family/school friends):

> Of course, the guide, the natural guide [*o fisikos odhigos*] for my own ideological direction, was my brother, who was then twenty-nine years old. And a couple of years before the occupation, both from books and from certain friendships, he had adopted leftist ideas. And from talking with him at home—I adored him then (and I still do)—all this affected me very much. He would give me books to read, by Marx, or the Tao, or books by Gorky, and so on the heels of those, my first steps to awareness, came the occupation. That is, my brother had primed me; I had been

prepared. I was first approached by some friends at school, because then all the girls went to separate schools and I went to the neighborhood girls' school. So, one day during recess, some of the older girls from two classes above me, called me over and said if I wanted to, I could help out in the resistance. And I said that I definitely wanted to, and they gave me a code name and so I joined the organization anonymously.

Rethymno, Crete (women's meetings sponsored by the organization):

I was an EPON liaison with the partisans who had been arrested and taken to jail by the Germans. Eventually I had to go into hiding. They hid me in town at different houses for a month or so, and then they couldn't hide me much longer, so they took me to different villages and eventually to Koxare. Koxare happened to be my mother's village. There we would have meetings with the village women and we would talk about the resistance, about the role of EPON, about the role of EAM, and we would scrounge up food for the partisans. They were of all ages, old ones, young ones, in Koxare many women took part and helped to cook, because Koxare was very near the ELAS mountain headquarters in that part of the White Mountains. Very often we would cook food and take it up to the partisans. But there were some Germans there in Koxare and after a while I was under suspicion because I wasn't from the village; that is, my grandmother still lived there and had a house, but still, I was basically a foreigner in the village and couldn't stay around too long. So they took me to Selia to another house, owned by the Katsaragakis family. They kept me there for a month, and there along with the other EPON girls we did the same thing with the village women, we cooked for the partisans and at the same time we would talk about social and political themes, about the resistance. I stayed there a month or so, and from there I went to another village, to Kisso, and there I did the same thing.

Another important route to joining the organization was through the neighborhood soup kitchens which arose in the winter of 1941 at the height of the massive starvation caused by Nazi requisitioning of food supplies. These kitchens enabled the organization to get the attention of a wide range of women and also offered many women the chance to meet women from other class backgrounds for the first time.

The various means of recruitment are discernible in many of the testimonies, a strong indication of the importance of organization for Gramsci's "modern prince." What is important to note here is that though women and girls took a range of paths into the organizations, recruitment was coordinated nationally. In contrast, in Italy recruitment of women and girls into resistance organizations was generally confined to the northern section of the country. Many Italian participants, moreover, came from the ranks of the students and factory workers of Milan, Turin, and Florence.[15]

Parental Reactions

Little attention has been paid to family reactions to women's decisions to engage in collective action even though this dimension is vitally important, particularly for younger women.[16] Clearly, negative family reactions carry more weight whenever customary ties to family life, subordinate status within the family, and widespread kindred expectations that girls will someday produce their own families are most pronounced. Naturally, when families are supportive, participation is far easier. If families are reluctant and women must defy them, the personal cost of involvement in the cause is higher and the motivation must be compelling. Sometimes, too, women and girls involved in the kind of collective action that one woman called earlier "resistance at home" may have the opportunity to modify the collective identities of dissenting parents or other crucial family members, thus activating the mobilization potential of older generations.

Before the EAM was formed, families nearly always disapproved of resistance work for women. Notable exceptions were the women who carried supplies through the Pindos Mountains to Greek troups in Albania and the women and girls who participated in the Battle of Crete in May 1941. Once the EAM was founded, however, many Greek families who supported its goals were willing to entrust the organization with the family honor, and the women of these families faced fewer problems at home. Nevertheless, many girls testify to joining secretly, and those whose parents found out reported unpleasant scenes and shouting matches. Still, there was the potential that the parents might change their minds, and many girls foresaw far-reaching benefits that made it worthwhile to defy parental authority. One respondent, who grew up in a middle-class neighborhood in Athens, the daughter of a civil servant, told me:

> My parents didn't know. And, naturally, not all parents were in agreement with all this. First of all, because of the physical danger involved, they didn't want their children to get hurt, because of the enormous danger; and second, often their ideologies were conservative, they thought you

[15] The former Italian women partisans I talked with in Turin in December 1985, confirmed this assertion.
[16] An exception is Doug McAdam's informative discussion in *Freedom Summer,* especially "The Biographical Roots of Activism" (35–65).

should just sit there, put your head down, and wait for us all to be liberated at some vague point in the future. But my parents did find out later. They found out in the meantime. Within a year they had learned of our involvement (mine and my sisters). They learned of it because we had to go out to participate in the activities. They never let us go out alone at night—never. So we eventually had to tell them, and at first it was a huge battle, but later they understood that it was something we had to do, that it was for a good cause. In the beginning they made scenes, they yelled, they tried to keep us inside, but they soon realized that they couldn't really hold us back. And the same thing happened in many other families. More often, of course, with the girls, because for the girls, this was the way that they opened the doors and went outside. But they didn't sneak out fearing their parents; they went out for something that was practical, and heroic, and grand. So along with this effort aimed at national liberation, the female species also got on the road to women's liberation.

Another woman, from a wealthy suburb of the capital, the daughter of a bank vice-president, said:

My father supported the monarchy, but not necessarily the king personally or the people who constituted the royal family at the time . . . but then, King Constantine, when he had left, when he had come back . . . Greece had been divided in half, let's say, as Greece has always been divided in two. And at that time, the EAM, because I can't really say . . . the other organizations, the rightist ones, were much smaller in strength and number and most people went with EAM, and with EPON, which was for the young people . . . but all of that "sat on our heads like a hat." We weren't at all interested in either the names or who was behind all of it, and it was really by chance and circumstances that we ended up in that organization and not in another. But of course, we (me and my friends) were in support of the poor people, and those wronged by society, and we wanted a kind of social justice to reign. Therefore, there is really no doubt that we were of the Left. But at that time, they didn't know that communism was connected with EAM. That is, most people weren't communists in the least, they were simply what we call Left (*Aristeros*). *Aristeros,* what does that mean? That is to say, with a social conscience, for some kind of justice to exist [*dhikaosini*] that people should not be oppressed [*na mi iparhei katapiesmenoi anthropoi*] by people with more power. . . . Of course, we didn't really know much about the details, since we were very young, fifteen, sixteen, seventeen years old. What did we know about politics? . . . We were active only to show our dislike of the *kataktitis.* Naturally, we didn't tell our parents that we were in EPON because they would've been so worried for our safety, and that's why my father was so shocked when the Germans came and they knocked on our door at four in the morning, and then he said to them, "I am her father and please take me and not my daughter, who's just a little girl."

Activities

As I have said, most of my interviewees had joined the EPON youth group, whose activities were among the most dangerous of the entire resistance and involved: ferrying guns and messages to various neighborhoods where contacts waited to receive them, announcing meetings and demonstrations through bullhorns, writing slogans of protest and defiance on public walls, holding recruiting and strategy sessions at designated houses, publishing news bulletins gleaned from BBC broadcasts heard on forbidden radios, receiving training in special military units in order to take part in battles. Of note here is that the activities of girls and boys were basically the same, and they brought girls and boys into contact with one another for the first time. If scholars' assertions that mobilizing activities that take place during formative adolescent years are also the most indelible, then surely the experience of "sleeping in Panayioti A.'s arms, but just to keep warm," must have made a lasting impression. One woman commented: "Me and my sister, before the war, neither one of us would have *dared* invite a boy to our house, but during the occupation, we would often shelter men who were in danger, or we would hold secret meetings at our house and boys would be there, or we would go to other houses and have planning sessions with the boys."

The following excerpts from the body of oral histories I gathered offer a fairly comprehensive and detailed version of resistance activities and their meaning for participants from several perspectives. Each narrator emplots her story through a series of fabula, highlighting the symbolic importance of particular episodes. I encourage readers to let themselves be drawn in, as I was, by the existential drama and meaning of these tales.

When war was declared, Anthoula was twelve years old and attending school in Kypseli, a middle- and working-class Athens neighborhood. She joined an EPON cell. The Germans arrested her in 1944, took her to Merlin Prison, and tortured her for several weeks. Eventually, they sent her to Ravensbruck Concentration Camp, where she stayed until the area was liberated in 1945. When I interviewed her in 1985 she was working as an administrative assistant in an architectural office. Her testimony typifies aspects of the Athens experience.

My father was a civil servant [*dhimosios ipalilos*]. Politically, my father was a very intense man, who used to be a very enthusiastic monarchist. He

loved King Constantine! and the generalship! and all the pomp and circumstance that went along with the royal family. But as things began to
change, he became more democratic. He changed when the resistance
came along and he saw all his children join EAM. That's when he began
to change. . . .

Because automatically, the minute you confronted the same danger as a
boy, the minute *you also* wrote slogans on the walls, the moment *you also*
distributed leaflets, the moment you also attended protest demonstrations
along with the boys and some of you were *also* killed by the tanks, they
could no longer say to you, "You, you're a woman, so sit inside while I
go to the cinema." You gained your equality when you showed what you
could endure in terms of the difficulties, the dangers, the sacrifices, and all
as bravely and with the same degree of cunning as a man. Those old ideas
fell aside. That is, the resistance always tried to put the woman *next to* the
man, instead of behind him. She fought a double liberation struggle. And
of course this embraced many women. How would you put it? It moved
many women who somehow began to think about how things had been
for them.

Each section was assigned different activities based on what kind of section it was, what "space" it occupied, that is, and where you lived. They
did certain kinds of work in the villages, and another kind in the cities.
We were in the capital, in Athens. We were organized in the schools, the
girls first in Eleftheri Nea [Free Young Woman], and then when EPON
was created, we automatically went into EPON. And so we were in the
students' section. Our activities were, first, we would meet, secretly of
course, and the older ones would give us a political direction, that is, the
theme that we would focus on during that time, regarding exactly how
we would confront the occupiers. As the occupation progressed, we grew
more and more hungry because in the beginning they had taken all our
food. They had taken all our supplies. The first winter was absolutely
tragic. People were dying of hunger. We had neither wood to heat our
houses nor food to eat. The Nazis had taken all the food from the villages
and either used it themselves or sent it outside the country. In the capital,
where we didn't have fields or gardens, we suffered the most. And so we
saw our first dead bodies, but they were people who had starved to death.
The second year, however, things had changed. There were big
demonstrations, organized by EAM.

And . . . we also started, from the first months, to write slogans on
walls. That was the other responsibility of the young people. And of
course making announcements with the bullhorns [*me ta honakia*].[17] It

---

[17] Literally, "little cones." They were usually made of cardboard or other crude salvaged
materials. This was one of the girls' specialties because it was thought that their voices carried

was a lot easier for the young people to go out and do that kind of thing. Four kids would go out together; two would write and two would stand guard on the sidewalk. One of the team would write and the other would stand on the sidewalk, whistling a tune. When you heard that tune, it was a signal that someone was coming. You would stop and you would hide your brush and pail, and the girl and the boy would come close together and pretend that they were a couple in love, out on a walk. As soon as it was confirmed that the coast was clear, you began to write on the wall again. The people in the neighborhood who saw us from their houses wouldn't betray us, nor would they chase after us. Everyone agreed and worked together, there was a consensus, [*oloi itan simphonoi*].

I remember one morning . . . because we would go out very early in the morning; we had a curfew then. We had to be in by ten at night, and we were allowed to circulate again at six in the morning. But in order to write on the walls, without people around, the streets had to be deserted. So we had to write a half hour before the nighttime curfew, and a half hour before they were out and about in the morning. And it was very dangerous, because they could arrest you just for being outside. They were arresting people solely for that reason. And I remember, one morning I had knocked on a door because my paint had spilled, the door of a milkman who had to be up early to prepare the milk, and I saw that the door was open, and I knocked and said, "Could you give me a little water for my paint?" And he gave it to me. Of course he said to me, "They'll kill you! You shouldn't be doing this!" And I said, "Don't you worry about that. Please, sir, could you just put a little water in the pail?" [laughs] I was very determined! And so he gave me the water.

So—we wrote on walls. We spoke into the honakia. With the "trumpet" [*me ton tilevoa*]. You would go up on the Lofos tou Strefi, up on Likabettos Hill, into the neighborhood squares, and you would shout with the bullhorn, slogans that would give people courage or that would mobilize them [*pou tha tous sesikonoune*]; and when there were to be demonstrations, you would announce those demonstrations. Or you'd yell out slogans that would prepare the people for resistance; that is, some of the things you wrote on the walls, you would also shout into the *honi*. For instance, we had to announce the public soup kitchens. That kind of thing we would shout with the horns. Or we had to demand more bread than they were giving us or if a strike were going to happen. All those things we would shout into the horn.

---

better than the boys'. Also, girls were able move about the streets more freely. Shouting with the honakia was mostly done in Athens, where such clandestine activities could be carried out far more easily than in the villages, and where large groups of people were regularly solicited for street demonstrations.

The strikes during the occupation! They were really something [*itan kati to megaliodhes*]. Today's strikes don't even come close to the strikes during the occupation. They were spontaneous, huge, and general. They weren't the trade union type [*dhen itan sintekniakes*], that is, with such-and-such branch striking for the sake of its own demands. They were national strikes [*ethnikes apergies*]. Employees, greengrocers, shopkeepers, merchants, workers, students—everyone struck on the same day. Public transportation came to a screeching halt. Everyone, all the working people, the public utilities, everything. And the public, without any means of public transportation, all set out on foot at the same time to go to the gathering place [*sto meros tis synkendhrosis*]. At the gathering place, ten minutes before, there wasn't one soul. So that the place wouldn't be revealed [to the occupiers]. At the *exact* time, almost to the second, each team captain from the school divisions had gathered everyone together; students from one class on this corner; from another class on the next corner; and on the next, and so on. Very few people in the organization knew where the gathering was to take place, only those at the very top of the hierarchy, and at the last minute they would send the word out to the ones below them, and everyone would begin to descend through the streets to the place. They had been told minutes before, and they would all start to gather. This person would speak to them, and as soon as they got the signal, they would go toward the center of town [*bros tous kendhrikous dhromous*].

The demonstration against the "work mobilization" [*kata tin epistratevsi*]—when the Germans announced that they would send people up to Germany to work in the munitions factories and the quisling government here agreed to the plan—there was a *tremendous* demonstration, on the fifth of March, against the *epistratevsi*. That day, everyone came into the center of town to protest, they came from Exarheia;[18] they came down from Likourgou; they came from Kolonaki Square;[19] there were people there from all the different neighborhoods. There were about seven huge demonstrations during the occupation; I went to all of them. I was always with a very good friend of mine. She was one year younger than me, in the next lower grade in school, and we always went together, together and forward. She's actually still alive and well and is now living outside of Greece. It was very dangerous. Yes, she became an archaeologist.

Anyway, that day, I remember it like it happened today [*san tora*], walking down Pattission Avenue to the place where the march was to be-

---

[18] A working-class neighborhood of Athens.
[19] A wealthy neighborhood in Athens.

gin. People were descending in little groups, and we all knew that we were going for the same purpose, but no one said a word to anyone else, we were laughing, we were talking among ourselves, and you would've thought we were just on our way to work. And there next to the Polytechnic University, there was usually a roasted chickpea seller, there with his cart. We went to buy a snack, and the cart was completely shut. Why? Because even *he* was involved! Even the roasted chickpea vendor. . . . That kind of universal [*katholiki*] discipline has never been seen again. . . .

Of the large EAM organizations, the one that owes the most to women is the relief organization, the EA. They were the ones who would gather up the dead and treat the wounded from the demonstrations. They were the ones who would scout around for food to feed those who had been forced to live underground [*stin paranomia*]. They found houses where such people could sleep. My friend's mother, today she's about eighty years old, was in the EA. And my sister who died,[20] she was also in the EA. They were the invisible heroines [*oi afanes iroides*]. They did wonderful, important work without carrying weapons and without making a big fuss. They were the ones who, silently, would be on the front lines during the street battles in Athens, secretly taking the wounded to the hospitals and retrieving the dead for burial. And they would give first aid, bring food to the fighters; their work was extremely heroic and they did it without asking for credit and without a lot of fanfare [*horis megali fasaria*]. The women of the Ethniki Allilengii.

As younger people, our job was also to transport various things. We never knew, at least *I* never knew, what the others were doing. We were told as little as possible what the others were up to. Many times I would be carrying weapons right in my schoolbag, but no one would know about it. In some ways my older brother undertook more serious work, but he was more suspect when he was out on the street; they would search him. So when he had something to transport, I would put it in my bag and go first, and he would walk ten meters behind me, and because I was so young, they wouldn't tend to suspect me at all. That happened from time to time with me and my brother. It wasn't even something that the organization told us to do. We did it on our own. We had our own little racket going! [laughing] Our actual organizational membership was elsewhere, but we had our own little group of two and we kept that one to ourselves!

[20] "Her health was always a bit fragile. After liberation, when they started to go after people who were in the EAM, especially those of us who had been in it from the start, a lot of people left the city and stayed outside. Because it wasn't safe to hang around. And she got sick right after she came back and died. She was twenty-two years old, my big sister."

What really distinguished us was our "code of silence" [*siganotikotita*]. That we were told never to say anything more than what was absolutely necessary, never to ask to know anything, not to ask names or talk about people using their real names. To act as though we knew nothing about each other. Many times, those of us who were arrested and tortured, next to you in the torture chamber was someone whom you had worked with, who you had written on the walls with, who went with you to clandestine meetings, and you would say, "No, I've never seen this person in my life." Because it was a very difficult thing. Sometimes people cracked under the torture. That was the job of the organization, to educate us about how to behave under those circumstances and to understand the tremendous responsibility we were undertaking by participating in the resistance. They would train you, and then send you on missions, eventually, to other areas of the city. That was the work of the organization. To spread the skill of resistance to as many people as possible.

Eventually, some of the kids who had been in the resistance began to disappear, some into hiding in the mountains, some executed, some arrested. And as for me, as luck would have it, my fate seemed to be that I was arrested by the Germans. It was the eve of our national holiday, the annual celebration of our liberation from Turkish rule in 1821, it was the twenty-fourth of March and the holiday is the twenty-fifth. The resistance always celebrated national holidays, secretly of course, and used those days as a chance to step up its activities, to distribute information because people would be out of their houses. It was an opportunity to buoy people's spirits. So that day was very full, I remember there were a lot of activities jammed into that day in preparation for the holiday. I was out early in the morning, writing on the walls. I spoke into the horn. I still remember it like it was yesterday, what I said. "People of Athens! The voice of EAM is speaking to you! Tomorrow is a day of national joy, of national freedom! No one is to go into the center of the city! No one is to take part in the parade planned by the Germans! Everyone in the neighborhoods, in the churches, in the squares, together with EAM and ELAS, we will celebrate the twenty-fifth of March together!" I distributed leaflets. There was a lot of work to do. I remember I went to a special meeting where they were giving patriotic speeches and stirring words of courage about the revolution. I remember that suddenly, someone asked me to say a few words, and I panicked, because I thought, "Oh, no! What am I going to say?" They said, "Come on, you're a student, you must know something! Say a poem!" And somehow, I thought of a poem I had once memorized about Ayia Lavria and the revolution and whatever, and I recited that, stuttering and blushing, and got by! I went home to pick up a list of names and was supposed to go out to a rendezvous and give it to my contact at 2:30. My mother had seen the list, and got frightened because it looked like a dangerous thing to be carrying around, and she locked me in my room. I screamed, "Give me the key, so I can leave! Give it to me, give me the key!" She wouldn't come and let me out. So I tied some sheets together, attached them to the bars of the balcony, and got out that way. I was *determined* to get out. My mother heard me doing this and she was yelling, "Don't! Don't! Don't make us look ridiculous [*mi ginoume rezili*)]! Here, take the key!" Because it didn't look very good for a girl to be climbing out the window that way. But I left with my list to go to the rendezvous, and that was the last time I saw my mother until after liberation.

Maria was from the village of Isteia on Evia Island, a large land formation situated at the southeastern corner of the Greek mainland. She was seventeen when the Nazis invaded Greece. A founding member of EPON in her area, in early 1944 she was chosen to be in a model girls' ELAS unit organized in Viniani, the capital of Free Greece. After liberation, she married a prominent journalist for the resistance press and publisher of the *Poseidon Codes,* the official list of statutes and decrees voted into law by the new citizens of the Government of the Mountains (PEEA). Maria escaped in 1948 while her husband was on death row in an Athens prison, going first to Tashkent and eventually settling in Moscow, where she lived for seventeen years until her husband was allowed to join her. At the time I interviewed her she had been back in Greece for about ten years; she was a cultural consultant and managed Soviet and Eastern bloc performing arts groups on tour in Greece. When I spoke with her she was busy arranging the visit of the Bolshoi Ballet, which was due in Athens the next week.

Her testimony is augmented in spots by that of Plousia, a close friend who was also chosen for the model girls' unit. When the interview was over, Maria telephoned Plousia, who stopped by for lunch and to chat more about their stint in the 13th Division Girls' Platoon. Plousia was from the Missalonghi area, where her father was a wealthy fisherman working in the Ionian Islands. "My father was very well-off," she said, "because that area is very rich in fish and he was in charge of dispensing the fish for the whole region. He was head of a kind of union." Politically, her father was a royalist, "but he was very clever and he could read and write, which was kind of rare. He came from a family that had the means to send him to study. And when they were stopped on an island for months at a time, he would teach the others to read and write." She continued, "My mother was from a well-to-do family. Her father owned several large ships that used to carry food and other goods for people. I don't know . . . politically . . . well, she was always on her kids' side, but really, she never spoke about politics. She married very young." Plousia was arrested in

1947 and spent five years in the island reeducation camps of Ikaria, Trikeri, and Makronisos. In 1985 she was teacher and manager of an ethnic dance group, which at the time of the interview, was rehearsing for performances in Chicago and New York.

Maria's testimony with Plousia's added comments illuminate an important facet of the mobilization of women and the conditioning of men to women's participation, as planned and carried out by the EAM leadership *from above*. Their histories also reinforce aspects of Anthoula's testimony with regard to parental reactions, the emphasis on the training and socialization of youth, the military-style, centralized discipline of the organization, the correspondence of male and female duties, and the ways in which participants' own agency helped shape the terms of the struggle.

> I was one of the first to join, first EAM-Neon, then in February 1943 when EPON was created, I became a member of EPON. My parents were very worried at first, because I was the only daughter. They worried because in the rural areas, at least at that time, girls grew up with very strict rules. For instance, I couldn't go anywhere without them knowing where I was going, whom I was going with, when I would be back. I never went anywhere alone. That is, until the occupation came and I joined the resistance. In the meantime, because we were right in the midst of the enemy, we had an underground press, there at the house we had a mimeograph and a typewriter and we published a little bulletin and we distributed it. It was very dangerous. And they were extremely worried about what might happen to us. In the beginning they were very much against it, but because they had democratic roots [*dhimokratikes rizes*], afterwards, they had to support us.
>
> My father was a merchant, petty bourgeoisie [*mikroastiki taksi*]. Afterward, they went through a lot, and he ended up being a farmer, but he was basically a merchant. My father had gone to America, at the time of the big emigration before 1912. One of his brothers had gone and my father had also gone, and he had become quite wealthy. But when war was declared here, that is, the First World War, he couldn't bear to think that here there was fighting going on, and he was sitting over there comfortable in America. So he abandoned it all and came back here to fight. And based on that example, when faced with the same situation, we kids felt that we couldn't do otherwise. Because he had left all that property and come back to fight for his country, we just couldn't do otherwise, me and my brother. But they did worry quite a bit, especially over me. I was a bit frail. They had me "wrapped in goose feathers," as they say [*sto poupoulo pou lene*]. And suddenly, I had begun to do something that wasn't exactly to their liking. But they realized we were doing something important, and because they were so worried about our safety, they started helping us.

For instance, they would stand watch for our underground press. They would go outside and look around and make sure no one was coming.

But we really hadn't conceived of the danger that we were in. My father was arrested by the Italians. And why had they arrested him? They had arrested him because I had gone to a secret meeting, held on the outskirts of town, and they told my father that if I returned—well, I was staying there outside of town, underground—and they notified him that if I came back, they wouldn't hurt me. And I came back to the house. The teacher had come, the priest, and various notables to say that they weren't going to harm me, they wouldn't arrest me, and I should go ahead and return. I came back to the house at night, and my parents told me that I shouldn't be there, and so I left that same night, and I went to another house to sleep, and that night they arrested my father. Someone had betrayed us. They got him, but they had really wanted me. They had taken him to a jail in Halkida, where my mother came to visit him. And they had told him, if your daughter comes, we'll let you go and nothing will happen to her. But he said that I wouldn't come under any circumstances, and that they were stuck with him. That is, he had changed. In that space of time, he had changed. Whereas before he was saying, "Come, they won't hurt you. What is all this? You, a girl, running all over the mountains, running here and there, what are people going to think? What will people say [*ti tha pei o kosmos*]?" And all that, just like a typical village man. But later on, he was saying, "Under no circumstances should you come and give yourself up."

And so around the time that the Italians left and the Germans came (around mid-1943), my life was in danger, so I went with my brother to Athens to get the Germans off my trail, and I continued to be active in the EPON organization in Athens. In the meantime, my brother was arrested for his resistance activities there in Athens. My father came to try to pull strings [*ta mesa*] to get my brother released. Finally, after about five months in Athens, we both returned to the village when the coast was clearer. I worked for a bit in the village organization again, but then I got restless and decided that I wanted to go and fight.

Because I was so young, they required permission from my parents in order for me to go to the resistance army. They had to give them a signed form that they consented for me to go to join ELAS. In the beginning, they didn't want to, but for one thing, they knew that somehow I would find a way to do what I wanted to do, and for another, I told them that I would go to my grandmother—my mother's mother was from Roumeli—and that I wouldn't "go to the mountain,"[21] and they gave in and gave their permission. They signed the paper saying that they agreed.

[21] That is, join the ELAS army fighting in the mountains.

Because they were very strict about the circumstances under which they would allow girls into that ELAS unit. With another girl and boy then, I took off. From the island, we crossed over to the mainland into Roumeli, and with various "adventures" [*peripeties*] we arrived in Karpenissi. Secretly. We passed through roadblocks; we passed through heavily guarded areas . . . oh yes, of course. It was extremely dangerous then to go anywhere in a boat. We left with a boy, who rowed us with the oars, and we . . . it was very dangerous because of the constant sea patrols, and we had to find just the right moment to cross over. We crossed over from a spot somewhere between Orei and Kanatadika. That's where we left from. And once we got across, we continued on foot. It took about two days for us to get there because we could only go at night. We had to traverse the National Highway [*na perasoume ton dhimosio ton Ethniko Dhromo, ton dhiaskisame*] to get over there. We had our identity cards, just in case. I had a student card, and the other girl was a village girl who had stayed in the house, nothing special.

We arrived in Karpenissi. And because we had our signed parental consent forms, the local ELAS personnel took care of us immediately. We went to the local headquarters, and they set everything in motion. Because our local EPON organization had also given us a document of introduction [*ena fyllo poreias*] a kind of identity paper, it was. And they had notified them of our impending arrival. The girls' unit had been created there in Karpenissi. Before, they had the girls scattered around in different sections. Each division of Aris's army had different regiments. They decided to centralize them and to create a section and that would then become a platoon. In the beginning there were ten girls in the regiment, and it would later become thirty. So as I said, in the beginning we had the regiment, and then others joined and we ended up with the platoon. With a chain of command. With drill sergeants. Exactly like an army unit.

Naturally, because it was an EPON platoon, a division with a platoon of EPON kids, they had to be young. Because they had divided them according to age, and that left the younger ones. The oldest ones were twenty-three or twenty-four, no older. There was one exception, however, and that was Thiella.[22] She was a little older than us, but not by much. She might have been about twenty-five. But all the others were under twenty. Each of our local organizations had chosen us, and had recommended us, saying that this person had potential, that you had done this,

---

[22] Thiella, meaning "Storm," was one of the most famous women resistance fighters in Greece.

and this, and this, and were well qualified to become an *andartis* [a partisan]. There was a whole selection process.

So first of all, they created separate branches because, as I said, they thought that with the example we set, more people would want to participate in the resistance, generally and second, they hoped to create a competitive standard [*mia amilla*] since a woman is, by nature, more organized. They would create some competition between the men and the women, and we succeeded in that area. Because there were two youth platoons, one for the women and one for the men, and we succeeded in performing very well at all the military contests, on organization, on discipline. We were much more disciplined than the men, and what was amazing was that they adjusted so quickly and so well. Because the army is the army, and at that time, ELAS had already become a tactical army. From the top right down to the last partisan. There was a whole set of written documents regarding how each division would be formed and what its duties would be. Sarafis had written it all down. Furthermore, it wasn't only that the division would fight but also that it would help in the town organization as well, in the gathering of food and other supplies and in their distribution. And a very important factor was that it would participate at the "civilizing" level [*ekpolitistiko tomea*]. Because in the villages things were very backward; they were very underdeveloped [*ipovathismena*]. That is, the people didn't know what "theater" meant; what "dance" was. They would dance, that is, when they had festivals [*panigyria*], but it wasn't in any organized fashion. So the occupation came along . . . and the resistance played a very big role in the cultural area.

The platoon had an outside standard [*eksoteriko kanonismo*] to conform to. With this competition that existed, we were constantly thinking of how we could become better. We had our program planned out from morning till night, and this schedule would be followed no matter what—that is, during peacetime, not when there were battles going on. That is, there were military exercises, lots of training drills. We got up very early in the morning. We had various lessons. All the girls were taught to read and write, because a lot of the girls were illiterate. Lessons in the arts and culture. We learned dances, we learned recitation. We learned . . . we put on plays. And all this stuff, the girls who came in knowing nothing realized that we all had talent in some area. In the course of all of these "manifestations" [*ekdhiloseis*].

We all know that at that age girls have reached physical maturity and they get their periods every month. That was a problem under those conditions in which we lived. A fair number of girls had problems; some of them stopped getting their periods altogether because of the hardships

Weapons instruction. Courtesy the Trustees of the Liddell Hart Centre for Military Archives, King's College London

and such. But we always tried to hide it because we didn't want the EP-ONites [the boys] to suspect a thing, because we usually went to the parades and the mock battles with the boys' platoon. We didn't want them to know át all—that such and such girl was "indisposed." We saw it as a kind of handicap, something that somehow would diminish us, as a sort of shameful thing. It was our own personal illness, that the problem was entirely ours and that no one should know that you had that problem on that particular day. We tried to confront the problem and keep it to ourselves as much as possible. If we couldn't, we would do things like try to carry the machine gun even though it was a strain. In that condition to lift a machine gun! They were really heavy. They were the heavy, Italian kind [Beta] of machine guns. But we didn't want anyone to suspect or think less of us. Because the machine gun is something you have to be taught; not just anyone knows how to do it. Things were very austere, especially regarding our conduct. For instance, they didn't allow us to go out with any of the boys. Romantic involvements [*romantikes skheseis*] weren't allowed at all. This was because our goal wasn't only to kick out the enemy [*na dhioksoume ton ekhthro*] but to serve as guide for the people, to . . . attract them to the resistance. There in Roumeli, where I was, everyone had taken part in the resistance. The majority of the people there. And we had to serve as a model. When a peasant woman saw a girl with a rifle, wearing the uniform, that girl had to set a good example. Because [the peasant woman] had her older, traditional perceptions which had been passed down to her through the generations. And because of that, at all times our behavior had to be above reproach.

In terms of the romantic involvements, I'll give you an example. We had a very beautiful girl in our platoon, and she was also very hot-blooded [*thermo-aimi*]. And a lot of the officers, the male officers, were attracted to her. In the end, we were forced to vote her out of the group, that is, once it became clear that she couldn't control herself, because there was a law stating that we weren't allowed to have any other kind of contact with each other beyond that which was platonic and comradely. Sexual contact was not permitted. We couldn't form any other kind of relationships. And we kicked her out. We had a general meeting, and we told her she had to leave, that she should go back and work in her local organization if she wanted to contribute something. It was very sad. She took it very badly. We all felt horrible, and she was very upset about it, especially when the time came for her to give up her weapon. It was a very depressing experience for us, but I tell you that example so you can see how severe the penalties were for that kind of thing. We were all supposed to wait until after liberation to have our romances. My husband and I had met there in Viniani. We knew each other, but we didn't have anything going. He proposed to me right after liberation.

One of the nicest girls in the unit was Thiella. Before, she had been with Aris, and then when they created the platoon, she came over to be with us. Thiella was from Athens. She was one of the first women to join ELAS; she had fought in many battles with Aris. The clothes she wore were *lafira*—that is, they came from dead German or Italian soldiers. And they needed clothes badly, so they would take them and wear them. She was a special case because she had left her three children back in Athens. She was one of the few real heroes, male or female [*itan ena ap' ta liga palikaria, anamesa se andhres kai yinekes*]. Unfortunately, Thiella was killed during the December Events. Around Omonia Square, at the National Theater. Her real name was Meni Pappailiou. Another case was Koula Danou, who had a child. She had fought with her husband, and was separated from him. She left her child with an aunt and came up to the mountains to fight in ELAS. And for all that time she couldn't see her child. After liberation, during the civil war, she was forced to flee, like a lot of us, to avoid arrest here. And she joined the Democratic Army, but she was wounded and they caught her. And they executed her in 1949. She was sentenced to death and they killed her. She was one of the last to be executed.

Each week we would have a general meeting and we would discuss all our problems. Whenever a group of people live together, there are bound to be some problems. Maybe I have this point of view, Plousia might have that one. Or maybe our ideas clash. Whenever such problems would appear, we would all talk about them together, democratically. I'll give you an example that had to do with Thiella. When she came to the platoon, as I told you, she was wearing *lafira* taken from a dead German soldier. Her pants were dark blue, her tunic was regulation green or khaki. But we were all wearing khaki. Thiella didn't want to take off the pants. And we all discussed it together in the meeting, and we decided that Thiella should follow the same rules of discipline, that she should take off the dark pants so that she didn't stick out from the others. It wasn't right that a platoon should be parading down the street and have someone stick out like that. So Thiella had to go along with that, but she didn't throw away the pants, and when she went down to Athens, she wore her blue pants.

Plousia: Of course you understand why she didn't want to give them up; she was emotionally attached to the pants, as she was to her rifle, which she started off with and had seen her through so many battles. She didn't want to change it, because it was the one she had always fought with, and she had gotten it by herself. That is, she killed someone and took it. And that's why she was so attached to it.

Maria: One other thing having to do with cleanliness, but also with femininity. As you can see from the photographs, we all wore braids. Because if we beautified ourselves too much, it would constantly be getting in our way, or distracting the men. And so we had braided our hair. So that we wouldn't be seen as female. That was one part, the other was the practical side. We couldn't comb our hair as easily as the men, and we didn't have combs. One comb made the rounds. We would braid our hair and it might have to stay that way for several days. Everything had to be just so, the uniform, the hair, everything in perfect military order, and we were to be as neat as the boys. But we had decided at the general meeting that we would keep our hair in braids until Liberation Day. Among ourselves, we decided that. And so we all arrived at the Liberation Day parade in Lamia with our hair cut and fixed up. We were women, and if we had gone to the parade with our braids, the people wouldn't have been able to distinguish us from the boys! They wouldn't have known who was passing by.

ELAS 13th Division (Model Girls' Unit) marching in formation in Liberation Day parade at Rendina. Courtesy Spiros Meletzis

Mairi was from the medium-sized town of Elassona, located at a strategic point on the National Highway, which ran from Athens to Larissa to Salonika. Her case was somewhat unusual in that the declaration of war in 1941 found her, having just completed high school, working as a typist in the office of the prefect of Elassona. Her father was employed at the public treasury, and Mairi had gotten the job through his personal contacts. Politically, "my father was a Royalist, but he wasn't a fanatic. Actually, I can't really say that he was especially politically oriented, but before the war he definitely voted monarchist." Mairi was arrested in 1947 and was in an Athens jail until 1961, with a brief period of release from 1953 to 1954. In 1985 she lived in Athens with her husband, a former ELAS partisan from the Athens neighborhood of Kaissariani, and was a member of the United Resistance survivor organization.

We rose up against what had happened and they [EAM] urged people to join in protest, and I tell you, our songs and our chants were so beautiful! And me and about ten other girls from our area went up together, to the village where the local ELAS unit was to enlist. We enlisted. I joined too, and we signed the necessary papers and they explained the rules and issued me a gun [*ena pistoli*]. And we began learning military maneuvers, doing gymnastics, and we became part of the life of the organization, the mess kitchens. We listened to the news on the radio and helped to issue bulletins, etc. etc. And every day or few days, we would go through military exercises and we would learn how to use the weapons, etc. This wasn't only girls, of course. There were also boys participating, but it was only we ten or so girls who had come up in a group from our area together to that general assembly of forces [*sinelevsi*]. We all decided to go together and we left immediately.

But I should go back a little and tell you that after I joined EPON and during the time that I was active in EPON, they [EAM] approached me and told me that I would be used elsewhere, in a difficult, serious, and dangerous mission. That is, what? They explained it to me.

Because Elassona was at a crossroads, and many of the troops entered Greece by this route, or would leave Greece that way, this meant that all the cars, all the tanks, all the armaments, all the soldiers, their weapons, their cannons, their machine guns, everything, would pass through Elassona—whatever didn't come by train but rather by road. And they showed me how I must count and to distinguish the different kinds of trucks, tanks, weapons, etc. etc., to the point where I had really learned this work very well, and I could distinguish them by their different marks and I had created a system. So I would put, this truck, this kind of transport, there; the other type, with its particular markings, there; there, so many tanks; there, the machine guns. And I would keep track of all kinds of transportation and the soldiers inside them. I knew that the carriage of a certain kind of transport vehicle held twenty people and I would count them. Because at my house . . . well, what would happen is, I would make these calculations, either during the day at my office—that was in the square and they would pass through there and I could see it all out the window—or from my house. Because my house was right on the road, and on one of the walls of the [outdoor] toilet that we used, there was a hole, and because it was up on a hill, and at a turn [in the road], they were outside our toilet a lot—toilet, "cabinet," that is—they spent a lot of time at that turn, taking things up and down the hill, and I had all that time to see, to count, that is, to write down. . . . I would put, for instance, one little mark here, as soon as I saw a truck, I would make a mark in the truck column; a mark, as I saw a tank, there, a little mark. And I would put down twenty soldiers, eighteen. And every day, in the evening, I would send a bulletin to the American Mission—of course the organization had introduced me to the American Mission. And every night, I would send my report to the American Mission. Of course, the organization had gotten me in touch with the American Mission—but they would know that I, Mairi ——, which was my name then, was Agent OO [*Praktoras Midhen Midhen*]. And I would send it to OI, another agent, and from OI it would go straight to the American Mission. So, my notebook was so up-to-date and so correct and meticulous all of this, that they sent me a dispatch, that is, a "bravo," that it really was very accurate and valuable work that I was doing for them; it was a service that they really needed at that time. And especially considering that the Germans were leaving Greece at that point and were evacuating the area and with regard to the forces that were coming in and were going out. So there was also that aspect to my duties.

I had, first, a very good partner [*kalos sintrophos*], who, I don't know why, left this work. He was the one who had set the whole thing up; he had coordinated it all, and he held the position until 1943. I don't remember, I don't know from when because I began after 1943, it must have been starting in the autumn of 1943, and it was one whole year, up until the autumn of 1944, because on 23 October the Germans left Athens, but Elassona, which is beyond Larissa, it's approximately four hundred kilometers from Athens, they withdrew little by little, they left Elassona, and Elassona was liberated. Until that time I sent notice of the enemy's movements and military capabilities to the resistance. And as well what they were doing in Elassona, because the Germans still . . . until September 1943, we had Italians, we had a very large number of Italian troops in Elassona.

Elassona was under Italian occupation; that is, they had concentrated the Italian occupying forces there. We had a whole regiment there. We had a colonel. We had a garrison. We had lots of troops. As for me, I was a civil servant. In Elassona, and precisely because there were these things, because of Elassona's military significance and value, we had many Italian troops stationed there. Exactly for that reason, an administrative division [*eparheio*] was created. It was one of the cities where they set up civil posts—that is, on a level slightly below the network of nomarchies. That is, Larissa was a nomarchy, but that couldn't cover the whole area because our region alone involved the administration of about sixty villages. Elassona, then, acquired the status of a civil administrative division, with a provincial governor, and I was the first employee, a typist. As for the work that went on in that office, it is impossible to describe: absolutely everything. But at the same time, the office helped with other things; for example, some sort of soup kitchen was needed. The children were suffering. They were hungry. It didn't matter that Elassona is right there in the middle of a wheat-producing region (they say that Thessaly is the "bread-basket" of Greece [*o sitagolonas tis Ellados*], at least then it was), we were still hungry. It was a time when we had no wheat whatsoever. During that time, 1941, 1942, we ate mostly potatoes and wild greens [*horta*]. Every day, I would go and gather wild greens as soon as I returned home from the office, I would leave my bag and I would go and gather wild greens up on the mountain. And my mother would clean them, and would make a sort of little pancakes with them [*pittes*]— pancakes, well, that is to say, with a tiny bit of cornmeal underneath so that they wouldn't stick and so that they would hold together, and a little bit on top, and that's what we would eat, constantly. So, anyway, what was I saying? I got off the subject. I started to say one thing and ended up with another. . . . Oh yes, so I was a public employee and from there, we helped in other capacities.

We had . . . the prefect of Elassona [*o eparhos*] was also president of the regional relief organization. That is, the International Red Cross would send, for instance, wheat, maize, beans, etc.—these would all go to this organization, that is the service of the state which collected such goods. The prefect of Elassona was president of this committee of the International Red Cross and he had the authority to distribute them to the villages. The eparhos of Elassona then became a nomarch. I don't really know why. And for a while, until another eparhos assumed the position, the authorities made me responsible for coordinating these operations.

So that's when I realized that we had enough quantity and that we had the capacity to move in the area of relief, and that we could also start a soup kitchen for the children. And we started at first using our own resources. . . . I would take a little gruel myself [*pligouri*]; Katina would get some sour milk noodles [*trahanas*]; Annetta would get a little bread, her family had some flour; and we started a soup kitchen. We went to a clinic, we obtained a clinic and we brought benches there from a school; we got a large cooking pot [*mia katsarola*]; we got some wood for tables from here and there, from our homes . . . and first we took eight kids, the poorest kids of the school, and the first day we did that, we gave them food. And the second day, we had thirteen. And the third, twenty, and afterward we reached two hundred kids. We went to the council of the regional organization and it gave us flour, it gave us all of those things, and we mobilized all the women of Elassona, and we wrote down, you will

EA food relief: Women distributing rations in an outdoor soup kitchen. Courtesy
Spiros Meletzis

cook, or you will be responsible for distribution [*dhianomi*]; you will keep
records, or I don't know what—and all the women in turn began to
come; there wasn't one woman who didn't. . . . and that way everybody
helped, all the women. . . . All the women, there wasn't . . . in this case,
everyone helped. Not one woman refused. Of course, there were some
who were afraid. Mostly fear, and that they didn't want to get mixed up
in such things, or that their husbands wouldn't allow them to leave their
houses. But the majority of women helped or at least didn't refuse us
when we would go and ask for their help in adding to the stores of food.
And because our records were so well organized and we did our job so
well, the International Red Cross congratulated us and told the local ser-

vice, "*You* should take lessons from the women of the Women's Committee of the soup kitchen!"

One fine morning, however, the regional organization cut our supply of flour; they cut our gruel; they cut our grain; and they left us only chickpeas, and whatever. They cut some of the flour we made bread from. And when the children heard about this, because we had told them that today there is no bread, there is only a half portion of gruel for each of you, and starting tomorrow there may not even be gruel, an uprising occurred. Something happened that had never happened before, not in Elassona, and I don't know where else. . . . they started a protest demonstration, the children [*kanane silalitirio ta paidhakia*] . . . and they began beating on their plates with their spoons and shouting, "We—are—hungry!! We—want—bread! Why did you cut off our food?!" [*Pina-me! The-loume psomi! Yiati mas kopsete to sissitio mas?!*] And it was something very beautiful! But the prefect of Elassona chased them away and refused to help them . . . and the children broke into the storage area and began to crawl under the crates and move stuff into the women's storage area, because we had our own pantry, whatever they could find, even wooden clogs [*chokara*], and they didn't even know that there were *chokara* there. They carried chickpeas and other things, although they didn't get to the box with the flour. But since they did it themselves, they didn't have any way of knowing exactly where things were. You can't imagine how much the children broke! But it happened and what can I tell you? It was something very shocking for Elassona. It had never happened before, that so many children should stage a demonstration, and should break storage crates, etc. . . . Of course, it caused some problems for me because they thought that I was responsible, and in the end, I had some problems with my service.

At any rate, the important thing is that we were successful, and [because of the demonstration] we were able to resume all of the original quantities, and the whole operation continued until liberation and beyond, and still even after that particular soup kitchen, up until liberation. It was a big undertaking and we women managed to pull it off. . . . We mobilized, and this is the important thing, we mobilized all of Elassona. . . . That is to say, until then, people would do things in an isolated way, sporadically . . . but with this opportunity, this women's movement reached the masses [*mazikopithike to kinima ton yinekon*], let's say, and we helped a lot of women to break away from their narrow mentality, their routine, and the usual problems that they had to contend with. They were simple women and, you could say, illiterate for the most part; those women helped a lot. The others who participated were the high-class types [laughs and makes mimicking gesture]. Thus, we continued until 1944.

And we had other duties. From Elassona, as you know, the young men couldn't work or live undercover because the place was small and everyone knew who was in the organization. So they left and went to the mountains or they would go to the political wing of the organization. There were the soldiers and there was the political wing, the political organizations in each village, town, and orchard, it seemed. . . . that is, EPON was the political organization for the youth. But there were also EPONites-ELASites, EPON-ELAS, or the military arm, you understand?

Anyway, something you were asking me about my father. . . . My father was a public employee—an agent of the treasury. But I didn't really get any flack from home about my joining the movement or working, even though I was. . . . we lived in the "provinces." Elassona then had three thousand inhabitants, now it has seven or eight, or maybe even ten thousand by now. But in spite of all of that, I finished high school and I didn't have problems. I would go out walking nearly every day, while the other girls in Elassona didn't go out at that time, forty years or so ago. They didn't usually go out every day; they would leave the house only in the summer every day, or they would usually only go out on Sundays, for the "weekly walk,"[23] Whereas I would go out every day. I didn't have problems; I had learned how to ride a bicycle, and my parents didn't really react badly, or even notice half the time. But when I joined the movement, they didn't want me to go to the *andartiko*, and they didn't want me to get mixed up in the whole thing because they were afraid, they were really afraid for my life. When the Germans started to withdraw, however, and we had a great deal of traffic on the road, then I wouldn't come back during the day or until late at night. . . . all night they would be passing by and we only slept for a few hours. My parents would even help there at the "post" in the toilet, my father and even my mother. Our toilet was outdoors in the yard rather than inside, and my father and my mother would sit in the yard all night gathering this information. We didn't have toilets in the houses then, but outside in the garden, and we would do shifts and they would also take turns until morning when I would go to work. So my family also watched, either from the balcony or

[23] Every evening (the most important day being Sunday), the *peripato* or *volta* would take place all over Greece. People of all ages would stroll up and down the main street of town, greeting one another, gossiping and socializing. The walk-around was an important ritual for girls and boys of marriageable age. This was where the family might decide on potential mates and one of the only times that young people were allowed to flirt openly, under the watchful eyes of their parents, relatives, and neighbors.

from inside the toilet, which was of course better because it wasn't as obvious.

Two other shorter examples demonstrate the scope of women's activities during the resistance period.

Xeni was from the Athens suburb of Kaissariani, known for its concentration of Asia Minor refugees. Because of its reputation as a "red" or Communist district, the Nazis had christened Kaissariani "Little Stalingrad." Because of the high degree of mobilization in that and other so-called eastern suburbs of the city, Kaissariani was rumored to be an area where German soldiers feared to tread. It was a district of small houses so crowded together that "it was difficult to tell where one stopped and the other began, and so there were a lot of hiding places," said Xeni. The neighborhood women were organized into a network to feed the ELAS soldiers, mostly teenagers and young men and women in their twenties. The smallest children were called *aetopoules,* or "eaglets," and their duties involved spying surreptitiously while playing on the streets and ferrying messages among the various ELAS units. Early in the war, neighborhood participants also took part in street battles with the Germans "using sticks, homemade weapons, rocks, and whatever they could manage to pull together."

Xeni was about fifteen when war was declared. Her mother died in 1939, leaving her father a widower and Xeni to serve as mother to her five younger sisters. Xeni was called "the little blond one" because of her straw-colored braids, but her innocuous appearance belied her more warlike actions during the resistance. Xeni was arrested in 1946 and spent eight years on death row in the Averoff Prison. She was released in 1954 and spent the rest of the decade coming and going underground. In 1985 she lived in Athens with her husband, a journalist and former ELAS member, whom she had met when they were being transferred in the same truck from the prison in Patras back to jail in Athens.

I had given a speech against the Italian and German occupation in school, and somehow word got back to the authorities and I had to be on the run for a while. I went into hiding at another house and soon joined an armed ELAS unit of high school students. We all lived in a large barracks together and fought and trained together; certainly, none of us could go back to our houses because it was too dangerous. They were searching for me everywhere, and whenever they found a girl with blond braids they would beat her thinking she was me. In fact, the Germans came looking for me and broke into our house. They beat my sister, who was also in the resistance, she was an *aetopoulo;* they were looking for me but they

An ELAS *andartissa,* 1944. Courtesy Imperial War Museum, London

found her and beat her and soon after she died from her injuries. It was very sad.

So I fought quite a bit with the weapons. I had my own guns. Because not everyone is suited to fight with a gun. It bothers some people, but it didn't bother me. And later on, after the Varkiza agreement when the resistance leaders agreed that we should all come forward and give up our weapons, we were all crying, even the men. I gave up my rifle, but I kept my handgun. I kept it in my bag. Not because I could foresee the future and that we would have to fight for our own protection later, but because I liked my gun and I didn't want to surrender it.

One time, during a battle in Kaissariani some friends of ours were killed. These were kids that we had been with just a couple of hours earlier. On our way down the hill, running to take part in the battle, we came upon those guys, lying there on the street with head wounds. I'll tell you exactly how it was, even though it was extremely sad for me. I was wearing a skirt, the girls' uniforms had skirts, and I went over to them, knelt down and covered their heads with my skirt. I didn't want them to die like that out in the open. Afterwards, our people came and gathered up their bodies and took them away. As I was leaving, I felt something on my legs. It was their brains and they were also all over my skirt. [begins to cry and continues crying for the rest of the story] When the battle was over, I was in horrible shape, and someone said to me, "What's the matter with you?" They weren't used to seeing me like that. And I said, "Please, let me just go into a house, I feel sick." They were all wondering what my problem was. And this guy said to them, "You know what happened; she covered the heads of those kids with her skirt. Something must have happened then." He said to me, "Tell us what happened," and I said, "I have Thanassi and Yiorgo's brains all over my legs and skirt. And I can't stand the thought of it." And the others around who had known them all started to cry too. And someone said, "Take her to a house so she can get cleaned up." And for days and days, I couldn't chase that image out of my head. I'm telling you this so you can see, even though a lot of those who took part in these battles during the resistance were young kids, carrying guns, going on missions, getting shot, in spite of all that, we were children, but we had to become tough. We all had to become tough at a very young age in order to survive, because in order to survive you have to change, to become tough like that. But at the same time we were kids, and we were very sensitive.

Another example was when a friend of mine was killed. He had been shot in the neck. I ran to him and held him as he died. He said to me, "Please, could you sing 'Forward ELAS for Greece' with me." And I sang it, along with another friend who was with me; we sang it with him until his voice stopped. And then we got up and left. Because even though it meant that we might be killed, we felt so much for each other, such *filotimo*, that we couldn't do otherwise.

But the people around, seeing us fighting like that, that was why they loved us and took care of us. Every morning up there in Kaissariani— there was a house next to our barracks where some little children lived, about three or four of them, and [laughing] every morning, these kids would get up, leave their mother, and come over to us. Their mother— then they had something called *thrapsini*. I don't know if you know it. It's a kind of sweet that they would make with bread. And it would basically be the main thing that she would have for her children to eat that day. She would make it, I guess, and say to the kids, "A slice for you, a slice for you, and one for ELAS." One day one of our friends was carrying one of them in his arms, and he took the little kid back over to the steps of their house, across the way. The mother had made some *thrapsini* that day and the kid offered him some. He said to the little boy, "I'll have mine and you'll have yours, too. We'll eat it together." And the little boy said very seriously, "First, ELAS." My friend said, "Wow, who told you that?" "My mother and father. They always say, *first* ELAS, then *we* eat."

I'll tell you though, if my mother had lived, I don't know if things would've been different for me. I might not have been able to do so much, because she was a very conservative woman about her children, she was from Asia Minor, she was very emotional about her children and very attached to us. I'm sure she would've tried to stop me because she would've been so terrified about my safety.

Tasia grew up on a farm outside of Rethymno, Crete. She was fourteen when war was declared, and she joined EPON in 1943 when it was created. Tasia was arrested in 1946. She was released six months later and immediately went to Athens to stay with her sister because it was no longer safe to stay on Crete. In 1950 she returned to Crete and married a man "with progressive ideas, although he hadn't been in the resistance." She added, "At first his people didn't want me because I had been in the resistance, but he prevailed." In 1985, Tasia ran a craft/tourist shop in Rethymno.

Later on, my whole family joined the resistance in some way. And my mother helped a lot. She hid people; she gave people food; she gave shelter to people. We had a house outside of the city and for that reason a lot of people passed through the house all during the occupation. My mother was a very nice person. She did it out of kindness, because she knew nothing about politics and resistance. But as a good person, she helped people quite a bit—people that were underground, partisans. . . . she even hid a stranger, a man from Macedonia, for a whole month in our orchard so that the Germans wouldn't catch him, and in order to feed him, she would put food in her harvesting basket and pretend that she was going to the orchard to cut grapes. Even my father didn't know that this stranger was in our orchard! That's how well my mother had hidden it. Only me and my mother knew. My father didn't know a thing about it. He was a very hardworking man and he did his work and didn't have time for anything else. Of course he was always antifascist. That was why, later on, when I had to go underground, neither did he yell at me, nor did he bother me about it at all. And one time I sent him a letter saying, "Papa, I don't have shoes." At that time it was very hard to get shoes and so people wore clogs made out of wood or animal skin, and he went and traded some of his wheat with someone in exchange for *stivanakia,* a kind of boots, which at that time *no one* was wearing, made out of leather. He gave me sturdy shoes so that I could walk around from village to village. I had to be able to get around because when I was in EPON, I was made a liaison [*sindhesmos*] with the partisans who had been arrested and taken to jail by the Germans. I would go to the jail, I would take messages from the prisoners, such as "Today the Gestapo are planning to get such-and-such person. Tell him to leave so he won't get caught." I saved a lot of people that way. I would bring them food to the jail, and I would take back the messages.

One time one of them escaped from the prison and became a traitor. He had planned his escape with the Germans, and I hid him at my house, without knowing that his escape had been faked and that the Germans knew that afterwards he would come and stay at my house and that I would help him. I hid him three days, but I couldn't keep him there any longer because we had some relatives staying at our house who already had someone in the prison and so our house was under suspicion as it was. So I called on a neighbor, M.G., and she helped me because she was a democratic-minded person and an antifascist, and we hid him at her house without suspecting that something was going on. And after a few days I was able to notify EPON that Mr. K. had escaped from the prison and that I was hiding him, and in turn they notified the partisans in the mountains, the ELAS army; two ELASites came down and waited at a spot lower down the mountain. They sent word to me that the ELASites had come for the man, and me and the other woman [*sinagonistria:* fellow fighter], G.'s wife, we disguised him. We put glasses on him; we made him a mustache; we put a suit on him and a hat; we walked arm and arm with him, pretending he was one of our family; we took narrow, out-of-the-way streets; and finally we made it out of town. There, another partisan took him to the ELAS men. Because usually we women didn't go all the way up the mountain, we stayed farther down.

Discussion of social issues was as much a part of collective instruction as lessons in military strategy and discipline. Moreover, a large number of teachers belonged to the EAM. In secret annexes and outdoor "classrooms," the curriculum included such subjects as literacy, history, politics, and geography. The 1944 appointment by PEEA decree of Irini Stratiki, also married to a teacher, as the first woman superintendent of public schools can be seen as the official expression of a revolutionary shift in this area. Several of the older women I talked to who had been members of the EAM and not EPON were teachers. They were placed in charge of recruitment and education for specific regions and, with the schools closed down for the duration of the occupation, they continued their teaching duties in the resistance. In the next chapter, I examine the pedagogical work of the resistance.

CHAPTER 6

Constructing the People's Empire

Marion Sarafis, widow of the military and strategic head of ELAS, Major General Stefanos Sarafis, has written in a footnote to his memoirs: "EAM's contribution to the liberation and politicization of Greek women was by no means the least of its achievements and perhaps one of the most enduring. The author himself was in no doubt that the progress achieved was also responsible for much of the post-war 'backlash' against the Left, especially in the countryside" (1980, 193). In a letter (16 December 1985), she notes:

> This footnote is the result of what I myself saw in Greece in 1952–8 and also of discussions with my husband, who said of EAM-ELAS' policy of equality for women: "We had to do it; but we suffered for it afterwards." We were at that time discussing how far the leadership of a progressive movement is justified in pursuing a policy in advance of public opinion and he instanced this as a case in point. He also had a very nice little anecdote on the subject which seems to have been current during the Resistance period: the peasant woman saying to her husband: "Mitso, put the baby to sleep and feed the pig; I'm going to the meeting."

Vasilis Barziotas was a member of the Central Committee of the EAM during the resistance and served as General secretary in the PEEA Government of the Mountains from 1943 to 1946. He comments on the status and participation of women in the EAM-ELAS and later in the Democratic Army during the civil war:

> Many have criticized us for using women in the Democratic Army to such a large extent. Our answer is that in a popular army, in a partisan struggle, the movement must involve women. Women fought well, very well, in the

Democratic Army both in attacking and defending! They showed a sense of responsibility, exemplary courage and self-sacrifice, and many rose to prominent positions in the Officers Training School. . . . Women were truly equal with men in all endeavors, in the battle for life and in death. (1981, 63–64)

Sarafis's comments, together with Barziotas's display of enthusiasm on the "woman question" and use of the plural personal pronoun (we), suggest some measure of consensus at the leadership level. Just how widespread this "structure of feeling" actually was is difficult to gauge. And whether in 1981 Barziotas chose to reconstruct his thinking in a self-serving way at a time when the ruling Socialist party hoped, partly for reasons of political expediency, to cast a positive glow around "state feminism" is even harder to discern. But in practical terms, this imagined social pact appeared to have had significant consequences, as leaders tapped into and created a national identity anchored in *defensive* nationalist enthusiasm. To the extent that male resistance leaders, in partnership with key women, were able to influence social policy within the organization and spread the word about the value of a more fully integrated female presence in the organization as well as in the polity of the future, they occupied a position comparable to that of political authorities during peacetime.

How in practical terms did the organization begin to prepare women to participate in the hypothetical postwar republic? How did a critical mass of women—one of the groups most blatantly excluded from the political system previously—grow to expect the full benefits of Greek citizenship? The organization generated these kinds of nationalist expectations in three principal ways: by providing an organizational structure that gave women a chance to participate; by establishing organizational authority and legitimacy among mass publics; and by propagandizing its vision of new forms of political intervention using a number of symbolic measures.

Making Enthusiasm Work: Gender and the Roots of Action

As we have established, the logistical organization of the EAM can be attributed to the popular front strategies favored by its small but sturdy network of Communist party founders. The highly synchronized cell structure described by respondents and the national-level coordination that in my study yielded the same kinds of testimonies from women residing at opposite ends of the country provide some evidence of the role played by organizational structure in mobilizing women cross regionally.

Here we might return for a moment to Gramsci and the elements that he asserts must converge for a party to exist and prosper. Once again, the affinity with actual EAM political praxis is striking. Gramsci specifies

1) *A mass element*, composed of ordinary, average men [*sic*], whose participation takes the form of discipline and loyalty, rather than any creative spirit or organisational ability. Without these the party would not exist, it is true, but it is also true that neither could it exist with these alone . . . 2) *The principal cohesive element*, which centralises nationally and renders effective and powerful a complex of forces which left to themselves would count for little or nothing. This element is endowed with great cohesive, centralising and disciplinary powers; also—and indeed this is perhaps the basis for the others— with the power of innovation (innovation, be it understood, in a certain direction, according to certain lines of force, certain perspectives, even certain premisses). . . . 3) *An intermediate element*, which articulates the first element with the second and maintains contact between them, not only physically but also morally and intellectually. In reality, for every party there exist "fixed proportions" between these three elements and the greatest effectiveness is achieved when these "fixed proportions" are realised. (1971, 152–53, "The Modern Prince")

Here, Gramsci is placing the "Modern Prince," or the revolutionary party, in the intermediary role. With regard to the EAM, L. S. Stavrianos describes analogous arrangements:

The base of the EAM structure consisted of its village organizations. In each village there were four EAM groups—the EA for relief work, the EPON youth body, the guerrilla commissariat or ETA [Epimeliteia tou Andarti], and the general EAM committee. The ETA collected taxes, mostly in kind, for the support of the ELAS forces. The secretary of the general EAM committee was the Ipefthinos or responsible one. His duties were to check the identification papers of travelers or newcomers to the village, provide recommendations to local villagers who wished to join ELAS, and execute the orders of his district superiors. It was through the Ipefthinos that the Communists exerted control over the EAM mechanism. The Communist party alone maintained a nationwide underground organization during the Metaxas dictatorship. When the occupation began, the great majority of the early EAM organizers were Communists. Thus it was usually a Communist who recruited the peasants into the village EAM unit and remained as the leading EAM functionary. The hierarchical form of EAM organization further increased Communist influence. The Ipefthinoi of a group of villages elected the *eparhia* or district EAM committee. The members of this committee, in turn, elected an Ipefthinos, and the Ipefthinoi of several district committees elected the *nomos* or prefecture EAM committee. The process was repeated, and the Ipefthinoi of several prefectures elected the *periohi* or regional committee, which represented a large section of Greece, such as Thessaly, Macedonia, or Peloponnesus. Each of these regions had one representative in the national EAM central committee. Large cities, such as Athens, Piraeus, Salonica, and Patras, likewise were represented by one delegate in the central committee, each being the Ipefthinos of his city's central committee. The latter was elected by the Ipefthinoi of the neighborhood EAM committees and of the functional EAM organizations—for lawyers, scientists, doctors, teachers, artists, civil servants, clerks, workers, and so forth. In this manner some twenty-five delegates were elected to the national central committee of EAM. These represented the constituent political parties (Communist, Socialist, Agrarian, etc.), the functional organizations (ELAS, EPON, EA, etc.) and the central committees of the regions and of the large cities. It is apparent that the Communist control over the Ipefthinoi insured a Communist majority in the national central committee, although only about a tenth of the total EAM membership were also members of the Communist party. (1952, 45–46)

In addition to its practical value, the sociolegal authority and symbolic message sent to the existing and potential membership by this kind of tiered organizational structure must have been considerable. For those previously uninitiated into the ways of organized politics and political culture, this mode of doing business created a lasting impression and engendered a set of expectations about participatory government which were at least competitive with what fascism propounded. For women and girls tied by tradition to the family, the assignment of an appropriate organizational category to virtually every member must have helped to cement loyalty to the cause. To quote conservative critic C. M. Woodhouse, commander of the Allied Military Mission, once more:

Followed at a distance by the minor organisations, EAM/ELAS set the pace in the creation of something that Governments of Greece had neglected: an organised state in the Greek mountains. All the virtues and vices of such an experiment could be seen; for when the people whom no one has ever helped started helping themselves, their methods are vigorous and not always nice. The words "liberation" and "popular democracy" filled the air with their peculiar connotations. Uneasy stirrings were breaking the surface everywhere, but only the KKE knew how to give them direction. (1985, 146–47)

The unique combination of centralization and decentralization helped to ensure that the administrative apparatus functioned smoothly and with some sensitivity to local issues. Theoretically, the ipefthinos-at-large could be a woman, although this was probably rarely the case. Tight organization coupled with the habitual validity accorded to male authority, however, contributed to the ability of local groups to carry out policy directions set at the top, notably with regard to the desirability of integrating women into the organization.

Returning for a moment to the case of women in Spanish anarchism, Temma Kaplan argues persuasively that the plans of male anarchists to integrate women into postrevolutionary Spain never extended beyond the theoretical level, as we noted earlier. Kaplan attributes blame to their "failure to envision women in more aggressively revolutionary roles, and their general failure to make Spanish anarchism more responsive to women's needs," partly due to inadequate organization. Although male leaders of the movement "were more sensitive to the connections between socialism and the liberation of women from tyrannical sexual and family relationships than any other European political group," they "seldom even promised greater female participation in the struggle. They never specified how females, whom they considered victims of traditionally oppressive relationships, would break free to become revolutionary comrades. In fact, reading anarchist publications, one has the distinct impression that male anarchists never seriously considered making women equals" (1977, 402–3). The trouble in Spain was that the main vehicle for social liberation was to be the worker's syndicate, where, it was vaguely hoped, women and men would work side by side. The syndicate was to supersede the two institutions in which Spanish women had previously been the most active and which consequently meant the most to them; the church and the family. The male anarchists maligned and sought to eradicate all so-called bourgeois conventions. Ironically, these were the only social organizations to which Spanish women had ever been exposed. This situation made it all the more imperative that a realistic alternative to women's traditional activities be found and that it be coupled with specific "remedial" measures. Yet, as I have noted, few concrete steps were taken to prepare either the women or, as important, the men for a radical new female presence in the factories. The one arguably vital Spanish women's organization within the movement, Mujeres Libres, was forced into a defensive role in its attempts to keep women on the agenda. Thus its own "movement within a movement" to create political space for women within the boundaries of the broader Civil War repeatedly met with frustration (see Ackelsburg 1986).

Although the Spanish and Greek cases differ in many other respects, perhaps the most significant contrast is that the EAM does appear to have made far greater use of the organizational resource, assuming a more proactive stance regarding the reconstruction of popular attitudes and seeking to condition both sexes for a *relatively* more equitable existence in postwar politics and society. The consciousness behind this strategy is partly traceable to Glinos's remarks in his Women's University inaugural speech in 1921. After 1917, he said, "suddenly thousands of girls turned up in the Greek schools and state gymnasia, affording the most radical, shall we say, solution to the problem of girls' training, but without any prior study, without any research into the program's implications, and in any case without any preparation for boys' and girls' cohabitation in the miserable cowsheds called Greek teaching institutions, with no real guidance concerning the completely natural lack of personal experience with the multifaceted problems of coeducation" (1971b, 58–59). Organizational pragmatism in this area is evident in an informant's description of the inauguration and purpose of the girls' protoorganization Eleftheri Nea.

I remember that we girls, in school, we had, how would one put it? . . . a disadvantage, because we had strict rules at home, because the boys were freer, because young women weren't allowed to pursue an education the way the boys could. That is, a girl finishing high school could only stay at home. Whereas a boy could go on to the university to study. . . .

I'll tell you something that happened to me personally. In 1941, before Eleftheri Nea had been formed, I was at a meeting at a house where there were seven or eight male students, and me. And we wanted to form a club. I had no idea whatsoever how clubs got formed, or anything of the kind [*Egho dhen eiha idhea, oute pos ginetai enas syllogos, oute tipote*]. I had somehow just ended up at this meeting. And I had nothing to say. I felt so horrible that I couldn't talk, that I had nothing to say, that I said to myself, "What in the world am I doing here?! Because I have absolutely nothing to say. I don't know anything." That kind of thing, for girls, among other girls, is more easily overcome. Because we don't feel as though another girl knows a whole lot more than we do, that she is more able, our girl friend, our female comrade [*i sinagonistria mas*], whereas we don't have the same perspective as the men.

In the spring of 1942, an organization called EAM Youth was formed. The reason it was formed was that, well, at that time, girls' chances of being able to join a mixed organization were very slim. Their mentality, the preconceptions, the difficulties they would encounter at home . . . that was the most important thing. . . . that is, they would first of all have problems at home, because they would be in the company of boys. Girls had very tight restrictions. Second, women, because they were so sheltered, it would have been much more difficult for them to gain any sort of recognition, to be heard, to be able to grow and change at all when among the men. The men "covered them over" with their dynamism, with the confidence which comes from having some leeway in society, with their experience, they were involved in politics, in everything. So this organization was concerned with helping girls to have the courage to speak up, not to be so hesitant, to talk when there were men around. It covered both of these problems. The ones that the girls would face at home, and the problems that had to do with timidity.

Thousands of girls were mobilized into this organization in Athens. It was a big step. The EN grew by leaps and bounds [*ihe mia almatodhi anaptiksi*] in Athens and in Piraieus. Thousands of junior high and high school students, and girls from the factories, and girls in the neighborhoods, who had been sitting in their homes. A lot of the schools formed EN chapters. The organization turned out quite a few leaders, many many leaders. But this was an organization that had a prescribed life-span, because later on it fed into EPON, but it had those ten or so months of activity, in that time it did wonderful work, it performed a miracle. The girls who had become leaders in EN could now enter EPON and they could undertake very serious work, and make a success of it. They could now do their resistance work very well. They now had self-confidence. Because it wasn't only that you took part in demonstrations, in some bold protest marches, and such. It wasn't only that. It was also the basic fact that at a particular time, we got together and talked about all those things. We had to make decisions, to plan, we had to think about all the old assumptions [*proipotheseis*], with that they wanted to put something in your brain, and we women, we who also had organizational abilities [*mia organotikotita*], because they kept house, the house and all of that, they often showed that in many ways they had resources that the men didn't have. And those qualities were going to be lost, because all they did was sit around inside.

So we took on more responsibility. But I'll tell you something. The most difficult thing of all was to change the relations between couples, inside the family. That was really the hardest thing. It was so much harder for us to reach the married women and change how couples related to one another.

This passage shows an awareness of cultural constraints on the political behavior of women and girls. Note also that the last line conveys some official concern about the relation between the public and private spheres. Those in charge of overall social policy had apparently recognized that the organization should begin to think about a way to regulate the "rules of the game" within the home. In this area it is quite possible that prewar feminist figures and Communist women either took the initiative or strategized with male leaders such as Glinos, Tzimas, Siantos, and others about the gender requirements of an effective cultural politics, helping to sanction initiatives closer to the ground. It appears that the second wave of the modern women's movement, though it popularized the phrase "the personal is political," was not the first to consider the concept.[1] Conceiving itself as mandated to address unequal rela-

---

[1] We must also take into account the narrator's own contemporary feminist conditioning as revealed in the way she lays out the issues she now recalls as momentous. Collective memory in this sense—"remembering" problems that might have been addressed in the past based on subsequent political lessons—can also be a factor.

tions within the family, the EAM offered to insure the risk inherent in altering the status quo. By inaugurating a protoorganization for girls, the leadership tried to put in place some sort of structural means to encourage normative value change as well as the extension of citizenship to young women.

Authority and legitimacy are crucial to successful policy implementation, and it is not only legally sanctioned governments that require the popular stamp of approval. Authority and legitimacy are also acutely necessary for socializing movements hoping to embed new concepts in the public consciousness. Organizational authority is defined here as the ability to command popular support and attention and to elicit certain behavior. Organizational legitimacy is defined as the perception on the part of critical numbers of people that the organization has the right to influence their own and others' actions.

The EAM's authority on matters of social policy can be seen in the testimony of Spiros Meletzis, the official resistance photographer, who began traveling around with the EAM-ELAS leadership in 1942 to record all facets of the resistance. His first photograph of a woman partisan was taken that year in the Arcadia region of the Peloponnese. It was captioned "Andartissa Annetta" (Partisan Annette). Meletzis also photographed the popular schools and courts, the resistance leaders with their wives, and women voting on the PEEA constitution. One of his photographs shows a woman in an ELAS uniform demonstrating the use of a rifle to an attentive group of men. On changing gender relations, he observed:

> When we first used to go up into the mountain villages, in Roumeli, in Thessaly, in Macedonia, we would often see couples on the road. The man would be riding on the donkey; the woman would be walking behind, loaded down with various things and knitting all the while. They would enter the village, the woman would be unloading the stuff and the man would be resting himself. He would never say to himself, "She's a woman; maybe she needs to rest too." *Filotimo* didn't extend to women. So the war found the woman in bad shape, a slave. But up there in the resistance, in the mountains, they would see how the men from the city, the leaders, behaved toward their wives, how they lived and slowly it gave them a lesson that the woman should also have rights. She shouldn't be a slave all her life. And slowly, they began to become more aware.
>
> And there were superstitions. We met women who were afraid of water. Women and men. They never washed. They thought that water would kill them. They were scared of it. There were men who from the time they were born till they died, they never washed. We taught them to use soap; when we boiled the water to wash the clothes of the partisans, then they learned to boil the water to wash clothes.
>
> Aris sent down the word to the male partisans not to bother the

Weapons instruction: Dismantling and reassembling a rifle in an ELAS unit. Courtesy
Spiros Meletzis

women, to respect them at all times. The older men, the ones in EPON,
all of them. Not to mistreat them in any way. No, that wouldn't do at all.
Because he didn't want the organization to get a bad name. And he punished one or two of them, as examples, to show everyone what would
happen if they seduced or raped the women. When I say he punished
them, I mean he executed them for it. Romances were not allowed. And
I'll give you a personal example. Once I had gone to a factory where
there were a lot of EPON girls, very working-class girls, and they would
come and go relatively freely. I had gone there to take pictures. And we,
me and some other guys, we would hang around and shoot the breeze
with the girls, flirting. And they wanted to flirt with us too—it wasn't

that they didn't want to—but they said to us, "It's not a good idea for us to talk to you like this. You'll be leaving, and we'll be left behind." And they were right. We learned that we should respect their wishes; we learned to respect all the girls. And we were afraid to push it. . . . We respected them.[2]

Whether purely allegorical or based on an actual incident, the rumor that resistance leader Aris Velouchiotis shot a man for violating the respect for women mandated by the organization was mentioned often in the interviews. The story became an important symbol of the EAM policies with regard to women. The "built-in" cultural sanction of "respect women or die" made constant vigilance by the organization unnecessary. Similarly, the legal prerogatives given to the "popular courts" in regions where only bandit justice had previously reigned served to extend the authority of the resistance and to enforce certain moral imperatives. The EAM sought to institutionalize a system of civil administration and popular democracy (*laokratia*) by setting up a paralegal infrastructure in rural areas designed to adjudicate local cases ranging from sheep stealing to property disputes to honor killings. A number of women were appointed to serve as judges, including a woman in the Peloponnese region famous for her decision to transcend family connections and "convict" her brother-in-law for his role in a controversy with a neighbor.

Further examples of disposable corporate authority can be seen in testimony from informants around Greece about relations between the sexes within the organization. From the Peloponnese:

> We girls and boys weren't really allowed to have romances. Of course, from time to time there were "flirts"—it couldn't be helped—but if you were going to get involved with someone, you were obligated to go together and tell the organization. In some cases, they would actually have them separated. They would send the boy to Messinia and the girl to Laconia. But mostly, we just repeated to ourselves, "Now we have the struggle. Now we have the struggle. We'll leave all the rest for after the war. Now we have the struggle."

From Athens:

> There existed a kind of equality [*mia isotimia*], a camaraderie, but I didn't have the problems of relationships yet, because I was young yet and I was

---

[2] Meletzis's remarks can also be read for what they indicate about class relations, both in modern Greek society, with its attendant ambivalence toward the subaltern, and also within the context of the resistance. Athens contingents, spurred on by such tone-setting documents as Glinos's pamphlet, undoubtedly saw themselves as fulfilling a kind of civilizing mission when they ventured into EAM-controlled mountain areas.

mostly with the girls who had been organized from my school. But I remember what the organization told us, though. They said, "It is early yet for you to be thinking about having romantic involvements or to be interested in boys, but when you get to be about eighteen or so, that is, physiologically these things start to happen. It's very important that you don't just go ahead and do it on your own. You should always check with your parents and discuss it with them. And afterwards with the organization. Don't sneak around and do it." Well, what did we know about all that at that point? That is, the organization played a guiding role [*kathodhigito*].

In other words, the EAM regularly asserted its authority on the matter of relations between girls and boys, and in so doing, it assumed a disciplinary role that normally fell within the parental domain. Because the organization actively policed sexual relations, it was in turn accorded a certain degree of legitimacy by those families who knew about their children's involvement and entrusted them to its care. For example, in requiring parental consent for girls' participation in EPON and seeking to guarantee the chastity of female members, the organization became guardian of the virtue that was so essential to social exchange under the dowry rubric for Greek women and their families. How this type of legitimacy was actually manifested can be seen in testimony about parents' reactions to their children's involvement.

The mentality was very conservative about women. That is, if the girl wasn't a virgin, it was death. And they usually couldn't come and go freely or have groups of friends [*parea*], and if they were seen flirting, the word would go around and she would get a bad name. It was "so-and-so is a prostitute," and she wouldn't be able to find anyone to marry her; it was. . . . So the point is, that if there hadn't existed such austere standards [*avstirotita*], neither women nor girls would have joined the organization, nor would the villagers ever have opened their homes to let cadre leaders, to let the partisans come in and sleep, nor would *I* personally have been able to leave my house and join the resistance. People knew that romantic involvements were forbidden. (Peloponnese)

A woman from Crete commented:

My father was always a democrat, a Venizelist democrat. But after the movement, he became even more than us, he almost seemed to believe in it even more than us. And that's why I didn't have any negative reaction [*dhen iha kamia andirisi, dhiladi*], neither from my father nor my brothers. My brothers were in the organization, too. That is, I didn't have the usual problems of my brothers saying, "Don't go here; don't go there," no, not at all. I would just say, "I'm on my way to a rendezvous" [*tha pao sindhesmos*], and they didn't ask. If the organization said to me, "You're going to go there," I would just go. Because it was okay, I was doing it for the resistance. So that's why I moved about much more freely, because my father and my brothers were in the organization and they knew why it was happening, and they knew that there weren't immoral things going on [*anithikotites*].

Another Cretan woman asked:

Well, what could my family do? My mother was by herself; my father had died. And maybe for that reason I had a bit more freedom. But I had an older brother who was very authoritarian [*poli avstiros*]. However, he was also in the organization. He was in the EAM, so he didn't cause me any problems. It was a higher cause, and so no one bothered me. And my mother accepted it. She accepted it like a duty. It was as though I was a son who had gone off to war. That's how it was.

It is important to note that organizational legitimacy was also related to the traditional value placed on children in Greece. Buttressed by the strong affective bonds of the Greek family, the legitimacy many parents gave the organization was often founded on the involvement of their own progeny. A woman from Thebes remarked:

My father had been a royalist [*vasilofronas*] from way back. Yes, of course he was a royalist. All over our house there were pictures of the royal family. But through our activity, we had started to change the household. My father was an older man, he couldn't just change overnight, but when we joined the movement and he saw that that's how things should be, he supported us. Both my mother and my father. And he would say. . . . they would say to him around the village, "How can you believe in those things now, how can you stand it, now that your children have all left and abandoned all you've worked to build?" Because we had lots of fields, and property, and he was worth quite a bit of money; everything stayed there and we all left. . . . It was, well, the two younger boys became partisans in the mountains, one was captured by the Germans and he escaped and came back and then went to fight in the mountains; he was executed at Corfu Prison during the Civil War; the other one was a partisan in the mountains, the other two older boys were in the political wing of the EAM and me and my little sister were in EPON, and we also ended up in the mountains eventually . . . and anyway, he would say back to them, "My children are the best. Whatever my children do is good, whatever

my children do is all right. My children will take the right path." That's
what he ended up saying, because in Greece, people worship their
children.

A Macedonian woman described a similar situation:

> My mother wasn't in the EAM herself, but she helped us. One time, I re-
> member, the police came to the house [*ilthe oi horofilaki*], and among my
> books was something called *The ABC of Communism*. My father owned a
> bookstore, and because we were a leftist family, I had gotten the book
> from the store, and I read it when I was going to the *gymnasio*. And so
> when they came upon it when they were searching through my stuff, they
> found it and said, "Aha! Here it is! This must be *her* book!" And my
> mother said, "No, no! It's *my* book! What do *you* need it for? It's a book
> of ABCs!" She said, "What does this here mean? I'm just learning how to
> read and this is my book." And they actually bought it! [laughing]
>   But the funniest thing was my grandmother. She was originally from
> Turkey. She was Pondian. And she was a very religious woman. She spent
> most of her time in church, confessing, crossing herself, tending the
> icons, etc. She was about eighty years old. When she saw these people
> that collaborated with the Germans, and then they collaborated with the
> English, and she would say, "I've lost My Eyes,"[3] because she had lost
> her only son. My father was killed fighting in ELAS. "I've lost six grand-
> children in the war," she would say. She went to the EAM-ELAS head-
> quarters. She told them, "Please use me however you can. I'll take
> messages to villages." "And what if you're caught, Granny?" "I'll swallow
> the messages!" she replied. And afterwards, after the war, we would kid
> her, saying, "Granny, which party do *you* belong to? Because you gave a
> lot to the struggle!" "Yes! That's right! And *I* did resistance! I did what-
> ever needed to be done!" "And which party do you belong to?" "What's
> a party?" "Oh, whatever, EAM, EPON, ELAS, KKE . . . what are *you*?"
> She'd say (she adored my brother; out of all of her grandchildren, he was
> her favorite), she'd gaze in his direction and say, "Yangos, which one is he
> in?" Yangos was twenty-two years old and he had been in EPON.
> "Yangos is in EPON." "Well me, too! I'm also in EPON!" Of course,
> EPON was the youth group. "And me, too! *I'm also* in EPON!" my
> grandma would say.

A final source of legitimacy for organizational policy on women's rights
concerned the efforts of the younger women in the organization. Traditional
culture classified women as weak and stupid (*mourles, hazes*) and men as

---

[3] "My eyes" (*ta matia mou*) is a common term of endearment.

intelligent and capable (see Du Boulay 1974, 100–120), but of course, not all girls had internalized such views. For example, one woman commented in an earlier passage that in setting up contests of military competence "the organization hoped to create a competitive standard [*mia amilla*], since a woman is, by nature, more organized." At times the young women expressed concern or indignation about the pace of the purported "revolution in values" within the organization. Looking back, a Theban respondent credited critical changes to women's own assertiveness:

> Listen, here, things like that . . . in some ways there was a great deal of consciousness [*katanoisi*]; there was equality, and in some ways there was oppression [*katapiesi*]. Oppression in the sense that the men always got to have the first word, and we fought that kind of thing, we women, in the organization. We fought the fact that we would do the same things and many times even more, and so why should they always have the first word? And we fought inside the organization; we also struggled for equality. Inside the movement, and inside the organization. We fought to have our own opinions and have them listened to. We said why we took the positions we took. We pointed out that our contributions were just as valuable as theirs. And slowly, I think they began to see our side more, because also the organization was saying that too. But lots of times, we had to fight within the organization to be heard.

It would be an exaggeration to claim complete success for EAM policies among the rank and file. Nevertheless, on the whole the trend initiated by the organization was inclusive and sensitive to women's plight. To some extent, we can only speculate about the consensual orientation of EAM-ELAS leaders regarding the need to counter age-old social barriers to subaltern advancement, since most are no longer available for comment and if actual minutes of wartime strategy sessions exist, they have yet to be discovered. Evidence of the priority given to expanding female membership and reorienting public belief systems can be discerned in a number of pragmatic reform initiatives, however. In other words, evidence will have to come from apparent behavior, rather than from concrete plans and written calculations. For example, as we have already noted, the intricate katharevousa, the formal Greek language spoken and read by the educated elite, was replaced by the more widely used demotic Greek for official resistance business and publications. The impact of this gesture was considerable, both politically and symbolically. The overall effect was to broaden the circles of communication to encompass much of the country's marginalized population, including many peasants and many women not conversant in the ceremonious katharevousa.

A further indication of the leadership's avowed interest in challenging traditional attitudes was the organization in 1942 of the Theater of the Mountains under the aegis of Vasilis Rotas, poet, writer, theater producer, and translator (of Shakespearean plays into Greek, for example), and one of the most prominent intellectuals in Greece before and after the war. Troupes of actors and singers traveled around the countryside. Among other duties, these players were charged with recruiting women and girls and with performing skits in which, for example, a character would denounce his wife, claiming that she was stupid and inferior. In the denouement, his remarks would be exposed and ridiculed, as members of the village audience jeered and stamped their feet along with the cast.[4]

Rotas's attempts to recruit talented young women into the theater troupes traveling through the mountains succeeded often enough, though they did not always achieve their aim. The following incident reveals much about the cultural biases and parental misgivings that might restrict girls' participation.

And Vasilis Rotas even passed through our village. He had some girls with him—a theater group. He wanted to find girls with good singing voices. That same evening, I had spoken into the bullhorn [*tilevoa*], and he had heard me. He asked, "Who is that girl with the crystalline voice? As soon as she finishes, bring her to me." They came to me and told me, "Rotas is looking for you." I went to him. He seemed to me to be about forty years old. He was slim and had a small beard. He said to me, "Why don't you come with me, comrade [*sinaghonistria*]?" "What would I do with you?" I asked him. "You have a beautiful voice," he told me. "We are organizing a singing theater troupe and we plan to entertain people."

I liked the idea, because I wanted to get out more, to do something different; I had a very lively, active spirit. I told him, "I would love to come. But my parents would never let me. My mother would die." "What a pity!" Rotas said. "But I can understand your mother's position. Put yourself in her shoes for a minute. That her daughter would leave, that she would be lost! That her child would become a starlet . . . or a degraded woman!" But, he repeated, he really liked my voice. "Won't you try again to talk to your parents about this?" Eh, I went and told them and "Po, Po!!" my mother began beating herself. "I will die! I'll go drown myself in the well!" And so much for my voice. (Grizona 1982, 18)[5]

---

[4] Documentary film, *The Theatre of the Mountains,* shown 13 November 1985 at the Center for Scientific Research, Athens. Theater of the Mountains' scripts are published in Mavroeidi-Papadaki, Rotas, et al. 1962. On the general phenomenon of the resistance theater, see Kotzioulas, 1980.

[5] One of my interviewees was known as the "Voice of Kaissariani" because of her bullhorn work. She had passed the exams to enter Rotas's Athens acting school before the war but was not allowed to join because she was too young at age ten.

EPON theater group in Rethymno, Crete, post-Liberation, 1944. Courtesy Spiros Meletzis

Certainly there is no overt reason to doubt Rotas's ethics. Still, the contemporary discourse that has illuminated subtler forms of sexual harassment makes this story vaguely unsettling. Even more strikingly, however, this incident shows the capacity of resistance organizers to validate and mirror people's essential fears as a means of gaining public trust. No doubt many were reassured and the use of such culturally sensitive communication skills helped win adherents to the cause. Even though the ultimate ideal of the partisan/citizen would be carved in a gender-neutral, if not masculine, image, crucial insight into the gendered byways of the culture contributed greatly to EAM's mobilizational success.

The *message about organized resistance* embedded in the *resistance message* radiated into many areas, encouraging challenges to hegemonic structures. An example is the near food riot by children in Elassona described earlier. Labor organizer, Fofi Lazarou, tells of another incident: "They told us that at the Spiropoulou Textile Factory, the workers are in an uproar. The wages are very low. No food is distributed. Things can't get much worse. The girls are ready to strike. They don't have an organization. Someone must help them. We worked together with textile worker Yiorgia Haralambidou-Yiorgiou, tobacco workers Elli Topika-Makri and Politimi Fardhi-Timoyiannaki . . . and other girls whose names I no longer remember, in organizing the Piraieus Light Industry Section of EPON. Also in the Papastratou and Krani tobacco factories, and textile factories of Retsina, Velka, Karella, Velisaropoulou, Sfaellou and others, in the districts of Levkas and of Neo Faliron. Places where the workers were almost exclusively women, and most of them young women" (1982, 28). Lazarou goes on to describe a subsequent strike organized and led by factory girls themselves, then notes:

> The war, the occupation, the resistance were all a cosmogony [*kosmoghonia*]. Life changed. And people changed, their brains, their perspectives. The young women factory workers found the strength to alter their own fate. They too felt the responsibility to fight for freedom and to break their chains, and these changes also took place within the bounds of the home. They joined organizations, they fought. And in the process they gained their own opinions, strength, self-confidence, fortitude. In the organization and in the struggle they discovered talents which had lain buried and unused deep within them and launched the battle to catch up in all areas, almost as though they wanted to shake off, all at once, the slavery and backwardness of centuries. (30)

In addition to breaking through the entrenched concentration of cultural stereotypes about women, a number of more formal political rights were bestowed. The most significant was the right to vote and the equal rights clause that appeared in the PEEA constitution in the spring of 1944. In some ways these new laws mark structural changes, but it is hard to separate formal aspects of this legislation from their symbolic message for women. In a BBC documentary called *The Hidden War* (1986), a village woman says: "I remember that the government made beautiful things happen and we were raised to a higher level. The other governments had neglected the peasants. Beautiful things happened, like voting. I voted. And we helped in the local government in any way we could."

Voula Damianakou was the widow of Vasilis Rotas. She met and married him soon after the PEEA government was established in the spring of 1943, and Rotas was named minister of culture.

> When I first went to Larissa, in Thessaly, in 1942, I found women who were in such a state that you said to yourself, "Are they mentally retarded?" They weren't morons. They simply hadn't really entered society; they hadn't ever played any real role in society; they were under the power of their husbands, their fathers and their husbands. But feminist movements aren't the same in every country. That is, in America it's one way, and in other countries it might be another way. These things come

EPON public meeting. The banner on the wall reads: "Forward with passion into the antifascist battles." Courtesy the College Archives, King's College London

in a variety of forms depending on the conditions that create this or that culture. So, this was the way that these women . . . the resistance happened, but things hadn't yet taken off for them. That is, they did whatever their husbands told them to do. They contributed to the struggle, and they didn't talk. There was a kind of retardation [*mia kathisterisi*].

But soon these women—how can I tell you what they did?—they took a step up and they were "warbling like birds" [*kai kelaidhousan*]. They were talking on a whole range of subjects. They were considering all kinds of issues. They were going to the popular courts set up by the resistance and they were bringing their own viewpoints to the discussion. When they were the judges, they decided all sorts of cases. And they often judged the cases more fairly than formally trained judges. And they participated; they learned how to read and write. Here and there I also tried to help. Both women and men would come, but the women were more illiterate than the men to begin with. And it was something to see. . . . there would be these, what today we would call "seminars." Then they called them "schools." But "schools" isn't really accurate either, but the struggle didn't allow us to do more. . . . it was . . . well, we would go into the woods and we would give lessons to the women. And I remember so many of them, holding their pencils, or writing on rocks with rocks, and trying to write. And quite a few learned how to write. And they considered it a really big thing, that. Then they could finally learn how to write . . . and they voted for the first time. They voted for the first time. It was the first time they voted. And to watch them walk up there with their ballots was really something.

We can see that resistance organizations played a crucial, indeed, a "make-or-break" role in the empowerment of women and girls. During the recruitment phase, it was the specific organization that very deliberately gave—or failed to give—women the message that it was acceptable for them to step outside the boundaries of traditional behavior and into the public sphere. The extent of attitudinal change was congruent with the general philosophy of sexual equality propagated by the particular organization and is clearly reflected in respondents' retrospective view of women's general and, by extension, of their own potential role in society.

The EAM message to women along these lines was the most radical because it was the most direct. It was also the most pervasive. In fact, after a fairly exhaustive search, I was able to find only four women who were in organizations other than the EAM. The scarcity of non-EAM women can be considered a statistic in its own right. It is safe to say, based both on my own evidence and on the historical record, that the women who were not in the EAM were probably exceptions to the rule. This was almost certainly due to the fact that EAM, in aspiring to become a populist organization, specifically targeted women for group mobilization, whereas the other organizations had less resolute reasons for recruiting women.[6] "My uncle did not believe in women," commented Evanthia Zervas, niece of General Napoleon Zervas, in our telephone conversation in November 1985. She quickly modified her assertion. "That is, he did not believe that women should take up arms and fight." The few women in the EDES, which Zervas headed, served as nurses. I have been unable to find firsthand accounts or archival material concerning the recruitment of women into the EDES in any capacity.

The one exception among rightist organizations was the PEAN youth organization in Athens, which was the only group with more than a few female

---

[6] Some used women simply because the occupying forces tended to be less suspicious of them. Indeed, this motivation was not absent in the EAM. Nazi ideology stressed domestic roles for women and very much discounted any possible public or military role for them. For this reason, the munitions plants of the Third Reich relied heavily on foreign labor. Thus, it took occupation authorities some time to "catch on" that women and girls might be involved in resistance missions. For accounts of the experiences of German women during the Nazi period, see Koonz 1987.

members. There were approximately 150 girls in PEAN and some effort was made to recruit female members. It was not uncommon for siblings of PEAN members to belong to EPON. "It just depended on which group the rest of your *parea* [friends] had joined," said one informant.

Perhaps the best way to end here is to look briefly at the resistance songs that inspired partisans of both sexes with their fundamentally populist messages. It is significant that the resistance song lyrics had the capacity to interpellate Greek citizens across gender lines.[7] The primacy of political populism—what Mouzelis calls a change in the relations of domination without, or at least prior to, a concomitant change in the relations of production—is apparent in the "spaces" left partially vacant by the movement in its broader mobilizing efforts. From another point of view, the absence of "hard-line" themes and the priority given to expressly Greek nationalist motifs is particularly striking when the official songs of the Greek and Yugoslavian resistance movements are compared (see Dedijer 1990). The Yugoslavian songs also stress nationalism, but it is of a different sort: an indigenous nationalism combined with orthodox Communist references. Virtually to a song in the Yugoslavian renditions I have come across, some mention is made of Stalin, Tito, the Communist party, or Mother Russia as the heroes of the struggle.[8] In contrast, Stalin, the KKE, and the Soviet Union appear much less often in the lyrics of the Greek songs, whose "superstars" are nearly always Greece, Freedom, the People.[9] Examples

[7] In some cases, Greek poets were commissioned to write songs for the movements; in others, members attached their own lyrics to old folk melodies. See K. Myrsiades 1983.

[8] The Yugoslavian songs are quoted in *The War Diaries of Vladimir Dedijer* (1990). For example: "Oh people of Lika and Kordun, / The time has come to rise up / Against your loathsome oppressors, / All of the Ustashe and all of the conquerors. / You fool, you who are called the Poglavnik, / The soil beneath you is shaking, / You won't be able to run, nor save your head, / Our strong hands will grab you. / Oh Stalin, you are the people's idol, / Without you they cannot live. / Come brothers, let's measure the Drina, / So we can build a bridge for Stalin. / Comrade Stalin and the red star / Will destroy the fascist nests. / Oh youth, the beloved of our race, / From you will dawn freedom. / On you will fall the weight / To eradicate this wretched fascism. / We will bear fortune and freedom / To the Croatian and Serbian peoples. / Or, / In the camp of the Bolsheviks / They say it is my love; / For three months, maybe more, / She has neither come nor written, / I was with them yesterday / On Durmitor's peak. / I sat by the camp / And watched the Bolsheviks, / Partisans all. / I saw beautiful sights / Among them is discipline / And the comradely life. / I listened to their reading, / Lenin's teachings, / And I watched my sister / How she spoke the truth. / I then gazed upon the standard: / The hammer and sickle, the five pointed star, / Beneath that two, three words, / Comrade Molotov's name. / Above all Stalin's promise: / Enslavement no more! / The sunshine shimmers, the dawn beams, / I depart down the mountain / And leave behind the Bolsheviks, / Stalin's workers."

[9] Other types of songs may have been sung among Communist party members in the EAM. Postwar repression and silencing of political options may have made it expedient to omit explicitly "red" lyrics from songbooks or memoirs. Nevertheless, members almost never mentioned that sort of content in recollecting on their experiences, and it is conspicuously absent from content analyses of popular resistance journals and Theater of the Mountains scripts. In

of the most popular Greek songs will serve to make the point, and we can use these songs as a device to imagine how we might process their "speech" if directed toward us. First is "The Official Song of the EAM," written by Rotas:

> Freedom, the beautiful daughter
> Descends from the mountain tops
> And the people embrace her
> And they sing and celebrate.
>
> EAM! EAM! EAM! EAM! Voice of the people!
> which stretches as far as the stars in the sky!
> EAM! EAM! EAM! EAM! it echoes.
> All Greece shall speak with one voice.
>
> Tell it to the birds and the winds
> That now the beast will tremble
> Black violence the time has come for you to leave
> And great punishment will befall you.
>
> And we shall be so happy and rejoice
> That we shall all see freedom together
> and we will live in brotherly love,
> Throughout the world, throughout the universe.

Another song is called "One Voice":

> One voice, one voice calls out to me,
> Giving me the signal to move forward.
> From the earth, it reaches to the sky,
> Whatever the people want! Whatever the people want!
>
> Down with thrones, down with violence,
> Down with dark, insidious fascism!
> Forward with democracy!
> So that the people may have whatever they want!
> Whatever the people want!

1975 two songbooks were published simultaneously: a major source of resistance lyrics (*To andartiko kai to epanastatiko traghoudhi*) and a companion volume entitled *Socialistika Traghoudhia: Kokkina traghoudhia* [first published in 1921] and *Epanastatika traghoudhia* [first published in 1928] (Socialist songs: Red songs and Revolutionary songs). These "facts," taken together, lead me to conclude that it was resistance culture and not fears of subsequent censorship that accounts for the lack of Soviet references.

Nikos Karvounis wrote "To Arms, To Arms":

> Mount Olympus thunders
> And lightning on Kiona,
> Agrafa rumbles, and Steria shakes.
> To arms! To arms! Forward into battle!
> For the most valuable thing of all, Freedom!
>
> The *armatoliki* has been revived,
> The arms iron, the spirit enflamed
> The foreign wolves crouch trembling
> At our avenging male[10] force!
>
> The Gorgopotamos sends proud salutations to Alamana
> Its a new resurrection, beat the drums
> Word of our uprising reaches Litromo.
> We break the ignoble chains
> That have been our deadly burden,
> We want our country free
> And universal human freedom.
>
> Mount Olympus thunders,
> And lightning bolts from Kiona.
> The flames leap over to Moria.
> To arms! To arms! Forward into battle!
> For the most valuable thing of all, Freedom!
>
> With joy and a song in our hearts
> The kids of EPON fight,
> A heroic generation goes united into battle
> For Democracy and for Freedom.
>
> In the mountains, on the plains and in the cities,
> Youth, you always go forward
> And with a flame in your breast
> A victorious freedom fighter.
> A hero of ELAS has been born.
>
> EPON, EPON, you are the enemy of fascism
> Valuable generation of hard workers
> The pride of the people EPON, EPON, EPON,
> EPON, EPON, a new day is dawning,
> the Generation of '21 lives again among the people.

---

[10] *Andrikia:* men's, manly, masculine, crushing.

The Greek and Yugoslavian resistance songs share such themes as the glory of the land, natural images, and the necessity of destroying the fascists, but a close reading reveals how different were the organizing principles of the two movements. Both movements attempted to mobilize a mass base, but the discourse of inspiration, its terms ultimately set by the leaders, gave members in the two countries very different messages about for what and whom they were fighting. The curriculum of the Greek People's Schools stressed literacy, personal growth, and voting as a universal, inherent right; in short, training members to become somewhat attenuated "good Greeks" rather than "good Communists," envisioned in sharper relief. My point here is not so much to make a normative judgment of either movement, as it is to emphasize the populism of the Greek movement and its concomitant reluctance to embrace more specific themes that might complicate matters. This hyperinclusiveness is indeed the cornerstone of populist nationalism and can, as I have said, be a mixed blessing.

An interesting passage from this perspective is Vladimir Dedijer's diary entry in which he describes a meeting of the international communist youth leagues which took place in Yugoslavia. Those groups that could not send delegates instead sent messages of support. Dedijer reports that the delegate of the French resistance, Raymond Obrac, spoke in the name of French youth: "We in France know that we are your comrades. We admire your people and your struggle. We greet Marshall Tito, who is the greatest symbol of your fatherland." In contrast to the message from France, and those from the Soviet Union and Bulgaria, the Greek message was brief and general: "Deeply touched by your invitation, we greet the congress of the Yugoslav Antifascist Youth, which is fighting heroically for the destruction of fascism. EPON, fighting with you, admires your successes and firmly believes in the fortunate resolution of the common struggle. It is impossible to participate in the congress because of the shortness of time. Our deep regrets" (1990, 3:283–84).

Referring to the song quoted above, Diamando Grizona waxes enthusiastic, her emotional pitch common to other nostalgic partisan narrators: "We worked all night long, because in the day the German cannons were trained on us—you just didn't dare. We got used to the dark. And what songs we sang while we worked! We moved heaven and earth! Everyone sang! And which ones didn't we sing! I will sing one now, 'Mount Olympus thunders, And lightening bolts from Kiona, Agrafa rumbles and Steria shakes, To arms! To arms! Forward into battle, For the most valuable thing of all, freedom!' Oh . . . I can't . . . Now I'm crying . . . For the most valuable thing of all, *for freedom*."[11]

[11] Grizona 1982, 15.

Worlds of Feeling: Nationalism as Patriotism

> When I was wounded, I said, "*Zito i Ellada—Elefteria*" [May Greece Live—Freedom] to myself, I said it, "whatever I do I do for Greece. I do it for Greeks." I didn't really feel afraid, at that moment, I thought, "Well, my life is over, and that, O.K., another Greek is leaving this life."
>
> —Martha

> I was drunk with resistance. [*Iha ena methisi*]
>
> —Anthoula

The poet George Seferis said of Greece, "Wherever I go it wounds me." The case of the women who joined the Greek resistance shows how strong and ubiquitous Greek nationalism actually cut across societal cleavages and offered powerful motivation for participation. In the interviews, women almost always cited their intense love of country as a reason for becoming active in a resistance organization. The prevailing normative consensus about the righteousness of collective resistance against outside invasion in many cases helped women and girls to circumvent convention. This was largely because defensive nationalism, or the willingness to defend Greece once a credible threat had been established, was (and still is) a central cultural value, attached to the more individual concept of *timi* (honor and self-worth). Often, the women who joined the EPON would comment that their parents allowed them to do so only because they were fighting to defend Greece against the Nazis. Presumably, husbands also made this distinction.

Andreas Psomas argues that the system of formal education played an important role in engendering a "positive image and ready identification with Greece as a nation" (1978, x). It is true that the most important age for political learning runs from childhood to late youth, when the subject is the most impressionable. Most of the women I interviewed were young adults at the time of the resistance, and many were attending junior high or high school. In many ways, in fact, the resistance was primarily a youth movement, not an attempt to resocialize those whose opinions were already formed. Even before the fall of 1941, the mobilization potential of the women was quite high in this regard, even though as part of a disfranchised group they had had limited prior exposure to the usual agents of political socialization, not only the educational system, (particularly in the villages), but also the practice of voting, discussions in the kafeneion, and the like.

The family played a significant part in the political socialization of women at this time. A majority of my interviewees mentioned that they identified most strongly with a male member of the household—father, grandfather, older brother—who was what they termed *pro-odheftikos* (progressive). Usually, what they meant was that these men valued learning, in the sense that Psomas means when he writes that "education has traditionally been referred to by the Greek people as the strong light which disperses the darkness of illiteracy, allowing one to proceed safely on one's own—thus rendering dependence on others unnecessary" (1978, 185). In some cases my informants meant that these male figures valued learning for women and girls, although the two meanings of *pro-odheftikos* were not necessarily always congruent. Nevertheless, one might surmise that instinctively progressiveness, desire for self-improvement, personal autonomy, and nationalism might intersect in the public consciousness. Insofar as these women identified with important men in their lives, men who, there can be little doubt, were symbolically committed to the phenomenon called "Greece," sentiments on nationalism were also transmitted to and absorbed by daughters, granddaughters, and sisters.

In addition, there were two other significant contributing factors. One was the connection made between the struggle against the Axis and the rebellion against Turkish rule in 1821. The image of resistance against the Ottomans as a righteous cause was well secured in the popular memory. The virtual canonization in nineteenth-century Europe of such figures as Lord Byron, who participated in that revolution, probably still fired the Greek imagination as late as the 1940s as a matter of collective pride. A second factor was the Greek victories on the Albanian front. The victory celebrations in the streets and in the schools had a tremendous effect on those young people who had not gone to the front. The rejoicing at each victory won by Greek forces on the Albanian front triggered a profound sense of pride and love of country among a cross section of the public, much like the winning of a gigantic soccer game. The collective self-adoration catalyzed during the 1940 battles would serve to augment the EAM's mass appeal as a resistance movement against any and all external threats to Greece's territorial sovereignty. This situation in turn created a ready-made "sentiment pool," which was then available to be mobilized.

For example, one woman and her sister were both members of EPON. On the subject of patriotism, she said:

> And another thing, because we were so hungry, there was a lot of activity around that. There was a path that went through a field across from our house and we would use it to go get bread at the bakery, you know, the kind of bread they would give us then, that horrible stuff that had wood shavings [*rokanidhia*] in it, and all anyone got of it was just a handful of pieces. And there, the Germans had their cars lined up all along the length of the field, from the road over to where we would go to the bakery. And one morning, I saw that the engine of one of the cars was running with the hood up (why no one was around, I have no idea) and I said to myself, "Gee, I should sabotage them." I thought of it on my

own, and I went back to the house and I got a pair of pliers [*mia pensa*] and I came back and I stuck my hand in and fortunately, my hand didn't reach the wires because it was very far; otherwise, I was prepared to cut the wires of the car! I tell you, people were crazy! [*trellos kosmos!!*] The point is, we weren't afraid! We were so—how can I put it?—we weren't the least bit worried that we would be killed. We didn't think about being caught. Of course we had no idea what death meant, or real slavery [*sklavia*] like being in a jail. . . . we had absolutely no reservations about what we were doing.

Also important in developing nationalist patriotism was the inordinate repression that characterized the Nazi occupation virtually from the beginning. Several elements activated popular resentment. Public outrage soared over the food requisitions, which lead to large-scale starvation in the winter of 1941; rigorous inspections of transportation conveyances and in other public venues; the arrest and torture of civilians in special facilities such as the Hotel Crystal and Merlin Prison in Athens; and hundreds of other such odious acts. "I remember when the Nazis marched into the main square of Missolonghi, and they were shouting and ordering old women around; thirteen I was then, and I remember that I was walking with my mother," said one woman. "I was furious. I *loathed* them. And I vowed to do something about it. Can you imagine? Who was I at thirteen to become so angry?" This leads us to a related theme in the testimonies, that of the mobilization potential of youth.

The Mobilization Potential of Youth

> We were at an age when we played it all or nothing. [*Imaste se ilikia pou ta paizame ola yia ola*]
>
> —Eleni

A major theme running through the oral testimonies is that many girls and some women also were beginning to despair over their confinement and truncated life choices. One woman's mother took the previously "unheard of" step of separating from her husband and, leaving the children in his care, joined the EAM as a nurses' aide. But as might be expected, such defiant behavior was more common among younger movement participants.

The political socialization literature, such as it is, is fairly definitive about the moral suasibility of youth. Just as "wars, industrialization, international political realignments, prolonged unemployment, and widespread demographic changes" are the disruptions which lead to social transformations at the macrolevel (McAdam 1988, 41), so youth may be viewed as an opening in the political opportunity structure on a micro-personal plane. It is a fairly intuitive matter for anyone who has traveled the path from childhood to adulthood that during this approximately fifteen-year transition individuals are inclined to rebel and attempt to affect situations in relatively risky ways.

The youthfulness of the participants, alluded to earlier, is one of the most striking, repetitious themes of the Greek resistance movement. The attributes associated with the age group ten to twenty-five—idealism, impressionability, impetuosity—all increased the likelihood that the young would adopt the EAM's radical agenda. Evidence of rhapsodic reactions and the general effects of youthful malleability can be seen in a number of the testimonies.

For example this woman, from Serres, Macedonia, displayed a juvenile defiance of authority that armed with a more seasoned perspective she might not have risked:

> One time I saw a girl I had gone to school with give a flower to a Nazi soldier. And I went berserk! I started to yell and went up to her and screamed, "Aren't you ashamed of yourself? How can you do that?" And the German jumped all over me and wanted to beat me, but a Bulgarian soldier held him back.
>
> Because the mother of one of my friends was letting a room in their house to a couple of Bulgarian soldiers, I had stopped going to their house. Because I refused to go with them there. I didn't trust myself. And one day that friend said to me, "Why don't you come over and eat with us? Come over to my house, come on," and my mother said, "Oh, go ahead, go on and go." And because we had some EPON business to do over at her house anyway, I went, and when it came time to eat, I saw food that we never got at our house. And there were the Bulgarians at the table. When I saw them, I went crazy, because my friend didn't tell me they were going to be there. We sat down to eat. So she says, "Do you know how beautifully Martha sings? She sings very well." And they requested that I sing a certain song, a Russian song. I stood up, I pulled myself up to a height, and I said loudly, "Next to my enemy, I shall *never* sing!!" And I went to leave. And one of the Bulgarians got up and congratulated me, saying, "We love our country, too. That's just what we would've done." And I said, "Well, have you learned something?" And I slammed out the door. I was pretty sassy. Of course, in the meantime I was starving! [laughing] And where was I supposed to eat? But it was the principle of the thing.

The following passage shows a similar zeal for the cause, partly (though not entirely) attributable to the obstinacy of youth:

When I left to join the resistance, they sent me into the mountains and I would go around to various villages making contact with the EPON groups in the Peloponnese. I even got as far as Zakinthos. But basically, I didn't come back to the house to live again until I got out of jail, in 1952. Anyway, when I left, my mother wasn't there. She had gone somewhere to exchange food, because we had an exchange economy then. At that time there wasn't much food in our area; for example, we had oil, and different things, but we didn't have wheat. So they would take the oil and go off to other villages that needed oil and had wheat and they would make exchanges. My mother had gone off to do something like that. I left her a note, saying, "I'm leaving." At the time we didn't have real shoes and we wore *chokara*, clogs of wood and animal skin. I needed shoes, and so a few weeks earlier my mother had traded oil for the shoes. I put on the shoes and I left. . . . And later on, when my mother came to see me during visiting hours at the Averoff Prison in Athens, she said to me, "Ach—this is all my fault, because I got you the shoes! [laughing] Because, if you hadn't had shoes, you wouldn't have been able to leave!!" And I said to her, "Mama, *barefoot*, I would've left *barefoot* if I had to!!" She said, "You left, and you never came back, except that one time wanting me to fix the soles on your *chokara*!" So, she wasn't at all happy that I left. But what could she do to stop me? I wanted to go.

Recall that Anthoula was arrested by the Gestapo partly because she defied maternal authority and kept an appointment with a resistance contact. As a result, she did not see her mother until after liberation:

So finally I ended up in Haidari Prison and they sent us from there to Ravensbruck. When we first got to Germany, they took us to a holding camp, where they gave us medical examinations. They made us wait outside in the snow, completely naked, then one of the Nazis would come and get you and you would go inside to be examined, they would poke at you, and look at your teeth, etc. And the older ones also got a gynecological exam. In case we were pregnant or something was wrong and we couldn't be productive workers. They finished with you, and then you would go back out into the snow from the warmth of the clinic, and have to stand there until they finished with all of the others. After two months, they took us to the factory. And there life was a nightmare. We were all young women who had been in the resistance, students, very good young women and very determined. And there the Greek women really stood out. The first night we got there, the very first night, we had a secret meeting. A secret meeting. To decide how we would confront the whole thing, these new conditions that required a new kind of resistance.

It was now going to be different from distributing leaflets, or writing on walls, or whatever resistance we had done before. This was something entirely different. So, what would we do to resist this new situation? And we decided: that we wouldn't eat garbage, the garbage they threw out, because it's degrading, it begins the process of losing your dignity, we wouldn't pick through the garbage; and we would do whatever we could to mess up our work, we wouldn't produce one bullet for the front. We wouldn't eat garbage, and we wouldn't assist the hand that was striking us.

There was a division with forty machines, and the other twenty were in the other factory opposite, we were sixty altogether, and that's how we were divided. And we produced various things, war supplies, these kinds of bullets, and they would keep track on a large board. One twelve-hour shift was made up entirely of Greek women; the other, out of the forty machines, was women from different countries, Polish women, Russian women, or whatever. The other shift produced a large number, but out of the Greek women, almost nothing. And this was completely unacceptable. They punished us for it, they put fifteen of the girls in a bunker, and when they came out, they were completely white, very very pale, from being locked underground in those dark cells with iron doors. Without food, etc. Then we realized that we could sabotage things by doing it wrong so that the machine would break down. If you put the bullet in the wrong way, then when it came time to press down, the machine would break. The *Meister*, the German supervisor, couldn't imagine that *I* was capable of sabotage. I looked very innocent, with my long braids, like a little milkmaid. And he would say to me, "*An*-toula! The bullet goes in from this side!" He was an SS man, but a civilian, not an SS soldier. "Nicht Verstehen! *An*-toula! Not that way," he would say patiently, "What did I tell you? This way! This way! Otherwise, the machine *kaput*!" [laughing] And that, of course, was exactly what I wanted!

The combination of youth and nationalism is obviously a heady one. Neither area has been studied very extensively in the social sciences; hence, empirical data are scarce. But recent cases—China, South Africa, South Korea—can provide insight into nationalist youth movements and associated political processes. I would imagine that such variables as timing; the organizational components of structure, authority, legitimacy, and message; and ideological roots may manifest themselves in comparable ways in myriad youth movements. On the one hand, contextual issues are certainly critical to a full reading of the narratives of these movements. On the other hand, nationalist, youth-centric movements do have certain generic qualities as well, which might be investigated for what they can tell us about the passions that work to produce important social transformations. We might begin with one of the most commanding emotions in such cases. Randall Collins, writing about the New Left of the late 1960s, summarizes this facet of youth movements from personal experience:

> After all, we had our "Berkeley-the-center-of-the-universe" self-image, full of not only the feeling that what we were doing was the most important thing of our own lives, but also the illusion that what we did rippled outwards and catalyzed followers everywhere else. With more detachment, one can say it is precisely that feeling that is the mark of a movement on the rise, and which constitutes one of its strongest attractions. (1988, 729)

Although not explicitly nationalist, that movement was very much concerned with political inclusion. The sentiment Collins refers to is utterly familiar to students of youth movements and suggests a need for further studies of the nexus of youth and politics.

Cracking the Code: Social Transformations

> The war was a lesson for all of us. [*O polemos itan ena dhidhagma yia olous mas.*]
> —Tasia

As skeptical of binarisms as the next person, nevertheless I find it useful to weigh the consequences of the resistance as a social movement from two basic perspectives: the macrolevel (political incorporation) and the microlevel (empowerment). Should we find ourselves in danger of committing to an overly rigid scheme, we might keep in mind that the narrative approach helps to add shades of meaning and virtually guarantees that all conclusions will in some sense remain speculative.

In macrohistoric terms women's political incorporation appears negligible at first glance, since many of the structures and social policies promoted by the resistance—including those aimed at women—were discontinued in the postwar era. To say, however, that these innovations were officially discredited should not be taken to mean that it made no difference to the Greek political system that there had once been a social movement cum popular regime from 1941–44. But we should be cautious.

In this regard, the case of France is partly instructive. One scholar has recently noted that French women's right to vote was endorsed as early as October 1944 by General Charles de Gaulle, then president of the Committee of National Liberation in Algiers, while the resistance was still in full swing

«... Ἡ λαοκρατικὴ θεμελίωση τῆς Πολιτείας, θὰ στηριχθεῖ σὲ μιὰ **πραγματικὴ αὐτοδιοίκηση καὶ στὴ λαϊκὴ δικαιοσύνη.**
Ἡ αὐτοδιοίκηση ἀναπτύσσει τὴν πρωτοβουλία στὰ πλατύτατα **λαϊκὰ στρώματα καὶ τὰ διαπαιδαγωγεῖ** στὴν ἐξάσκηση τῆς ἐξουσίας...»

Resistance organizing pamphlet.
Self-government
"... The popular political foundation of the State will be grounded in actual self-government and in popular justice.

"Self-government develops the initiative of the broad popular strata and educates people about how to exercise power ..."

Λαϊκή Δικαιοσύνη

«... Ὁ θεσμὸς τῆς λαϊκῆς δικαιοσύνης μὲ λαϊκοὺς δικαστὲς ποὺ θὰ βοηθιοῦνται ἀπὸ εἰδικοὺς νομικούς, θὰ ἐξασφαλίσει μ' ἔναν ἁπλὸ μηχανισμὸ διαδικασίας, ἀπονομὴ δωρεὰν οὐσιαστικοῦ δικαίου, ἐξυπηρετικοῦ γιὰ τὰ συμφέροντα τοῦ λαοῦ, μὲ δημοκρατικὲς λύσεις σ' ὅλα τὰ προβλήματα τοῦ ἰδιωτικοῦ καὶ δημοσίου βίου...»

Popular Justice
"... Institutions of popular justice staffed by popular judges who will be assisted by legal experts will guarantee, through simple legal procedures, the donation of essential free counseling that will serve the interests of the people, providing democratic solutions to all the problems of private and public life ..."

back at home (Rossiter 1986, 223). A standard official narrative is that this gesture and the issuance of the ordinance of 21 April 1944 which enfranchised French women were partial payment for their contributions to the partisan movement, especially the Forces Françaises Combattantes.

Of course what was different about the Greek case was that women were enfranchised in the PEEA constitution of 1944 as the culmination of a larger social agenda advanced by EAM leadership throughout the resistance period. The Government of the Mountains was the legal articulation of EAM's vision of the postwar Greek political system. It is probably fair to assume that the practice of incorporating women into the political system would have been a major priority had the authors of that constitution retained any power after the war and had things in general turned out quite differently. Even as inevitable fissures began to appear in the edifice of popular democracy, this goal might have remained on the agenda for a time. As one woman commented, "After the war, we expected equal relations to continue. We wanted a 'people's government' like they had created in the mountains."

Although the framers of the 1944 constitution did not remain in power, Greek women were enfranchised in March 1952 by the semiliberal Plastiras government. The issue of whether there was a direct connection or even a crude quid pro quo at work in France or in Greece will always be open to dispute. It is possible that policies successfully initiated during the Greek resistance somehow left an impression in the more conservative halls of government and that women's activism during the resistance and its temporary extension of citizenship rights had pointed out an important political constituency, which, for purely opportunistic reasons, leaders wished to exploit. In a practical sense, the issues raised by the 1944 PEEA constitution (and the 1946 Panhellenic Women's Convention organized by the EAM) were not to play such a preeminent part in national politics for another thirty years, until after the fall of the colonels' dictatorship in 1974. Furthermore, it is perhaps not merely coincidental that article 4, paragraph 2 of the 1975 Greek constitution, although written by a center-right government, reads "Greek men and Greek women have the same rights and obligations," its wording a striking reminder of the 1944 law. Thus, although it is difficult to prove, there are hints that postmortem, the EAM's influence as a social movement along with its inclusive, nationalist ideologies may have influenced subsequent gender discourse. However, considering the simultaneous existence of political prisoners, brutal repression and antiresistance legislation in the aftermath of the war, the connection may be remote and in any case it is hard to see how something like this could be established to any tenable degree.

Broader ideological changes and attitude transformations are clearly indicated in the personal narratives of the women I interviewed, as is the possibility of cross-generational change. On some themes, attitudinal changes were similar to those experienced by women and girls in other kinds of social movements, or they could simply be the product of crisis, war, and national defense. Other themes, however, were specific to membership in the EAM as a national socializing movement.

"How is it possible," ask Fred Greenstein and Sidney Tarrow, "to trace the course of development through childhood and into the adult years of various political and politically relevant dispositions?" (1971, 51) Women's comments on how the resistance experience affected their personal ideological development fall into three several main categories. These are political education, moral development, and the breakdown of social barriers (of class and New Greece/Old Greece cleavage).

On Political Education

Most girls received what they considered their first real exposure to the workings of political life in the resistance, although some had been members of the compulsory Metaxas youth groups organized in all primary and secondary schools during the late 1940s. Some women felt that the resistance had changed their perspective on the world. This reaction was similar to Rosa Park's analysis of her educational experiences at the Highlander Folk School in 1962. "At Highlander I found out for the first time in my adult life that this could be a unified society, that there was such a thing as people of differing races and backgrounds meeting together in workshops and living together in peace and harmony. It was a place I was very reluctant to leave. I gained there strength to persevere in my work for freedom, not just for blacks but all oppressed people" (quoted in J. Williams 1987, 64). Similarly, a woman from the Peloponnese who was in her late thirties during the war recalled:

> Look, without the resistance, I would have been a nobody. Eh, I was a teacher, but I can honestly say that without the ideals of the resistance I would have been nothing. I mean, I would have continued as a teacher and, let's say, a good teacher, going from village to village in my area of the Peloponnese. But the resistance gave us wings [*mas edhose ftera*]. It gave me a perspective on the world, and I realized that Greece wasn't the center of the world; our area wasn't the center of Greece; and our problems were part of something greater. It opened our eyes to things like justice and the equality of women. Some women learned to read and write and we talked for the first time about the problems of equality.

The EAM's 1940s version of what would later come to be called consciousness raising in the modern women's movement appears to have had a great

Maria Svolou speaking to partisans at PEEA gathering. Courtesy Spiros Meletzis

effect on women and girls who were hearing some of these ideas for the first time. The motivation and power behind consciousness-raising as a strategy used in the American women's movement has a familiar ring: "Consciousness-raising—studying the whole gamut of women's lives, starting with the full reality of one's own—would also be a way of keeping the movement radical by preventing it from getting sidetracked into single issue reforms and single issue organizing. It would be a way of carrying theory about women further than it had ever been carried before, as the groundwork for achieving a radical solution for women as yet attained nowhere."[12] Although it has been claimed that consciousness-raising was a specific response to the power struggles within the New Left and the women's movement in the late 1960s, the Greek case

[12] Kathie Sarachild, "Consciousness-Raising: A Radical Weapon," in *Feminist Revolution,* ed. Redstockings (New York: 1975), 131, quoted in J. Freeman 1983, 202.

suggests that the technique was not unprecedented. It was linked not so much to what Temma Kaplan (1982) calls "female consciousness" as to a more expanded weltanschauung.

On Moral Development

According to one observer, the most significant antecedents of adult moral life begin to develop sometime around the age of ten. (Coles 1986). Morality—the capacity to distinguish right from wrong and to make consequential links between one's individual behavior and its implications for a wider community—takes on a political hue for children who are thrown into highly disruptive and politicized situations for prolonged periods. The effects of such experiences are particularly salient during this pivotal early phase. The sacrifice of wartime or intense social movement activity as well as the direct and ongoing contact with death greatly affects adolescent development, and all subsequent political decisions tend to be filtered through these narrative referents.

For women in Greece, moral training before the war was very straightforward. The requirements of "moral womanhood" (*na isai timia yineka*) were inculcated early, and they had little to do with institutional politics. In fact, girls' moral training usually had little to do with the public sphere at all, except to the extent that girls were admonished never to commit acts which might ultimately besmirch the family name. Tasoula, however, recalled new kinds of politically relevant influences:

> We met people whose bravery made them role models. And just that was enough for me to keep going. It was enough. One of my first cousins, Stelios Frangelakis, was arrested by the Germans and executed in Agia. I went to the jail in Agia to see him. We knew he was going to be executed in two days, and when I saw him, I started to cry. He said to me, "Tasoula, don't cry. I don't want you to feel badly about this at all, no matter what happens to me. That's the last thing I want you to do." And two days later he was dead. You know, the sort of people who really set an example.

Anthoula told me:

> I was drunk with resistance. I also learned to have my ideals, my moral framework, if you will, and always to try and live a centered existence, to filter whatever I decided to do through the control of my ideals to make sure it matched up, to live according to some plan. But you know, it hit

me, coming back across the Yugoslavian border from the work camp in Germany . . . and we could see all the destruction and burned out buildings from the window of the train, and I thought of the Polish girl in the work camp who had died in my arms and I hadn't even realized it because we all slept that way to keep warm. . . . I thought to myself—mind you, a girl of sixteen I was then—"Who are the winners? They don't exist. War has only victims." And it made a great impression on me. Now, sometimes at work, they'll say to me, "What political party do you support, A.? Who are you with, tell us, say one way or the other." And I say, "With the dead of Kaissariani.[13] If you can dig up their bones and they tell you they're with KKE or PASOK, or Nea Democratia, then I'll chose a party, too."

On the Breakdown of Social Barriers (Class)

The temporary disintegration of class barriers in otherwise stratified societies is common in wartime. For women who had generally led sheltered lives until the advent of the war, associating with others from different backgrounds was a novel experience. For example, a woman trained in the Air Transport Auxiliary as England prepared for the anticipated Luftwaffe attacks commented, "We were a mixed bag, really. We'd have girls with titles, and nobody ever asked them what they were and nobody cared" (Saywell 1985, 16). A woman from the Peloponnese described a similar phenomenon:

> The interesting thing about the EAM was that we had poor people and we also had rich people. We had lawyers and doctors, and then we had people like my father, who had a mule and used to carry things from village to village for people and get paid for it. And the one didn't necessarily look down on the other.
>
> There was a man from my village and Grigoris Christakou was his name. He had become a lawyer, and the family went to live in Githio. They were originally from the village, though, and they would come back quite often, for Christmas, for the summer, for Easter. . . . he was also a successful merchant, and president of the Lawyer's Guild in Githio. He had a wife who happened to be very very fat. She was also from a wealthy merchant family, and so they were very rich people. They would come to the village, and they were what you might call the aristocracy. She was a very good person, and Dimetra was her name. She would wave to people in the street, simple people, and she was kind to everyone, but at the same time, they were something different from us. They were the rich

[13] Where several hundred people were executed in 1944.

people. The occupation came along and her husband joined the EAM, he became a local EAM leader [*stelehos*]. And Dimetra joined too, and they came back to the village. Whoever had relatives in the village would come back because of the food scarcities in the cities. Because we weren't quite as badly off as they were in the cities. Okay, we didn't have things like sugar, but we had the kinds of things villages have—oil, wheat, vegetables. Dimetra joined Ethniki Allilengii, and she was such a nice person, we felt like she was one of us, because she would wear the same wooden clogs as us, and before the war, the soles of her feet were white, whereas those of the village girls were all dark and stained and scratched up from walking around in the country without shoes, carrying loads of branches, etc. And at that time, when there would be German raids, they would gather us all in the square, men and women, and someone up on a balcony would talk and from below the others would answer, etc. And Dimetra also would sit down below with the rest of us. When an ELAS party would come into the village, Dimetra would take over and give orders, "You, give us pillows for them," or, "Yes, we'll use the school, the boys need somewhere to sleep," and things like that. She became one of us. They killed her, during a raid, in 1944. The collaborators with the Germans, the security battalions [tagmata asfaleias), they killed her in another village. And I remember Dimetra, she was a wonderful person, like a cartoon figure, but in the struggle, she was a fighter in spite of her social position.

On the Breakdown of Social Barriers (New/Old Greece)

After the 1922 Asia Minor disaster and resulting population exchange and well into the late interwar period, a "national schism" developed between newly arrived refugees and more long-term residents, pitting community against community. The schism was expressed politically in the division of Greece into "two worlds," one that supported the liberal, republican, vaguely socialist leader Eleftherios Venizelos and one lined up behind the monarchy, headed by King Constantine in coalition with the old nineteenth-century Greek parties. This split was largely responsible for the vitriolic political polarization that showed no signs of abating until the EAM populist coalition united disparate elements against a common enemy. "With respect to the state," George Mavrogordatos writes, "the Schism reflected a territorial division between the New Lands, acquired after 1912, and Old (pre-1912) Greece. With respect to the nation, it reflected a bitter conflict between, on the one hand, the newly liberated Greeks in the New Lands together with unredeemed Greeks elsewhere and, on the other hand, the majority of Old Greece. The national aspirations of the former were embodied in Venizelism. The war-weariness and defensive patriotism of the latter found their political expression in Antivenizelism" (1983, 28).

Because girls and boys were thrown together in the course of resistance activities, friendships and marriages were often the inevitable result. It is unlikely that this was part of any deliberate strategy on the part of the leadership; as we have seen, if anything, the organization officially discouraged all but the most platonic contacts. The wider social implications of the breakdown of this critical social barrier, however, can be seen in the following testimony of a woman from Kilkis, Macedonia:

> First of all, we refugees, a lot of us had come over in '22. All these refugees, when they came, they gave a new breath to Greece and to her people, a breath of progressiveness. And that was the kind of thing that some of those already here really didn't like, and they tried to make the Greek people fight among themselves. They would say that the refugees were taking bread out of their mouths; they sent the police after us for the slightest thing, they pitted Greeks against one another. So for years and years . . . for instance, when my mother learned that I was going to marry a man from Old Greece, a guy from Laconia in the Peloponnese [*ena palioeladhitis*]! She had a fit!! Oh, my!! [sucking in her breath in horror] "Oh, my god, you're going to marry a *palioeladhiti*!!" Yes. That kind of thing existed then. And we had a whole war right there in the house. So, the war came along, and all that stopped. The people were finally one, united, Old Greeks, New Greeks, refugees and everyone. EAM managed to pull it off. They managed to unite all those people against the Nazis, and also said that popular determination should reign. The spirit of the resistance lasted in some ways.

Finally, the results of the resistance experience are evident in two other areas, in narratives about the reconditioning of parental views and attitudes toward women in society, and about the modern women's movement. Additional changes that were specific to the women political prisoners will be dealt with in the next chapter when we take a look at the effects of demobilization.

On the Reconditioning of Parental Views

Earlier I alluded to the mobilization potential of parents when children are accorded a high status and families are closely knit. Under such circumstances, when offspring become involved in movements and to an even greater extent when they begin to suffer or die, parents are often mobilized in support of the cause themselves. For example, Jeffery Paige notes that the assassination of Pedro Joaquin Chamorro, editor of the newspaper *La Prensa*, helped to radicalize a somewhat complacent agrarian bourgeoisie during the Nicaraguan revolution. "One does not kill people of a certain social condition," was one response. But just as significant at the personal level were incidents such as the machine-gun murder of the son of a prominent coffee grower and his friend by the National Guard. "A decade later," writes Paige, "there was still a tone of profound sadness in Victor Robles' voice as he described his son's lost potential. 'He was such a brilliant boy, brilliant. He won a national competition to study in Switzerland and then came back to Nicaragua and helped run the estate. He had been here for two years when he was killed. He was 21'" (1988, 33).

The Nicaraguan revolution, a nationalist struggle as well as a youth movement, resembles the Greek case on a number of dimensions and is comparable on this issue. Women were also mobilized into the Nicaraguan revolution on a mass scale, although, of course, as the years go by, the constructed meaning of any movement changes in popular memory. In her 1981 study Margaret Randall interviewed the mother of Commander Monica Baltodano. She writes that

> early in her life Zulema was concerned with the need for social justice, but she began to participate only when faced with the choice of supporting her daughter's commitment or abandoning her. Zulema lost her sixteen-year-old daughter in a bombing, looked after another daughter whose hands were severed making contact bombs, and lived for months without knowing if Monica was alive or dead. "It helped being more politically aware. It helped later when I had to bear up under the hard blows I received. If I hadn't been clear politically I might have reacted the way many mothers did. Some are still resentful. Its their lack of political consciousness." (1981, 186–87)

Similarly, a Greek resistance fighter described the changed consciousness of her widowed father:

> My father was pretty upset about my participation at first. For a while, "he chased me around from behind," [*me kiniga ena dhiastimo apo piso*]. "What in the world do you think you're doing?" and "That's not for girls like you to do," etc., etc., etc. But what kid listens to their parents when they've really decided from their very roots [*apo themelio*] that they're determined to do something? You understand? But he did change. Let's just make a parenthesis here. He did change, because when I was in jail and he came to see me and they told him to pressure me to sign a statement of repentance [*dilosi*],[14] he

14 A certificate of "correct political views."

said, "Never. Never. Under no circumstances is that what I would want for my daughter. She did nothing that she should be ashamed of."

On the Contemporary Women's Movement

I tried to ascertain the value of the resistance experience for the women, first, by asking them to imagine what their lives might have been like had the resistance, occupation, and war not come along; and second, by asking them their views of the women's movement today. It was difficult for the former partisans to answer the second question without unfavorably comparing the contemporary women's movement to their own experiences during "the *real* feminist movement."

> Of course there are still men who tell you to sit there and shut up, but there are also men who learned from the resistance. Today, I cook; my husband cooks; only my daughter doesn't cook! (Kilkis, Macedonia)

> Today, when they go on about equality and autonomy and self-determination, it's nothing new to us. We *lived* those things in the resistance, and we lived them as ordinary people. The women's movement carries on about mothers for peace, peace is a woman's issue, and all. What has that got to do with it? What, the people, the men who get slaughtered in war don't care about peace, too? (Peloponnese)

> Women must fight every minute to avoid being "little wifies," [*yinekoules*]. Sometimes the woman has better ideas than the man, but she defers to him; she's afraid to come out with them. It's time that women had their rights and that they don't have to wait around for men to say no to them; sometimes the men just say no out of egotism [*eghoismos*], or the woman does a better job, and the man pretends not to notice because it bothers him, it threatens his pride. But it's time for us to get out of this "misery behavior" [*to miseristiko*] or this "womanliness" [*yinekistiko*] that says we can't speak up or be what we want to be, what we dream of. I tell you, since the time of the resistance, I haven't thought much about the words "turn back." And you say it to me, and I don't really hear you, because I don't have the time. And my age doesn't bother me so much as not being able to give what's inside of me. (Crete)

> How do I feel about the women's movement in Greece? The women's movement in Greece is nice enough, but it could become even nicer. Listen, my girl [*Akou na dheis, kopella mou*], people generally, whether we're

talking about a man, or a woman, grow, gain strength depending on the environment and the time that he or she lives. I happened to grow up at a time when we had the occupation and the resistance, and that taught me more than my mother could and more than my father could. You understand what I'm saying? It made a great deal of difference what period of history I was living through at the time. Now, today, you see all these people milling around at the beach, or in the town squares, or kids killing themselves on their motorbikes, and you say to yourself, "What a pity they don't have a cause to fight for. Because there doesn't exist any goal, or any ideal. What are *they* going to fight for?" (Crete)

Although memories of the resistance itself were usually favorable, sentiments about its consequences for women were sometimes more critical. Some reflected the conventional wisdom about systems once open to change that shut women out when wartime conditions no longer require their active participation. One woman spoke to this dilemma:

But, perhaps even though of course we suffered, we were lucky in that. . . . I often think to myself, "You really lived through something unique then. You lived, let's say, through a time of such enthusiasm, brotherhood, a time with dreams and visions for something better, to confront cruelty and fascism" . . . and it was something that not many people get a chance to live. And that's what we were able to live. We thought that when the war was over, oh, how happy we're going to be when the war is over, and we thought that all our ideals and dreams were going to come true as soon as the war was over—that we'd be so incredibly happy, we Greeks, and people in other countries too. We'd all live with such intensity, in such harmony. In terms of the men, well, I'll tell you, we women that went to the exile camps, we kept the dream of glory with us and it helped us survive. We kept a kind of "glitter" in some people's eyes, because of what we did in the resistance, and we suffered right along with the men afterwards. Some of us were executed just like the men, and so they saw us as equal at the time. But slowly, in the family, the women when they went back to their houses, weren't they the same ones who were in the mountains, and in the jails, and in the resistance? Now they had become little housewives [*nikokiroules*] again, they had become the mothers of children, they became spouses, and slowly, let's say, in one way or another, the old climate of the Greek family returned. And so, in a way, they won. And the women themselves began to ask, "Could that have been *me*? Was that *me* who held a rifle, or that had such a position? Could that have been *me* [*Araghe, imoun ekini*]?

Finally, Marion Sarafis, English widow of General Stefanos Sarafis, tells the story of campaigning with her husband for parliament after the war. They were invited to dinner at the house of a man who had been an important EAM-ELAS leader in Salonika, Mr. P. His wife and daughter, "and his daughter was even a qualified lawyer," served the meal and then, instead of sitting down at the table with them, retired to the kitchen. "Well, the first time *I* experienced that in his house, I found it highly embarrassing. I felt awful sitting down at table and these women, not!" The next time the couple went to dinner, the women sat down to eat with them. "Yes, well I think Sarafis had said something to them. This shocks me and it shocks my English wife! This'll never do!! Or something along those lines. He was an elderly man, so I don't think the resistance had changed him in any basic way." Or had Sarafis reminded Mr. P. of the legacy of the resistance? "Now as for how much the resistance had changed the men of EDA?[15] All right, they *said* 'equality,' and all right, they had a women's section, but most of the men I encountered during the fifties were *completely* unreconstructed in their behavior toward their women! Completely! It was only on paper! Now to what extent was EAM successful in changing public opinion about equality and all that? Well, what I think they did, was I think they encouraged the *women*! They encouraged the women to find their own resources rather than changing the men. I mean what had happened with the men was that they'd had to accept this theoretically, and well, after that it was for the women to make them accept it practically!"

In the years following the Iranian revolution, the same women who passionately and vocally joined the protest that ultimately tumbled the Shah's regime were systematically stripped of their civil rights. Indeed, Iranian women couldn't have fewer rights than they do now: nine-year-old girls are summarily married off; women are not allowed to sing in public, lest their voices excite men and cause them to lose control; the chador, which so clearly demarcates the boundaries between private and public has been reintroduced with a vengeance. Somewhere between ethnocentrism and apologism for me lies an outraged reaction to this tragic situation. Recently, a student of the effects of the Iranian revolution on women wrote with obvious bitterness that women are now "free to begin again from nothing" (Nategh 1987, 60). But we can reframe that statement for the case of women in the Greek resistance and say that, as a result of the resistance Greek women were now free to continue from something.

[15] The Eniaia Dhimokratiki Aristera, the United Democratic Left (EDA) was the only legal party on the Left until the 1967 junta government outlawed all political organizations.

CHAPTER 7

After the Fall, 1945–1964

Repression . . . as a process, [is] any action by another group which raises the contender's cost of collective action. . . . political repression [involves] the relationship between contender[s] and government[s].

—Tilly 1978, 55

The state also functions as a social agent, either of reaction or of change, of support for the dominant classes or, conversely, of support for a new ruling class or popular movement.

—Touraine 1981, 117

From 1941 to 1944 the resistance arbitrated between women and popular culture and managed to add important new dimensions to the normative discourse about female and subaltern behavior in the public/political sphere. In this regard, Keith Legg has written that "the resistance movement filled the vacuum left by the suppression and exile of the traditional Greek political leaders; it reached the younger Greeks as no other political movement had done, and inspired them with a great sense of their own importance. Not only was the traditional authority of the father over his children questioned, but in many cases, women were called upon to perform tasks in the name of the nation that might not have been sanctioned by their husbands and fathers in the past" (1969, 58).

However, once the resistance was discredited by public authorities after the war and was no longer able to disseminate legitimate political models, the same moral standards were reversed and turned back on the newly conscious women. The "women's movement" that was embedded in the resistance was consequently now vulnerable to a changed and less hospitable political opportunity structure. The alternative "regime of truth," which had facilitated the creation and growth of the EAM, was rapidly transformed. During the demobilization period, another state was now the source of moral authority, and that state had declared war on the resistance.

Anthony Oberschall analyzes the trajectories of various movements of the 1960s and traces the dynamics of three kinds of outcomes, citing internal weaknesses that undermine and ultimately destroy the movement; repression that "disappears" vital human and material resources, making it impossible for the movement to continue to function with any sort of coherence; and success sufficient to take away the movement's raison d'être, as activists drift away or are somehow absorbed into the "system," their fundamental goals met and demands normalized within the dominant political culture (1978, 257–89).

According to this scheme, the main source of movement decline in our case clearly resides in the second category. Demobilization was accomplished through a network of state repressive measures, to which Greek culture added its own unique stamp. Between 1944 and 1945, the costs of participation in the EAM increased precipitously. The structure of national political authority was completely transfigured, and "sympathizers" were forced into a far less favorable relationship with a whole new regime. P. Nikiforos Diamandouros summarizes these broader discursive changes: "It was not, however, until the dramatic events of the 1940s, and especially of the civil war (1946–49), that anti-communism was transformed from a mere instrument of state legislation to the governing principle of an aggressive strategy of social demobilization and of social control designed to safeguard the closed nature of the Greek political system, to reinforce it, and, above all, to ensure its perpetuation" (1981, 7).

Little scholarly attention has been given to repression as a type of demobilization. Repression is often interpreted as a particularly abrupt ending to a case of mobilization and as an unequivocal sign of movement failure. I maintain however, that there is a great deal to be learned from closer scrutiny of periods of repression. The techniques selected in particular settings, the choice of some groups and not others, and the ways in which stories of key episodes are emplotted by key "authors"—all contain important clues about factors that produced the movement itself and the cultural politics now working to dismantle its gains.

Repression, in fact, signals more than dramatic change in the fortunes of its immediate victims. Governments have gone to the considerable trouble of using repression and have been willing to pay the high cost in lives and general disruption and to court possible international sanctions for a reason. That the changes proposed by a given movement justify such extreme measures in the minds of authorities exposes the fabric of bigger structural and ideological conflicts, as hegemonic political regimes double their efforts to prevent further flare-ups in revolutionary activity. In Gramscian terms, culture and formal structures of state domination—jails, police, and other midrange institutions that do not always publicly advertise their activities—combine to act as the agents of social control. The submerged nature of the partnership often obscures the meaning and deployment of repressive tactics, which is of course entirely consistent with how hegemony tends to function. In these less flagrant instances, testimonies about personal experiences, aggregated, provide crucial narrative evidence about how hard authorities have worked to dismember insurgencies.

Discrediting the Historic Bloc

From 1947 to 1950, American foreign policy makers were anxious to demobilize "communism" in Greece thoroughly enough to leave the Greek government able to shoulder the fight alone. Valuable resources could then be diverted to other areas in the world where communist-based movements appeared to be gaining strength. Truman had had a tough time pushing the Truman Doctrine legislation through Congress. But during the fight on Capitol Hill, the President had managed to convince American lawmakers that communism posed a looming threat.

Prewar Greek leaders were still smarting from the affront to their own power—and collective honor—which the mass popular movement represented, especially after Middle East troops rallied in support of the EAM in the spring of 1944. Furthermore, the intensely anticommunist guiding philosophy of the British and American governments strongly colored the postwar reconstruction process in Greece. The Domino Theory narrative foretold the successive fall of vulnerable states to communist bandits and urged strong measures to avert the social disorder that was sure to follow. Torture and execution were consequently justified on grounds of national security (Crockatt and Smith 1987). This stance toward the "Red Peril" encouraged the new Greek regime, now back from exile in Cairo, to initiate an extensive crackdown, which in turn emboldened members of the parastate.

I do not want to claim that the anticommunist sentiments of British and American postwar leaders were solely responsible for Greek policy during this period. The powers-that-be in Greece, from the monarchy to state officials to the Greek Orthodox clerical elite, were all sufficiently anticommunist in their own right. On the other hand, Churchill and Special Operations Executive (SOE) personnel had made no secret of their view that Britain's designated role was to keep Greece from falling into communist hands at all costs. That mantle of vigilance was effectively passed on to the Americans with the end of the war and the demise of the British Empire as a major player. American presence in Greece increased dramatically once the Truman Doctrine was approved by Congress in 1947. Also in 1947, the U.S. House Un-American Activities Committee began its hearings into the political activities of American citizens, notoriously infringing on the civil liberties of the accused. That there was an ideological component of American relief efforts (from the Marshall Plan in Europe to the MacArthur Plan in Japan), has long been established. Announcing the terms of the Truman Doctrine to Congress in March 1947, Truman referred specifically to Greece in making the classic formulation of American Cold-War ideology: "I believe that it must be the policy of the United States to support free peoples who are resisting attempted subjugation by armed minorities or by outside pressures." There was no question in policymakers' minds that the EAM exemplified the latter and not the former.

In keeping with this strategy, the national government of Greece connected membership in the EAM with communist conspiracy, danger, and sinister plots and worked hard to establish these convictions in the interstices of the public imagination. According to the operative narrative, repressive policies were necessary to wipe out the spectre of communism, which threatened to overrun Greece and the rest of the Balkans if bold mass initiatives and reconstituted political culture were allowed to flourish unchecked. As we have seen, fears about the EAM's popularity were not at all unfounded. Even conservative historians agree that "the movement did clearly enjoy genuine mass support" and that "EAM was set to destroy the tradition of patronage and substitute a modern habit in social relations" (Clogg 1979, 150; Woodhouse 1976, 12).

During the Civil War and the 1950s, female resistance participants were demobilized as part of the return to exclusionary politics and the evaporation of public support for the kind of women's emancipation espoused by the EAM. In 1947, Public Law No. 509 was passed. Its purpose was to protect Greek national security against fallout from EAM's alleged secret plans to link Greece with the Soviet Union by force. As a result, mass arrests, trials, and executions began in earnest (Alivizatos 1981, 220–28). Women and girls who had participated in the EAM with open enthusiasm were now in great danger of being raped, maimed, or killed by the fanatical right-wing gangs that were terrorizing the Greek countryside unchecked, as the government alternately encouraged their exploits and "looked the other way." From 1948 to 1950, seventeen women were executed in the Averoff Prison in Athens for "subversive activities" and for refusing to sign *dhiloseis,* "statements of repentance," in which signers renounced all participation in the resistance, declared themselves traitors for joining the EAM, and promised thereafter to be "good Greeks." Those who refused to sign ran the risk of being executed (until 1950), and many remained in prison until 1963 or longer. Local authorities were supplied with the names of EAM members by neighborhood informers, among other means, and girls as young as twelve were tried, arrested, and incarcerated in jails and prison camps, in some cases for twenty years or more. "I went in a child and came out a woman," recalled Maria Sideri. She was arrested at age fifteen in 1947, and fourteen years later, emerged from the Averoff Prison in Athens; evidence that, instead of heroes and heroines, for much of the postwar era, the government of Greece considered these former resistance fighters to be "dangerous to the public welfare" (*epikindhines*) and "official enemies of the State and the Greek family." This view would begin to change only after 1974. A journalist and former EPON member who spent the years from 1947 to 1952 on the prison island of Trikeri spoke of the resignation: "We had decided that we were going to die: that much was obvious. Our real fear was not of death, but of not knowing how and when we would die." Mobilized women who had not fled or been sent to prison were left with the options of joining the women's organization of the EDA (United Democratic Left), the only authorized left-wing party; working in underground organizations; or bowing out of politics altogether.

One factor that gives this case a special coloration is the severity of the political repression that followed these life-transforming events and the duration—several decades—of the resistance experience. Subsuming all of the individual stories of torture, sexual violation, homelessness, and unemployment, Greek ex-partisans faced a more universal problem. Regardless of family background or socioeconomic status, participants in the EAM were automatically designated as pariahs within the context of a highly conformist society. Those members of EAM not willing to sign dhiloseis were forced to conceal wartime activities from authorities, neighbors, and acquaintances for most of the postwar period. Often relatives were also arrested for refusing to "sign." Children might be harassed by their teachers. Students were habitually forced to write essays calling their parents "traitors" (*prodhotes*) for having been active members of the EAM. Whole families remained in hiding for fifteen years or more under false names.

It was difficult to challenge the label of "political renegade," both implied and official, on an individual basis. Many political prisoners' cases were left pending for years, while family resources were depleted by lawyers' fees and the requirements of sheer survival. The a priori equation of resistance to communist insurgency often left little recourse within the Greek legal system. Furthermore, since, as Constantine Tsoucalas has pointed out, Greece was a nominal democracy until 1967, the international community remained tragically uninformed of this mean season in Greece. Regarding the ideological consequences of this period, Tsoucalas comments:

> If any culture is in its essence a class culture, in the sense that it represents the attitudes and outlook of the dominant group in society, the mechanisms for minimizing or emasculating dissent usually work through control of information—or, more subtly, by capturing dissident ideas and assimilating them within the system itself. But the specific feature of the Greek cultural system was that criticism and dissent were forcibly reduced to total silence by the class in power; all fundamental political and social alternatives were banished. . . .

He continues,

> If the inevitable aftermath of any civil war is repression of the defeated by the victors, in Greece the repression went beyond the scope of politics. Not only were the victims expelled, persecuted and exterminated, but also, as in Spain, the post-war regime imposed its culture as well as its material power. However, unlike Franco's Spain, Greece remained—in the formal sense at least—a democracy. (1969, 114–15)

The repressive tactics used to demobilize EAM were particularly effective in the Greek context. The formal aspects of political displacement of the Left during this period were quite extensive. EAM leaders and members were exterminated, exiled, or imprisoned in a manner that Tsoucalas has written "can only be compared with the sombre fate of the Spanish intelligentsia" under Franco.[1] Once released from prison, most were obliged to check in with the security police at regular intervals, sometimes weekly. With the Communist and Socialist parties outlawed, the only legal alternative was the EDA, which often had negligible influence in the political arena.

At the cultural and ideological levels, the effects were no less debilitating. The social consequences of public humiliation were enormous, particularly in light of the pivotal role that honor (*timi*) played for an individual as an extended family member dealing with outsiders. A tarnished reputation meant social ostracism. Thus, during the 1950s, the publication of the family name in a regional newspaper in connection with political "crimes against the State" could mean that a person who was a child during the resistance might later be denied a job or be singled out at school. For women and girls, whose world still revolved around building and nurturing a family, one purpose these tactics served was to equate participation in the movement with moral degeneracy. This represented a serious social liability. A good family name and "irreproachable" conduct, however that might be defined, were especially vital to girls of marriageable age under the dowry system.[2] Participation in EPON or subsequent imprisonment, for instance, could call into question a young woman's virginity, an important part of an honorably drawn-up marriage contract. Postwar propaganda suggested that women in the EAM organizations spent the war engaged in prostitution. For example, a song called "To the EPONitisses" (girls of EPON), sung by parastate groups, claims:

[1] Tsoucalas, 115.

[2] The dowry (prika) system, very important in Greece, was officially eradicated only in 1983. A girl without a dowry was handicapped in the marriage market. In fact, one of the activities of charitable women's organizations was to provide dowries for poor girls whose dowry property was destroyed during the war. Most of these efforts were not aimed at girls who had been in the EAM, however. On the importance of the dowry and its postwar evolution, see Allen 1979, 142–56; and Du Boulay 1983.

Now that the Germans are here,
your belly is flat
and when the Russians come
your belly will grow

Babies and many other gifts
the Greek mountains give you
with swollen bellies and
your string of cartridges
you are the heroines of ELAS.

(*Traghoudhia* 1975)

As a result of repressive techniques that were well grounded in local social realities, the general message given to women and girls during the thirty-year period following liberation was that their most legitimate life choice was to return home and stay there. This was, not coincidentally, in keeping with the philosophy that sent Rosie the Riveter out of the factory and back to the kitchen in the postwar United States. From 1941 to 1944, political participation had become more inclusive, riding on a broader popular base. But at the end of the war, the old political guard returned, bringing with it traditional values. Quickly, political structures shrank to their original, prewar size. Mobilization into the resistance had raised women's expectations for an expanded role in the public sphere. One goal of the demobilization process administered by the postwar Greek state and in part carried out by terrorist gangs was to deflate these expectations and, once again, to encourage women to choose more traditional lifestyles.

The Politics of Dissuasion

For the most part, evidence suggests that when women are recruited into wars, resistance struggles, and revolutions, their demobilization is every bit as resolute as their mobilization. Types of demobilization range along a continuum of coercive strength. Take the case of America's Rosie the Riveter, where an abrupt change in propaganda created an entirely different cultural frame regarding the female presence in the factory. But violence wasn't required. In spite of evidence that 75 percent of wartime Rosies would have preferred to continue working, for the most part American women cooperated by leaving the factory and making the effort to conform.[3] In the cases of Iran

---

[3] See Gluck 1987, 16. Gluck quotes the 20 February 1943 issue of the *Saturday Evening Post* in which Harold Ickes, secretary of the interior under Franklin Roosevelt, says: "I think that this is

and Zimbabwe, women were censured much more forcefully (Seidman 1984, 419–40). Algeria provides an additional case of ultrademobilization. Many women who fought long and hard in the anticolonial war against the French were soon left with any hopes of continued participation extinguished (Knauss 1987).

Yet negative findings on this score have also been used to argue that women's participation in war and resistance movements is invariably fruitless. This assumption may partly stem from the problem that our "ways of knowing" have not always been inductive enough to capture important textures of experience. For some, this has led to a certain premature closure on the subject of women in war and to fatalistic assumptions about outcomes. Thus, in spite of the apparent "failure" in this case and hard as it is to ignore the crushing effects of a repressive demobilization process, I have also tried to show that, even where structural opportunities were revoked, EAM's legacy is more complicated.

In the remainder of this chapter I want to show, first, how repression in the Greek context affected the women I talked to and, second, how women continued to resist a different enemy—the tripartite forces of state, parastate, and culture—and what sorts of factors lay behind their stamina.

The Interim Context: 1944–1946

What was the political climate for women as liberation approached and during the two years that preceded the official start of the Civil War in 1946? I will try to recreate the postwar mood in Greece with the help of the women who lived to tell about their experiences.

The Nazis evacuated Greece in mid-October 1944, though German troops stayed on Crete six more months, until May 1945. Although many recalled the autumn of 1944 as a festive time, the women were subdued when they talked of liberation day. Their accounts of the celebrations were overshadowed by a great sense of sadness about what happened afterward.

As early as 1943, traces of what would later erupt into the Civil War were evident. The so-called security battalions (*tagmata asfaleias*), recruited and trained by the Germans to assault members of the resistance and terrify the population generally, were raging through the country unencumbered by the

---

as good a time as any . . . to warn men that when the war is over, the going will be a lot tougher, because they will have to compete with women whose eyes have been opened to their greatest economic potentialities." Gluck notes, "The alarm was sounded when the results of Women's Bureau interviews with thirteen thousand women about their postwar plans were announced. The *Wall Street Journal* ran a banner headline declaring that 75 percent of working women wanted to continue to work after the war."

The first annual Antifascist Congress of EPON, 13–19 February 1946, Athens. The Central Committee takes a break from the proceedings at Cape Sounion. Courtesy Spiros Meletzis

rule of law. The origins of the parastate countermovement can be traced to the social infrastructure of collaboration instituted by the Nazis.[4] Right-wing fringe groups such as the X-ites in Athens and other areas,[5] the PAOzides in the north central region, and the Papayanakides in western Crete were much dreaded by anyone who had participated in the EAM. This atmosphere of terror was breeding even as Operation Noah's Ark, the Allied plan to harass the Germans out of Greece with the help of the resistance, was being carried out.

For a time, the idea of popular participation (*laiki dhimokratia*) seemed to persist. Anxious not to lose valued legal prerogatives and to fight the misogynous attitudes of the increasingly repressive postwar climate, women resistance leaders organized the first Panhellenic Women's Conference, held in Athens 26–29 May 1946. Delegates from newly formed women's groups in villages and towns all over Greece attended this convention, including Maria

[4] For an evaluation of the countermovement phenomenon, see Zald and Useem 1987. On *tagmata* operations, see Hondros 1988.

[5] Formed by Colonel Grivas, or Colonel "X." The X gang, or X-ites were violently anti-EAM and were responsible for raping, killing, and maiming many former EAM-ELAS partisans.

Svolou, a PEEA deputy and Ruling Council member, and the prominent educationalist and prewar feminist Rosa Imvrioti. The goal of the conference was to reemphasize the importance of women's rights and women's solidarity on a national scale. Unfortunately, any optimism was marred by reports of repression in the delegates' home districts. For example, a photograph from the League for Democracy in Greece archives at King's College, the University of London shows broken glass, splintered wood, a typewriter in pieces, paper torn and scattered on the floor, and signs demolished. The caption reads, "Women's Centre at Karditsa, wrecked April, 1945."

One of the delegates to the conference stood up and began her speech:

> I would like to direct the attention of our delegates to the following question which I consider to be extremely serious and to invite this body to take a formal stand on the matter. We all know that our country is, from every angle, experiencing difficult times and our people are suffering a lot. Naturally, our purpose here is not to lay blame or to make accusations of responsibility. But I would like to say this. The difficult lives of our people have taken an even more dramatic turn as a result of the killings and murders that are happening among us for political reasons. With each passing day, these take on more horrific proportions and are threatening to turn into a bona fide civil war if something is not done.[6]

Delegates from Kalamata in the Peloponnese testified:

> We are witnesses to the fact that, even though we sacrificed our children, our men, our brothers and sisters [adhelfia], our homes, and our lives for the freedom and independence of our country, we have been overlooked by the legal and social life of our country and we are not allowed to express our opinions or to contribute to the reconstruction of our country. Besides that, we have been subjected to the most incredible persecutions, humiliations, tortures. They kill us, they rape us, they shave our heads, they publicly ridicule us. Our lives have become a constant trial.[7]

Tasoula, of Rethymno, Crete, described to me the post-Liberation mood:

> After the Germans left, that's when we really began to pay a high cost for being in the resistance. After all those who fought and paid with their lives, and who we were never to see again, after all that, those of us who

---

[6] Documented from the archives of Rosa Imvrioti, Conference Secretary, *A Panelladhiko Synedhrio Yinekon—Athina, Mais 1946* (First Panhellenic Women's Conference—Athens, May 1946), proceedings published by the Greek Women's Federation (OGE), Athens, 1985, 154.
[7] Ibid., 152.

survived, who were left behind, they didn't see us as patriots who fought against the conquering armies [*kata ton kataktiton*], but they saw us as evil spirits [*san miasmata*] as they called us, they saw us as evil communist spirits. That's what they called us, *miasmata*. I couldn't leave my house, and even though they claimed that *we* were the immoral ones, it was really *they* who were immoral. *They* were the ones who would proposition me on the street; *they* were the ones who shouted dirty words at me; they insulted us and claimed that we had participated in orgies and other things that we had never even heard of before. I would go out of my house and I couldn't even walk a few steps without them following me from behind, shouting filthy words at me [*vromologa*], they asked me to do disgusting, unethical things with them; they followed me constantly. But I just let them yell those things at me, and kept going. I tried to ignore them, or make a joke out of it, to make fun of them back, and just keep doing what the organization needed me to do, I tried to just keep doing my duty.

Eleni, originally from Kilkis, Macedonia, was in Athens as a student member of EPON. Her memories of the growing terror in the capital city are similar.

After the liberation, in 1945, we saw that things were very bleak. And from then on, we were . . . we, who had *fought* the occupation, *we* were the bad guys, and those who had collaborated with the Nazis, they were now the good ones. The government rewarded them and punished us. And so we were the bad ones. We still worked in the organization, but underground. I was the editor of *Fititiki foni* [Student voice], the newspaper of the students. At one point, finally, in 1947, I was left completely alone in the office. One person had escaped to the mountains, another had been murdered, and I was all alone. And I had to gather the news from around the city, edit it, print it out, and even distribute it. And they came and arrested me, finally, in 1948. They came right to my dorm there, and they were shouting, "You whore! [*Poutana!*] You should be in the students' dorm in Sofia, not here! You, who are fighting the national government!" And you who did this, and that, and the other. . . . And they took me down to the police station and from there I was sent to the island camps, first Tinos, then Chios, Trikeri, Makronisos, Trikeri.

Despina described her life and that of her EPON comrades after 1945:

Well, I was arrested in 1946. They tracked me to Salonika and my sister. After Salonika, six months in the local jail, one month in the women's prison. After 1946, three years in the Averoff Prison here in Athens. . . .

Then I was taken to prison in Patras, the Italian School prison for another three years there. From Patras to Averoff again, then to the Kastron Prison in Piraeus, then to Averoff again. Then I was released in September 1955. In a few words [*Me liga loghia*].

As far as our EPON group, as I have already told you, we were disbanded and scattered. The leaders were gone; some to the mountains, others had left. Of those of us who remained out of, to begin with, a three-member office of EPON: I left, was taken to prison, the way things had evolved. Another member, Maria, a good girl, suffered a psychological crisis and a blow. When they were all chased out of the village by the army, at first, they were placed behind bars, later on they went off to Lamia, etc. Maria, too, went off to Lamia. When she returned to her village, she found everything in ruins. The rightists were in power, all the leftists had gone to prison, or were in exile on the islands, or killed. The years went by meanwhile. She was growing old. Her parents had aged; they were starving, suffering, working hard. As a result, she went through a psychological crisis, took nitric acid and killed herself; she died in Lamia. The third one, Georgia, one or two days after I'd left, she was abducted from her home by the rightists, by those gangs. She was beaten up and had her hair sheared. She had not been able to go into hiding because her parents would not let her leave home. She left the village and went to Piraeus to live with her aunt. She met a man, a member of ELAS, who fell in love with her, but he left to go abroad and died there. Later on she married a sailor, not of the same ideology but a fine young man. She never took any interest in signing a dhilosi.

The remaining EPON women from our village, some married men without regard to their political ideologies just to settle down. Others went into exile. Three of them, a mother and daughter and one more were taken to the same prison where I was in Patras. I found them when I got there. Another one, Koula, a good EPON woman, was blinded. Some say that she was hit by a grenade; others say that she had been tortured. She doesn't want to talk about it. Maybe she is afraid. She's been blind for thirty-four years. And yet, she never lost her courage or changed her mind; she has no regrets for what she did, only sorrow for what happened. Now, all of us try to help her out and look after her to the best of our ability. She collects a farmer's pension, seven thousand drachmas and another ten thousand from her father's pension. Her father was a war veteran. So, such was the state and the situation of the women's EPON organization.

Others recalled the macabre incidents of this period, the violently charged atmosphere, and the bewildering cognitive dissonance it generated. These parts of the interviews were often very emotional. A man from the Peloponnese remembered his family's ordeal. Despite changed circumstances, he felt the traditional responsibility of a brother to protect the welfare and honor of his sisters until their marriages.

My brothers and sisters and I were all active in EAM and ELAS in our area. My little sisters were in EPON. Around the time of the German withdrawal, the "chasing" really got much much worse, the *tag-matasfalites* were very active in our area. It's impossible to describe the kinds of things they were doing to people. I'd prefer not to even give details, it was so horrible. After the Varkiza Agreement in 1945, I managed to get to Athens, where I stayed until about 1947 or so. I took my older sister to Athens, because she was in great danger because of her activity; she was one of the founding members of the EAM in our area, and she would've been one of the major targets of the *tagmatasfalites* to be killed or raped. We had managed to hide her for a while in the village, and then she came to Athens where we went from house to house, trying to hide there. After Varkiza, it was much harder for us to defend ourselves, and so we were forced to hide for about two years in Athens. Well, we certainly weren't the only ones hiding in Athens! There were thousands and thousands of us. There was no kind of organized protection for us, to protect us from those people. And they were working with the local police so you could also be arrested. Just a brief conversation with a *tag-matasfaliti* condemned you to death. It happened to many people. They would come, and take them out and execute them right there and then. And of course they would never be punished for their crimes, and they knew that. Or, they [the *tagmatasfalites*] would have the people arrested, people that is, who had participated in the resistance.

In another description of the interim postwar environment, Anthoula recalled the reception that awaited her at the border on her return from Ravensbruck concentration camp in 1945:

Well, you know, when all that was happening, the Germans leaving Greece, the December Events, the Varkiza Agreement in 1945, we were still up there working in the munitions factory in Ravensbruck. And when we did come back in the fall of 1945, it was to a completely different Greece, a Greece now under a different kind of occupation, a rightist-monarchist occupation [*mia Ellada deksiokratoumeni-vasilikia*]. We arrived at the border—I remember it well—and, perhaps our ideology, my ideology, had become international [*diethnismos*], you know the term, that people don't really come from different countries, maybe all of that was within me, inside of me, that was my theoretical position on social questions, but your own country has a place in your life, it grows inside you like a living organism [*san vioma*], and I understood that when we came back. Whereas before, I hadn't realized it, I would say, "Greeks, Ethiopians, Bulgarians . . . we're all brothers and sisters, all of us," and I still believe that today. But when we arrived at the border, one kilometer before the line of demarcation there was a zone where cars and trains didn't pass so we had to come in on foot. And when we arrived at the border, and they lifted the wooden bar so that we could pass through, without really even thinking, I bent down and I kissed the ground.

There were customs guards there at the border, and they all had the symbol of the crown on their caps. We embraced and they cheered us and said that we were the first Greeks that had made it back from Germany. We kissed, but I said quietly to the others, "Oh no, the crown again! Who ever thought we would return to this?" And later on they slaughtered a lamb for us, the officers, and they arranged a nice meal for us with our Greek dishes, they welcomed us, that is to say, like real patriots. Even though they wore the crown on their hats, and they no doubt suspected us of being communists. The next day, they put us in trucks to go back to our homes. And when we got off at the Larissa station for a rest stop, that's when the first "postoccupation slaps" began [*efera ta prota meta-katohika skabilia*]. The security police [*i asfaleia*] came to write down our names. And to ask us what and where. And suddenly, "Where do you live?" Where is my house? How should I know where it is, what has happened there after so much time? It was very hard for us emotionally after so much time to answer questions like "Where do you live." "Your name." Plus we hadn't had any news of our families in Germany. And the guy slapped me two or three times and said, "You'd better shape up because now you're talking to the police!" That was the reaction of our country when we returned. And from that moment began a new kind of persecution . . . which didn't stop for years. "*Why* were *you* in a German prison camp?" "*Why* were you arrested *so young?*" That's what they said to me personally, because when I came back I was only about seventeen or eighteen. "*Obviously* you were a communist!" And so on, *why* this, *why* that. And what you were actually guilty of was taking part in the resistance.

Thus, the political climate for resistance participants had progressively worsened. During the Civil War, ELAS partisans faced the grave choice whether to join the remnants of the resistance, the Democratic Army, or be drafted into the Government Army and forced to fight against their former comrades. Institutional structures of politics, a framework of trials, courts-martial, prisons, island exile camps, and dhiloseis were aligned with a now deeply divided and reactionary culture, which added moral insinuation and a politics of shame. The countermovement, consisting of the Greek National Army, parastate terrorist gangs, and government officials, saw itself as acting appropriately to eliminate dangerous elements in the Greek polity. Thus, the country faced the postwar era with open political wounds that would take thirty years to begin to heal.

Women's Resistance, the Second Wave: 1947–1964

Averoff Women's Prison
Christmas Carol, 1949

Merry Christmas and Happy Holidays
That's what the drums mean
When children and mothers
Embrace each other most tenderly.

We are celebrating Christmas
Behind our iron bars
Far from brothers and sisters and parents
Far from our children.

We celebrate here in prison
And we are of one heart, of one mind:
That soon our day of freedom shall come.

This spring has gone
and winter has come again
And we will remain soldiers
Where the struggle needs us most.

Next year may we celebrate
Far from these prison walls
Our houses await us patiently
Our families endure without us.

On death-row, the sun of peace
does not shine
But outside the birds
sing sweetly of harmony.

To the sky, to the earth
To the far seas
Our songs will echo
Throughout the golden universe.

The demobilization experiences that are the most important symbolically for women and about which we have the most complete information, are the Averoff Women's Prison in Athens and the island exile camps of Trikeri and Makronisos. The women sent to these places were considered to be among the most dangerous; yet ironically, they were more likely to survive the postwar terror (with notable exceptions). Many of the women who remained in the villages were killed outright during the Civil War, having been denied access to the capricious court system of postwar Greece.

In the women's section of the Averoff Prison, seventeen executions were carried out in 1948 and 1949. The youngest to die, Maria Repa, was sixteen years old. The story of Matina Papadhiamandhopoulou, an Athens liberal arts student executed 7 March 1949, is particularly tragic. Matina happened to be the niece of then prime minister Voulgaris. Matina was charged with forging false passports for EPONites who were trying to leave the country. According to Maria Sideri, several of the Averoff women got up the nerve to tell Matina's father, during visiting hours, that his daughter was scheduled to be executed, "but she had a father who didn't want to hear by any means that the Greek state [*to Elliniko kratos*] was capable of killing anyone. He began to yell at the woman who had brought him the news, calling her a Bulgarian slut [*Voulgara sikofantria*]. 'I'm warning you,' she said, 'things aren't as you think. If you want to save your daughter, go to your relative and have him get you a stay of execution. Otherwise, your daughter might be dead in three days.'" Matina was executed several days later (Sideri 1981, 158–60).

Although the movement's political and social achievements were seriously damaged, they were not completely reversed. New modes of collective action were employed by jailed activists and their relatives, by underground groups, and within the EDA party, the only legal political alternative on the Left from 1951 to 1967. The women of the Trikeri and Makronisos island exile camps, of the Averoff Prison in Athens, of the Patras and Kerkyra (Corfu) prisons, and of other regional detention centers sustained a type of collective action that was not, as might be expected, blatantly political. Survivors of these difficult times say that their resistance activity provided a clear motivation to survive.

Women of the Averoff

Among the most cohesive groups of female political prisoners that the Greek Civil War created was the aforementioned women of the Averoff Prison in Athens. Many spent between one to fifteen years in prison. The repressive postwar climate, however, has erased these women from the collective memory, except in certain activist communities. Questions about exactly how and why the women of the Averoff managed to resist torture and the continual pressure to sign statements of repentance renouncing their resistance activity (*dhiloseis*) remain largely unanswered. My interviews indicate that two factors were key to the remarkable stamina of the women of the Averoff. First, the organization cum guiding ideology of the EAM created a kind of "resistance momentum" that helped sustain these women through the hard times. This spirit of resistance continued to be fueled by their common experiences and decisions in prison. Second, the prisoners (at one time numbering as many as five hundred women) were fairly representative in terms of age, region, and socioeconomic class. A kind of social microcosm formed that gave these women living proof that the participatory ideals fostered by the resistance could be carried out in practice.

In the testimony of the women of the Averoff, we can observe several kinds of resistance strategies typical of jails, prisons, and island exile camps all over Greece. These tactics were collectively conceived during the early period from 1947 to 1949, when most of the long-term detainees were arrested and when seventeen women were executed. During this time, the women agreed not to sign dhiloseis, even if it meant death. Those selected for execution would not show fear, in order to give the others courage and to make a statement to the jailers. They would sing and dance around the large palm tree in the prison courtyard (the *Finikas*) along with the condemned woman on the eve of her execution. Teachers would conduct lessons in their areas of expertise, including literacy, French, mathematics, literature, the classics. A singing group was organized and inmates wrote and performed plays, usually of classical works and myths. Responsibilities were divided and delegated to various inmate committees in the areas of, for example, cleanliness, package distribution, recreation or amusement [*psyhaghoghia*].

Maria Sideri from the Kozani region, spent fourteen years in the Averoff Prison. She was arrested in 1947 in Kozani and was sentenced to death there, the sole condemned female in a group of seventeen boys and men. (Many of the men were the fathers of sons who had been in the ELAS, arrested and sentenced to death because their sons could not be located.) One of the charges against Maria was that she refused to reveal the name of another EPON member who escaped to the Kozani region in 1946 and was using the alias "Eleni." Maria was tortured and questioned repeatedly about Eleni's true identity, information that she was unable to supply because of standard organizational security procedures.

When the day of execution arrived, Maria had, according to prison custom and with the help of the other women, prepared her things: her farewell letters to her family were ready, her possessions in order, her hair combed and braided. Word came from the men's prison by way of a crude communications system, which involved talking through a hole in the wall, that ten of the eighteen had been taken away. Maria, mentally prepared to die, remembered being disappointed. She paced the cell restlessly for the rest of the afternoon, anxious to be taken away to meet her fate. Maria describes a tragicomic moment when an old woman, jailed because her son had been in the resistance, attempted to comfort her by saying, "There, there, my child, don't worry. Don't be upset. Maybe *tomorrow* they'll come for you." With an ironic smile, Maria recalled, "It was her way of soothing me."

Maria was then transferred first to the Yedi Koule Prison in Salonika and then to the Averoff Prison in Athens, where she remained on death row for twelve years. Her testimony emphasized the politics of the execution process. As an extra torture, a few days before an execution was to take place, prison officials would let the word out that several inmates were to be chosen, but the names would not be disclosed. Over the next few days, each woman prepared her things and wrote her good-bye letters in anticipation of being chosen. On the eve of the execution, a guard would finally come and announce the name(s), putting an end to the suspense.

Facing the executions resolutely was part of an overall strategy of collective action and survival. References to other coping mechanisms abound in the testimonies of the women political prisoners. For example, Maria described the prison lessons:

> Out in the sun, we would either do lessons, like foreign languages, which were allowed, and the literacy lessons, which were also allowed. We weren't allowed to study things like political economy and other theoretical subjects, but we did do those in secret. But all this without paper. We had to do it by memory, for the most part. And that's why we were in large groups. I would forget something, and you would chip in. Or vice versa. And we did those lessons outside.

Other prison activities helped the women to face torture collectively:

> When we didn't have lessons, because we didn't have the same lessons every day, we would do crafts, knitting, embroidery, we would sell those things later.
>
> If we hadn't had organization in prison, either we would have had to make concessions or we would have had many more mental breakdowns because they were also pressuring us from the outside, our parents, our relatives, "Sign a dhilosi, so that you can be released! Sign a dhilosi, so that they'll release you!" That's why the organization gave us a sense of security with lessons. And for instance, we had many illiterate women;

One of the few demonstrations against the Greek executions, New York, 1948. Courtesy the Trustees of the Liddell Hart Centre for Military Archives, King's College London

they didn't know how to write their own names. They learned to read and write in prison. Especially the old grannies.

Some of the inmates wrote plays, and we would put on performances. They [the authorities] would watch us closely. We did it with "watchguards." We would go to the "deepest chamber" in the prison. We had a large chamber up on an upper floor. We called it the EPON chamber, because it was where all the young kids stayed, and that's where we held the performances. We would post guards, and they would keep a lookout. And the old women would be given such duties. And what a thrill it was for them, to be given that kind of work! [laughing] It made them feel worthwhile, to be doing something. They couldn't really do gymnastics. Of course the older women could do some things, but many of them were over eighty years old. We would tell them, "Granny, you sit here and make sure no prison guard comes along." "What are you going to do, *yiayia?*" "I'll start coughing! I'll begin to cough!!" And, that's what kept us going, it kept up our strength. That way, we didn't have time to get depressed.

Look, we didn't have time to sit around dreaming [*na oneiropolisame*], to say "Oh, how wonderful it would be to be out of here, ah, if only I was out, I would do this or that. . . ." We didn't have time. Because from the time that we got up in the morning, we would get up and do gymnastics, we would make our beds; we would make tea; we would clean up and arrange things. Our beds had to be made, the windows cleaned, etc. I would do gymnastics with three groups, I did it with the fat ones [laughing], even though I was just a little thing, I did it with the sick ones, that had consumption [*fimatiosi*], and I did it with the regular group. After that, we had washing and ironing to do, lessons, our leisure activities [*psyhagogia*]. We had rehearsals [*ihame proves*]. We wrote our own plays; we didn't have books or scripts to go by; we had to write our sketches right there. And that's what kept us going, it kept up our strength [*mas kratousane*]. That way, we didn't have time to get depressed. For instance, the time that we were allowed outside was very short. They had us locked inside most of the time. We had to take advantage of the time we had outside in the sun. Inside it was all wet cement. Water was dripping down the walls, from all those people jammed in there breathing [*ap' tis anapnoes*]; they never dried out. The floors were all cement. So we were anxious to be out in the sun.

"Oh, yes," I said to her, "Asimina gave me something, a piece of lace that she had made then."

Yes, lace trim [*me saita*]. I painted little dolls. I'll look and see if I have any of them left to give you, because you know how it is, I keep giving them away [*dhose, dhose, dhose*] [laughing]. I don't think I have any more left! I have some that are unfinished and I still have to paint in the eyes and mouth. I'll see if I have any finished to give you. I painted. I made doll heads, little black ones, and here, this one, Ho Chi Minh, that I was making. I made that one in prison because the war in Indochina was going on at the time.

"And you had to hide all this?" I asked.

Oh, definitely, definitely. The guards were illiterate. Because they didn't know what it was. They would conduct searches of our cells and take things from us. They would take our crafts. They would steal everything from us [*mas kataklepsane*]. And so, we did such things in the sun. They would make out a plan for us, the prisoner committee, they would say, for instance, those doll heads that you painted, you'll get fifteen drachmas per day. Fifteen drachmas was a lot of money, then—fifteen drachmas, and you had sold a lot. Or I must paint fifty of those kind of doll heads, or twenty, accordingly. Or with those lace things, lace collars or knitting, of the round ones, I should make seventy, per day, or per week, or whatever. And that's how we met the requirements of our plan.

And in order to go beyond our plan, we would walk around the courtyard to stretch our legs; we would knit and repeat our lessons. We would walk around and recite our lessons. In order to have time to fit everything in. To sit around, saying "Imagine us being free . . . ," we didn't have time! [laughing] We had far too much work to do! Imagine, hanging around all day, and saying, "Shall we go outside? Shall we stay in?" lounging around and not working, and then going to sleep. How could we do that? We were running all the time! In order to fit everything in! There were too few hours in the day. Inside when it got dark, we couldn't see. What could we do then? And they turned the lights out early, and anyway, with one little lamp for sixty women—it was a large room, what could you see? And the old women, with their poor eyes, how were they supposed to see? And they turned the lights out early, by ten o'clock, the lights were out. We were in bed by ten. So to read a book, at least those that were allowed, or to make those things that we secretly made and sold, we hurried to fit it all in.

Usually we did things collectively. We had a communistic life, a socialistic life. A communal way of life. That is, I didn't really have anything of my own. We owned everything in common. Because I had been away from home so long, I didn't have any underwear. The committee took care of that and found me some underwear. If someone didn't have shoes, they scrounged around and found them shoes.

"Yes, I remember the story you told about the *andartissa* who didn't have any clothes when they brought her to the jail," I said.

Yes, well that was in Kozani. Up there things weren't nearly as well organized as they were here. But in the Averoff Prison, we had a kind of socialism. Packages from home would come for us with food, with clothes, and they would all be gathered in one place and the goods would be distributed to those who needed them. I never would know exactly what my family had brought me. Many times, though, they [the distribution committee] would tell us the specifics so we knew what to thank our families for; and there were women who designated what would go where. That is, this will go to someone who is sick, who needs it; this will go to the youngest girls who need it to grow; this will go to the elderly women who no longer have good teeth to chew because it's soft . . . and to women whose families lived far away or were dead and couldn't send them things, or for the children who were inside with their mothers.

The village women would get a package every twenty days, every month, at the most, whereas the ones from Athens would get one twice a week. Usually they would bring something for their child or relative; they couldn't bring it for everyone. But they began adding an extra plate so that the less fortunate ones could also have a little something too. Also we divided into groups. It would be, let's say, five village women who didn't get packages often, or at all, and two Athenian women, or from nearby, from Megara, from Elefsina, from Piraeus, who got packages, so that everyone would have a chance to eat something hot, something home-cooked—a little, maybe one forkful, but it was something.

The themes of the resistance—political education, moral development, and the breakdown of social barriers—are evident in the testimonies. The horrors of prison life produced a kind of leveling effect, which proved conducive to the formation of relationships that cut across boundaries of age, geographical region, and class. Similar phenomena were at work in the other domain of state repression, the island exile circuit.

Island Concentration Camps

Nicos Alivizatos describes the origins of these prison camps:

After the beginning of the civil war . . . the political persecutions against the left occurred mainly over and beyond the existing legal framework. The "emergency" measures either dealt only with some aspects of the political persecutions or tried to legalize them retroactively. . . . [An] example is the very existence of the concentration camp of Makronisos. By a law issued by the first Sophoulis government in February 1946, the concentration camps of the Metaxas period were officially abolished. The concentration camp of Makronissos was established in the beginning of 1947; all male deportees, with almost no exception, started being taken there "under disciplined regime," in the winter of 1948–1949. It was only in October 1949, that is to say, a month after the end of the actual hostilities, that the status of Makronissos and to some extent the methods applied there for the "reconversion" of the deportees were legalized by a special Constitutional "Resolution." (1981, 223–24)

Starting in 1946, women also began to be arrested, sentenced, and transported to island detention centers as punishment for holding "incorrect political beliefs." Those sent to island exile camps (and female prison populations in general) included women who had been actual EAM members as well as the female relatives—mothers, grandmothers, aunts, daughters, sisters—of the men and boys who had participated in that resistance organization. In addition, mothers brought their children with them into "exile" (*stin exoria*).

The exile camp circuit usually started with deportation to the "sorting" islands of Tinos and Ikaria. After processing, several thousand women were shipped to Chios, where army barracks awaited them, and after several months they continued their journey to Trikeri, a tiny island off the tip of the Pelion Peninsula. The women were under constant pressure to sign dhiloseis. In early 1950 those twelve hundred "incorrigibles" who, despite horrendous torture and hardship, still refused to "sign" were sent to Makronisos, where stepped-up measures were administered by a notorious crew of "experts." After six months of particularly fierce indoctrination and abuse, the six hundred or so women who still refused were brought back to Trikeri in 1951. Many were released in 1952, when the milder Plastiras government assumed power.

The Greek government's version of what it hoped to accomplish with the exile camps was congruent with American Cold War ideology. The camps' goals are well documented in a feature article in the December 1949 issue of *National Geographic Magazine* entitled "War-Torn Greece Looks Ahead" (M. O. Williams 1949). The first picture is captioned, "Queen Frederika, Young, Beautiful, and Democratic, Is the Idol of Greek Soldiers: The German-born, English-reared Queen has won her adopted country's affection by caring for its refugee children. She rides the shoulders of repentant Communists on Makronisi." The opening two pages of this article evince the philosophy underlying the repressive political framework.

On the once-barren island of Makronisi, off the tip of Attica, I watched tough Greek Army officers play the role of the good shepherd.

It is a strange reversal of the Biblical story, in which the good shepherd goes into the hills to find one stray sheep while the other ninety and nine are safe in the fold. For in this instance the ninety and nine are out in the hills away, fighting for Hellas. The lost one, who persists in staying that way, enjoys here the shelter of the strangest fold I have ever seen.

Makronisi, meaning Long Island, has been converted into a novel "concentration camp" where thousands of Communist sympathizers and former guerrilla fighters are being transformed into loyal, democratic citizens.

When the Greek Army found Communists or "fellow travelers" among its recruits, the high command decided to isolate them. About two years ago this camp was founded to receive them. Hundreds of captured or surrendered guerrilla fighters were added.

At the time Col. George Bairaktaris conceived the idea of Makronisi, his own brother was a Communist. Knowing his brother's basic loyalty, the colonel sought some way to let him, and thousands like him, prove it.

Of the 21,800 men who have been exposed to its course in regeneration, only 800 have been adjudged incorrigible. There is no harsh or "silent" treatment for those who refuse to swear allegiance to their homeland. There is a general feeling that time is on the side of the right.

At the time of my visit, some 7,800 "Pioneers" had returned to the ranks, to fight or die for Greece. Many helped free the Peloponnesus from Communist bands. Thousands now fight in the north. Others, unable to qualify for the Army, have returned to peaceful civilian pursuits.

Long Island is marked with patriotic slogans in whitewashed rocks, visible from miles away. "Hail to King Paul," shouts one steep hillside. "Hail to Hellas," echoes another.

With Col. James H. Philips, Chief of Staff with the Joint U.S. Military Advisory and Planning Group; Dowsley Clark, Director of Information of the Economic Cooperation Administration; and Mrs. Clark, I went to the island to see this Greek experiment in regeneration.

A Queen's Triumphal Ride

As we reached the mess hall, decorated with Greek, British, and American flags, hundreds of Pioneers flocked up the hill. Here on this barren isle they seemed to be living an abundant life with spirit, vigor, and enthusiasm.

When Queen Frederika visited Makronisi, these men lifted her to their shoulders and paraded her through the camp. Some conservatives humped their eyebrows when the picture was published, but the multitude have taken the petite, hard-working queen to their hearts.

Colonel Bairaktaris's first step at the camp was to create an atmosphere of civilized behavior, within which neither officer nor comrade could reproach a Pioneer for his past. Then, within this favorable environment, each individual is encouraged to "find himself" and develop his talents to the full.

While the leaven is working, Communist propaganda is honestly met in discussion. Makronisi has its own 40-page newspaper and a broadcasting station.

When a Bulgar radio invited the Pioneers to "leave the servitude of camp for the good guerrilla life," Greece's alert Minister of the Press, Michael Ailianos, sparked back:

"I've seen to it that every man on Makronisi has heard your plea. Are you doing the same for your boys?"

Probably not, for despite added help from Albania and Bulgaria, the "good guerrilla life" these days, is not so good.

We entered the mess hall with the men, to drink our ceremonial coffee.

Suddenly the sound of magnificent group singing flooded the hall. The composer of the battalion song now fights in the Grammos Mountains. His stirring words express the common sense:

"To Hellas's sun and waves and much-loved land we pledge ourselves. Our strong Hellenic heartbeat drives us on."

"Christ is risen" pennons, left over from Easter, lent a festive touch. Beside a cardboard bell tower paper swallows had built their nests. Between portraits of King and Queen was a life-sized Christ.

Our luncheon host, a major, was magnetic, handsome, and realistic: his approach that of conviction: "I was a Communist, too, but I got over it. For, despite everything, I am a Greek."

Few malcontents can resist that appeal, although I interviewed some who still do.

Like most of Greece, one man was "tired of fighting." Unlike Greece, he had quit. I could not pry from any of these men any good reason he had for holding out.

In direct contrast to this glowing portrayal are the reports of actual "pioneers," such as Natalia, a teacher from the Peloponnese whose husband was one of the original Makronisos inmates. She spent three years in exile with her children and was in the group transferred to Makronisos in 1950. Her testimony captures most of the main features of the island-exile experience for women. Natalia talked about life in the camps with children, whose very presence was a source of both comfort and torture for mothers. Food and medical treatment were often withheld from the camp's young, and prison authorities regularly threatened to kill the children as a way of forcing confessions and statements out of the women. The manipulation of the food supply was also common, as were torture in the form of beatings, forced labor, and lengthy harangues by guards in the scorching sun. The force of the women's will to resist these conditions is underscored in the following testimony. As in the Averoff Prison, various resistant measures were collectively agreed upon and used for mutual encouragement, such as lessons, plays, and singing, and the general organization of life by means of an elaborate committee structure. The women in exile also found ways to supplement their starvation diets through the resourceful gathering of wild foodstuffs.

So the point is, it was an enormous problem to be in exile with two children, without having anything to call my own, with absolutely no support. And the Red Cross didn't recognize the children of political prisoners, and they didn't apportion them food as they did for the adults. So imagine how hungry the children were, with no bread and no food. But our cooks, because some of us were appointed as cooks, from among us exiled women, we would cook the food ourselves, what little they gave us; that is, macaroni and dried beans. Potatoes. From the large cooking pot, they managed to save a portion for each child, a little plate of food for each child. Somehow we managed.

So the kids were with me, right there in the camp. When we got to Chios, they put us up in barracks. They had erected them for the soldiers and for us, I guess. Three large buildings, with two stories, and that's where they had us staying. We slept on the cement because most of us didn't have cots or bunk beds; so we slept on the cement floor. It got really bad when my little boy got very sick with meningitis and they wouldn't give permission for me to take him out to the hospital there in Chios; they said I had to sign a dhilosi first, and I fought very hard to be allowed to take him out to the hospital. But I refused to sign a statement. Finally I succeeded, and a miracle happened and my baby lived. And today he's a grown man. He's a professor.

After that incident, we stayed a year in Chios. And after Chios, they loaded us into three boats and they took us to Trikeri. At Trikeri, there was a monastery building, but that was where the administrative personnel stayed. They kept those buildings for their offices. And they wouldn't allow us to go up there. After a thousand struggles we were able to get a room for our sick and one room to use as an infirmary, and a dental clinic, we had some women there who were dentists, or nurses trained in dentistry, and they would treat us there, and we also had two women among the exiles who were trained pathologists who could look after us. Naturally it was difficult, a very tough fight to get that much out of them, because they refused to acknowledge that we were ever sick, and besides that, our own doctors weren't really in a position to treat us, without proper supplies or anything. For instance, we wanted X rays [aktines]. Where were we to have X rays? We had to go to the hospital in Volos and there conditions were frightful and they treated us like criminals.

So our life at Trikeri was . . . horrible. We stayed in tents, outside in tents. In the summer we suffered from the heat. And of course there were terrible flies; it was terribly hot and the canvas absorbed the heat and we couldn't do much about it. When the first rains started, you know the first rains of winter, when they finally start they're very very strong, with howling winds . . . and a couple of times, they blew away our tents, and we were forced to request that they let us rebuild our tents up on the hill, close to the monastery where it was more sheltered from the wind. So we did that, and they came a couple of times and destroyed those tents, forcing us to rebuild them again each time. And they beat us around, and made us sleep in the mud, even with the children, to force us to give in and sign statements. We had a lot of sick women, young girls like you, who got amenorrhea. They didn't get their periods at all and they had all kinds of gynecological problems, spending their young years in that way.

And would you believe it, the administration, besides all of that, the torture, the beatings and the hunger, the administration on top of all that had the nerve to steal our food! Our oil, our food, and money . . . because the Red Cross gave twenty-five hundred drachmas per day per prisoner. And they took some of it! We were a thousand women, twelve hundred women. So it was a large sum. And they would take some of it and instead of buying us food, they would. . . . for example, we would go to cook fifty kilos and there would only be ten kilos. Imagine, one afternoon we had to tell the children that we had no food to give them, it wasn't even a matter of the cooks reserving a bit for the children like on Chios. Now there was nothing for any of us. We had to skip that meal entirely.

We had ways of surviving, however. For example, fortunately for us, there were a lot of olive trees around there and we would gather them and soak them in seawater brine. And we would eat those olives, because you know that olives are very healthy, they give you strength. Also there were wild mushrooms growing around the base of the olive trees, and we'd pick those. I would say to the children, "Come on, now you're going to eat *sikotakia*."[8] And those few olives and the mushrooms helped us get through the hunger. Of course, there were girls who received packages from home, with food.[9] But I was one of the ones that had no way of getting anything, because, as I said, my people were in such bad shape themselves, being hounded. When they arrested us, they had also arrested them.

Things got really bad in 1949, when the Democratic Army surrendered, in the summer, in August 1949. And the police took over the administration. And they started with renewed force to pressure us into signing dhiloseis, so that we could leave and they could dissolve the prison camp. But many of us *still* refused to sign statements, and that made them furious. There was a lot of torture then, with threats and all, that you're all going to die now, we're going to cut off your food and make you eat snakes, etc. And then they brought in our own partisans, people who had been in EAM-ELAS but had caved in and signed statements and were induced to serve the other side, to pressure us as a "reformed" communist. There was one man, he had been an officer in the Democratic Army and his name was "Poulos." And they gathered us all together, and he started to shout at us, "What are you all doing here? Your leaders are criminals, and they're this and that, and there's no hope left, the struggle is lost,

[8] A delicacy, fried lamb's liver.

[9] Poet Victoria Theodorou tells the story of receiving a box from home and refusing to share it with the others. "I'm ashamed of it now, but you know I was so young [seventeen or eighteen] and I had had so little to call mine up until then, with the sacrifices of the occupation and resistance, and now exile. . . . I guess I just wanted something to keep all to myself."

give up now while you have the chance, etc. etc." And the whole camp then, with closed mouths, they started to hum, "Mmm-mmm-mmm . . . mm-mmm," like that. And can you imagine, to hear twelve hundred women doing that, he became apoplectic! "Mmm-mmm-mmmm . . ." And one day, at one of those public haranguings, an elderly woman started to sing in a wild voice a song, "Aman, aman. . . ." It was a non-sensical song. And all the women started to dance to the tune. Until they started beating us for it. That is to say, the collective morale was very high. Very high. And to think that with all that torture, the women still managed to put on plays, and have singing groups, it was like they carried the resistance over into the camps, a kind of political mood, a spirit of de-fiance. With the written word, with laughter, and with song, we "raised a fist in the darkness," to let a little ray of light into our lives. And we did resistance, a passive resistance.

Finally, they transferred us to Makronisos. We left for Makronisos 27 January 1950. And it was quite a feat for us to prepare ourselves to be transported, because we had to do it ourselves, we women, and the sick, and the old, everybody. In the winter weather, cold rains and snow. We had to bring all the camp materials down to the boat and load them, cooking pots, food, canvas, utensils, etc. And they put us in a transport boat, about a thousand women and the children, about twenty children. Me, with my own kids, I had finally been able to send them out. When they announced that they were transferring us to Makronisos, they left with a woman from our area who had signed a statement and was free to leave, and she took them with her and they went to stay with my mother, who was out of jail by then. Because I knew what Makronisos meant, what a horror it was going to be. It was notorious.

We arrived at Makronisos after a rough voyage, and they gave us three days to rest up. And then on 30 January, which is the holiday of the Three Wise Men, and is celebrated as Children's Day in Greece, the Holi-day of Education as we say, because the three were teachers, the Three Wise Men. They put us in a theater, a so-called theater, a closed-in area like an athletic field, it was. And they lined up the machine guns, pointed at us, and they said, "Either you sign statements, or you will die. There is no other choice. You will sign statements, whether you want to or not. You will sign statements or we start shooting." The morale at the camp was still high. Not one woman got up to sign a statement. We sat there on the dirt, on the cold earth, the January earth. And not one woman got up. Then they got wise. There were about ten mothers with about twenty children among them. And they started shouting with the microphone that the Greek Army was taking children from unfit mothers. "You aren't mothers, you aren't Greeks, you are traitors. You are whores!" that's what they said, the *alfamites,* these were the police, they had little white strips on their pants' legs, they were the torturers of Makronisos, the ones who beat people were called the *alfamites.*

That's when the really heartrending scenes took place, because they were grabbing the children from the arms of their mothers, they were trying to pry them away. That's when a lot of women signed; they were screaming and crying, and they said to you, "They're taking the children. They're going to kill our children. If they kill the children, they're really going to kill us all." And so a lot of women . . . many of the old women peed on themselves then, right there on the ground, from the trauma of it all, the poor things. And also, they had gotten us up at six in the morning, and they hadn't let us go to the bathroom. It was a kind of psychological torture, to break our nerves, as we say, and it worked to some extent. So some women went up and signed dhiloseis then. And they continued to pressure even more those of us who were left. But the rest wouldn't budge. So then we were left with about six hundred women, out of a thousand or so, out of about twelve hundred. And two hundred weren't with our group; they were from somewhere else, those women.

One old lady from Crete, when they were beating and shoving her around, shouting, "Come on! We're going to get you to sign a statement, you old hag?! What are you doing still here?! Come on and sign a statement!" And she said with her Cretan accent, it was a very moving moment, "I'm not a slave, and I won't sign! I didn't bow down to the Turks, so now I'm going to let *you* enslave me?" It was beautiful.

So they left us there about six months, and then they took us back to Trikeri. And we stayed there, some of us another year, others another two years. And some got released the third year, that is '50, '51, '52. And afterwards, they gave us all permission to leave. The camp was disbanded, and whoever was left, they took them to Ai Strati, another island camp, along with the men. And there they stayed, the women, for quite a while, some of them until 1960, or so. I left early, that is, relatively early. I was allowed to leave in 1952, from Trikeri. And then I came here to Athens and was reunited with my mother and the children. My husband also got out early, in 1952. He had been in Makronisos.

When we went back to Trikeri, though, the conditions were different. They went a little easier on us. And so we were able to do a lot of lessons. All the teachers, because a lot of the teachers were still there, like me. We had a lot of illiterate women, and we were able to give them lessons, and also to the girls. There were about fifty-four teachers there, and we taught about 350 illiterate women to read after a fashion. And we had fifteen girls who were high school age, and we had to prepare them for university—girls such as Victoria Theodorou, the poet from Crete; she was there and wanted to go to the university when we got out. And there were some very important teachers and educationalists there, such as Liza Kotou, a famous professor, a woman of letters who had studied outside of Greece, in Paris and in Germany. She was an art historian. She gave lessons in fine arts and art history to us. It was really wonderful.

Another woman reflected:

We continued to resist afterwards, in jail. When you believe in something and you sit there inside a jail and you can't accept what it is that the others are, it's resistance. Isn't it? . . . As for me, as soon as I came down from the mountains, they locked me up in jail. They accused me of numerous murders and of charges I knew nothing about, nor had I even been to those places. And subsequently I was sent into exile for five years. In the beginning of 1947 they took me to Ikaria, from Ikaria to the camp on Chios. A lot of women passed through Chios. We ended up with about two thousand women in three buildings, all crushed on top of each other, in barracks. After that we went on to Trikeri. From Trikeri we went to Makronisos. After Makronisos, they took us back to Trikeri and after Trikeri, slowly they began to let us go. Naturally life there was indescribable. And the worst thing was that after the intense life we had led, after what the resistance had taught us, we weren't able to give anything back to society; they wouldn't let us. I believe that that was the worst part of the punishment. It was something completely different from what we had become used to.

But, even though it was difficult, in spite of the horrible things we went through, we always tried to organize our lives in order to stay efficient [*boreti*]. In order to be able to live in that hell, places that could literally be described as hellholes, especially Makronisos, where so many things happened. The one year that we stayed there, it was literally like living in hell. But we kept up the leisure activities [*psyhaghoghia*] there in the camp. We did a lot of things. I threw my whole self into that *psyhaghoghia*. There I learned dances from all parts of Greece, and songs from all over, we would teach each other our native songs and dances. I danced, I sang, I was in plays, I joked my way through.

And of course, this wasn't only for myself, because I had made it my business to help some of the others who also had been brought there. For those women, the women who had lost their families. Because every day we had news of executions. We would learn that so-and-so's son had been executed, so-and-so's daughter had been executed, somebody else's husband or father had been caught and executed. And in that kind of atmosphere, you tried to give something, not just to make yourself feel better.

It was a sweet note in the life of a grief-stricken mother who had just lost her son. That's why I had made it part of my program in exile. I had given all of myself to that purpose, exactly for that reason. I made up my mind, and so did a lot of the girls, of the forty or so of us who were the youngest. I was about sixteen. We had decided to do these things to cheer up the rest of the camp. Secretly, of course. Because many times when they caught us singing or doing something, later we paid for it in wood,[10] with beatings or being shut up in solitary. Of course that didn't bother us because the next day we did the same thing. We didn't just stop as they wanted us to. Everything was forbidden, everything, everything. Well, since everything was forbidden, you would have had a nervous breakdown, you would have been driven crazy if you did nothing. And that was their goal, naturally. But we, no, we never put the banner down. Nope, the next day, we would keep doing the same things. I would be released from solitary and I would start singing again, and back to solitary it was for me. In and out. Camp and solitary.

The Averoff Prison and the island exile circuit experiences are significant in three ways. First, these centers of detention brought women from all backgrounds into contact with one another, forcing them to forge a life together that might somehow help them cope despite torturous conditions. Detainees created an underground political network of individuals who still maintain contact even today. Although some of the women said that relations among the prisoners weren't always completely smooth, for the most part, a consensus emerged based on a common fate and cause.

Second, the camps and prisons in effect became educational institutions, since a number of teachers and even professors were serving time. Lessons learned in a variety of disciplines could then be put to good use upon their release. Some girls were able to pass their high school equivalency exams after being in prison. Thus, the emphasis on broadening the perspectives of potential citizens which EAM initiated was continued by the political prisoners.

Finally, the best evidence that the EAM had managed to spark the mobilization potential of a variety of women can be seen in their tenacious will to resist signing dhiloseis. Although some buckled under the strain or were forced by extenuating circumstances to put their signatures to confessions of guilt, a politically significant number of others also refused on pain of death. It would thus appear that the mobilization efforts of the EAM were in some measure successful far beyond the resistance years.

[10] The Greek expression *fau ksyllo* literally means to "eat wood" or be beaten.

Fables Redux

Experience which is passed on from mouth to mouth is the source from which all storytellers have drawn. . . . The story-teller takes what he tells from experience—his own or that reported by others. And he in turn makes it the experience of those who are listening to his tale.

—Benjamin 1976, 278, 281

If a prologue professes a moral point or forecasts a book's major motifs and an epilogue is the end of a fable where the moral is asserted, then this is the place to revisit some of the themes with which I began this book. However, I will stop short of drawing the single set of conclusions that this classification scheme implies. The person finishing this text, unlike the political science graduate student who began the project nearly ten years ago, is now, I hope, more attuned to the multiple, context-bound, contested and contestable meanings that can be extracted from any case study. Beside postmodernism's function as a device helpful in conceptualizing the comparative significance of "modern" culture, this may be the most appropriate role for the postmodern perspective to play: as an echo of intellectual conscience in a struggle against analytic fundamentalism rather than as a doctrine, method, or vocabulary in its own right, entirely adequate to the concerns of empirical research. When attempting, as authors, to represent or speak for others, the internal dialogues that in turn shape our texts must now, it seems, be different, because a different moral regime now prevails: in our knowledge claims, we are publicly accountable both to our subjects and to our own psychological impulses. Although "modernist" thinkers (the Frankfurt School, for example) warned of uncritically accepting packaged mythologies and iconographies, awareness of our own social and political positionings has put a fresh spin on the reflexivity concept. "New times," thus writes Stuart Hall, "require us to radically rethink the link between history and subjectivity" (1991, 62).

What continue to interest me are the larger implications and patterns of mobilizational politics emerging out of specific historical cases, and related cross-national comparisons. Pursuing universal, "scientifically" replicable behavioral theories, as I was once advised to do, no longer appeals. Among the things I have learned is that research may generate insights with transhistorical applicability, but the shoals of ahistoricity always lurk as a potential hazard for the producers of generalizations.[1] Lack of balance in the effort to remain true to context can lead to elaborate and baroque accounts with limited relevance. A healthy compromise brings even contemporary social research to take account of historical contingency, and allows traditional narrative history to embrace sociological approaches. In any event, the schizophrenia that many social science historians feel in attempting, on the one hand, to contextualize meaningfully and, on the other, to isolate broader social configurations may simply come with the territory.

In the wake of the scholarly journey that this book represents and a recent trip back to Greece after a considerable absence, I want to return to several points of inquiry raised in this text about consciousness as a political process and to offer some further reflections on the stories we tell.

Modernizing Nationalism

Gramsci recalls the work of the factory councils:

This element of "spontaneity" was not neglected and even less despised. It was *educated,* directed, purged of extraneous contaminations; the aim was to bring it into line with modern theory—but in a living and historically effective manner. The leaders themselves spoke of the "spontaneity" of the movement, and rightly so. This assertion was a stimulus, a tonic, an element of unification in depth; above all it denied that the movement was arbitrary, a cooked-up venture, and stressed its historical necessity. It gave the masses a "theoretical" consciousness of being creators of *historical* and institutional *values,* of being founders of a State. This unity between "spontaneity" and "conscious leadership" or "discipline" is precisely the real political action of the subaltern classes, in so far as this is mass politics and not merely an adventure by groups claiming to represent the masses. (1971, 198, "The Modern Prince")

As a student of collective action, Gramsci remains one of the leading opponents of the theory of "spontaneous combustion." Such divergent camps as the radical Marxist, the liberal idealist, and the far right have held to the enduring fallacy that spontaneous eruption from discontented masses doth a social movement make. Although his Leninist side posits a role for collective energy in destabilizing entrenched interests, Gramsci denies that "spontaneity" alone is a sufficient pretext for sustained protest. Ever the strong critic of the

---

[1] An extremely useful discussion of the temporal implications of social-historical research is Ron Aminzade 1992, 456–80.

mechanistic view and of popular political development left to chance, the empirical roots of Gramsci's convictions were the factory council experience and his observations about the ease with which fascism had taken hold in the popular imagination.

This idea reinvokes one of the main conclusions of this book, namely, that organization becomes a central factor in socializing movements, defined by their long-term transformative aspirations. The modern period was marked by a mass surge into national political activity, public sphere growth, and the articulation of civil societies. Vital objects of study for the nineteenth and twentieth centuries, then, are the organizations that served both as channels for collective political expression and as models for other movements. Many of these movements embodied alternative definitions of modernity, conceived to subvert the structural integrity and viability of old regimes. If not already in place, modernizing elites hoped to maneuver their way into a position from which they could somehow shape the course of state and nation building. In leaders' imaginations, this would be accomplished through the deployment of "rational," "enlightened" technologies of social engineering and would depend on their capacity to tap the critical resource of organized mass political power.

One of the resources available to nineteenth- and early twentieth-century modernizers involved the manipulation of popular consciousness, which was central to the burgeoning and increasingly significant public sphere. Their ambition was to demonstrate to political initiates the ways that traditional regimes remained mired in self-serving and "backward" goals and to substitute demands for inclusion, participation, and rights accruing from national citizenship. These citizenship narratives originated in the Enlightenment and the French Revolution, as well as in ideals about ancient Greek democracy characteristic of a proper "modern" education, and were molded to serve particular authors' needs in creating utilitarian images of "progress." If, as Gramsci astutely observed, political power in a state-building context involves both domination and consent, a key aspect of the modern nationalist project was the bid to establish and manipulate mass compliance. The race was on to impress, mobilize, educate, guide, and reform the common folk.[2]

One of the points that I make in this book is that modern nationalists were not just bourgeois liberals, in the sense that the literature on this period often presumes, even though so-called liberal ideals were a foundational part of their narratives. Claimants to the nation state–building process also included communists such as Stefanos Sarafis or Dimitris Glinos who envisioned their own

---

[2] Probably the best analysis of the dialectics of this process in comparative perspective is still Hroch 1985.

various "third-way" narratives, emplotted with scenes of how *else* communism might function. Similarly, as a political strategist, Gramsci's main allegiance was not to a vague "world revolution" but rather to the political possibility of finding more equitable solutions to *Italy's* problems of modern nationhood—a labor to be structured by internationalist guidelines. Furthermore, if we keep in mind that for many influential leaders, misguided and bigoted though some occasionally were, the driving narrative behind collective action was quest-romantic rather than shrewdly criminal, we can more easily understand why they so often drew from a bag containing assorted solutions. Thus, the non-cynical view of political motivation during the modernist era would recognize both the mixed quality of the leadership ontologies that fused radical, liberal, conservative, communist, social democratic, and various other possibilities (and these were often different from their avowed memberships and allegiances) and the essential idealism that tends to undergird the political enterprise in general.

To the extent that modernist nationalism sought to organize a basic core of legal citizens and was traceable to the popular mobilizational ambitions of the Enlightenment, it can be distinguished from other kinds of more reactionary national insurgencies. Clearly such nationalisms have little in common with, for instance, the fascism of any era. Here, we are also reminded that the Serbian nationalism presently raging away in Bosnia-Herzegovina is worlds apart from our present case. Nation building—training future citizens, emphasizing commonalities, inclusiveness, participation—and racist enlistment built on a platform of national superiority, are clearly different enterprises, and yet both often use the "nation" as their common mobilizational denominator. Thus the notion in recent cultural critique that all nationalisms are dangerous is questionable. Opposing "good" and "bad" nationalisms may not be especially fruitful. Yet Gramsci and others who lived through the fascist period might argue that it is the absence of certain *kinds* of nationalism that can be considered dangerous. This recalls a parallel debate about the legacies of the resistance in Italy. As Adrian Lyttelton observes in a review of Claudio Pavone's controversial book, "Partisan justice was undeniably rough justice; but one ordinary partisan gave a memorable answer to a judge who asked him why he had failed to observe legal procedures: 'Signor giudice, it's true, only you weren't there, and so I had to do my best.'"

Like Pavone, I am "not seeking to write a general history of the period, but to explain the motives and mentality of those who did choose sides and who took action in consequence." Pavone's conclusion, rendered by Lyttleton, also captures the soul of the present work: "Cultural and political motives dictated a greater respect for life and a greater humanity on the Resistance (as opposed to fascist) side. The partisans were more conscious than their opponents of 'the weight of evil,' as Italo Calvino put it, which inevitably burdened all those who killed; the ultimate justification could only be found in the fight for liberty" (Lyttelton 1992, 28).

Historically, national insurgencies were characterized by their participatory logic and social justice–seeking agendas. Such movements were seen by the significant number of new recruits to be formations for which they, as Anderson expresses it, would "willingly . . . die." Examining such movements ontologically, to ascertain their origins, development, allies, strategies, tactics, and modes of organization is an especially useful way to gauge what motivated participants to become and continue as activists. A central factor in movement organization is leadership, whose role it is to delineate a narrative conception of the movement, thus pushing collective activity in particular directions. I have paid special attention to this aspect in analyzing the case of the Greek resistance movement spearheaded by the EAM and have maintained that it was a logical continuation of an earlier eighteenth- and nineteenth-century prospectus.

Bringing in Gender

Gender is always in some way a constituent element of any nationalist cause. Interactions and power differentials between female and male participants, official policy commitments as compared to concrete changes in divisions of labor, visions of ideal male and female activists, practical variations in activities, and the regulation of participant sexuality are among the important gendered dimensions of national political movements. Because of its stronger traditional presence in politics, the male gender has in most cases been the one to inaugurate mixed movements, a situation that has also favored largely androcentric notions of activism (see, e.g., Mullaney 1990). As we have seen, ontological narratives are often logically prior to the creation of situational mobilizational narratives. In this regard, Carole Pateman raises an important aspect of the gender question that is applicable to the Greek resistance. In *The Disorder of Women,* she maintains that in so-called Western societies, which most nationalist intelligentsias sought to emulate or somehow reconcile, the political norm for

citizenship has been made in the male image. . . . it is precisely these marks of womanhood that place women in opposition to, or, at best, in paradoxical and contradictory relation to, citizenship. Women are expected to don the lion's skin, mane and all, or to take their place among and indistinguishable from, the new men postulated in radical democratic theory. There is no set of clothes available for a citizen who is a woman, no vision available within political theory of the new democratic woman. Women have always been incorporated into the civil order as "women," as subordinates or lesser men, and democratic theorists have not yet formulated any alternative. The dilemma remains. All that is clear is that if women are to be citizens as *women,* as autonomous, equal, yet sexually different beings from men, democratic theory and practice has to undergo a radical transformation. (1989, 14)

Similarly, the most significant and typical aspect of the radical nexus between gender equality and the EAM was the usage of a masculine or even "neutered" model of citizenship. In terms of a national citizenship, women qua women were an under- and untheorized category. For the most part standards encompassed only "traditional" women and women qua honorary men. This raises crucial concerns about what kinds of political change are possible given the long-standing and still-current rubrics of gender equality and democratic collective action. To look for resolution of this question in a modern domain of struggle when, as I have argued, a characteristic of the era was to avoid deconstructing silences on questions of diversity may be an anachronistic expectation. It is probable, nevertheless, that even in the light of an earlier discourse some women "noticed" their interpretive exclusion and the various subtle impediments and glass-ceilings that were still in place even as their hopes for a new order were being raised. Of course we are reminded that at the turn of the twenty-first century the problem of the womanist citizen has yet to be resolved on any significant scale. Indeed, this also raises the very vexing question of the so-called sameness/difference paradox, which has consistently posed problems for the democratic political process and will no doubt continue to do so. At issue is how justice and diversity can intersect: if constitutive differences are recognized and somehow incorporated, equal treatment is then compromised; but if communities marked by difference are read as equal, then their relevant characteristics and specific problems cannot also be taken into account without contradiction. Particularly relevant to our case is how this paradox was played out in the formative gender debates of the nineteenth and twentieth centuries between such figures as August Bebel and Clara Zetkin.[3] In light of this dilemma, this book has been an effort to excavate *attitudes* about citizenship, the fulfillment of socialist ideals, and inclusion held by influential EAM leaders, as well as to suggest ways in which movement authors were led to "engender" nationalist narratives in a fashion that was typically both enabling and constraining for women.

Particularly relevant to gender in social movements are the operative norms and referents of male leaders as they constructed their own masculinity in the political arena. Whom did these men perceive as judges of their political acceptability—as, for example, "modern" (anti–Second International?) socialists and in the Enlightenment legal problematic, as "reasonable men"?

[3] See J. W. Scott 1988b on the Sears Case; also Lopes and Roth 1993.

Many leaders were convinced that gender equality was the mark of a modern nation, and progress on that score was deemed necessary for Greece to begin to reverse its image in the world community. Also, as Sheila Rowbotham maintains, "nationalism and antiimperialism pulled women into public action because they were needed by the nation. Their emancipation was less an individual right than a public duty. The individual was to find realization through the nation. Nonetheless in the process some men and women questioned the domestic and sexual control of men over women. However, nationalist movements had a profound ambiguity about the proper place of women" (1992, 108).

A full prosopographic reading would have to take into account both the "personal as political" and the general exposure of modern political generations to fluctuating and ambivalent norms about female participation in public sphere activity. Just as abiding prejudice colored the actions of some, admiration for the "New Woman" critically influenced how others stretched policy in certain directions and tightened it in others.[4] Thus, without accepting the individualist assumptions of traditional psychohistorical approaches, we might seriously consider factors such as Sarafis's close relationship with and deep respect for his mother's "coping skills," which played a crucial role in his contribution to the gender-equal goals of the movement.[5] We would also want to note the policy effects of the close associations that leaders such as Glinos maintained with prominent Greek women in the demotic movement, among them the most important feminist activists of the prewar period. Unfortunately a lack of data and space considerations have prevented me from further teasing out how resistance leaders may have been implicated in the gender narratives of the day.

[4] For a provocative discussion of this general phenomenon, see Hobsbawm, 1987, 192–207, "The New Woman." Also Angela Davis's treatment of Frederick Douglass in *Women, Race and Class.*

[5] On the broad-minded tenor of Sarafis's attitudes toward women, in contrast to prevailing culture, see M. Sarafis, 1990. Marion Sarafis wrote to me: "One can only really answer your questions by trying to reconstruct Sarafis' way of thinking. He didn't consider himself a 'thinker.' He greatly under-estimated himself intellectually, but he had a habit of seizing on to anything said by others which seemed to express his own way of thinking. Thus, he found his unexpressed ideas of Balkan solidarity given expression by the early socialist politician Papanastasiou and followed him when he found Venizelos going too much to the right. In the same way, I imagine he heard 'equal rights for women' as a KKE slogan in the Aegina prison lectures and felt: 'Yes. That's what I have always thought.' And it drew him to them. Now his two brothers, though they shared the respect for their mother, were quite normal, unreconstructed old-fashioned provincials. I never heard anything about women's equality from them and indeed the younger, having made a disastrous marriage, spoke of women most disparagingly" (23 August 1990). In another letter, she wrote: "A typist-secretary who had him as boss pre-war in the Defence Ministry adored him because she said he was the only boss who had respected her and never harassed her sexually, though she had been terrified when she was told that her new boss was unmarried" (22 September 1990).

Another important consideration is the "control factor." How did anxieties about women's behavior and their own affect the standards leaders set? In what ways might fears about the extent of their own or colleagues' self-control have affected key decisions? For example, the widow of an ELAS political leader reflected on inconsistencies in the movement's sexual code: "They discouraged romances [*romantikes skheseis*], but only for the common people. Those same ones who laid down the law about it always had a woman themselves, and this was inhuman." When I commented that many male leaders apparently brought their wives with them to the mountains, ostensibly to demonstrate the revolutionary value of stable family life, another observed, "This is Greek common sense. It was the only way to keep the leadership off the village girls, which could have destroyed the resistance. [My husband] did not mince his words on the trouble he had from some of them." She added: "As I knew them, they all said 'equal rights,' and none of them really acted on it, with possibly one exception, a German-trained pediatrician and friend, Dr. George Spiliopoulos, but he came to the resistance from the Right."

The following depiction of the personal politics of everyday life during a thirty-year exile in Eastern Europe is not atypical. When asked, "Did your husband also help you around the house?" the first woman responded, "Well, to some extent, but you know men. . . . Well, let's just say that he also spent quite a bit of time sitting in the kafeneion talking with the others." Yet if certain social paradoxes were widely known, it is also probably true that some situations were tolerated as culturally accepted "facts of life" in, after all, an era before the second wave of the women's movement, when sexual power relations were problematized more explicitly. The unspoken and also often unrecognized need to neutralize women's real or imagined power raised by Nancy Chodorow's work (1978, 1989) should be taken seriously in evaluating the complex roots of male political behavior. It is important, moreover, to consider the role played by individual but highly influential personalities, as Marion Sarafis's comments suggest,[6] but remembering that such biographical variables are useless if removed from the broader structural context of gender relations and social discourse.[7]

In the EAM gender equality was of course not always uppermost in the minds of military authorities, nor were efforts in that direction always an unqualified success. For example, during the Civil War, which participants generally viewed as a continuation of the enlightened gender policies of the resistance, Loula Tzavara and Stathoula Plithikioti of the 103d Brigade complained to the battalion directorate: "We cannot understand why you under-

---

[6] It can be difficult to judge the merits of clearly partisan testimonies given by close family members if they are the only available source of information, but perhaps no more difficult than deciding whom to believe from a more general point of view.

[7] Carolyn Steedman (1990) makes this point eloquently.

estimate us and refuse to send us on any serious missions. Have we not fought and do we not continue to fight beside the guys? We write to you because we have observed that the missions going behind enemy lines consist only of young men and never of young women. This devalues all the girls. We are hoping that action will be taken soon on this matter."[8]

It is hard to know what gender conflicts signify about the movement. Although the lack of adherence to gender-equal norms testified to above may appear to subvert a basic argument of this book, I read the matter differently. Not all male participants were able to change their views and behavior miraculously in the course of a few years; nevertheless, the evidence is still fairly strong that a novel reconstruction of gender and participatory norms had created unprecedented changes. This is demonstrated by the fact that, for instance, the young women of the Democratic Army possessed such robust opinions about inconsistencies that might violate the movement's integrity and, moreover, expressed them in the language of "equal rights," in accord with expectations they were undoubtedly taught by the movement itself.

Difficult as it is to extract a fair picture of how the gender politics of the men in power may have affected the movements they created, several recent studies have usefully focused on the archaeology of male gender ideology and leadership in national movements.[9] What has not been studied sufficiently is the construction of masculinity and how it relates to leadership. How does masculine self-image affect the ontological narratives that produce specific mobilizational narratives? These core mobilizational narratives are emplotted to emphasize subjective realities that fall within a certain comfort zone and to silence those that threaten aspects of male "collective unconscious."[10] Cynthia Enloe, among others, has foregrounded the issue of nationalism constructed in response to threats against a composite masculinity, arguing that "nationalism typically has sprung from masculinized memory, masculinized humiliation and masculinized hope. Anger at being 'emasculated'—or turned into a 'nation of busboys'—has been presumed to be the natural fuel for igniting a nationalist movement," (1990, 44). Enloe's point raises vital questions about how seriously one can take the archetypal nationalist claim to represent the harbinger of social justice, given such partially submerged agendas. Here, in addition to a creative use of Freudian theory, insights from the "men's movement," assem-

---

[8] From the archives of Ioanni Mavrou, *Eleftherotipia*. Saturday, 23 December 1978, 9. I am grateful to John Iatrides for sending me this and other materials from the same series.

[9] See Chatterjee 1993b; Kandiyioti 1989; Layoun 1992; and Katrak 1992. For discussion of sexuality and political authority, see Gruber 1987, 1991; Mosse 1985; Padgug 1979; and Stoler 1992.

[10] Alexander 1994; and Gay 1985. For example, it would be worthwhile to consider leadership struggles and conflicts of interest from the perspective of intermale power dynamics.

bled by men for men, might help illuminate the nexus of masculine ego and political authority.[11]

On a related but more general note, the Greek national movement, like any other, was significantly shaped by the ontological narratives of influential figures. Here we have considered, as part of a prosopographic profile, Dimitris Glinos, Stefanos Sarafis, to a lesser extent Nikos Zachariades, and by historical analogy, Antonio Gramsci, but there is considerable room for further work in this area, and a full treatment of other leaders from this perspective remains to be done. In imagining a starting point for such multivalent analysis, we might recall Louis Althusser's assertion that "ideology 'acts' or 'functions' in such a way that it 'recruits' subjects among the individuals . . . or 'transforms' the individuals into subjects . . . by that very precise operation which I have called *interpellation* or hailing, and which can be imagined along the lines of the most commonplace everyday police (or other) hailing: 'Hey, you there!' "

The point is that it is worth keeping in mind such questions as who, or what, would founding members have wanted to be "hailed" as and why? Moreover, how might the story of "Identities I Relish Least" read? These and other heuristic, even metaphorical, exercises that I have advocated are incompatible with those social science methodologies that attempt to tightly pattern themselves after scientific inquiry, based on objectivity writ large. Such styles of positivism provide less than satisfactory "ways of knowing" about social transformations, and we would want to keep our critical stance toward the modernist metanarrative that asserts its religious faith in lawlike generalizations. At the same time, fantasy-structural cum narrative analysis should not constitute a license to, as one scholar says, "invent documents at will" (Eley forthcoming), but can help to create an opening for assimilating new insights about dilemmas of social causality. Overall, to recapitulate an earlier point, the use of such methods requires an interdisciplinary philosophy capable of uniting sociological with literary, anthropological, psychological, and other approaches. Such an academic worldview is predicated on a belief in the value of thinking through problems, as I call it, "in spite of the disciplines."

Finally, back to what I have sought to contribute to the historical record regarding this case so touched by distortions in cold war historiography. In his discursively influential text *The Right of Nations to Self-Determination*, Lenin asserts that "The bourgeois nationalism of *any* oppressed nation has a general democratic content that is directed *against* oppression, and it is this content that we *unconditionally* support" (1979, 8). On this question, Tom Nairn writes, "The crux of Lenin's view was that nationalism could constitute a

---

[11] For example, Pleck 1989; and Goode 1989. For an investigation of such issues by a sociolinguist plainly attempting to listen to the "other side," see Tannen 1990. For a fascinating Freudian interpretation of nationalist narratives, see Hunt 1992.

detour in some degree valid—contributing to the political conditions and general climate favourable to the break-through, undermining the conservatism and the inertia of old regimes" (1977, 90). What we most want to emphasize here are the concepts of breakthrough and potential dislodgment of the complacent State, which Lenin's narrative addresses. In Greek political development, the "inertia of old regimes" was from a popular point of view buttressed by the misleading results of the 1821 revolution, analogous to the effects of passive revolution that Gramsci stresses in his critical review of Italian history. These were, as elsewhere, augmented by fascism which, on the horizon of the 1920s, had come into full view by the 1930s. Over the course of decades, political lethargy, acquiescence, and repression had combined to create a political bottleneck.

The EAM movement fostered a breakthrough and also, following Gramsci, a site for the construction and reconstruction of political culture. Greek World War II nationalism was forged in the crucible of indigenous socialism as a destabilizing force, which underscores the importance of political openings, one of the major lines of argument in this book. Breaks in the opportunity structure, as I have noted, involve not just formal political opportunities such as elections but also reconstitutive political events during periods of crisis or, figuratively, *what else* happens when the normal stays of politics are loosened.

Within the context of resistance against the occupation, significant priority was placed on the institution of a viable set of democratic participatory values to counter existing exclusionary hegemonies. From this point of view, the chaos of the war created a moment of opportunity when the forces of a war of position—albeit a vaguely constituted populist one—were given license to advance. In a popular manual issued by the People's Library: "Popular democracy [*laiki dhimokratia*]," proclaims the caption under a sketch of a mixed group of citizens, with eyes raised toward the future and posed under a sun-drenched Greek flag, "is power that incarnates the alliance of workers, farmers, professionals, industrialists, intellectuals, the petty bourgeoisie, and the middle classes. Popular Democracy is a new type of Democracy, which destroys the political oppression of the exploited and in which power is in the hands of the People." The back cover of the same pamphlet portrays a patriot trenchantly planting a flag inscribed with the words "Popular Democracy" on a mountain called Ellada (Greece).[12] Benedict Anderson has noted the significance of the proliferation of print media in the spread of nationalism. An indication of how symbiotic the concepts of nationalism and popular democracy were, is the Office of Strategic Services classified document dated 1

---

[12] *Levkoma apo to Programma tis Laikis Dhimokratias tou politikou sinaspismou ton kommaton tou E.A.M.* (Guidebook from the People's Democracy Program of the political coalition of the parties of EAM).

EAM organizing pamphlet. A patriot plants the flag on a mountain called "Greece."

August 1943, which lists thirty-nine clandestine newspapers operating in the Thessaly region and the body each represented, with titles such as "O Rigas" (after revolutionary patriot Rigas Ferraios); "Voice of EAM; "People's Democracy"; "Worker"; "Women's Struggle"; "Everyday News"; "Truth"; "The Voice of Olympus"; "New Horizons"; "Voice of the People"; "New Life"; "Farmer's Voice"; "Field of Freedom"; "The Lighthouse"; "Free Mountain"; "Revolutionary Voice"; "Voice of the Countryside"; "Passion" (Karditsa EPON). The populist logic is patent in this list.[13]

It is precisely the themes of cohesiveness overriding diversity and of generative politics, and as Gramsci put it, of the new relationship between "the leaders and the led" that drew adherents to the movement and that for many, symbolized the nationalist cause for which they found themselves willing to die. The staying power of an inclusionary narrative can, for example, be seen in the case of the Spanish Civil War. Many international veterans justified their continued support for the communist cause, in the face of profound disaffection during the 1950s with Stalinism, based on a nostalgic loyalty to the ideals of the Spanish "moment." Whatever patriotism or love of country may already have been in place when the Nazi invasion of Greece occurred, a less static notion of *nationalism*, derived from a social and historical *analysis* of the meaning of participation in the nation, was advertised and ingested in the course of the resistance as a political event.

Here, it is worth noting the distinction between nationalism and patriotism. Nationalism is a *learned* allegiance, whether through explicit political instruction, media inculcation, or experiential metamorphosis. Its narrative terms may be richer than those of patriotism. Thus the nationalist narratives considered here, while built on a patriotic foundation, contained additional scenes and fields of analysis: about injustice, about deserving constituencies, about civic duties and rights, about international hierarchies and relevant historical events. In this view, nationalism is marked by the range of definitions it contains: of gender roles, of economy, of legal and political process. Patriotism is activated from a different and far less comprehensive level of judgment and collective memory. Clearly EAM tapped into preexisting patriotic sentiment; in addition, it fostered a learning opportunity and enhanced public discourse about the meaning of the Greek nation.

On the issue of how women themselves experience and narrate the predominantly male fields of war, resistance, and politics, the present work amplifies rather than decisively settles questions that other books have also raised. There is the question of how women's internal agency should be weighed against the external and often paternalistic control of movement leadership. There is the issue of differences among the women who participate in such movements in terms of age, class, and political background, which in turn

[13] Documents courtesy of the Lagoudakis Collection, Boston University Library.

destabilize pretensions to generalizability. There is the question of whether movements that seek, as a matter of policy, to politically empower women can be labeled "feminist" or if the fact that potential transformations originate in the policy initiatives of men requires a different conceptual category, since proposed changes are not introduced by women, for women. There is the problem of the explanatory power of collective action versus individual personality regarding the extent and type of activity undertaken by particular women. When asked about the empowering value of feminism, for example, one woman replied: "Oh, I wouldn't have many problems anyway, Janet dear, because me, I *always* speak my mind" (*dhen prokietai na vrisko provlimata, Ioanna mou, afou egho, eh, panda leo ti gnomi mou*). The same woman was reputed to be one of the boldest and most fearless members of her battalion, whose lack of hesitation in using her shotgun against enemies and collaborators alike was legendary.

And what about the methods used to make sense of female participation? Has the methodological sieve been invented that can separate movement ideology from "life experience," considering that the two are sometimes the same and sometimes different? Are the women who say their experience has been a good one necessarily victims of false consciousness and the researcher who trusts them hopelessly naive? What indicators do we use to count and measure the extent of women's participation—the existence, degree of influence, numbers of women among the leadership? membership statistics? testimony? analogy? What kinds of conclusions can be drawn from the jubilant pride that often marks informants' accounts? And what kinds of tentative predictions can be made regarding what the political future might hold for female combatants who have fought "alongside the men"? To be sure, the case of Nazi women reminds us that a female presence in war is not a priori a sign of cultural breakthrough.

In the end, perhaps the one dependable assertion that can be made, even as feminist theory and gender as a category of analysis have transformed and continue to transform all documented readings of social processes, is that no transcendent theory of women in any particular social domain is tenable. The so-called "first wave" of feminism, stemming as it did from the modernist Enlightenment project, is often equated with the explicit pursuit of universal womanhood suffrage. The Greek case makes it clear, however, that the same wave of political controversy about citizenship rights and women contained other, less readily recognizable facets. Women as a category were politically incorporated and empowered in a variety of ways besides through formal political channels, namely acquiring the right to vote. Understanding the problem of suffrage historically is, of course, very necessary, but so is looking at broader issues of participation, legitimacy, and citizenship that surrounded suffrage debates. In considering the "woman question" and the EAM in relation to those larger debates, I have tried to extend narrower definitions of politics while continuing to recognize the crucial role played by traditional institutions and conceptions of political process. When I began this research, there was very little secondary literature on the subject from any angle. The increase in articles and books focusing on women in nationalism, resistance, war, and revolution are for me not only interesting but moving, considering that these topics have been important sites for the study of gender politics and also deeply tied to my own personal and professional development.

Reflexive Moments

Finally, in (re)search of the self, I began this book with certain premises about authorial experience drawn from the literature on autobiography. Paul John Eakin sums up one aspect of those suppositions well: "When we settle into the theater of autobiography, what we are ready to believe—and what most autobiographers encourage us to expect—is that the play we witness is a historical one, a largely faithful and unmediated reconstruction of events that took place long ago, whereas in reality the play is that of the autobiographical act itself, in which the materials of the past are shaped by memory and imagination to serve the needs of present consciousness" (1985, 56). In writing this book, I have tried to think through the question of intellectuals and how they become engaged in the business of cultural critique. I believe that national histories veer in certain directions and not in others based on exactly who produces, consumes, and interprets knowledge about political development(s).

It is still true, it seems to me, that the civil society bracing the state is vulnerable when insufficiently articulated and can, as in Gramsci's famous formulation, be dangerously "primordial and gelatinous." The modernist in me still believes in the normative possibility of "a proper relation between State and civil society," so that when the state "tremble[s] a sturdy structure of civil society [is] at once revealed. The State is only an outer ditch, behind which there [stands] a powerful system of fortresses and earthworks" (1971, 238, "State and Civil Society"). The test, as Gramsci also notes and as I believe the Greek case shows, comes during times of crisis, "when the immediate situation becomes delicate and dangerous, because the field is open for violent solutions, for the activities of unknown forces, represented by charismatic 'men of destiny'" (210). It is at such times that political intuition comes into play: "Political intuition is not expressed through the artist, but through the 'leader'; and 'intuition' must be understood to mean not 'knowledge of men,' but swiftness in connecting seemingly disparate facts, and in conceiving the means adequate to particular ends—thus discovering the interests involved, and arousing the passions of men and directing them towards a particular action" (252).

At the same time, a recognition of the age-old problems of alliance and collaboration should help siphon off any natural tendency toward blind idealism and overly centered political interpretations. There is clearly a dearth of long-lasting success stories in the social movement literature. In fact, the best way to maintain a healthy skepticism about coalition building as an antidote to exclusionary politics is to study the global history of social movements. Although the issues that social movements put on the social and political agenda and their leverage may continue through time, as actual live entities they are virtually always short-lived, deteriorating as a result of factionalism, repression, co-optation, megalomania, and various other less-than-satisfactory outcomes. Ironically, at the same time that participant collective memories often bespeak a triumph and the facilitation of important oppositional narratives, it is also axiomatic that someone, as often as not a former supporter, is left feeling bitter and abused.

Modernism can best be understood as a time of building foundations; postmodernism has raised the possibility that those foundations are critiquable and, in fact, need critiquing. Here is where it seems to me that we still need Gramsci, first, to help remind us that although the enemy is no longer as clear as, for example, "the ancien regime" or "the fascist machine," some of the same narratives continue to threaten us profoundly. Second, it is not just material achievement but also political education, the fight against ignorance about historical and international political realities and the cultivation of the ability to disaggregate political relationships, which will help us toward some resolution of the myriad political impasses faced by contemporary societies. Although we should no longer assume a universal foundation, the existing infrastructure still needs some combination of installment, change, and repair. It is collaboration of intellectuals, "traditional" (in that they are in a position to influence the political education of the young) and "organic" (in that their links to particular communities of origin are a major source of training and inspiration), which will bring the necessary rigor to the process of cultural and political critique and will feed into the battles in a postmodern "war of position."

I sat on the British Airways flight on my return trip from Athens, listening to the drone of the engines and contemplating some of the ways in which I and my impressions of Greece had changed in the eight years I had been away. In the meantime the world had been rocked by huge political changes: Berlin, 1989, Nelson Mandela's release and the crumbling of apartheid in South Africa, the Persian Gulf War, the Bosnian civil war, face-to-face negotiations between Israel and the PLO. Greece had itself changed considerably: the loud and humiliating fall of the Socialist party from office in 1988, leaving in its wake a deep popular cynicism about politics and political possibilities; new border and ethnic conflicts on the horizon; and increasing numbers of, and diversity among, groups that will have to find a way to live together under the Greek national umbrella, such as ethnic and Greek Albanians; Africans; the community of Philippine women (*filipinezzes*) who serve as maids and nannies to the bourgeoisie. CNN, MTV, and a variety of new channels are now available on Greek television. Many more telephones are now in use, and one rarely has to wedge messages in the doors of households that haven't yet been able to purchase a line. Common Market membership and whether to expel the American military are no longer burning issues of the same magnitude that they were in 1985. In Greece, as elsewhere, a mood of confusion, disillusionment, fear of further destabilizations, even nihilism prevails. The record on addressing diversity and recognizing the ways in which "race matters" is, I would say, just as spotty as it is in other countries, especially when it comes to incorporating cautionary tales about the importance of tolerance and unconditional respect into public discourse.[14] And as elsewhere, regimes of political commodification—the Bennetton–video culture variety—seem to be socializing the Greek young, with disturbing implications.[15]

The aims and accomplishments of the Socialist party, so widely appreciated when I first lived in Greece, are now deprecated by a much larger segment of the population. In some quarters, the evaluation of the EAM movement is linked to the failures of PASOK, even though for various historical and political reasons, impressionistic and visceral knowledge about the EAM rather than studied understanding is the order of the day. When I identified my topic, I would often hear one or two schematic anecdotes, from which the narrator would generalize certain macrostructural conclusions about the resistance movement. Implicit in these rhetorical "speech acts" was the assumption that information about a resistance participant who had cheated on his wife or a niece who had allegedly been shot by ELAS, coming from Greeks, ought somehow to be privileged over research, especially by a non-Greek. As life and politics become more precarious and as cynicism becomes epidemic, some of the previous openness seemed to be vanishing. In my social imagination, such receptivity did exist in the mid-1980s, but that now seems to have been replaced by a brand of closure I hadn't noticed before. Regarding EAM specifically, the most important point here is certainly that owing to decades of repression, the movement was rarely discussed openly and never incorporated into school curricula. A friend told me that she had not learned of her parents' involvement until she was nearly twenty, when she joined the antijunta movement in the late 1960s. Interrogated by the police, she was told that her

[14] See West 1993; Panourgia 1993, 1992; Dimitras 1993.
[15] See discussions of these and related phenomena in hooks 1992.

father's name was on file for "antinational" activities. Neither parent had dared risk revealing their involvement, even to their children. Now, several generations have had virtually nothing but hearsay to go on. The symbolic and inspirational value of the movement has never really been tapped. Unlike the American Civil Rights movement, the EAM has remained either a shadowy failure or a local version of the "Evil Empire" story in many eyes.

Narrative and history are deeply enmeshed. The stories that are told about the past change as each new and significant event is incorporated into popular narratives. To achieve legitimacy, the plots of the mobilizational narratives that political authorities use to gain compliance are adjusted to fit the requirements of the times. Since with each passing decade, the decade before actually becomes *history*, crucial lessons for historical research lie in identifying those narratives that have "serve(d) the needs of present consciousness" (Eakin 1985, 5) for individual scholars and for whole communities during the eras when they were written. Likewise, gaping fissures open when earlier narratives threaten regimes in power or when they no longer resonate for particular generations. The effects of exempting particular narratives were brought home to me by a letter from Marion Sarafis (14 June 1993). I had written to tell her of my trip to Greece, a research venture in which I planned to talk to the children of partisans to learn what aspects of the resistance had survived into the next generation. Sarafis wrote back: "I had been struck by the way knowledge had *not* been passed on, as I saw it in Greek students here (in London) and I felt the need to investigate this. . . . I had concluded that because of post Civil War persecution, for a whole generation parents had just not talked to their children about past history. . . . My own impression (particularly from the Sarafis centenary in Athens and Trikkala in 1990) is that this generation of silence has created a real 'generation gap.' Crowded meetings: 400 and 700 at two Athens meetings and over 1,000 in Trikkala and not a young face to be seen. A man of 28–30 who had known me here as a post-graduate student, looked as though he came from another planet." In a deep-structural sense, what does it mean that the Trikeri political exile camp is now a picnic spot where no plaque commemorates its tragic events? Or that every day thousands of cars pass the site where the Averoff Prison stood in Athens and have no idea that young resistance fighters with national ideals and futures spent their final hours before execution there? Such yawning silences remind us of the possibility that nihilism and the impoverishment of collective memory often occupy the same acrid territory.

Intellectual architect of the EAM, Dimitris Glinos, once wrote: "The only way for a person to live and die as a human being is to live and die for an ideal" (*O monos tropos yia na zisei kai na pethanei kaneis san anthropos inai na zisei kai na pethanei yia ena idhaniko*). Such was the EAM to many of its participants, female and male alike. The fact that Glinos, Gramsci, and some of the other characters who have made appearances throughout this book also occasionally displayed signs of the racialism, sexism, and other blindnesses and ordered "Otherings" common to their generation is of less concern to me than it probably should be. That the movements they took part in have been accused of perpetuating aims in direct opposition to the kind of social justice they advocated, is not enough to derail my basic belief in the good that emerged from communist and communist-led movements. That the personal lives of members of the African National Congress or the Civil Rights movement or the Socialist party of Greece reveal stains cannot diminish my broader macrostructural faith in the rightness of the kinds of social problems they have placed on the public agenda for resolution. A more disturbing notion is that it is possible to exist cut off from the kind of ideal and example this project provided me, and the kind of psychic nourishment, creative subversion, and constructive problem solving that social movements and moments of political opportunity provide.

The narratives we choose to tell about the past will always ring true for some, while false for others, and there will certainly be those who are guardedly skeptical. But since history serves as a resource pool for lessons aimed at the uninitiated and is used to justify massive and often irreversible acts, it is my hope that we continue to keep in perspective what critical trust is placed in the hands of the weavers of fables.

On the road to Karpenisi from Ay. Yiorgi, village burned by the Germans, 1944. Resistance graffiti reads: "FREE LIFE AND KNOWLEDGE LEARNING CULTURE SPIRIT ROAD FORWARD." Courtesy Spiros Meletzis

References

Ackelsberg, Martha. 1986. "Women and the Politics of the Spanish Popular Front: Political Mobilization or Social Revolution?" *International Labor and Working-Class History* 30 (Fall): 1–12.
——. 1991. *Free Women of Spain.* Bloomington: Indiana University Press.
Adamson, Walter. 1980. *Hegemony and Revolution: A Study of Antonio Gramsci's Political and Cultural Theory.* Berkeley: University of California Press.
Al-Azmeh, Aziz. 1993. *Islams and Modernities.* London: Verso.
Alexander, George M. 1981. "The Demobilization Crisis of November 1944." In *Greece in the 1940s: A Nation in Crisis,* ed. J. O. Iatrides, 156–166. Hanover, N.H.: University Press of New England.
Alexander, Sally. 1994. "Women, Class, and Sexual Differences in the 1830s and 1840s: Some Reflections on the Writing of a Feminist History." In *Culture/Power/History: A Reader in Contemporary Social Theory,* ed. Nicholas Dirks, Geoff Eley, and Sherry Ortner, 269–96. Princeton: Princeton University Press.
Ali, Moiram. 1987. "The Coal War: Women's Struggle during the British Miners' Strike," In *Women and Political Conflict,* ed. Rosemary Ridd and Helen Callaway, 84–105. New York: New York University Press.
Alinsky, Saul. 1972. *Rules for Radicals.* New York: Vintage.
——. 1989. *Reveille for Radicals.* New York: Vintage.
Alivizatos, Nicos C. 1981. "The 'Emergency Regime' and Civil Liberties, 1946–1949," In *Greece in the 1940s: A Nation in Crisis,* ed, John O. Iatrides, 220–28. Hanover, N.H.: University Press of New England.
Allen, Peter. 1979. "Internal Migration and the Changing Dowry in Modern Greece," *Indiana Social Studies Quarterly* (Spring): 142–56.
Althusser, Louis. 1971. *Lenin and Philosophy and Other Essays.* New York: Monthly Review Press.
Aminzade, Ronald. 1992. "Historical Sociology and Time." *Sociological Methods and Research* 20 (May): 456–80.
Anderson, Benedict. 1983. *Imagined Communities: Reflections on the Origin and Spread of Nationalism.* New York: Verso.
Anderson, Kathryn, and Dana C. Jack. 1991. "Learning to Listen: Interview Tech-

niques and Analyses." In *Women's Words: The Feminist Practice of Oral History*, ed. Sherna Berger Gluck and Daphne Patai, 11–26. New York: Routledge.

Anderson, Kathryn, et al. 1990. "Beginning Where We Are: Feminist Methodology in Oral History." In *Feminist Research Methods: Exemplary Readings in the Social Sciences*, ed. Joyce McCarl Nielsen, 94–112. Boulder: Westview Press.

Anderson, Perry. 1976–77. "The Antinomies of Antonio Gramsci." *New Left Review* 100 (Nov.–Jan.): 5–78.

——. 1988. "Modernity and Revolution." In *Marxism and the Interpretation of Culture*, ed. Cary Nelson and Lawrence Grossberg, 317–33. Urbana: University of Illinois Press.

Auerbach, Erich. 1953. *Mimesis: The Representation of Reality in Western Literature*. Princeton: Princeton University Press.

Augustinos, Gerasimos. 1977. *Consciousness and History: Nationalist Critics of Greek Society, 1897–1914*. New York: Columbia University Press.

Avdela, Efi, and Angelika Psarra. 1985. *O feminismos stin Elladha tou mesopolemou* (Feminism in Greece during the interwar period). Athens: Gnosi Press.

Bachofen, Johann Jakob. 1967. *Myth, Religion, and Mother Right*. Princeton: Princeton University Press.

Bailey, F. G. 1971. *Gifts and Poison: The Politics of Reputation*. Oxford: Basil Blackwell.

Bakhtin, Mikhail. 1981. *The Dialogic Imagination: Four Essays*. Ed. Michael Holquist. Austin: University of Texas Press.

Bal, Mieke. 1985. *Narratology: Introduction to the Theory of Narrative*. Toronto: University of Toronto Press.

Banac, Ivo. 1988. *With Stalin against Tito: Cominformist Splits in Yugoslav Communism*. Ithaca: Cornell University Press.

Barthes, Roland. 1972. *Mythologies*. New York: Noonday Press.

Barziotas, Vasilis. 1981. *O aghonas tou dhimokratikou stratou Elladas* (The struggle of the democratic army of Greece). Athens: Synchroni Epohi.

Bataille, Georges. 1985. *Visions of Excess: Selected Writings, 1927–1939*. Ed. A. Stoekl. Minneapolis: University of Minnesota Press.

Bathrick, David. 1990. "Max Schmeling on the Canvas: Boxing as an Icon of Weimar Culture." *New German Critique* 51 (Fall): 113–36.

Bauman, Richard. 1986. *Story, Performance, and Event: Contextual Studies of Oral Narrative*. New York: Cambridge University Press.

Bauman, Zygmunt. 1989. *Modernity and the Holocaust*. Ithaca: Cornell University Press.

——. 1992. *Intimations of Postmodernity*. New York: Routledge.

Belli, Mihri. 1984. *Rigas dedigi* (What Rigas said). Athens: Themelio Press.

Benjamin, Walter. 1976. "The Storyteller and Artisan Cultures." In *Critical Sociology: Selected Readings*, ed. Paul Connerton, 277–300. New York: Penguin.

Bergson, Henri. 1983. *Creative Evolution* (1911). Lanham, Md.: University Press of America.

Bermeo, Nancy. 1986. *The Revolution within the Revolution: Workers' Control in Rural Portugal*. Princeton: Princeton University Press.

Bernal, Martin. 1987. *Black Athena: The Afroasiatic Roots of Classical Civilization*. London: Free Association Books.

Bernstein, Jay. 1991. "Right, Revolution, and Community: Marx's 'On the Jewish

Question'" In *Socialism and the Limits of Liberalism,* ed. Peter Osborne, 91–119. New York: Verso Books.

Bertaux, Daniel, ed. 1981. *Biography and Society: The Life History Approach in the Social Sciences.* Beverly Hills: Sage.

Bettelheim, Bruno. 1989. *The Uses of Enchantment: The Meaning and Importance of Fairy Tales.* New York: Vintage Books.

Bien, Peter. 1989. *Kazantzakis: Politics of the Spirit.* Princeton: Princeton University Press.

Birkett, Dea, and Julie Wheelwright. 1990. "'How Could She?' Unpalatable Facts and Feminists' Heroines." *Gender and History* 2 (Spring): 49–57.

Bloch, Marc. 1949. *Strange Defeat.* London: Oxford University Press.

———. 1966. *French Rural History: An Essay on Its Basic Characteristics.* Berkeley: University of California Press.

Bobbio, Norberto. 1988. "Gramsci and the Concept of Civil Society." In *Civil Society and the State,* ed. John Keane, 73–99. New York: Verso.

Borland, Katherine. 1991. "'That's Not What I Said': Interpretive Conflict in Oral Narrative Research," In *Women's Words: The Feminist Practice of Oral History,* ed. Sherna Berger and Daphne Patai, 63–75. New York: Routledge.

Bourdieu, Pierre. 1977. *Outline of a Theory of Practice.* Cambridge: Cambridge University Press.

Brandes, Stanley. 1985. *Metaphors of Masculinity: Sex and Status in Andalusian Folklore.* Philadelphia: University of Pennsylvania Press.

Braungart, Richard, and Margaret M. Braungart. 1986. "Life-Course and Generational Politics." *Annual Review of Sociology* 12: 205–31.

Brewer, E. C. 1978. *The Dictionary of Phrase and Fable.* New York: Avenel Books.

Bridenthal, Renate, Atina Grossmann, and Marion Kaplan, eds. 1984. *When Biology Became Destiny: Women in Weimar and Nazi Germany.* New York: Monthly Review Press.

Briet, Martien, Bert Klandermans, and Frederike Kroon. 1987. "How Women Become Involved in the Women's Movement of the Netherlands." In *The Women's Movements of the United States and Western Europe: Consciousness, Political Opportunity, and Public Policy,* ed. Mary F. Katzenstein and Carol M. Mueller, 44–63. Philadelphia: Temple University Press.

Brown, Elsa Barkley. 1990. "Womanist Consciousness: Maggie Lena Walker and the Independent Order of Saint Luke." In *Unequal Sisters: A Multi-cultural Reader in U.S. Women's History,* ed. Ellen C. DuBois and Vicki Ruiz, 208–23. New York: Routledge.

Bukharin, Nikolai. 1969. *Historical Materialism: A System of Sociology* (1921). Ann Arbor: University of Michigan Press.

Bukharin, Nikolai, and Evgeny Preobrazhensky. 1988. *The ABC of Communism: A Popular Explanation of the Program of the Communist Party of Russia.* Ann Arbor Paperbacks for the Study of Communism and Marxism. Ann Arbor: University of Michigan Press.

Burke, Peter. 1978. *Popular Culture in Early Modern Europe.* London: Temple Smith.

Burton, Antoinette. 1991. "The Feminist Quest for Identity: British Suffragism and 'Global Sisterhood,' 1900–1915." *Journal of Women's History* 3 (Fall): 46–81.

Buttigieg, Joseph. 1992. Introduction to *Antonio Gramsci: Prison Notebooks*. New York: Columbia University Press.

Campbell, John K. 1964. *Honour, Family, and Patronage*. New York: Oxford University Press.

———. 1983. "Traditional Values and Continuities in Greek Society." In *Greece in the 1980s*, ed. Richard Clogg, 184–207. London: Macmillan, in association with the Centre for Contemporary Greek Studies, King's College, University of London.

Caplan, Jane. 1989. "Postmodernism, Poststructuralism, and Deconstruction: Notes for Historians," *Central European History* 22 (Sept.–Dec.): 260–78.

Card, Claudia. 1993. Book Review, *Signs* 19 (Autumn): 252–56.

Carr, E. H. 1964. *The Twenty Years' Crisis, 1919–1939*. New York: Harper and Row.

Chatterjee, Partha. 1989. "Colonialism, Nationalism, and Colonized Women: The Contest in India." *American Ethnologist* 16 (Nov.): 622–33.

———. 1993a. *Nationalist Thought and the Colonial World*. Minneapolis: University of Minnesota Press.

———. 1993b. *The Nation and Its Fragments: Colonial and Postcolonial Histories*. Princeton: Princeton University Press.

Chodorow, Nancy. 1978. *The Reproduction of Mothering: Psychoanalysis and the Sociology of Gender*. Berkeley: University of California Press.

———. 1989. *Feminism and Psychoanalytic Theory*. New Haven: Yale University Press.

Christ, Carol. 1979. "Why Women Need the Goddess: Phenomenological, Psychological, and Political Reflections." In *Womanspirit Rising*, ed. Carol Christ and J. Plaskow, 273–87. New York: Harper and Row.

———. 1980. *Diving Deep and Surfacing: Women Writers on Spiritual Quest*. Boston: Beacon Press.

Clogg, Richard. 1979. *A Short History of Modern Greece*. Cambridge: Cambridge University Press.

Cohen, David William. 1985. "Doing Social History from Pim's Doorway." In *Reliving the Past: The Worlds of Social History*, ed. Olivier Zunz, 191–235. Chapel Hill: University of North Carolina Press.

Coles, Robert. 1986. *The Moral Life of Children*. New York: Houghton Mifflin.

Collins, Patricia. Hill. 1991. *Black Feminist Thought: Knowledge, Consciousness, and the Politics of Empowerment*. New York: Routledge.

Collins, Randall. 1988. "Searching for the Structure of the Sixties." *Contemporary Sociology* 17 (November): 729–33.

Cowan, Jane. 1990. *Dance and the Body Politic in Northern Greece*. Princeton: Princeton University Press.

Crockatt, Richard, and Steve Smith. 1987. *The Cold War: Past and Present*. London: Allen and Unwin.

Dalven, Rae. 1990. *The Jews of Salonica*. Philadelphia: Cadmus Press.

Davidson, Alastair. 1977. *Antonio Gramsci: Towards an Intellectual Biography*. London: Merlin Press.

Davis, Angela. 1983. *Women, Race, and Class*. New York: Vintage.

Davis, J. C. 1986. *Fear, Myth, and History: The Ranters and the Historians*. Cambridge: Cambridge University Press.

Dedijer, Vladimir. 1990. *The War Diaries of Vladimir Dedijer*. Vols. 1–3. Ann Arbor: University of Michigan Press.

Degras, Jane, ed. 1971. *The Communist International Documents.* Vols. 1–3. London: Frank Cass.

De Grazia, Victoria. 1992. *How Fascism Ruled Women: Italy, 1922–1945.* Berkeley: University of California Press.

della Porta, Donatella. 1988. "Recruitment Processes in Clandestine Political Organizations: Italian Left-Wing Terrorism." In *From Structure to Action: Comparing Social Movement Research across Cultures,* ed. Bert Klandermans, Hanspeter Kriesi, and Sidney Tarrow, 155–96. International Social Movement Research: A Research Annual (1). Greenwich, Conn.: JAI Press.

Delta, Penelope. 1992. *Stohasmoi peri tis anatrofis ton paidhion mas* (Reflections on the upbringing of our children). Athens: Eleftheri Skepseis.

Denitch, Bogdan. 1976. *The Legitimation of a Revolution: The Yugoslav Case.* New Haven: Yale University Press.

Denzin, Norman K. 1989. *The Research Act: A Theoretical Introduction to Sociological Methods.* Englewood Cliffs, N.J.: Prentice-Hall.

Diamandouros, P. Nikiforos. 1981. *The 1974 Transition from Authoritarian Democratic Rule in Greece: Background and Interpretation from a Southern European Perspective.* Bologna Center Occasional Paper no. 37 Baltimore: Johns Hopkins University, October.

Dimitras, Panayiotis Ilias. 1993. "I elliniki alvanofovia" (Greek Albanophobia). *O Politis* 122 (April–July): 38–42.

Djilas, Milovan. 1977. *Wartime.* New York: Harcourt Brace Jovanovich.

Dolar, Mladen. 1991. "The Legacy of the Enlightenment: Foucault and Lacan." *New Formations* 14 (Summer): 43–56.

Dubisch, Jill, ed. 1986. *Gender and Power in Rural Greece.* Princeton: Princeton University Press.

Du Boulay, Juliet. 1974. *Portrait of a Greek Mountain Village.* New York: Oxford University Press.

———. 1976. "Lies, Mockery, and Family Integrity." In *Mediterranean Family Structures,* ed. J. Peristiany, 389–406. Cambridge: Cambridge University Press.

———. 1983. "The Meaning of Dowry: Changing Values in Rural Greece." *Journal of Modern Greek Studies* 1 (May): 243–70.

Dunn, John. 1989. *Modern Revolutions: An Introduction to the Analysis of a Political Phenomenon.* Cambridge: Cambridge University Press.

Eakin, Paul John. 1985. *Fictions in Autobiography: Studies in the Art of Self-Invention.* Princeton: Princeton University Press.

———, ed. 1991. *American Autobiography: Retrospect and Prospect.* Madison: University of Wisconsin Press.

Eisen, Arlene. 1984. *Women and Revolution in Vietnam.* London: Zed Press.

Eley, G. 1981. "Nationalism and Social History." *Social History* 6 (Jan.): 83–107.

———. 1984. "Reading Gramsci in English: Observations on the Reception of Antonio Gramsci in the English-Speaking World, 1957–82." *European History Quarterly* 14: 441–77.

———. 1988. "Nazism, Politics, and the Image of the Past: Thoughts on the West German *Historikerstreit,* 1986–1987." *Past and Present* 12 (Nov.): 171–208.

———. 1989. "Labor History, Social History, *Alltagsgeschichte:* Experience, Culture, and the Politics of the Everyday—a New Direction for German Social History?" *Journal of Modern History* 61 (June): 297–343.

———. 1991. *Reshaping the German Right: Radical Nationalism and Political Change after Bismark*. Ann Arbor: University of Michigan Press.

———. 1994. "Nations, Publics, and Political Cultures: Placing Habermas in the Nineteenth Century." In *Culture/Power/History: A Reader in Contemporary Social Theory*, ed. Nicholas Dirks, Geoff Eley, and Sherry Ortner, 297–335. Princeton: Princeton University Press.

———. Forthcoming. "Is All the World a Text? From Social History to the History of Society Two Decades Later." In *The Historic Turn in the Human Sciences*, ed. T. J. McDonald. Ann Arbor: University of Michigan Press.

Eley, G., and Keith Nield. 1980. "Why Does Social History Ignore Politics?" *Social History* 5 (May): 249–71.

Enloe, Cynthia. 1990. *Bananas, Beaches, and Bases: Making Feminist Sense of International Politics*. Berkeley: University of California Press.

Epstein, Barbara. 1991. *Political Protest and Cultural Revolution: Nonviolent Direct Action in the 1970s and 1980s*. Berkeley: University of California Press.

Eudes, Dominique. 1972. *The Kapetanios: Partisans and Civil War in Greece, 1943–1949*. London: NLB.

Evans, Sara. 1979. *Personal Politics: The Roots of Women's Liberation in the Civil Rights Movement and the New Left*. New York: Vintage.

Fendrich, James Max. 1989. Review of Doug McAdam, *Freedom Summer*, in *Contemporary Sociology* 18 (March): 227–28.

Fiori, Giuseppe. 1973. *Antonio Gramsci: Life of a Revolutionary*. New York: Schocken.

Flax, Jane. 1990. *Thinking Fragments: Psychoanalysis, Feminism, and Postmodernism in the Contemporary West*. Berkeley: University of California Press.

———. 1992. "The End of Innocence." In *Feminists Theorize the Political*, ed. Judith Butler and Joan W. Scott, 445–63. New York: Routledge.

Fleischer, Hagen. 1978. "The Anomalies in the Greek Middle East Forces, 1941–1944," *Journal of the Hellenic Diaspora* 3: 115–36.

Forgacs, David. 1984. "National-Popular: Geneology of a Concept." In *Formations of Nation and People*, 83–98. London: Routledge and Kegan Paul.

———, ed. 1988. *An Antonio Gramsci Reader: Selected Writings, 1916–1935*. New York: Schocken.

Foucault, Michael. 1980. *Power/Knowledge: Selected Interviews and Other Writings, 1972–1977*. New York: Pantheon Books.

———. 1988. *Politics, Philosophy, Culture: Interviews and Other Writings, 1977–1984*. Ed. Lawrence D. Kritzman. New York: Routledge.

Fourtouni, Eleni. 1984. *Greek Women in Resistance: Journals—Oral Histories*. New Haven: Thelphini Press.

Freeman, Jo. 1983. "A Model for Analyzing the Strategic Options of Social Movement Organizations." In *Social Movements of the Sixties and Seventies*, ed. Jo Freeman, 193–210. New York: Longman.

Freire, Paulo. 1992. *Pedagogy of the Oppressed* (1970). New York: Continuum Press.

Friedl, Ernestine. 1962. *Vasilika*. New York: Holt, Rinehart, and Winston.

———. 1986. "Fieldwork in a Greek Village." In *Women in the Field: Anthropological Experiences*, ed. Peggy Golde, 195–217. Berkeley: University of California Press.

Gagnier, Regenia. 1990. "Feminist Postmodernism: The End of Feminism or the

Ends of Theory?" In *Theoretical Perspectives on Sexual Difference*, ed. Deborah L. Rhode, 21–30. New Haven: Yale University Press.

Gates, Jr., H. L. 1987. *Figures in Black: Words, Signs, and the "Racial" Self*. New York: Oxford University Press.

——, ed. 1991a. *Bearing Witness: Selections from African-American Autobiography in the Twentieth Century*. New York: Pantheon Books.

——. 1991b. "'Authenticity'; or, The Lesson of Little Tree." *New York Times Book Review*, November 24, 1991, 1, 26–30.

——, ed. 1986. *Race, Writing, and Difference*. Chicago: University of Chicago Press.

Gay, Peter. 1985. *Freud for Historians*. New York: Oxford University Press.

——. 1988. *Weimar Culture: The Outsider as Insider*. New York: Peregrine.

Gerlach, Luther, and Virginia H. Hine. 1970. *People, Power, Change: Movements of Social Transformation*. Indianapolis: Bobbs-Merrill.

Gibson, Mary. 1990. "On the Insensitivity of Women: Science and the Woman Question in Liberal Italy, 1890–1910." *Journal of Women's History* 2 (Fall): 11–41.

Giddens, Anthony. 1990. *The Consequences of Modernity*. Stanford: Stanford University Press.

Gitlin, Todd. 1987. *The Sixties: Years of Hope, Days of Rage*. New York: Bantam.

Glinos, Dimitris. 1944. *Ti einai kai ti thelei to Ethniko Apelevtherotiko Metopo* (What is the National Liberation Front and what does it want?). Athens: Ellinika Themata, O Rigas.

——. 1971a. "Dhimiourgikos istorismos" (Creative history) (1920). *Eklektes selides* (Selected works), 13–34. Athens: Stohastis Press.

——. 1971b. "Yinekeios anthropismos: Enas logos yia tin arhi enos ergou" (Women's humanism: Speech on the beginning of a project) (1921). *Eklektes selides* (Selected works), 35–61. Athens: Stohastis Press.

Gluck, Sherna Berger. 1987. *Rosie the Riveter Revisited: Women, the War, and Social Change*. Boston: Twayne.

Gluck, Sherna Berger, and Daphne Patai, eds. 1991. *Women's Words: The Feminist Practice of Oral History*. New York: Routledge.

Goffman, Erving. 1963. *Stigma: Notes on the Management of Spoiled Identity*. New York: Simon and Schuster.

——. 1986. *Frame Analysis: An Essay on the Organization of Experience*. Boston: Northeastern University Press.

Goldberg, Harvey. 1962. *The Life of Jean Jaurès*. Madison: University of Wisconsin Press.

Goode, William J. 1989. "Why Men Resist." In *Men's Lives*, ed. Michael S. Kimmel and Michael A. Messner, 43–58. New York: Macmillan.

Gordon, Linda. 1990. "Family Violence, Feminism, and Social Control." In *Unequal Sisters: A Multi-cultural Reader in U.S. Women's History*, ed. Ellen Carol DuBois and Vicki Ruiz, 141–56. New York: Routledge.

Gordon, Robert. 1981. "Historicism in Legal Scholarship, *Yale Law Journal* 90: 1017.

——. 1988. "Law and Ideology." *Tikkun* 3 (Jan.–Feb.): 14–18, 83–86.

Gramsci, A. 1971. *Selections from the Prison Notebooks*. Ed. Q. Hoare and G. Nowell-Smith. New York: International.

——. 1985. *Antonio Gramsci: Selections from Cultural Writings*. Ed. D. Forgacs and G. Nowell-Smith. Cambridge: Harvard University Press.

——. 1988. "Passive Revolution, Caesarism, Fascism." In *An Antonio Gramsci Reader: Selected Writings, 1916–1935.* Ed. David Forgacs New York: Schocken.

——. 1990. *Selections from the Political Writings.* Vols. 1–2. Ed, Q. Hoare. Minneapolis: University of Minnesota Press.

Greenstein, Fred. I., and Sidney Tarrow. 1970. *Political Orientations of Children: The Use of a Semi-projective Technique in Three Nations.* Comparative Politics Series 1. Beverly Hills: Sage.

Grimshaw, Anna, ed. 1992. *The C. L. R. James Reader.* Cambridge: Blackwell.

Grizona, Diamando. 1982. "Eh, kai ti na protothimitheis!" (Eh, and what do you remember first?). In *Yinekes stin andistasi: Martiries* (Women in the resistance: Eyewitness testimonies), 11–23. Athens: Kinisi "I Yineka Stin Andistasi."

Gruber, Helmut. 1987. "Sexuality in 'Red Vienna': Socialist Party Conceptions and Programs and Working-Class Life, 1920–34," *International Labor and Working-Class History* 31 (Spring): 37–68.

——. 1991. *Red Vienna: Experiment in Working-Class Culture.* New York: Oxford University Press.

Habermas, Jurgen. 1974. "The Public Sphere: An Encyclopedia Article" (1964). *New German Critique* 3: 45–55.

——. 1975. *Legitimation Crisis.* Boston: Beacon Press.

——. 1981. "Modernity versus Postmodernity." *New German Critique* 22 (Winter): 3–14 and comment by A. Giddens, "Modernism and Postmodernism," 15–18.

——. 1989. *The Structural Transformation of the Public Sphere: An Iquiry into a Category of Bourgeois Society.* Cambridge: M.I.T. Press.

Hall, Stuart. 1991. "Brave New World," *Socialist Review* 9 (Jan.–March): 57–64.

Hankiss, Agnes. 1981. "Ontologies of the Self: On the Mythological Rearranging of One's Life-History." In *Biography and Society: The Life History Approach in the Social Sciences,* ed. Daniel Bertaux, 203–9. Beverly Hills: Sage.

Haraway, Donna. 1988. "Situated Knowledges: The Science Question in Feminism and the Privilege of Partial Perspective." *Feminist Studies* 14 (3): 575–99.

Harding, Sandra. 1986. *The Science Question in Feminism.* Ithaca: Cornell University Press.

Hart, J. 1990. "Women in the Greek Resistance: National Crisis and Political Transformation," *International Labor and Working-Class History* 38 (Fall): 46–62.

——. 1990. "Women in Greek Society." In *Background to Contemporary Greece,* ed. Martin Eve and Marion Sarafis, 95–121. London: Merlin Press.

——. 1992. "Cracking the Code: Narrative and Political Mobilization in the Greek Resistance." *Social Science History* 16 (4): 631–68.

Haupt, Georges. 1986. *Aspects of International Socialism, 1871–1914.* Cambridge: Cambridge University Press.

Haviaras, Stratis. 1984. *The Heroic Age.* New York: Simon and Schuster.

Herzfeld, M. 1983. "Semantic Slippage and Moral Fall: The Rhetoric of Chastity in Rural Greek Society." *Journal of Modern Greek Studies* 1 (May): 161–72.

——. 1985. *The Poetics of Manhood: Contest and Identity in a Cretan Mountain Village.* Princeton: Princeton University Press.

——. 1987. *Anthropology through the Looking-Glass: Critical Ethnography in the Margins of Europe.* New York: Cambridge University Press.

Higginbotham, Evelyn Brooks. 1993. *Righteous Discontent: The Women's Movement in the Black Baptist Church, 1880–1920.* Cambridge: Harvard University Press.

Higonnet, Margaret Randolph, et al., eds. 1987. *Behind the Lines: Gender and the Two World Wars*. New Haven: Yale University Press.

Hirschon, Renee. 1983. "Women, the Aged, and Religious Activity: Oppositions and Complementarity in an Urban Locality." *Journal of Modern Greek Studies* 1 (May): 113–29.

Hobsbawm, Eric. 1976. "Forty Years of Popular Front Government." *Marxism Today* (July): 221–28.

———. 1989. *The Age of Empire, 1875–1914*. New York: Vintage.

Hobsbawm, Eric, and Terence Ranger, eds. 1983. *The Invention of Tradition*. Cambridge: Cambridge University Press.

Holst-Warhaft, Gail. 1991. Introduction to *Journal of Modern Greek Studies* 9 (Oct.): 141–43.

Hondros, J. L. 1981. "The Greek Resistance, 1941–1944: A Reevaluation." In *Greece in the 1940s: A Nation in Crisis*, ed. John O. Iatrides, 37–47. Hanover, N.H.: University Press of New England.

———. 1983. *Occupation and Resistance: The Greek Agony, 1941–44*. New York: Pella Press.

———. 1988. "'Too Weighty a Weapon': Britain and the Greek Security Battalions, 1943–1944." *Journal of the Hellenic Diaspora* 15 (1 and 2): 33–47.

hooks, bell. 1981. *Ain't I a Woman: Black Women and Feminism*. Boston: South End Press.

———. 1990. *Yearning: Race, Gender, and Cultural Politics*. Boston: South End Press.

———. 1992. *Black Looks: Race and Representation*. Boston: South End Press.

Horn, Gerd-Rainer. 1990. "The Language of Symbols and the Barriers of Language: Foreigners' Perceptions of Social Revolution (Barcelona, 1936–1937)." *History Workshop Journal* 29 (Spring): 42–64.

Hoy, David Couzens, ed. 1986. *Foucault: A Critical Reader*. Oxford: Basil Blackwell.

Hroch, Miroslav. 1985. *Social Preconditions of National Revival in Europe: A Comparative Analysis of the Social Composition of Patriotic Groups among the Smaller European Nations*. New York: Cambridge University Press.

Huggins, Nathan. 1971. *Harlem Renaissance*. New York: Oxford University Press.

Hunt, Lynn. 1992. *The Family Romance of the French Revolution*. New York and Los Angeles: University of California Press.

Iatrides, John O. 1981. "Civil War, 1945–1949: National and International Aspects." In *Greece in the 1940s: A Nation in Crisis*, ed. John O. Iatrides, 195–219. Hanover, N.H.: University Press of New England.

Irokawa Daikichi. 1985. *The Culture of the Meiji Period*. Princeton: Princeton University Press.

Jacques-Garvey, Amy, ed. 1969. *Philosophy and Opinions of Marcus Garvey*. (1923) New York: Atheneum Press.

Jaggar, Alison M. 1989. "Love and Knowledge: Emotion in Feminist Epistemology." In *Gender/Body/Knowledge: Feminist Reconstructions of Being and Knowing*, ed. Alison Jaggar and Susan R. Bordo, 145–71. New Brunswick: Rutgers University Press.

Jameson, Fredric. 1981. *The Political Unconscious: Narrative as a Socially Symbolic Act*. Ithaca: Cornell University Press.

———. 1990. *Late Marxism: Adorno; or, The Persistence of the Dialectic*. New York: Verso.

Jancar, Barbara. 1981. "Women in the Yugoslav National Liberation Movement: An Overview." *Studies in Comparative Communism* 14 (Summer–Autumn): 143–64.

Janeway, Elizabeth. 1981. *Powers of the Weak*. New York: Morrow Quill.

Jayawardena, Kumari. 1989. *Feminism and Nationalism in the Third World*. London: Zed Books.

Jelavich, Peter. 1982. "Popular Dimensions of Modernist Elite Culture: The Case of Theater in Fin-de-Siècle Munich." In *Modern European Intellectual History: Reappraisals and New Perspectives*, ed. Dominick LaCapra and Steven L. Kaplan, 220–50. Ithaca: Cornell University Press.

Jennings, M. Kent. 1987. "Residues of a Movement: The Aging of the American Protest Generation." *American Political Science Review* 81 (June): 367–82.

Johnson, Chalmers. 1962. *Peasant Nationalism and Communist Power*. Stanford: Stanford University Press.

Judt, Tony. 1986. *Marxism and the French Left: Studies on Labour and Politics in France, 1830–1981*. New York: Oxford University Press.

Jusdanis, Gregory. 1991. *Belated Modernity and Aesthetic Culture: Inventing National Literature*. Minneapolis: University of Minnesota Press.

Kandiyoti, Deniz. 1989. "Women and the Turkish State: Political Actors or Symbolic Pawns?" In *Woman-Nation-State*, ed. Nira Yuval-Davis and Floya Anthias, 126–49. New York: St. Martin's Press.

Kaplan, Temma. 1977. "Other Scenarios: Women and Spanish Anarchism." In *Becoming Visible: Women in European History*, ed. Renate Bridenthal and Claudia Koonz, 400–21. New York: Houghton-Mifflin.

———. 1982. "Female Consciousness and Collective Action: The Case of Barcelona, 1910–1918." *Signs* 7 (3): 545–59.

Katrak, Ketu H. 1992. "Indian Nationalism, Gandhian 'Satyagraha,' and Representations of Female Sexuality." In *Nationalisms and Sexualities*, ed. Andrew Parker et al., 395–406. New York: Routledge.

Kaufman, Robert. 1974. "The Patron-Client Concept and Macro-Politics: Prospects and Problems," *Comparative Studies in Society and History* 16 (3) (June): 284–308.

Keane, John, ed. 1988. *Civil Society and the State*. New York: Verso.

Kelley, Robin D. G. 1990. *Hammer and Hoe: Alabama Communists during the Great Depression*. Chapel Hill: University of North Carolina Press.

Kelman, Mark. 1987. *A Guide to Critical Legal Studies*. Cambridge: Harvard University Press.

Kenna, Margaret. 1991. "The Social Organization of Exile: The Everyday Life of Political Exiles in the Cyclades in the 1930s." *Journal of Modern Greek Studies* 9: 63–81.

Kennedy, Ellen. 1987. "Nietzsche: Women as *Untermensch*." In *Women in Western Political Philosophy*, ed. Ellen Kennedy and Susan Mendus, 179–201. New York: St. Martin's Press.

Kitroeff, Alexander. 1985. "Documents: The Jews in Greece, 1941–1944, Eyewitness Accounts." *Journal of the Hellenic Diaspora* 12 (Fall): 5–32.

———. 1987. "Greek Wartime Attitudes towards the Jews in Athens." *Forum* 60 (Summer): 41–51.

Klandermans, Bert, and Sidney Tarrow. 1988. "Mobilization into Social Movements: Synthesizing European and American Approaches." In *From Structure to Action:*

Comparing Social Movement Research across Cultures 1: 1–38. Greenwich, Conn.: JAI Press.

Knauss, Peter R. 1987. *The Persistence of Patriarchy: Class, Gender, and Ideology in Twentieth-Century Algeria.* New York: Praeger.

Kokkini, Evangelia. 1989. *Dimitris Glinos, 1882–1943: I epohi, i zoi kai to ergo tou* (Dimitris Glinos, 1982–1943: His times, his life and his work). Athens: Ekdhoseis Filoppoti.

Koonz, Claudia. 1987. *Mothers in the Fatherland: Women, the Family and Nazi Politics.* New York: St. Martin's Press.

Kotzioulas, George. 1980. *Theatro sta vouna: To theatro tou aghona* (Theater of the mountains: The theater of the struggle). Athens: Themelio Press.

LaCapra, Dominick. 1983. *Rethinking Intellectual History: Texts, Contexts, Language.* Ithaca: Cornell University Press.

———. 1987. "Rethinking Intellectual History and Reading Texts." In *Modern European Intellectual History: Reappraisals and New Perspectives,* ed. Dominick LaCapra and Steven L. Kaplan, 47–85. Ithaca: Cornell University Press.

Laclau, Ernesto, and Chantal Mouffe. 1985. *Hegemony and Socialist Strategy: Towards a Radical Democratic Politics.* New York: Verso.

Laitin, David. 1986. *Hegemony and Culture: Politics and Religion among the Yoruba.* Chicago: University of Chicago Press.

———. 1988. "Political Culture and Political Preferences." *American Political Science Review* 82 (June): 589–93.

Lakoff, George, and Mark Johnson. 1980. *Metaphors We Live By.* Chicago: University of Chicago Press.

Landes, Joan. 1988. *Women and the Public Sphere in the Age of the French Revolution.* Ithaca: Cornell University Press.

Laqueur, Thomas. 1989. "Bodies, Details, and the Humanitarian Narrative." In *The New Cultural History,* ed. Lynn Hunt, 176–204. Berkeley: University of California Press.

Lash, Scott, and Jonathan Friedman, eds. 1992. *Modernity and Identity.* Cambridge: Basil Blackwell.

Laska, Vera, ed. 1983. *Women in the Resistance and in the Holocaust: The Voices of Eyewitnesses.* Westport, Conn.: Greenwood Press.

Lavin, Maud. 1992. *Cut with the Kitchen Knife: The Weimar Photomontages of Hanna Hoch.* New Haven: Yale University Press.

Layoun, Mary. 1992. "Telling Spaces: Palestinian Women and the Engendering of National Narratives." In *Nationalisms and Sexualities,* ed. Andrew Parker et al., 407–23. New York: Routledge.

Lazarou, Fofi. 1982. "Ena ergostasio ston Peiraia organonetai" (A factory in Piraeus becomes organized). In *Yinekes stin andistasi: Martiries* (Women in the resistance: Eyewitness testimonies), 28–34. Athens: Kinisi "I Yineka Stin Andistasi."

Lefkowitz, Mary, and Maureen Fant, eds. 1982. *Women's Life in Greece and Rome: A Source Book in Translation.* London: Duckworth.

Legg, Keith. 1969. *Politics in Modern Greece.* Stanford: Stanford University Press.

Lemarchand, Rene, and Keith Legg. 1972. "Political Clientelism and Development: A Political Analysis." *Comparative Politics* 4 (Jan.): 149–78.

Lenin, Vladimir I. 1979. *The Right of Nations to Self-Determination.* Moscow: Progress.

——. 1987. *Essential Works of Lenin: "What Is to Be Done?" and Other Writings*. Ed. H. Christman. New York: Dover.

Leon, George B. 1976. *The Greek Socialist Movement and the First World War: The Road to Unity*. New York: Columbia University Press.

Lerner, Gerda. 1986. *The Creation of Patriarchy*. New York: Oxford University Press.

Lewis, Earl. 1991. *In Their Own Interests: Race, Class, and Power in Twentieth-Century Norfolk, Virginia*. Berkeley: University of California Press.

Lloyd, Christopher. 1986. *Explanation in Social History*. New York: Basil Blackwell.

Locke, Alain, ed. 1992. *The New Negro: Voices of the Harlem Renaissance* (1925). New York: Macmillan.

Loizos, Peter, and Evthymios Papataxiarchis, eds. 1991. *Contested Identities: Gender and Kinship in Modern Greece*. Princeton: Princeton University Press.

Lopes, A., and G. Roth. 1993. "Marxism's Feminism: Bebel and Zetkin in Opposition." *Rethinking Marxism* 6 (Fall): 66–78.

Loulis, John. 1982. *The Greek Communist Party, 1940–1944*. London: Croom-Helm.

Lovenduski, Joni. 1986. *Women and European Politics: Contemporary Feminism and Public Policy*. Amherst: University of Massachusetts Press.

Lurie, Alison. 1990. *Don't Tell the Grown-ups: Why Kids Love the Books They Do*. New York: Avon.

Lutz, Catherine A., and Lila Abu-Lughod, eds. 1990. *Language and the Politics of Emotion*. New York: Maison des Sciences de l'Homme and Cambridge University Press.

Lyttelton, Adrian. 1992. "Line of Resistance." Review of Claudio Pavone, *Una Guerra Civile: saggio storico sulla moralitá nella Resistenza*. *Times Literary Supplement*, September 25, 28–29.

Marcus, George E. 1986. "Ethnography in the Modern World System." In *Writing Culture: The Poetics and Politics of Ethnography*, ed. James Clifford and George E. Marcus, 165–93. Berkeley: University of California Press.

Marcus, George E., and Michael M. J. Fischer. 1986. *Anthropology as Cultural Critique: An Experimental Moment in the Human Sciences*. Chicago: University of Chicago Press.

Matsas, Joseph. 1991. "The Participation of the Greek Jews in the National Resistance, 1940–1941." *Journal of the Hellenic Diaspora* 17 (I): 55–68.

Mavroeidi-Papadaki, Sofia, Vasilis Rotas, et al. 1962. *Theatro: 19 Monoprakta*. Athens: Politikes kai Logoteknikes Ekdoseis.

Mavrogordatos, George Th. 1981. "The 1946 Election and Plebiscite: Prelude to Civil War." In *Greece in the 1940s: A Nation in Crisis*, ed. John O. Iatrides, 181–94. Hanover, N.H.: University Press of New England.

——. 1983. *Stillborn Republic: Social Coalitions and Party Strategies in Greece, 1922–1936*. Berkeley: University of California Press.

Mazower, Mark. 1993. *Inside Hitler's Greece: The Experience of Occupation, 1941–44*. New Haven: Yale University Press.

Mazrui, Ali. 1991. "Dr. Schweitzer's Racism." *Transition* 53: 96–102.

McAdam, Doug. 1982. *Political Process and the Development of Black Insurgency, 1930–1970*. Chicago: University of Chicago Press.

——. 1988. *Freedom Summer*. New York: Oxford University Press.

McCormick, Richard W. 1993. "From Caligari to Dietrich: Sexual, Social, and Cinematic Discourses in Weimar Film." *Signs* 18 (Spring): 640–68.

McCarthy, John D., and Mayer N. Zald. 1987. "Resource Mobilization and Social Movements: A Partial Theory." In *Social Movements in an Organizational Society,* ed. J. D. McCarthy and M. N. Zald, 15–42. New Brunswick, N.J.: Transaction.

McClintock, Anne. [n.d.] "'No Longer a Future Heaven': Women and Nationalism in South Africa." *Transition* 51: 104–23.

Melzer, Sara E., and Leslie W. Rabine, eds. 1991. *Rebel Daughters: Women and the French Revolution.* New York: Oxford University Press.

Middleton, Peter. 1990. "Vanishing Effects: The Disappearance of Emotion from Postmodernist Theory and Practice." *New Formations* 12 (Winter): 125–42.

Migdal, Joel. 1974. *Peasants, Politics, and Revolution.* Princeton: Princeton University Press.

Mills, C. Wright. 1959. *The Sociological Imagination.* New York: Oxford University Press.

——. 1984. "Situated Actions and Vocabularies of Motive." In *Language and Politics,* ed. M. Shapiro, 13–24. New York: New York University Press.

Minces, Juliet. 1978. "Women in Algeria." In *Women in the Muslim World,* ed. Lois Beck and Nikki Keddie, 159–171. Cambridge: Harvard University Press.

Minehan, Philip. 1983. "Dependency, Realignment, and Reaction: Movement toward Civil War in Greece during the 1940s." *Journal of the Hellenic Diaspora* 10 (Fall): 17–34.

Mink, Louis O. 1978. "Narrative Form as a Cognitive Instrument." In *The Writing of History: Literary Form and Historical Understanding,* ed. Robert H. Canary and Henry Kozicki, 129–49. Madison: University of Wisconsin Press.

Moe, Nelson J. 1990. "Production and Its Others: Gramsci's 'Sexual Question.'" *Rethinking Marxism* 3 (3–4): 218–237.

Morris, Aldon. 1984. *The Origins of the Civil Rights Movement: Black Communities Organizing for Change.* New York: Free Press.

Morris, Aldon, Shirley Hatchett, and Ronald E. Brown. 1989. "The Civil Rights Movement and Black Socialization." In *Political Learning in Adulthood: A Sourcebook of Theory and Research,* ed. Roberta S. Sigel, 272–305. Chicago: University of Chicago Press.

Mosse, George. 1985. *Nationalism and Sexuality: Middle-Class Morality and Sexual Norms in Modern Europe.* Madison: University of Wisconsin Press.

Mouffe, C. 1990. "Radical Democracy or Liberal Democracy?" *Socialist Review* 20 (April–June): 57–66.

——. 1991. "Pluralism and Modern Democracy: Around Carl Schmitt." *New Formations* 14 (Summer): 1–16.

Moutzan-Martinengou, Elisavet. 1989. *My Story.* Trans. H. Kolias. Athens: University of Georgia Press.

Mouzelis, Nicos. 1976. "Greek and Bulgarian Peasants: Aspects of Their Sociopolitical Situation during the Interwar Period." *Comparative Studies in Society and History* 18: 85–105.

——. 1978. "Class and Clientelistic Politics: The Case of Greece." *Sociological Review* 26 (3): 471–97.

——. 1985. "On the Concept of Populism: Populist and Clientelist Modes of Incorporation in Semiperipheral Polities." *Politics and Society* 14 (3): 329–48.

Mullaney, Marie Marmo. 1990. "Women and European Socialist Protest, 1871–1921."

In *Women and Social Protest*, ed. Guida West and Rhoda L. Blumberg, 103–119. New York: Oxford University Press.

Myrsiades, Kostas. 1983. "A Theory of Resistance Poetry during the Greek Occupation, 1941–1944." *East European Quarterly* 17 (1): 79–88.

Myrsiades, Linda Suny. 1977. "Greek Resistance Theatre in World War II." *Drama Review* 21 (March): 100–106.

Nairn, Tom. 1977. *The Break-up of Britain*. London: NLB.

———. 1982. "Antonu Su Gobbu." In *Approaches to Gramsci*, ed. Anne Showstack Sassoon, 159–79. London: Writers and Readers Press.

Nategh, Homa. 1987. "Women: The Damned of the Iranian Revolution." In *Women and Political Conflict*, in Rosemary Ridd and Helen Callaway, 45–60. New York: New York University Press.

Newman, Louise M. 1991. "Critical Theory and the History of Women: What's at Stake in Deconstructing Women's History." *Journal of Women's History* 2 (Winter): 58–68.

Newton, Judith. 1987. "Making—and Remaking—History: Another Look at 'Patriarchy.'" In *Feminist Issues in Literary Scholarship*, ed. Shari Benstock, 124–40. Bloomington: Indiana University Press.

Nimni, Ephraim. 1989. "Marx, Engels, and the National Question." *Science and Society* 53 (3): 297–326.

O'Ballance, Edgar. 1966. *The Greek Civil War, 1944–49*. London: Faber and Faber.

Oberschall, Anthony. 1978. "The Decline of the 1960s Social Movements." In *Research in Social Movements, Conflicts, and Change*, vol. 1, ed. Louis Kriesberg, 257–89. Greenwich, Conn.: JAI Press.

Offen, Karen. 1990a. "Feminism and Sexual Difference in Historical Perspective." In *Theoretical Perspectives on Sexual Difference*, ed. Deborah L. Rhode, 13–20. New Haven: Yale University Press.

———. 1990b. "Women's Memory, Women's History, Women's Political Action: The French Revolution in Retrospect, 1789–1889–1989." *Journal of Women's History* 1 (3): 211–30.

Ortner, Sherry. 1989. *High Religion: A Cultural and Political History of Sherpa Buddhism*. Princeton: Princeton University Press.

Osborne, Peter, ed. 1988. *Socialism and the Limits of Liberalism*. New York: Verso.

Padgug, Robert. 1979. "Sexual Matters: On Conceptualizing Sexuality in History." *Radical History Review* 20 (Spring–Summer): 3–23.

Paige, Jeffrey. 1988. "Revolution and the Agrarian Bourgeoisie in Nicaragua." *CSST Working Paper 8* (Oct.). Ann Arbor: University of Michigan, CRSO.

Panourgia, Neni K. 1992. "O ratsistikos logos stin Ellada: Ithageneis stohasmoi" (Racist speech in Greece: Native thoughts). *O Politis* 117 (Jan.): 38–42.

———. 1993. "If Greece Is the Mother of Europe . . . Autochthony and the Development of Racist Discourse in Greece." Unpublished paper.

Passerini, Luisa. 1988. *Fascism in Popular Memory: The Cultural Experience of the Turin Working Class*. New York: Cambridge University Press.

Pateman, Carol. 1989. *The Disorder of Women: Democracy, Feminism, and Political Theory*. Stanford: Stanford University Press.

Patterson, Thomas C. 1989. "Post-structuralism, Post-modernism: Implications for Historians." *Social History* 14 (1): 83–88.

Peristiany, John G., ed. 1965. *Honour and Shame: the Values of Mediterranean Society.* London: Weidenfeld and Nicolson.

Petropoulos, John. 1981. "The Traditional Political Parties of Greece during the Axis Occupation." In *Greece in the 1940s: A Nation in Crisis,* ed. John O. Iatrides, 27–36. Hanover, N.H.: University Press of New England.

Pippin, Robert. 1991. *Modernism as a Philosophical Problem.* Cambridge: Basil Blackwell.

Piven, Frances Fox, and Richard A. Cloward. 1977. *Poor People's Movements: Why They Succeed, How They Fail.* New York: Vintage.

Pleck, Joseph. 1989. "Men's Power with Women, Other Men, and Society: A Men's Movement Analysis." In *Men's Lives,* ed. Michael S. Kimmel and Michael A. Messner, 21–29. New York: Macmillan.

Pollis, Adamantia. 1965. "Political Implications of the Greek Concept of Self." *British Journal of Sociology* 16 (1): 29–47.

——. 1980. "Greek Women: The Struggle for Individuality." Unpublished paper.

Pollock, Griselda. 1988. *Vision and Difference: Femininity, Feminism, and the Histories of Art.* New York: Routledge.

Pomeroy, Sarah B. 1976. "A Classical Scholar's Perspective on Matriarchy." In *Liberating Women's History: Theoretical and Critical Essays,* ed. Berenice Carroll, 217–23. Urbana: University of Illinois Press.

Portelli, Alessandro. 1991. *The Death of Luigi Trastulli and Other Stories: Form and Meaning in Oral History.* Albany: State University of New York Press.

Pring, J. T. 1982. *The Oxford Dictionary of Modern Greek.* Oxford: Clarendon Press.

Psomas, Andreas I. 1978. *The Nation, the State, and the International System: The Case of Modern Greece.* Athens: National Center for Social Science Research.

Psychoundakis, George. 1955. *The Cretan Runner.* London: John Murray.

Rabinbach, Anson. 1977. "Unclaimed Heritage: Ernst Bloch's *Heritage of Our Times* and the Theory of Fascism." *New German Critique* 11 (Spring): 5–21.

Randall, Margaret. 1981. *Sandino's Daughters: Testimonies of Nicaraguan Women in the Struggle.* Toronto: New Star Books.

Reif, Linda Labao. 1986. "Women in Latin American Guerilla Movements: A Comparative Perspective." *Comparative Politics* (Jan.): 147–69.

Reiter, Rayna. 1975. "Men and Women in the South of France: Public and Private Domains." In *Toward an Anthropology of Women,* ed. R. Reiter, 252–82. New York: Monthly Review Press.

Richter, Heinz. 1975. *1936–1946: Dhio epanastaseis kai andepanastaseis stin Ellada* (1936–1946: Two revolutions and antirevolutions in Greece). Athens: Exantas Press.

——. 1981. "The Varkiza Agreement and the Origins of the Civil War." In *Greece in the 1940s: A Nation in Crisis,* ed. J. O. Iatrides, 167–80. Hanover, N.H.: University Press of New England.

——. 1986. *British Intervention in Greece: From Varkiza to Civil War.* London: Merlin Press.

Robinson, Cedric. 1990. "Du Bois and Black Sovereignty: The Case of Liberia." *Race and Class* 32 (2): 39–50.

Rosaldo, Michelle. 1980. "The Use and Abuse of Anthropology: Reflections on Feminism and Cross-Cultural Understanding." *Signs* 5 (3): 389–417.

Rosaldo, Michelle, and Louise Lamphere, eds. 1974. *Woman, Culture, and Society.* Stanford: Stanford University Press.

Rosaldo, Renato. 1989. *Culture and Truth: The Remaking of Social Analysis.* Boston: Beacon Press.

Rose, Sonya O. 1992. *Limited Livelihoods: Gender and Class in Nineteenth-Century England.* Berkeley: University of California Press.

Rossiter, Margaret L. 1986. *Women in the Resistance.* New York: Praeger.

Rowbotham, Sheila. 1992. "Nationalist Movements and Women's Place." *Women in Movement: Feminism and Social Action.* New York: Routledge.

Safilios-Rothschild, Constantina. 1968. "'Good' and 'Bad' Girls in Modern Greek Movies." *Journal of Marriage and the Family* 30 (3): 527–31.

———. 1969. "'Honour' Crimes in Contemporary Greece." *British Journal of Sociology* 20 (2): 205–18.

Sakellariou, Haris. 1984. *Andistasiaka paidhika dhiigimata* (Selections from children's war writings). Athens: Kedros.

Salecl, Renata. 1992. "Nationalism, Anti-Semitism, and Anti-Feminism in Eastern Europe." *New German Critique* 57 (Fall): 51–65.

Samuel, Raphael, and Paul Thompson, eds. 1990. *The Myths We Live By.* New York: Routledge.

Sarafis, M. 1980. "Stephanos Sarafis: Biographical Memoir." In S. Sarafis, *ELAS: Greek Resistance Army,* xi–ci. Ed. M. Sarafis. London: Merlin Press.

———. 1990. *O Stratigos Sarafis opos ton gnorissa* (General Sarafis as I knew him). Athens: Kastanioti Press.

———. 1994. "Army, Constitution, and People in Greece." *Thetis* (Mannheim) 1: 95–103.

Sarafis, Stefanos. 1980. *ELAS: Greek Resistance Army.* Ed. M. Sarafis. London: Merlin Press.

Sassoon, Anne Showstack. 1980. "Gramsci: A New Concept of Politics and the Expansion of Democracy." In *Marxism and Democracy,* ed. Alan Hunt, 81–99. London: Lawrence and Wishart.

———. 1987a. *Gramsci's Politics.* Minneapolis: University of Minnesota Press.

———. 1987b. *Women and the State.* London: Unwin Hyman.

Saywell, Shirley. 1985. *Women in War: First-hand Accounts from World War II to El Salvador.* New York: Viking Press.

Schick, Irvin C., and Ertugrul A. Tonak. 1987. *Turkey in Transition: New Perspectives.* New York: Oxford University Press.

Schmitt, C. 1976. *The Concept of the Political.* New Brunswick, N.J.: Rutgers University Press.

———. 1988. *The Crisis of Parliamentary Democracy.* Cambridge, Mass.: M.I.T. Press.

———. 1990. "The Plight of European Jurisprudence" (1943–44). *Telos,* no. 83 (Spring): 35–70.

Schneider, Jane. 1971. "Of Vigilance and Virgins: Honor, Shame, and Access to Resources in Mediterranean Societies." *Ethnology* 10 (Jan.): 1–24.

Scott, Bonnie Kime, ed. 1990. *The Gender of Modernism: A Critical Anthology.* Bloomington: Indiana University Press.

Scott, Joan W. 1988a. *Gender and the Politics of History.* New York: Columbia University Press.

———. 1988b. "Deconstructing Equality-versus-Difference; or, The Uses of Poststructuralist Theory for Feminism." *Feminist Studies* 14 (1): 33–50.

———. 1991. "The Evidence of Experience." *Critical Inquiry* 17 (4): 773–97.

Seidman, Gay. 1984. "Women in Zimbabwe: Postindependence Struggles." *Feminist Studies* 10 (3): 419–40.

Sideri, Maria. 1981. *Dhekatessera chronia* (Fourteen years). Athens: Ermis Press.

Sigel, Roberta, ed. 1989. *Political Learning in Adulthood: A Sourcebook of Theory and Research.* Chicago: University of Chicago Press.

Skliros, George. 1977. *To kinonikon mas zitima* (Our social question). *Erga* (Works), 80–358. Athens: Epikairotita.

Skocpol, Theda. 1989. "Reconsidering the French Revolution in World-Historical Perspective." *Social Research* 56 (Spring): 53–70.

Skouteri-Didaskalou, Nora. 1984. *Anthropologika yia to yinekio zitima (4 meletimata)* (Anthropological thought on the woman question [4 studies]). Athens: Politis.

Smith, Dorothy. 1989. *The Everyday World as Problematic: A Feminist Sociology.* Boston: Northeastern University Press.

Smith-Rosenberg, Carol. 1989. "Discourses of Sexuality and Subjectivity: The New Woman, 1870–1936." In *Hidden from History: Reclaiming the Gay and Lesbian Past,* ed. Martin B. Duberman, Martha Vicinus, and George Chauncey Jr., 264–80. New York: New American Library.

Snow, David A., and Robert D. Benford. 1988. "Ideology, Frame Resonance, and Participant Mobilization." In *From Structure to Action: Comparing Social Movement Research across Cultures,* ed. Bert Klandermans, Hanspeter Kriesi, and Sidney Tarrow, 197–217. International Social Movement Research: A Research Annual (1). Greenwich, Conn.: JAI Press.

Snow, D. A., et al. 1986. "Frame Alignment Processes, Micromobilization, and Movement Participation." *American Sociological Review* 51 (Aug.): 464–81.

Somers, Margaret. Forthcoming. "Social Theory after the Historic Turn: Knowledge Cultures and Historical Epistemology." In *The Historic Turn in the Human Sciences,* ed. T. J. McDonald. Ann Arbor: University of Michigan Press.

Stallybrass, Peter. 1990. "Marx and Heterogeneity: Thinking the Lumpen-proletariat." *Representations* 31 (Summer): 69–95.

Stallybrass, Peter, and Allon White. 1986. *The Politics and Poetics of Transgression.* Ithaca: Cornell University Press.

Stavrakis, Peter. 1989. *Moscow and Greek Communism, 1944–1949.* Ithaca: Cornell University Press.

Stavrianos, Leften Stavros. 1948. "The Jews of Greece." *Journal of Central European Affairs* 7 (Oct.): 256–69.

———. 1952. "The Greek National Liberation Front (EAM): A Study in Resistance Organization and Administration." *Journal of Modern History* 24 (1): 42–55.

———. 1958. *The Balkans since 1453.* New York: Rinehart.

Stavrianos, L. S., and E. P. Panagopoulos. 1948. "Bibliographic Article: Present-Day Greece." *Journal of Modern History* 20 (June): 149–58.

Steedman, Carolyn. 1990. *Childhood, Culture, and Class in Britain: Margaret McMillan, 1860–1931.* New Brunswick, N.J.: Rutgers University Press.

Steedman, Carolyn, Cathy Urwin, and Valerie Walkerdine, eds. 1985. *Language, Gender, and Childhood.* London: Routledge and Kegan Paul.

Stewart, C. 1991. *Demons and the Devil: Moral Imagination and Modern Greek Culture*. Princeton: Princeton University Press.

———. 1994. "Syncretism as a Dimension of Nationalist Discourse in Modern Greece." In *Syncretism/Anti-syncretism: The Politics of Religious Synthesis*, ed. Charles Stewart and Rosalind Shaw, 127–44. New York: Routledge.

Stoler, Ann. 1992. "Sexual Affronts and Racial Frontiers: European Identities and the Cultural Politics of Exclusion in Colonial Southeast Asia." *Comparative Studies in Society and History* 34 (3): 514–51.

Stone, Lawrence. 1987. "Prosopography." In *The Past and Present Revisited*, 45–73. New York: Routledge and Kegan Paul.

Svoronos, Nicos. 1981. "Greek History, 1940–1950: The Main Problems." In *Greece in the 1940s: A Nation in Crisis*, ed. John O. Iatrides, 1–14. Hanover, N.H.: University Press of New England.

Szporluk, Roman. 1988. *Communism and Nationalism: Karl Marx versus Friedrich List*. New York: Oxford University Press.

Tannen, Deborah. 1990. *You Just Don't Understand: Women and Men in Conversation*. New York: Ballantine.

Tarrow, Sidney. 1967. *Peasant Communism in Southern Italy*. New Haven: Yale University Press.

———. 1988. "National Politics and Collective Action: Recent Theory and Research in Western Europe and the United States." *Annual Review of Sociology* 14: 421–40.

Thompson, E. P. 1966. *The Making of the English Working Class*. New York: Vintage.

Thompson, John B. 1984. *Studies in the Theory of Ideology*. Berkeley: University of California Press.

Tilly, C. 1978. *From Mobilization to Revolution*. Reading, Pa.: Addison-Wesley.

———. 1984. "Social Movements and National Politics." In *Statemaking and Social Movements*, ed. C. Bright and S. Harding, 297–317. Ann Arbor: University of Michigan Press.

To andartiko kai to epanastatiko traghoudhi (Songs of resistance and revolution). 1979. Athens: Mnimi.

To ethniko mas provlima kai to Kommounistiko Komma tis Elladas. Ekdhosi KOMEP (1943). Athens: Mnimi Press, 1985.

Tomeas Filosofias, Filosofikis Skolis Pan/miou Ioanninon. 1983. *Dimitris Glinos: Paidhagogos kai filosofos* (Dimitris Glinos: Educator and Philosopher). Athens: Ekdhoseis Gutenberg.

Touraine, Alain. 1981. *The Voice and the Eye: An Anaysis of Social Movements*. New York: Cambridge University Press.

Traghoudhia tis andistasis kai tou emfiliou (Songs of resistance and civil war). 1975. Athens: Ellinika Themata.

Traverso, Enzo, and Michael Lowy. 1990. "The Marxist Approach to the National Question: A Critique of Nimni's Interpretation." *Science and Society* 54 (2): 132–46.

Tsoucalas, Constantine. 1969. *The Greek Tragedy*. London: Penguin.

———. 1981. "The Ideological Impact of the Civil War." In *Greece in the 1940s: A Nation in Crisis*, ed. John O. Iatrides, 319–41. Hanover, N.H.: University Press of New England.

———. 1991. "'Enlightened' Concepts in the 'Dark': Power and Freedom, Politics and Society." *Journal of Modern Greek Studies* 9 (May): 1–22.

Tyler, Stephen A. 1986. "Post-modern Ethnography: From Document of the Occult to Occult Document." In *Writing Culture: The Poetics and Politics of Ethnography*, ed. James Clifford and George E. Marcus, 122–40. Berkeley: University of California Press.

van Boeschoten, Riki. 1986. "Myth and History in Greek Folk Songs Related to the War of Independence." *Journal of the Hellenic Diaspora* 13 (Fall–Winter): 125–141.

Van Dyck, Karen. 1989. "The Poetics of Censorship: Greek Politics since 1967." Ph.D. diss., Oxford University.

Varika, Eleni. 1987. *I exegersi ton kyrion: I yenesi mias feministikis sinidhisis stin Ellada, 1833–1907* (The revolt of the ladies: The birth of a feminist consciousness in Greece). Athens: Division of Research and Education of the Commercial Bank of Greece.

Vlavianos, Haris. 1989. "The Greek Communist Party: In Search of a Revolution." In *Resistance and Revolution in Mediterranean Europe, 1939–1948*, ed. Tony Judt, 157–212. New York: Routledge.

———. 1992. *Greece, 1941–49: From Resistance to Civil War.* Oxford: Macmillan.

Vogel, Lise. 1991. "Telling Tales: Historians of Our Own Lives." *Journal of Women's History* 2 (Winter): 89–101.

Vukmanovic, Svetozar. 1985. *How and Why the People's Liberation Struggle of Greece Met with Defeat* (1950). London: Merlin Press.

Walker, Alice 1983. "The Civil Rights Movement: What Good Was It?" In *In Search of Our Mothers' Gardens.* New York: Harcourt Brace. 119–129.

Walker, Rebecca. 1992. "Becoming the Third Wave." *Court of Appeal: The Black Community Speaks Out on the Racial and Sexual Politics of Thomas vs. Hill.* The Black Scholar. New York: Ballantine.

Wall, Irwin. 1986. "Front Populaire, Front National: The Colonial Example." *International Labor and Working-Class History* 30 (Fall): 32–43.

Wasserstrom, Jeffrey, and Liu Xinyong. 1989. "Student Protest and Student Life: Shanghai, 1919–49." *Social History* 14 (1): 1–29.

Weingrod, Alex. 1968. "Patrons, Patronage, and Political Parties." *Comparative Studies in Society and History* 10 (4): 377–400.

West, Cornel. 1993. *Race Matters.* Boston: Beacon Press.

Wheeler, Mark. 1989. "Pariahs to Partisans to Power: The Communist Party of Yugoslavia." In *Resistance and Revolution in Mediterranean Europe, 1939–1948*, ed. Tony Judt, 110–56. New York: Routledge.

White, Hayden. 1973. *Metahistory: The Historical Imagination in Nineteenth-Century Europe.* Baltimore: Johns Hopkins University Press.

———. 1987. *The Content of the Form: Narrative Discourse and Historical Representation.* Baltimore: Johns Hopkins University Press.

Williams, Joan C. 1991. "Domesticity as the Dangerous Supplement of Liberalism." *Journal of Women's History* 2 (Winter): 69–88.

Williams, Juan. 1987. *Eyes on the Prize: America's Civil Rights Years, 1954–1965.* New York: Viking Penguin.

Williams, Maynard Owen. 1949. "War-Torn Greece Looks Ahead." *National Geographic Magazine* 96 (6): 711–44.

Williams, Raymond. 1977. *Marxism and Literature.* New York: Oxford University Press.

——. 1983. *Keywords: A Vocabulary of Culture and Society.* New York: Oxford University Press.

——. 1989. "When Was Modernism?" *New Left Review* 175: 48–52.

Wohl, Robert. 1979. *The Generation of 1914.* Cambridge: Harvard University Press.

Woodhouse, C. M. 1976. *The Struggle for Greece, 1941–49.* London: Hart-Davis MacGibbon.

——. 1985. *The Apple of Discord* (1948). Reston, Va.: W. B. O'Neill.

Zald, Mayer N., and Bert Useem. 1987. "Movement and Countermovement Interaction: Mobilization, Tactics, and State Involvement." In *Social Movements in an Organizational Society,* ed. John D. McCarthy and Mayer N. Zald, 247–72. New Brunswick, N.J.: Transaction Books.

Zei, Alke. 1969. *Wildcat under Glass.* London: Gollancz.

Zukin, Sharon. 1977. "Mimesis in the Origins of Bourgeois Culture." *Theory and Society* 4 (3): 333–58.

Index

The Wilder House Series in Politics, History, and Culture